ALBION

The Origins of the English Imagination

===

PETER ACKROYD

Chatto & Windus
LONDON

Published by Chatto & Windus 2002

2 4 6 8 10 9 7 5 3 1

© Peter Ackroyd 2002

Peter Ackroyd has asserted his right under the Copyright, Designs and
Patents Act 1988 to be identified as the author of this work

First published in Great Britain in 2002 by
Chatto & Windus
Random House, 20 Vauxhall Bridge Road,
London SW1V 2SA

Random House Australia (Pty) Limited
20 Alfred Street, Milsons Point, Sydney,
New South Wales 2061, Australia

Random House New Zealand Limited
18 Poland Road, Glenfield,
Auckland 10, New Zealand

Random House (Pty) Limited
Endulini, 5A Jubilee Road, Parktown, 2193, South Africa

The Random House Group Limited Reg. No. 954009
www.randomhouse.co.uk

A CIP catalogue record for this book
is available from the British Library

ISBN 1 85619 7212

Papers used by Random House are natural,
recyclable products made from wood grown in sustainable forests.
The manufacturing processes conform to the environmental
regulations of the country of origin

Typeset by SX Composing DTP, Rayleigh, Essex
Printed and bound in Great Britain by
Clays Ltd, St. Ives PLC

Contents

List of Illustrations

Colour plate sections

625–30 AD (gold, garnet and millefiore glass) (British Museum, London UK/Bridgeman Art Library)

'King Edgar between the Virgin Mary and St Peter dedicates the Charter Christus', Anglo-Saxon illuminated manuscript, c. 966 (AKG/British Library)

Driven by the Spirit into Wilderness: panel from the 'Christ in the Wilderness' series, 1939, by Stanley Spencer (1891–1959) (Stanley Spencer Gallery, Cookham, Berkshire, UK/Bridgeman Art Library)

'And hast thou slain the Jabberwock?', illustration by Sir John Tenniel for *Through the Looking Glass* by Lewis Carroll (Copyright © 1911 Macmillan Publishers Limited. Illustrations coloured by Harry Theaker and Diz Wallis)

Sir Ian McKellen in the 2001 film of Tolkien's *Lord of the Rings* (Lord of the Rings: Fellowship of the Ring, New Line/Saul Zaentz/Wing Nut. Courtesy Kobal)

'Event on the Downs', c. 1934, by Paul Nash (1889–1946) (Old Admiralty Building, Whitehall, London UK/Bridgeman Art Library)

'Seascape Study with Rainclouds' by John Constable (1776–1837) (Royal Academy Photographic Archive)

Durham Cathedral, the nave, c. 1093 (London/Bridgeman Art Library)

'The Wilton Diptych', portable altarpiece for the private devotion of Richard II, c. 1395–9 (National Gallery, London)

'Canterbury Tales': illuminated initial, with a portrait of Geoffrey Chaucer holding a book, c. 1400 (AKG/British Library)

St Leonard with crozier and manacles, St Agnes or St Catherine with sword and book. Two saints, from a screen in St John's Maddermarket, Norwich, mid 15th century (V & A Picture Library)

Miniature by Nicholas Hilliard: Queen Elizabeth I, 1572 (National Portrait Gallery, London)

'The Fairy Feller's Master-Stroke' by Richard Dadd, unfinished in 1864 (Tate, London 2002)

'A Hilly Scene' by Samuel Palmer, c. 1826–8 (Tate, London 2002)

'Daniel Delivered out of Many Waters' by William Blake, c. 1805 (Tate, London 2002)

'Sir Galahad, Sir Bors and Sir Percival' by Dante Gabriel Rossetti, 1864 (Tate, London 2002)

'Gawain', production at the Royal Opera House, Covent Garden. Music by Harrison Birtwistle, libretto by David Harsent, based on the story of Sir Gawain and the Green Knight (Clive Barda/Performing Arts Library)

John Milton, c. 1629, artist unknown (National Portrait Gallery, London)

Edward Gibbon, by Henry Walton (National Portrait Gallery, London)

Mrs Gaskell, 1851, by George Richmond (National Portrait Gallery, London)

Ralph Vaughan Williams, 1958–61, by Sir Gerald Kelly (National Portrait Gallery, London)

'Self-Portrait' by William Hogarth, c. 1757 (National Portrait Gallery, London)

'The Shrimp Girl' by William Hogarth (National Gallery, London)

Samuel Johnson by Sir Joshua Reynolds, 1756–7 (National Portrait Gallery, London)

Kemble as Hamlet, 1801, painted by Sir Thomas Lawrence (Tate, London 2002)

'No reasonable offer refused': Widow Twankey (V & A Picture Library)

Front cover of the music score for 'The Doctor' sung by Dan Leno (colour litho) by H.G. Banks (19th century) (Private collection/Bridgeman Art Library)

'Mr and Mrs Andrews' by Thomas Gainsborough (National Gallery, London)

'Mr B finds Pamela writing', illustration from Richardson's *Pamela* by Joseph Highmore (1692–1780) (V & A Museum, London UK/Bridgeman Art Library)

Pegwell Bay, Kent, 'A Recollection of October 5th 1858' by William Dyce (Tate, London 2002)

'Margate from the sea' by J.M.W. Turner (National Gallery, London)

'The Great Day of His Wrath', one of the three pictures in John Martin's Judgement series, 1851–3 (Tate, London 2002)

'Chatterton', by Henry Wallis, 1856 (Tate, London 2002)

'Stroud: An Upland Landscape', painting of the Malvern hills by Philip Wilson Steer in 1902 (Tate, London 2002)

'An experiment on a Bird in the Air Pump', 1768, by Joseph Wright of Derby (National Gallery, London)

Main block, designed by Richard Rogers (photo), Lloyds of London, Lime Street (London UK/Roger Last/Bridgeman Art Library)

For Murrough O'Brien

Chronology

Inigo Jones (1573–1652) Arc
Thomas Browne (1605–1682) W
John Milton (1608–1674) W
Peter Lely (1618–1680) A
Andrew Marvell (1621–1678) W
John Bunyan (1628–1688) W
John Dryden (1631–1700) W
John Locke (1632–1704) W
Christopher Wren (1631–1723) Arc
Aphra Behn (1640–1689) W
Godfrey Kneller (1646–1723) A
Henry Purcell (c.1659–1695) C
Daniel Defoe (1660–1731) W
Nicholas Hawksmoor (1661–1736) Arc
John Vanbrugh (1664–1726) Arc
Jonathan Swift (1667–1745) W
Thomas Archer (c.1668–1743) Arc
Joseph Addison (1672–1719) W
Richard Steele (1672–1729) W
James Thornhill (1675/6–1734) A
Colen Campbell (1676–1729) Arc
James Gibbs (1682–1754) Arc
John Gay (1685–1732) W
William Kent (c.1685–1748) Arc
Alexander Pope (1688–1744) W
Samuel Richardson (1689–1761) W
Richard Boyle, 3rd Earl of Burlington (1694–1753) Arc
William Hogarth (1697–1764) A
Henry Fielding (1707–1754) W
Samuel Johnson (1709–1784) W
Laurence Sterne (1713–1768) W
James Stuart (1713–1788) Arc
Richard Wilson (1714–1782) A
Thomas Gray (1716–1771) W
Nicholas Revett (1720–1804) Arc
Tobias Smollet (1721–1771) W
Joshua Reynolds (1723–1792) A
William Chambers (1726–1796) Arc
George Stubbs (1724–1806) A
Paul Sandby (1725–1809) A

Thomas Gainsborough (1727–1788) A
Robert Adam (1728–1792) Arc
Johann Zoffany (1734–1810) A
Joseph Wright of Derby (1734–1797) A
James Macpherson (1736–1796) W
Edward Gibbon (1737–1794) W
Benjamin West (1738–1820) A
James Boswell (1740–1795) W
Henry Fuseli (1741–1825) A
George Dance (1741–1825) Arc
Henry Holland (1746–1806) Arc
James Wyatt (1746–1813) Arc
Thomas Chatterton (1752–1770) W
John Nash (1752–1835) Arc
John Soane (1753–1837) Arc
Thomas Rowlandson (1756–1827) A
William Blake (1757–1827) A & W
Mary Wollstonecraft (1759–1797) W
John Opie (1716–1807) A
Ann Radcliffe (1764–1823) W
Thomas Lawrence (1769–1830) A
William Wordsworth (1770–1850) W
Walter Scott (1771–1832) W
Samuel Taylor Coleridge (1772–1834) W
Jane Austen (1775–1817) W
Charles Lamb (1775–1834) W
Joseph Mallord William Turner (1775–1851) A
John Constable (1776–1837) A
William Hazlitt (1778–1830) W
Robert Smirke (1781–1867) Arc
David Wilkie (1785–1841) A
Thomas De Quincey (1785–1859) W
Lord Byron (1788–1824) W
C. R. Cockerell (1788–1863) Arc
Percy Bysshe Shelley (1792–1822) W
John Keats (1795–1821) W
John Clare (1793–1864) W
Charles Barry (1795–1860) Arc
Mary Shelley (1797–1851) W
Thomas Babington Macaulay (1800–1859) W

Samuel Palmer (1805–1881) A
Elizabeth Barrett Browning (1806–1861) W
Alfred Tennyson (1809–1892) W
Elizabeth Gaskell (1810–1865) W
William Makepeace Thackeray (1811–1863) W
Sir Gilbert Scott (1811–1878) Arc
Augustus Welby Northmore Pugin (1812–1852) Arc
Charles Dickens (1812–1870) W
Robert Browning (1812–1889) W
William Butterfield (1814–1900) Arc
Charlotte Brontë (1816–1855) W
George Frederick Watts (1817–1904) A
Emily Brontë (1818–1848) W
George Eliot (1819–1880) W
John Ruskin (1819–1900) W
William Powell Frith (1819–1909) A
Matthew Arnold (1822–1888) W
George Edmund Street (1824–1881) Arc
William Holman Hunt (1827–1910) A
Dante Gabriel Rossetti (1828–1882) A & W
John Everett Millais (1829–1896) A
Frederick Leighton (1830–1896) A
Richard Norman Shaw (1831–1912) Arc
Philip Webb (1831–1915) Arc
Lewis Carroll (1832–1898) W
Edward Burne–Jones (1833–1898) A
William Morris (1834–1896) A & W
Algernon Charles Swinburne (1837–1909) W
Thomas Hardy (1840–1928) W
Arthur Seymour Sullivan (1842–1900) C
Gerard Manley Hopkins (1844–1889) W
Robert Louis Stevenson (1850–1894) W
Oscar Wilde (1854–1900) W
George Gissing (1857–1903) W
Joseph Conrad (1857–1924) W
Edward Elgar (1857–1934) C
Arthur Conan Doyle (1859–1930) W
Walter Richard Sickert (1860–1942) A
Frederick Delius (1862–1934) C
Rudyard Kipling (1865–1936) W

W. B. Yeats (1865–1939) W
Ernest Dowson (1867–1900) W
Edwin Lutyens (1869–1944) Arc
Aubrey Beardsley (1872–1898) A
John Cowper Powys (1872–1964) W
Ralph Vaughan Williams (1872–1958) C
Somerset Maugham (1874–1965) W
Augustus John (1878–1961) A
Lytton Strachey (1880–1932) W
Giles Gilbert Scott (1880–1960) Arc
Virginia Woolf (1882–1941) W
Percy Wyndham Lewis (1882–1957) A & W
D. H. Lawrence (1885–1930) W
Ezra Pound (1885–1972) W
T. S. Eliot (1888–1965) W
Paul Nash (1889–1946) A
Edward Wadsworth (1889–1949) A
Agatha Christie (1890–1976) W
Stanley Spencer (1891–1959) A
J. R. R. Tolkien (1892–1973) W
Wilfred Owen (1893–1918) W
Aldous Huxley (1894–1963) W
Henry Moore (1898–1986) A
William Walton (1902–1983) C
George Orwell (1903–1950) W
Evelyn Waugh (1903–1966) W
Graham Greene (1904–1991) W
Michael Tippett (1905–1998) C
Samuel Beckett (1906–1989) W
W. H. Auden (1907–1973) W
Francis Bacon (1909–1992) A
Benjamin Britten (1913–1976) C
Frank Auerbach (1931–) A
Bridget Riley (1931–) A
Howard Hodgkin (1932–) A
David Hockney (1937–) A

INTRODUCTION
Albion

Of the English imagination there is no certain description. It has been compared with a stream or river, in the same manner as English poetry. It may be a fountain perpetually fresh and perpetually renewed, as in the Marian hymn of the early sixteenth century: 'Haill! fresh fontane that springes new . . .' It can also be seen in close affinity with the flow of English poetical cadence:

> In the hexameter rises the fountain's silvery column;
> In the pentameter aye falling in melody back

It can be compared to an aeolian harp, of which

> . . . the long sequacious notes
> Over delicious surges sink and rise

These words of Coleridge suggest in turn the drawn-out melodies and vast chromatic harmonies of the English musical tradition. And yet, if a literary metaphor is required, then the most powerful may be taken from Henry Vaughan in the seventeenth century: 'Like a great *Ring* of pure and endless light'. The English imagination takes the form of a ring or circle. It is endless because it has no beginning and no end; it moves backwards as well as forwards.

Albion is an ancient word for England, *Albio* in Celtic and *Alba* in Gaelic; it is mentioned in the Latin of Pliny and in the Greek of Ptolemy. It may mean 'the white land', related to the whiteness of the cliffs greeting travellers and suggesting pristine purity or blankness. But the cliffs are also guardians and Albion was the name of the primaeval giant who made his home upon the island of Britain. He is the 'elemental and emblematic giant' whom G. K. Chesterton observed in his study of Chaucer, 'with our native hills for his bones and our native forests for his beard . . . a single figure outlined against the sea and a great face staring at the sky'. His traces can be seen in the huge white horses which populated the primitive landscape, inscribed in the chalk of the hills. Today, like those fading memorials, Albion is not so much a name as the echo of a name.

There is clear evidence that the concept of Englishness – the 'English-ness' of the Anglo-Saxons, as opposed to the 'Britishness' of the Celts – circulated widely in the Anglo-Saxon world. Bede composed *Historia Ecclesiastica Gentis Anglorum* (The Ecclesiastical History of the English People), where the 'Gens Anglorum' were deemed to be a specific and identifiable race sprung out of Saxon and Old English roots. In Bede's history, 'the English were God's new "chosen" nation elected to replace the sin-stained Briton in the promised land of Britain'.[1] (This belief in God's providential choice, most ably expounded by Milton in the seventeenth century, survived until the latter part of the nineteenth century.) The notion of Englishness itself was a religious one from the moment Pope Gregory sent Augustine to England with the mission of establishing a Church of the English, in the light of his celebrated if apocryphal remark *'non Angli sed angeli'* ('Not Angles but angels'). A late seventh-century biography then declared that Gregory would lead *'gentem Anglorum'* into the sight of God at the time of the Last Judgement. One of the reasons for the success of the Reformation, and the formation of the Church of England, lies in this national zeal.

King Alfred is associated with 'the councillors of all the English race' in a late ninth-century treaty, and defined himself as *'rex Anglorum et Saxonum'*. In the preface to the translation of Gregory's *Cura Pastoralis* he alludes to *'Angelcynn'*, or Englishkind, and *'Englisc'*. The 'D' and 'E' texts of the *Anglo-Saxon Chronicles* evince the spirit of English nationalism with reference to 'this nation', 'all the people of England' and 'all the flower of the English nation'.[2]

The nationalism of the Anglo-Saxon period has been maintained by the fact that no other European nation has kept its boundaries intact over so many centuries. English literature, too, is among the oldest in Europe. It has been remarked that the heroic poetry of England after 900 strikes a singularly patriotic note, and we may regard that date as significant.

Archbishop Wulfstan's 'Sermon of the Wolf to the English', of 1014, continually invokes *theodscipe* or the nation in an act of sympathetic if admonitory communion. As one historian has put it, 'Englishness was the creation of the Anglo-Saxons, and it was they who made England'.[3] It was of crucial importance, in this context, that many charters and wills were composed in Old English; the language itself becomes an image of unity and identity. In that most important of Old English poems, *Beowulf*, the voices possess 'eloquence and understatement', a 'melancholy' and 'firm resolve',[4] which were bequeathed to subsequent English literature. In the art of the ninth and tenth centuries, too, there is an unmistakable Englishness in the employment of light and delicate outline. In the architecture of the same period irregularity and the pragmatic assembling of parts have also been deemed to be essentially English in spirit.

Yet from the beginning there are ambiguities and paradoxes. In painting, for example, the Anglo-Saxon style was inspired and modified by continental models before it could achieve maturity; the insular idiom was most fully expressed and developed precisely in relation to Mediterranean art of the same period. It could not exist without its continental counterpart. The power of Anglo-Saxon culture springs in part from absorption and assimilation, thus emphasising a more general point concerning 'the susceptibility of the English artist to alien influences . . . and his willingness to tolerate and even adapt to his own purpose any acceptable new elements'.[5] This has been the pattern of the centuries, and indeed it can be maintained that English art and English literature are formed out of inspired adaptation; like the language, and like the inhabitants of the nation itself, they represent the apotheosis of the mixed style.

We may identify here a sense of belonging which has more to do with location and with territory, therefore, than with any atavistic native impulses. There has been much speculation on the subject of location theory, in which the imperative of place is more significant than any linguistic or racial concerns. In *The Spirit of the People: An Analysis of the English Mind*, published in 1912, Ford Madox Ford suggested that 'it is absurd to use the almost obsolescent word "race"'. He noted in particular the descent of the English 'from Romans, from Britons, from Anglo-Saxons, from Poitevins, from Scotch . . .' which is perhaps the best antidote to the nonsensical belief in some 'pure' Anglo-Saxon people. In its place he invoked the spirit of territory with his belief that 'It is not – the whole of Anglo-Saxondom – a matter of race but one, quite simply, of place – of place and of spirit, the spirit being born of the environment'. In Ford Madox Ford's account that tradition is in some sense transmitted or communicated by the territory. It is a theory which will also elucidate certain arguments within this book.

And so the enterprise is begun. This study will concern the origins, and not the history, of the English imagination. It will not deal pro-portionately, therefore, with every period and every author or every artist. Beginnings will be granted more importance than endings. I will mention other literatures only in passing, and for this I offer no excuse. There will no doubt be many errors and omissions, to which I plead guilty in advance. I am fully aware that certain qualities defined here as peculiarly English are not uniquely so. Russian melancholy, and the Persian miniature, are cases in point. Yet such qualities flourish within an English context in singular and particular ways; I have simply endeavoured to trace their formation. There may also be faults of a native hue. If this book is diverse and various, digressive and heterogeneous, accumulative and eclectic, anecdotal and sensational, then the alert reader will come to realise that the author may not be entirely responsible.

Peter Ackroyd,
London,
May 2002.

Patterns of eternity

'Trees V: Spreading Branches', 1979, by Henry Moore.

CHAPTER I

The Tree

When William Wordsworth invoked 'the ghostly language of the ancient earth' he spoke more, perhaps, than he knew. The mark or symbol of the hawthorn tree is to be found in the runic alphabet of the ancient British tribes, as if the landscape propelled them into speech. The worship of the forest, and of forest forms, characterised the piety of the Druids in whose rituals the spirits of the oak, the beech and the hawthorn are honoured. According to the texts of the classical historians the centre of the Druidical caste was to be found in Britain, from whose shores the practitioners of magic sailed to the European mainland. The forest worship of the northern and Germanic tribes, who were gradually to conquer Britain from the fifth to the seventh centuries, may derive from the Druids' ministry. That is why Hippolyte Taine, the French critic and historian who in the 1860s completed a capacious history of English literature, hears the first music of England in the fine patter of rain on the oak trees.

The poetry of England is striated with the shade that the ancient trees cast, in a canopy of protection and seclusion. Thus John Lydgate, in the fifteenth-century 'Complaint of the Black Knight', remarks of

> Every braunche in other knet,
> And ful of grene leves set,
> That sonne myght there non discende

where the charm of darkness and mystery descends upon the English landscape. In the nineteenth-century Tennyson recalls how

> Enormous elm-tree boles did stoop and lean
> Upon the dusky brushwood underneath
> Their broad curved branches . . .

and in that tremulous dusk the trees themselves are images of peacefulness and protection.

In the penultimate chapter of *Jane Eyre*, before her final awakening, the heroine passes through 'the twilight of close ranked trees' like a 'forest aisle'. 'The Knight's Tale' of Geoffrey Chaucer is set in Athens

3

but the funeral pyre of Arcite there is adorned with the trees of England rather than those of ancient Greece – 'ook, firre, birch, aspe, alder, holm, popler' – in a refrain which was in turn adopted by Spenser in the first book of *The Fairie Queene* where 'the builder Oake', 'the Firre that weepeth still' and 'the Birch for shaftes' are among 'the trees so straight and hy'. For Spenser in the late sixteenth century the trees prompt mythical longings, as if their ancient guardians might still be summoned by the vatic tone of English epic. The hawthorn was the home of fairies, and the hazel offered protection against enchantment; the great oak itself descended into the other world. It is Milton's 'monumental Oke'. As a child William Blake saw angels inhabiting the trees of Peckham Rye; as a child, too, his disciple, Samuel Palmer, was entranced by the shadows of an elm tree cast by the moon upon an adjacent wall. Wordsworth stood beneath an ash tree in the moonlight and was vouchsafed visions

> Of human Forms with superhuman Powers.

The same poet saw among yew trees 'Time the Shadow', and wrote other verses upon 'The Haunted Tree'.

The magical talismans of Puck, in Rudyard Kipling's *Puck of Pook's Hill*, are the leaves of the oak, the thorn and the ash which afford the children access to earlier times. As the Roman poet, Lucan, apostrophised the Druids of the English isle in the first century – 'To you only is given knowledge or ignorance (whichever it be) of the gods and powers of heaven; your dwelling is in the lone heart of the forest.' In *Piers the Plowman*, composed in the fourteenth century, the divine edict of a later god ensures that 'Beches and brode okes were blowen to the grounde'.

These sources fill with vigour and energy the legends of Robin Hood, hiding himself among the trees of Sherwood Forest; he may be descended from the English imp, Robin Goodfellow, but he is more akin to the formidable figure of the Green Man. The fable may have begun in 1354 with the incarceration of a 'Robin Hood' for the poaching of venison in the forest of Rockingham, but no local or secular origin can account for the power which this green figure among the trees has been granted.

By 1377 the 'rymes of Robyn Hood' were as familiar as household tales, and as late as the sixteenth century the local festivals of the Thames and Severn Valleys, and of Devon, were still associated with plays of Robin Hood. It is not necessarily an old, or forgotten, piety. In

Women in Love D. H. Lawrence's twentieth-century characters, Ursula and Birkin, drive among 'great old trees'. '"Where are we?" she whispered. "In Sherwood Forest." It was evident he knew the place.' He knew it spiritually, atavistically. '"We will stay here", he said, "and put out the lights."'

And then in the darkness they may have seen the Ash Tree of Existence, the Tree of Jesse and the Golden Bough. The Tree of Jesse was 'the first design to be integrated in England to fill a large window'.[1] As part of the mournful decorations upon English tombstones, shields hang from trees. The palm-tree vault in Wells Chapter House, begun c.1290, endures as a memorial of sacred stone beyond the depredations of rain and wind and frost. In the biblical narrative of the *Cursor Mundi*, composed in English in the early fourteenth century, there are holy trees which owe more to English folklore than to biblical tradition; a heavenly light shines upon them, and they have an innate virtue which wards off evil and heals sickness. In an old English carol Jesus talks to a tree while still in his mother's womb, and images of the cross in English art are generally those of a lopped tree-trunk. In *The Dream of the Rood*, a meditation upon the crucifixion of Christ, the tree speaks:

> *ic waes aheawen holtes on ende . . .*
> *Rod waes ic araered . . .*
> *   eall ic waes mid blode bestemed*

> 'I was cut down, roots on end . . .
> I was raised up, as a rood . . .
> I was all wet with blood.'

Some lines from this Anglo-Saxon tree poem were carved in runes upon the great Ruthwell Cross, one of the English stone crosses which create a sacred topography of the nation. The Ruthwell inscription can be dated to the late seventh century, while in its surviving state the poem is believed to derive from eighth-century Northumbria; yet still the stone speaks, and the tree sighs.

On the territorial charters of Anglo-Saxon kings a hawthorn tree is generally employed as a boundary marker; it becomes the root of time and space, as a measure of continuity and ownership. In *The Child that Books Built* Francis Spufford remarks that 'there was a forest at the beginning of fiction, too. This one spread for ever.'[2] The tree encloses a communal memory – 'beyond the memory of anyone now living', as the medieval rubric was later to express it – and from it derives that sense of place, of literal rootedness, which is one of the great themes of the English imagination.

So in *The Mill on the Floss* George Eliot describes a country town 'which carries the traces of its long growth and history, like a millennial tree'. In 'The Hollow Tree' John Clare, the nineteenth-century poet who laboured with the land, celebrates the 'battered floor' of an anciently hollowed and hallowed ash:

> But in our old tree-house rain as it might
> Not one drop fell although it rained all night

Constable claimed that he could see Gainsborough 'in every hedge and hollow tree'; the remark expresses an identification with the offspring of the earth itself, that local genius or deity to which we are bound and towards which we ineluctably travel. Of Gainsborough's landscapes, of trees and forests in profusion, Constable also wrote: 'on looking at them we find tears in our eyes and know not what brought them.' Gainsborough himself remarked that there 'was not a picturesque clump of trees, nor even a single tree of any beauty . . . that I did not treasure in my memory from earliest years'. And what of Constable's own paintings? 'The trees', he wrote, '. . . seem to ask me to try and do something like them.' An enthusiast once created an enclosure in which were to be planted all the trees of Shakespeare's plays.

The destruction of trees creates dismay and bewilderment among the English poets. When Clare's favourite elm trees were condemned, he explained that 'I have been several mornings to bid them farewell.' There is an English legend of a dying stag, sobbing when for the last time it enters its own familiar glade; this, too, is part of the *genius loci*. When Gerard Manley Hopkins watched an ash tree cut down, 'there came at that moment a great pang and I wished to die and not to see the inscapes of this world destroyed any more'. 'Inscape' is of Anglo-Saxon derivation, from '*sceap*' meaning creation with a passing obeisance to '*instaepe*' or threshold. The ash represents a threshold of creation, for Hopkins in the nineteenth century no less than for the ancient priests of Britain. There is, here, a continuity. In sixteenth-century tapestry the antlers of stags resemble the trees upon a hillside, as if all nature were animated by one aspiring spirit; fifteenth-century English mystics saw trees as men walking, a vision recalled by Tolkien in his legend of moving trees or Ents in *The Lord of the Rings*. 'Ents' derives from the Old English word meaning 'giants'. Tolkien also refers to them as the 'shepherds of the trees', thus reintroducing the shepherd as another figure beloved in the English imagination.

It was remarked of Thomas Hardy, in 1883, that he 'is never more reverent, more exact, than when he is speaking of forest trees'. The tree represents life itself, and his characters are often identified by it. There is, for example, Gabriel Oak in *Far From the Madding Crowd*. In *The Woodlanders*, Hardy himself dwells upon the 'runic obscurity' of the language of trees, yet 'from the quality of the wind's murmur through a bough' the local inhabitants could name its species. In *Far From the Madding Crowd*, humankind 'learn how the trees on the right and the trees on the left wailed or chaunted to each other in the regular anti-phonies of a cathedral choir'. It is not difficult to understand, therefore, how the trees of the ancient landscape became images of British liberty and of primitive Christianity itself.

When Tess of the D'Urbervilles remarked that the trees had 'inquisitive eyes' she was exclaiming upon that same preternatural insight which the 'Tree of Truth' possesses in nineteenth-century panto-mimes; whenever a character told a lie, a large acorn fell upon his or her head. When Jane Eyre accepts Rochester's fanatical passion, 'little Adele came running in to tell me that the great horse-chestnut at the bottom of the garden had been struck by lightning'.

The folklore of England has many interesting ramifications. When in 1922 D. H. Lawrence wrote that 'I would like to be a tree for a while', he was expressing his need for deep and yet deeper absorption into the earth; it represents that descent into the layers of past time which is very like the journey into his own inner self where all unacknowledged fantasies and unknown powers lie hidden. That is why, in ancient poems, the woods are places of refuge and sanctuary. When Will Brangwen, in *The Rainbow*, carved two angels out of wood they 'were like trees'. In Blake's 'A Vision of the Last Judgement', Jehovah is 'The I am of the Oaks of Albion'. So the tree grows through the literature of the English.

CHAPTER 2

The Radiates

In 'A Letter to a Friend upon Occasion of the Death of His Intimate Friend', composed in the 1670s, Sir Thomas Browne noticed the change in the human countenance just before death; the man about to die began to resemble his uncle 'the Lines of whose Face lay deep and invisible in his healthful Visage before'. Thus before our mortal end 'by sick and languishing Alterations, we put on new Visages: and in our Retreat to Earth, may fall upon such Looks which from community of seminal Originals, were before latent in us'. Our ancestors shine through at that moment of quietus and we are but a palimpsest of past times.

And is this the condition of the world itself? As the lachrymose eighteenth-century poet Edward Young asked, in his *Conjectures on Original Composition*, 'Born originals, how comes it to pass that we die Copies?' It is a question of absorbing interest for those who contemplate the persistence through time of certain patterns of behaviour or expression. It has often been remarked how the inhabitants of the Scottish Highlands retained such a primitive way of life that they remained in the ninth century for many hundreds of years. But more unequivocal evidence was discovered in Gough's Cave, Cheddar Gorge. Here was found the skeleton of a man who had expired at some moment in that great expanse of time known as the Middle Stone Age; his mitochondrial DNA was subsequently tested, and a close match found with a history teacher residing in the late twentieth-century Cheddar village. Thus a genetic link can be directly established over a period of approximately eleven thousand years. But can it also pose a question of place, rather than of tribe or family? Can dwelling become a form of indwelling or imaginative life? To attempt to elucidate the characteristics of the English imagination, over a period of two thousand years, may not then be a futile or unworthy task.

For over one thousand years the Celtic tribes were established all over England; these separate British tribes, or kingdoms, or *civitates*, survived *in situ* from the pre-Roman Iron Age to the sub-Roman period and the Saxon invasions. Their verses of prophecy and legend remain

8

in the Irish, Welsh and Cornish vernaculars but in no other source. While extant inscriptions and symbols 'make it certain that sub-Roman [British] literacy included both letters and poems'[1] none of them has been found in England; just as there are almost no Syriac manuscripts dating from the Macedonian occupation of Syria, no British Celtic texts survive from either the Roman or Saxon periods. One British manuscript survives, the *Vergilius Romanus* of the early sixth century which is 'the earliest British book known to us today'.[2] It is of course composed in Latin. Those who had mastered writing naturally preferred to employ the 'prestige' language. No music remains and, since early British churches were constructed of wood, no public architecture.

Yet the presence of a thousand years can never wholly die; it lingers still in the words that spring most easily and fluently to the lips, among them 'kick', 'hitch' and 'fudge'. Celtic words lie buried in the landscape, like their quondam speakers immured in round barrows, in such familiar names as Avon and Cotswold and Downs. The names of London and the Isle of Man are Celtic.

The settlement of the Saxon invaders was a more gradual and intermittent process than has generally been acknowledged; new scholarly emphasis is upon assimilation rather than conquest, and, for example, Celtic patterns of farming have been found in medieval surroundings.

There may have been some compact or understanding, then, between the indigenous population of the island and the invading Anglo-Saxon tribes of the fifth and sixth centuries. There is evidence, both in place-names and in personal names, of absorption or intermingling; there was an Anglo-Saxon term, '*wealhstod*', meaning one who can understand and translate native Celtic (British) speech. In the bleak and forbidding landscapes of the north, the Celts (the British) were often left within their own communal areas; there seem to have been British settlements just north of the Thames, also, and in the forests of West Suffolk and Essex. It is possible that the British language was being spoken as late as the end of the seventh century, in Somerset and Dorset. There are many who claim that in Northumbria, for example, there are still Celts, distinctive in appearance and even in behaviour, among the local population.

There are deep patterns of inheritance and transmission still to be found etched in the stone or metal of surviving Celtic objects. We need not call it 'art' because it furnished the texture of life itself. Consider the characteristic motif of the spiral in Celtic workmanship both secular and spiritual; there are reverse spirals or whirls, and trumpet spirals, and 'hair-spring' spirals, circling like some persistent pattern or obsessive secret. It may come as no surprising revelation, therefore, to note the presence of the same spirals, or 'rings', carved upon sandstone rocks of the earlier Neolithic period. Here, chipped with hard stone tools, are the same symbols upon cremation covers or cist covers or outcrop rock, in locations such as Broomridge and Goat's Crag and Hare Law. They are sometimes known as 'radiates', and indeed they seem to shine from prehistory into the annals of recorded time. Some of them, marked upon stones beside burial cairns, were never meant to be seen; but they rise again, like the twelfth-century spiral markings in the church of St Laurence Pittington, Durham.

This is no archaeological reverie, however. The paganism of the Anglo-Saxon English, which survived for many centuries after Augustine had brought Christianity to England in 597, may in turn be traced to much earlier beliefs. The idols and demons, the spells and amulets, of the Anglo-Saxons may derive some of their power from Neolithic avatars. Just as the spirals are found within the Durham church, so concealed within the fabric of the church of St Albans were discovered rolls which contained magical invocations and the details of pagan rites.

The lineaments of a style and sensibility which have over the centuries been characterised as entirely English can be traced to Celtic work. The motif of the spiral, for example, is deployed within a severe and abstract patterning. The tendency towards elaborate pattern, aligned to surface flatness, will become increasingly apparent in this narrative of the English imagination. The vision of the Celts was an intense and graphic one, executed with a grave sense of form and a majestic, almost numinous, style. Theirs was not an art based on the representation of nature but one rooted in the essential truths behind appearance. Animals are depicted in long, flowing, ribbon-like movements; they become zoomorphs, or images of life as part of the calligraphy of significant form. This visionary capacity of the Celts is of the utmost importance in understanding the English genius.

There have been many theories about the persistent Celtic presence in native art and literature, the most eloquent of them embodied in *The Study of Celtic Literature* by Matthew Arnold in 1867. He proffers the observation that even if we no longer hear of the Celts after the Roman and Saxon invasions, that by no means proves they had ceased to exist; conquerors make their own history, while the vanquished must endure in silence. There is no record of extermination or general exodus (despite the tendency of the old Britons to move westward) so that 'one would suppose that a great mass of them must have remained in the country . . . their blood entering into the composition of a new people'. Arnold noted among these early Britons 'a singular inaptitude for the plastic arts' yet also a 'turn for melancholy' and 'natural magic' together with a 'passionate, turbulent, indomitable reaction against the despotism of fact'. In his somewhat deterministic vocabulary this natural temperament of the Celts is different from that of the Anglo-Saxons which is 'disciplinable and steadily obedient within certain limits, but retaining an inalienable part of freedom and self-dependence', with a propensity for 'spending its exertions within a bounded field, the field of plain sense, of practical utility'. Succeeding chapters of this book will suggest the extent of this 'practical' or empirical genius, but it is worth noting that according to Arnold the conflation of Celtic and Saxon in the national temperament has produced a kind of awkwardness or embarrassment – a tendency to understatement – in the characteristic productions of England. We may trace it through Chaucer and Auden, and will find one of its earliest manifestations in the verse of *Beowulf*.

12th century spiral markings: church of St Laurence Pittington, County Durham

Old English

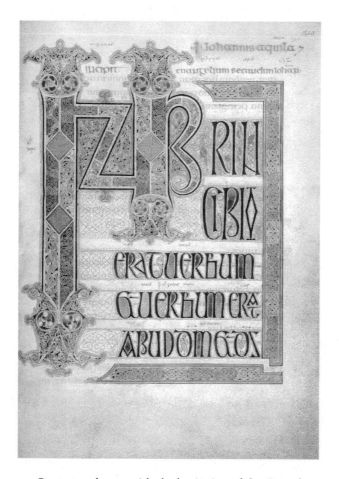

Ornamental page with the beginning of the *Gospel according to John*. From the Lindisfarne Gospels

CHAPTER 3

Listen!

In the beginning was the poem. It is of some 3,182 lines and is written in the language of the Anglo-Saxons known to us as 'Old English'. The events related in *Beowulf* can be dated approximately to the early decades of the sixth century, and to that period when the Frisians, Danes, Swedes, Franks and Geats were engaged in their occupation of England. The period in which it was actually written remains in dispute, although the most recent scholarship suggests a date in the tenth century. Yet *Beowulf* is so instinct with life and spirit that, on its discovery, it was believed to have been composed at the time of the events themselves. It is an act of the historical imagination, and may be seen as one of the earliest triumphs of historical consciousness.

The poem begins with a call for attention: '*Hwaet!*' – What! or Listen! Immediately invoked are the '*gear-daga*s', the days of old, a threnody which will become a constant passion among the English. There then follows a description of the funeral of Scyld Scefing, '*beaga bryttan*' or the Lord of the Rings, whose body is carried down to a great ship and despatched upon the whale-road and wave-domain of the sea; the sea is a constant presence in the poem, moving within the four beats of the alliterative line in an insistent rhythm which will affect the whole subsequent movement of English poetry. The grandson of Scyld Scefing, the warrior Hrothgar, builds a great '*heal-aern*', or hall-building, in order to memorialise his own triumphant career; this is a place of warmth and light, of food and drink, wide-gabled and lofty. It is a wine-mansion and gold hall of men. In a world of danger and of darkness, it represents human felicity. There is an Anglo-Saxon term, '*seledreorig*', meaning 'sad for a hall' (perhaps a longing for home); it is a harbinger of English melancholy.

Within this hall the '*scop*', or bard, chanted the song of creation when the '*Aelmihtiga*' created the earth and the waters, as well as the '*sunnan ond monan*' which grant light to humankind. And so good fortune reigned over Hrothgar's kingdom until a '*feond on helle*', a moor-dweller and border-wanderer, the monster Grendel, fell upon the bright hall and devoured thirty of Hrothgar's retinue. Grendel was descended from Cain, just as Alfred the Great's line was traced to

Adam himself. The feud of Cain and Abel was in direct and powerful relationship to the Anglo-Saxon culture from which *Beowulf* sprang; events did not necessarily take place in time but were endlessly fore-shadowed in the texts of sacred or spiritual teaching. The fraternal feud, then, might be seen as the most significant event in English history. It anticipates the sense in which later writers treated biblical history as a form of historical redaction.

Thus Grendel, the seed of Cain, was a '*death-scua*', or death shadow, a '*hel-rune*' who in the depths of night traversed the '*mistige moras*', or misty moors. Here, too, are the first traces of that delight in the strange and the occluded which marks the English imagination. The wonderful and the terrible stalk the '*mistige moras*' of subsequent poetry and fiction, with a particular conflation of horror and pathos which has become so characteristic and so familiar.

The monster was an exile and a wanderer, a state which the Anglo-Saxons feared and hated in equal measure. For twelve winters – note how, in this landscape, time is measured by winter – the monster pursued a campaign of extirpation and carnage against Hrothgar. Some of his men and counsellors offered sacrifices in propitiation to the pagan gods, and prayed to the '*gast-bona*', or devil, but the narrator consigns them to doom and damnation. *Beowulf* is a Christian poem concerning pagan warriors. This is a world in which the forces of elemental myth and of Christian typology are not necessarily distin-guished. It is not a question of the Christian and pagan elements opposing or modifying each other; they are equivalent in a poem of formal contrasts in which pathos and savagery, humour and celebration, are mingled. It is an inclusive English narrative.

After these twelve winters the thegn, Beowulf, came over the sea to assist Hrothgar. A watchman above the shining cliffs and high hills rides down to confront him. 'I have watched by the sea for many years,' he tells him, ' and have never witnessed such a host of armed men.' Then Beowulf unlocks his 'word-hoard' and speaks of his quest against the fiend. '*Beowulf is min nama*.' He takes up arms against Grendel and, in one desperate fight, the monster is fatally wounded by the warrior. Beowulf then severs the head of Grendel's monstrous mother. At a later time, he himself is delivered a fatal wound by a guardian dragon. The pattern is completed. The poem ends, as it begins, with a funeral ceremony. It is a high chant. It resembles an oratorio, and may be compared with John Milton's *Paradise Regained*. It is wrought at an intricate and formal pitch even though it springs out of melancholy and a sense of transience. It has the violence and intensity of Celtic work with the formality and fluency of Old English. The heart of the attentive listener may well break, but the *scop* keeps on singing.

The musical instruments of the Anglo-Saxon world, known to us, are the six-stringed harp or lyre, the horn, the bagpipe, the viol, the cymbals, the hand-bell and the reed flute. The association between music and poetry, however, is a matter of speculation. It is indeed possible that *Beowulf* was sung, and that the peculiar marks in the manuscript of the poem act as musical notations. The Latin word signifying singing, '*cantare*', is translated into Old English as '*the hearpan singen*', or sung to the harp. The phrase, '*swutol sang scopes*', appears. Yet the poem may have been chanted or intoned, to the accompaniment of the '*hearpan*'; it may even have been recited without the aid of any music. That its oration demanded a rigorous and formal performance is not in doubt; the *scop* was a significant figure in any lord's retinue, since he was both poet and historian of the community. The subsequent history of English poetry is so entwined with music, however, that the notion of musical accompaniment is a pleasing one. From the plaintive lyrics of the early Tudor court to the collaborations of Dryden and Purcell, Auden and Britten, the combined line of word and melody is persistent and continuous. It conjures up the image, expressed in an Old English *Life of St Dunstan*, of a harp sounding a melody – a song of joy – of its own accord.

Like many works of the English imagination, *Beowulf* has left its mark upon the landscape. The ancient site of Belbury Castle in Devon was known as '*bigulfesburh*', or 'Beowulf's burgh', and the name of '*grendlesmere*' appears in a Wiltshire charter of 931. The association of specific places with fatality is indeed an ancient one; the sites of pre-Saxon communities were generally held to be blessed or cursed, and until recent times there was a marked reverence for fairy circles and standing stones. There is a more elusive, but perhaps more significant, continuity. It is appropriate that in one sense *Beowulf* is a saga of origin, an attempt to animate or revive the culture from which the English believed they had sprung. Within the body of Anglo-Saxon writing itself lie the origins of subsequent English literature, whether in the form of dream-vision or riddle, history or travel, biography or elegy, verse moral or pastoral. There is also the matter of epic.

Beowulf itself survives in only one manuscript, its provenance unknown, but its fortuitous discovery is an intimation of the fact that there may have been other Old English epics which are now lost irretrievably; extant references suggest, if they do not prove, that there were long verse narratives concerning mythological figures such as Wade or Weland the Smith while fragments of the 'Battle of Brunanburh', the 'Battle of Finnsburh' and the 'Battle of Maldon' point to a relatively large corpus of lost and forgotten epic narrative.

That attraction to the epic form has persisted among the English poets. There are of course the great examples of Spenser's *The Faerie Queene* and Milton's *Paradise Lost*, of Hardy's *The Dynasts* and the fragment of *The Fall of Hyperion* by Keats. The epic ambition is to be found in Sidney's *Arcadia*, in Malory's *Le Morte Darthur*, in Tennyson's *Idylls*, in Browning's *The Ring and the Book*, in Blake's *Jerusalem*, in Wordsworth's *Prelude*, in Byron's *Don Juan*, in Shelley's *Prometheus Unbound*. One scholar of the English epic, E. M. W. Tillyard, cites Langland's *Piers the Plowman* as a worthy successor of *Beowulf* but refers to other examples in order to demonstrate 'the kinship of them all'.[1] He places *The Pilgrim's Progress* in this company, but then broadens his theme by arguing for the inclusion of Defoe's *Robinson Crusoe* and Gibbon's *The History of the Decline and Fall of the Roman Empire*. The case of Gibbon is instructive. In his childhood he had read Pope's translation of Homer, and Dryden's translation of Virgil; he was aware of the facility with which English poets could appropriate the epic tradition. In similar fashion he conceived of his *History* as a didactic and exemplary undertaking, and of himself as the true heir of Spenser and of Milton. The epic strain is deeply rooted.

One central preoccupation, however, might have been taken from *Beowulf* itself – that of a national epic celebrating the foundation and development of the race. Milton wished to 'rasp out a British tune' or Arthurian epic before he ever contemplated *Paradise Lost*; Dryden lamented his inability to write an epic upon a national subject, while Pope contemplated a blank verse narrative upon the theme of Brutus and his discovery of Albion. Coleridge had surmised that 'I should not think of devoting less than 20 years to an Epic Poem', but then surrendered the idea to Wordsworth who believed that only epic 'can satisfy the vast capacity of the poetic genius'. The epic mood was endemic, therefore. 'There is a *chaunt* in the recitation both of Coleridge and Wordsworth,' one contemporary noted, 'which acts as a spell upon the hearer.' The ancient chant of *Beowulf* is heard across the generations.

There is also a steadiness and intensity of tone which later poets have inherited. Here is a passage translated from the 'Battle of Finnsburh':

> Around him lay many brave men dying. The raven whirled about, dark and sombre, like a willow leaf. There was a sparkling of blades, as if all Finnsburh were on fire. Never have I heard of a more worthy battle in war.

Here is a passage from Siegfried Sassoon, on another battle, in 'Counter Attack':

> The place was rotten with dead; green clumsy legs
> High-booted, sprawled and grovelled along the saps
> And trunks, face downward, in the sucking mud

There is the same understated vehemence, the same directness and passion. It is reminiscent of Carlyle's remark that in the obstinacy and stolidity of the nineteenth-century labourer lay the lineaments of the Saxon warrior. When David Jones invoked his own experiences of the First World War, within *In Parenthesis*, he placed them in the context of Anglo-Saxon and Celtic mythology. As Taine puts the question (of the Anglo-Saxons), 'Is there any people which has formed so tragic a conception of life? Is there any which has peopled its infantine mind with such gloomy dreams?. . . Energy, tenacious and mournful energy, an ecstasy of energy – such was the chosen condition.'

The poetic life of approximately four hundred years survives now in only thirty thousand lines, snatched fortuitously from the oblivion of time; they are to be found in four manuscripts, one of them still located in the cathedral library of Vercelli near Milan, where no doubt it was left by a wealthy pilgrim on a journey to Rome. They were transcribed in the latter part of the tenth century, as part of the monastic revival of that period, when the scriptoria of the cathedrals and great monasteries were involved in a programme of educational and administrative reform. It was a question of preserving the inheritance of the race, at a time when its destiny and identity were being threatened by the Norsemen. But if it was a manner of affirming historical identity, it was also an act of piety; the poetic corpus transmitted by the monks was of an overwhelmingly Christian character, thus establishing the visionary religious tradition within all subsequent English poetry. The sacred histories of *Genesis, Exodus, Daniel, Judith, The Fate of the Apostles,*

Christ and Satan all furnish the homiletic material of the later English poets.

The dates for the composition of these Anglo-Saxon poems cannot now be ascertained and we may hazard any period between the sixth and tenth centuries; although most of the extant poetry has been transcribed in the West Saxon tongue, there are dialectical differences in the range of Old English which emphasise the provenance of different kingdoms. From Northumbria come the hymn of Caedmon, *The Dream of the Rood* and Bede's verses in the last hours of his life. Bede, who characteristically wrote in Latin, reverted to his native tongue *in extremis*, just as the scholar Aldhelm sang in the vernacular upon a bridge to attract and edify the English. From Mercia are supposed to spring two long poems on the life of St Guthlac, the hermit of Crowland among the fens of Lincolnshire, while *Beowulf* itself contains certain Mercian references. From Kent may derive a version of the 'Finnsburh' fragment; from the West Saxons 'The Ruin'. In such a sophisticated society there was a range of expressiveness. In the Cynewulf *Christ*, homage is paid to the singer of 'wise poems'; another bard may chant before heroes, while others are concerned with singing of sacred law or of the course of the heavens.

All employed the alliterative line, that great pounding force which is created by two half-lines divided by a caesura, with two principal stresses or 'lifts' in each half-line. It has been well noted that it emphasises the qualities of intense or loudly enunciated speech; it is measured by a firm and heavy beat. It does not run and cannot be rushed; it is intense because it harbours an ecstasy and energy forced to dwell in measure. The pattern of two alliterative words in the first half of the line, followed by one in the second, creates a cadence as if of thought or contemplation. The listener or solitary reader is obliged to pause – as it were – in order to comprehend the meaning. Its syllabic momentum courses so powerfully through the lines of later poets that the beat of the pentameter and the octosyllabic couplet, two of the dominant forms within English verse, can be supposed to spring directly from this oral source. Like English speech, it has a falling rhythm. It is a 'high' language, a call or summons like a great bell; the line-break and the pattern of stresses allow for a complete interrelation between parts in a series of oppositions and contrasts. The language employed is, by the tenth century, deliberately archaic and 'poetic' with a reliance upon encrusted ornamental diction as well as a repertoire of phrases; the sun is 'the candle of the world', the sea is 'the chalice of waves', the helmet is the 'castle of the head'. It is what William of Malmesbury declared to be 'English magnificence'.

One of the most interesting features of these tenth-century recensions is the manner in which they were transcribed; the poetry is written in the long lines of prose, as if no certain or intrinsic difference could be distinguished between verse and prose narrative. In similar fashion the prose homilies preserved in the Vercelli book borrow alliterative and general metrical features from Anglo-Saxon poems; this is of the utmost significance in dealing with examples of English prose and poetry from much later writers where, in many instances, there is again no clear distinction between the forms. The meditations of John Donne or Thomas Browne may best be understood as forms of allusive poetry, while parts of Browning or Clough move towards the dominant nineteenth-century mode of the novel. There is no necessary boundary. There is none, also, between the various genres of Anglo-Saxon poetic activity. Little distinction is made between the poetry of natural observation and of religious narrative, for example, which in turn suggests that there is very little perceived difference between religious and secular poetry. In a society once thoroughly paganised, where ravens spoke and stones moved, how can there be such a difference? And in a society where the values of early Christianity came to prevail over heathen reverence, the whole world remains a spiritual force replete with miracles and changed by prayer. It was, and is, an island of visions.

There was also no distinction between Latin and Christian verse, between classical and religious texts which were studied with equal attention; the eighth century was, in particular, a great age of learning in which the works of Virgil, Statius and Lactantius were inscribed alongside those of St Jerome and St Augustine. The monastic system of education trained not only prelates but princes, since both secular and religious leaders were generally interconnected and interrelated. This may account for the 'high' and artificial style of a poetry in large part composed for, and addressed to, a sophisticated audience. The pleasure of *scop* as well as listener lay less in the modern shibboleth of invention than in elaborating upon the impersonal authenticity and authority of ancient texts. We read continually of exile and of transience, of kinship feuds and the necessity of loyalty, of the isolated wanderer; we witness the giving of gifts in the mead hall, the blizzards of winter, the effigy of the boar; we are reminded of fate and of destiny, of the wilderness world, of the strongholds of city dwellers, of the surging salt sea, of the raven, of the eagle and the wolf. It has been suggested that we still dream of dark woods in memory of the Druids; in turn the fascination with old ruined dwellings in writers as disparate as Wordsworth and Dickens may have its deep source in the Anglo-Saxon preoccupation with deserted or empty buildings, all their warmth displaced by '*wintres woma*', or the awful sound of winter.

The nature of this poetry, then, does not encourage individual utterance; but it does not altogether preclude it. In the late eighth or early ninth centuries a cleric concealed his name in runes towards the conclusion of four poems. A rune was a symbol of the ancient Germanic alphabet used by the Saxon tribes long before the Romans came, in which each sign represented a letter or an object. Thus the cleric's name, Cynewulf, becomes in sequence torch, bow, necessity, horse, happiness, man, sea, wealth. His signature was a cryptogram, one of those aenigmata so congenial to the Anglo-Saxon imagination. The works where the runes are inserted are all of a homiletic nature – *Elene*, *Juliana*, *The Ascension* and *The Fate of the Apostles* – some 2,600 lines altogether, established upon Latin originals or, as Cynewulf puts it, 'as I found it in book'. The fact that his own name is distributed among the closing lines suggests that his is a work intended to be read rather than heard and, perhaps, to endure beyond the memory of his own civilisation. In the '*faecne hus*', or treacherous house, of the body he has been wholly intent upon '*wordcraeft*' or '*leothcraeft*', the art of poetry. One great Anglo-Saxon scholar, Kenneth Sisam, has described him as the first English 'man of letters . . . whose name and works are known',[2] and in that there is perhaps some distinction.

CHAPTER 4

Why is a raven like a writing desk?

It would be profoundly mistaken to underestimate the sophistication of Anglo-Saxon literature; there is no progress in English writing but, rather, a perpetual return to the original sources of inspiration. The ninety-five riddles in the manuscript known as *The Exeter Book*, for example, composed in the early eighth century, afford direct and unmediated access to a complex and suggestive culture in which elaboration, difficulty and highly wrought obscurity are qualities assiduously to be pursued:

> I stretch beyond the bounds of the world,
> I'm smaller than a worm, clearer than the moon . . .[1]

The verses contain the occasional refrain that the 'wise' or 'clever' man will 'say what my name is' or 'say what I am called'; in this example it is creation itself that is being announced in cryptic and enigmatic form.

It seems that one of the Anglo-Saxon definitions of intelligence lay precisely in the ability to unravel complex significations. The whole pursuit of art and literature is to find vital formal or spiritual meanings within the disparate array of the material world; the economy of means chosen bears some relation to Anglo-Saxon art, while the abiding interest in paradox and contrast is an aspect of that violence of expression which is also intrinsic to the Anglo-Saxon sensibility. The combination of austerity and brilliant subtlety is one of the profound gifts of that sensibility which subsequent English writers have learned to share. From where else do the *Paradoxes and Problems* of John Donne, and the riddles of Lewis Carroll, spring? That great elucidator of English literature, Jorge Luis Borges, was well aware of its Anglo-Saxon derivations – particularly as an intellectual game, or an intricate pattern or puzzle.

Some of these riddles may be related to folk-charms, but most of them are highly literary and extravagant exercises in word play which are part of the fascination for ornamentation of every kind in runic signatures and gnomic verses. Yet it would be wrong to suggest that there is nothing 'naturalistic' about this literary style; the keen curiosity and vivacity of the Anglo-Saxon imagination keep on breaking through. The manuscript volume in which the riddles are inscribed has the stains of daily use upon it; there are the marks of knives and the indentations of cups on the first folio as a fitting accompaniment to verses that celebrate the presence of household objects.

There are condensed metaphors here for the ink-well and the quill, the onion and the wine cup, the loom and the well-bucket, the bellows and the book-case; here also are lancets and helmets, swords and ploughs, oysters and weathercocks, all of them announcing their identities in the first person – 'I travel onward; I have many scars',[2] confesses the plough – as if the whole world were instinct with life. The poem then becomes a magical act of reclamation.

There is another active principle in these poems, with their propensity for crude or lewd humour; the jokes about male and female pudenda abound. So 'I grow very tall, erect in a bed'. When a girl recalls our meeting 'Her eye moistens'.[3] The answer might be an onion or, on the other hand, it might not. The Anglo-Saxons initiated a tradition of 'blue' humour and innuendo which has flourished in England ever since.

There is another inheritance, by way of English paradox. Although it would be fanciful to suggest any direct connection between the Anglo-Saxon Aldhelm's *Enigmata* and Elgar's *Enigma Variations* of 1899, other associations may tentatively be made. Certain sixteenth-century epigrams of Thomas Wyatt, such as

> A lady gave me a gift she had not
> And I received her gift which I took not

also bear witness to the delight in puzzle and 'wit-spell' which continued well into the twentieth century. Musical riddles were also popular devices in the sixteenth century with the fashion for 'puzzle canons', often for three voices; according to one musical historian, they seem 'to be a purely English invention'.[4] A Tudor chronicler notes that Henry VIII 'made to the Ambassadors a sumpteous banquet with many riddels and much pastyme', and Jane Austen depicts the early nineteenth-century English delight in anagrams and acrostics. We are not so far from Arthur Bliss's *Knot of Riddles*, performed in 1963, nor from the musico-mathematic illogic of Lewis Carroll. 'Why is a raven like a writing desk?'

The intricacy of Anglo-Saxon verse is suggestive in another sense because it affords access to an entire phase of English culture; it is one

24

of the tenets of this book that no art or activity need be seen in isolation, and that all partake of the same continuum of perception and desire. The structure of *Beowulf*, for example, is as ornate and intricate as that of the Anglo-Saxon riddle; patterns of repetition and variation, parallel and antithesis, are woven as tightly within the fabric of the poem as the echoes and anticipations of alliterative sound. It represents the fascination with what is difficult, and the resistance to easy interpretation. In the narrative itself the *scop*, or bard, is reported to '*wordum wrixlan*', or vary words, in precisely this sense. The poet Cynewulf describes the same effect with his announcement that '*ic . . . wordcraeftum waef*', or 'I wove my word-craft'. In the composition of *Beowulf* scenes and episodes are similarly 'woven' into a pattern of contrast and recapitulation so that the effect is of formal intricacy and immediacy rather than any linear development. The association with the weaving of tapestry is apposite here, and the poetic technique has become known as that of 'interlace'. The 'interlace structure' has thus been defined as expressing 'the meaning of coincidence', the recurrence of human behaviour, and the circularity of time[5] as the thread of words crosses and recrosses itself in endless weaves and knots.

It is not simply a technique, therefore, but a vision of the world. The great stone crosses of Northumberland and Cumberland, hewn in the early eighth century, are carved with abstract interlace patterns in which bands or threads or vines turn back upon themselves to form woven intersections or knots. They may be symbols of eternity, like the spirals upon even more ancient stone, but they seem also to display a delight in intricacy or ornament for its own sake. Ivory caskets, sword-hilts, brooches and rings are emblazoned with the same labyrinthine device; a large gold buckle, discovered during the excavations at Sutton Hoo and dated to the early seventh century, has an interlacing of snakes and birds' heads wrought upon it. It was what the *Beowulf* poet described as '*hring-boga*', ring-coiled. The manuscript illuminations from the seventh and eighth centuries are irradiated by interlace; the initial pages of the Lindisfarne Gospels are peculiarly rich in this art, with one page bearing several thousand 'intersections' while in another only two threads or bands are employed to create an entire and effortlessly detailed 'carpet-page'. The pattern occurs at a later date. When one Middle English poem, known as *The Owl and the Nightingale*, is depicted in terms of 'chain-stitch'[6] the relation to the 'carpet-page' of the illuminated gospels is reinforced. If it is indeed a vision of the world, it is one which has no beginning and no end; there is no sequence and no progress, only the endless recapitulation of patterns and the constant interplay of opposing forces. Thus 'interlace' has variously described Malory's *Le Morte Darthur* and Spenser's *The Faerie Queene*, Langland's *Piers the Plowman* and the penitential lyrics of the thirteenth century. The term has been used to define the novels of Charles Dickens.

In an embroidered alb of the twelfth century, humankind is depicted as a man caught in the interlaced coils of a dominant absorbing pattern. The nature of the embroidery here reveals another design – that is to say, the design of Englishness itself. In the late thirteenth and early fourteenth centuries the most rich and elaborate embroidery was known throughout Europe as *opus anglicanum*; England's most famous luxury and most celebrated export was finely wrought silk with gold patterns and coloured grounds. There are 113 examples in the Vatican inventory of 1295 and various feats of English workmanship are to be found in France, Spain, Belgium and Italy. It was truly a native art, with origins at least as early as the ninth century. It is perhaps no accident, then, that 'complex part writing' for the organ has been described as a 'fine native tradition'[7] or that the 'polyphonic carol' is 'a uniquely English phenomenon'.[8] Throughout this volume the English interest in pattern and elaborate decoration will become apparent; it is aligned with the affection for bold outlines and complex surface coverings in which frames and figures are interlaced or interwoven.

Art, therefore, is known to be artifice; it may eschew interiority or depth for the sake of striking ornament and exciting contour. But it may not lack significance, since the art of the surface is itself a bold one. Consider what interlace may mean in a different context. It has been often said of Elizabethan theatre, for example, that it was distinguished from all other European drama in its capacity to interweave comic and serious episodes; popular drama of the sixteenth century is prodigal of scenes and characters which, as it were, exist simultaneously. One historian of that drama has described the interplay between comedy and tragedy with the further reflection that, when 'strand eventually coheres with strand, the effect recalls Spenser's "interlacement" in *The Faerie Queene*'.[9] These writings are all of a piece, with many figures in view; the concern is for elaboration and 'intrigues' rather than principle or emotion.

In turn *The Faerie Queene* has been compared with a manuscript illumination, with a tapestry, and with a stained-glass window in an English church, because of its delicate links, its interconnecting scenes, and its profusion of principal and subordinate figures; in that poem there is no single or intense emotional stress, since 'the conflict of character and motive is undeveloped'.[10] The 'interest in exact detail and love of pattern are traditional in English art from its earliest appearance, and are to become firmly established as time goes on'.[11] In architecture, too, 'the characteristic English development lay in decoration rather than in pure architecture';[12] in stained glass the passion was for the 'ornamental patterns' of the windows in Salisbury Cathedral and Westminster Abbey,[13] while the eloquent prose of Sir Thomas Browne is preoccupied with 'the making of mosaic patterns with fragments of knowledge'.[14]

What manner of imagination is this? It is one that eschews purity of function for elaboration of form, that strays continually into anecdote and detail, that distrusts massiveness of conception or intent, that avoids 'depth' of feeling or profundity of argument in favour of artifice and rhetorical display. The twentieth-century architectural historian, Sir John Summerson, has remarked that Renaissance art made its way in England only 'as a mode of decorative design';[15] the diamond patterning to be seen at St John's College, Cambridge, is typical in this respect, and sixteenth-century portraiture in all its elaboration of ornamental detail comes close to abstract and decorative pattern.

In the earliest examples of architecture this passion for decoration may in part be regarded as the horror of vacuity, of blankness, that emerges in the poetry of the Anglo-Saxons. Has this something to do with their horrified refusal of the blank landscape all around them? Art is then the alternative to nature. It has, in fact, been suggested that 'the special gifts of the Anglo-Saxons may have lain in decoration rather than in architecture',[16] and the same predilection can be seen in the decorated patterns of the great nave at Ely and the richly inscribed stone of Durham Cathedral no less than in the eight bands of carving within the south porch of Malmesbury Abbey. There is a concern for 'rich surface display'[17] in Wells Cathedral which anticipates the ornamental coverings of Victorian upholstery and the flatness of Pre-Raphaelite painting. It can also be seen in the rococo of the Georgian period, in the ornamental ironwork of the Great Exhibition, in the floral wallpaper of William Morris. The open elaboration of the Lloyds Building and the Pompidou Centre, by Richard Rogers, can also be understood in this context. It is everywhere in the English sensibility. We seem to have come a long way from Anglo-Saxon art and poetry but, in the imagination, there is no distance at all.

CHAPTER 5
A rare and singular Bede

The Venerable Bede was born in a small and obscure village near Jarrow, in Northumbria, in or about 672, and nothing is known of his parents except that according to early commentators they were of humble origins; he was not the first English writer whose modest beginnings spurred an ambition and aspiration towards great achievement. At the age of seven he was taken to the monastery at Wearmouth; someone must have recognised his abilities, therefore, and caused him to be enrolled in what was then an orthodox course of education.

At this early age he began to memorise the Latin psalmody and hymnal, with the help of an Anglo-Saxon gloss, so that he might participate in all the Divine Offices of the monks; he then began to work upon Latin grammar and metrics, so important for the understanding of plainchant. He suffered from an impediment in his speech, however, but he was cured while writing about the miraculous relics of St Cuthbert. This personal experience should be recalled when examining his many descriptions of miraculous healing which purblind readers have ascribed to credulity or superstition.

He was educated under the tutelage of Abbot Benedict, and later of Abbot Ceolfrid, both of them important figures in seventh-century England. The young oblate was transferred to the neighbouring monastery of Jarrow, where he was to remain for the rest of his quietly exacting life. At the age of nineteen he became a deacon, and the fact that he was appointed some six years before the customary time suggests that he was already notable for his learning. He was ordained priest at the age of thirty and, by his own testimony, then began his commentaries upon the Bible. From that time forward he rarely travelled beyond the confines of the monastery, and never left Northumbria; he was one of those English writers of whom it can confidently be said that he saw the universe within the context of a specific geographical place. Like Blake and Bunyan he was granted intimations of the spiritual world upon his own spot of earth, and the writing poured forth as from a spring.

At the close of his *Historia Ecclesiastica Gentis Anglorum* Bede added a short autobiographical passage in which he declared that for almost thirty years he had laboured in his cell and had produced on a rough calculation some sixty-eight 'books', including commentaries upon Mark and Luke as well as Isaiah and Daniel, histories of the saints and books of hymns and epigrams, histories and text-books on poetry and chronology. It was a noble achievement. His was a life devoted to reading and chanting, writing and teaching; although he was well aware of events in the outer Anglo-Saxon world, with the death of kings and the rivalry of abbots, nothing could affect his dedication to his constant and assiduous work; he might almost have been born a scholar and writer, and he persevered in this course until the very close of his life.

The remains of Jarrow still stand, with stone walls, small squared windows and carved stone; the dedication stone, marking its foundation in 685, can be found in the wall above the arch of the chancel. Housing some two hundred monks Jarrow was a large foundation which, according to Benedictine rule, had independent status as a house of prayer and learning. Something of the old tribal structure remained, with an abbot, normally of royal lineage, ruling his band of brothers as 'chieftain to the community'.[1] On the abbot's death the leadership of the monastery was given to one of his kinsmen. Thus the society within the walls of the religious establishment copied the wider governance of England. The Latin word for town, *civitas*, was in turn applied to monasteries. But just as the observances of Celtic (that is, British) Christianity were being supplanted by the Benedictine (that is, continental) rules of the Anglo-Saxon monks, so the ethos and purpose of English monasteries were slowly being transformed. A letter of Bede's to Egbert, Bishop of York, condemns those bishops 'given to laughter, jokes, idle tales, feasting and drunkenness' who are at once lazy and unlearned, and denounces those who purchase monasteries in order to fill them with their own followers and concubines; all these abuses the Benedictine rule was designed to extirpate. There were of course centres and occasions of Celtic piety, particularly within the hermitic tradition, but the ancient order of faith had degenerated through the very fact of its longevity. The Benedictine dispensation was in turn responsible for, and responsive to, a fresh movement of devotion to learning. It is the single most important context for the transmission and preservation of Anglo-Saxon literature.

There was a common dormitory and common refectory at Jarrow but Bede, given his high occupation as commentator and historian, was granted a separate hut or cell of stone in which to live and work.

Situated somewhere to the south of the principal buildings, between the church and the river, it was approximately ten feet square with a wooden screen separating the space for prayer and meditation. In the area adjoining lay, perhaps, the codices upon which he worked. Bede would have recited the Divine Office each day, but whether he engaged in the normal routine of husbandry and field labour is open to doubt. There must also have been a larger scriptorium which he visited and used each day; here a few monks would be engaged in translation, transcription and manuscript illumination, preparing the Word of God and contributing texts for a select and devout audience. Here, again, lie some of the origins of English literature.

The monastery with its scriptorium was truly what King Alfred called, at a later date, a house of knowledge. In Anglo-Saxon literature, there are accounts of burnished books, inscribed in letters of gold and covered with precious jewels; they are treasures of 'gold and godweb' designed to illumine and glorify the scriptures but also powerfully to impress the sensibilities of the pagan English. In themselves they became sacred objects; water used to be poured over the Book of Durrow before being collected and given to ailing cattle. The *Codex Amiatinus* was created at Jarrow; the skins of 1,550 calves were required in order to provide the parchment, and two men were needed to carry it. It served as a reliquary or casket as well as a text. Sometimes, too, the book would speak – 'the bird's feather often moved over my brown surface, sprinkling meaningful marks'.[2] The art of illumination makes the English tradition paradigmatic of the whole Western spiritual tradition which, unlike that of the East, favours learning rather than looking. The parchment would have been tanned and then scraped with a knife before being smoothed with a pumice-stone; it was whitened with fine particles of chalk, and then ruled with lines before pen and ink were devoted to its illumination. The scriptorium itself represented 'contempt of earthly things', a sacred concept of writing which survived until the twentieth century and into W. H. Auden's 'cave of making'.

Yet the world kept on breaking through. There are marginalia, or doodles, upon the edge of Anglo-Saxon manuscripts which provide some evidence of circumambient life. A dog trots across the bottom of one page of *Andreas*, a long poem on the ministry of St Andrew, while a later page is marked with the half-erased name of 'Eadgith' or Edith. In the margin of another manuscript are found the words '*Writ thus odde bet; ride aweg; Aelfmaer Patta fox, thu wilt swingan Aelfric cild*' which may loosely be translated as 'Write like this or better; ride away;

Aelfmaer Patta the fox, you will flog the boy Aelfric'. Patta is the teacher and Aelfric the pupil set to work upon transcription. 'Ride away' may suggest the child's longing to be gone.

There are passages in Bede's *Historia Ecclesiastica Gentis Anglorum* which also evoke the true nature of the Anglo-Saxon world, and of its monasticism in particular. One of them concerns the departure of the abbot of Monkwearmouth, Ceolfrid, on a final pilgrimage to Rome. On Thursday morning, 4 June 716, he stood upon the altar of the monastic church with a burning censer in his hand; he bade the monks farewell and gave them the kiss of peace, but the sound of loud weeping from the assembly interrupted the chant of the litanies. An age of violence was also an age of ready emotionalism. He and the brethren then advanced in procession to the bank of the Wear, where the monks fell upon their knees as he and a few close companions boarded a boat. 'The deacons of the church embarked with them, carrying lighted candles and a golden cross. After crossing the river, he venerated the cross, mounted his horse and rode off.'[3] There is revealed here, in the carrying of the golden cross and the lighted candles across the river, an intrinsic respect for ritual and display; in a world racked by storms of every description, where life itself may be short and harsh, the glowing gold and the candlelight afford a fleeting vision of sacredness.

The quiet life of Bede was succeeded by a no less peaceful death. In his sixty-third year he knew that he was dying; he continued to teach his monastic pupils but spent the rest of each day and most of each night in song and prayer. He chanted the Latin scriptures and repeated by heart many old English poems – perhaps those he had learnt as a child near Jarrow – but when he reached the words of one antiphon, 'Do not leave us orphans', he burst into tears. His pupils wept with him, crying even as they studied under his instruction, but until almost the moment of death he kept them at their work of dictation. 'Learn quickly now, for I don't know how long I shall live . . . write quickly.' Here is an indication of his fervour for learning. He distributed his few 'treasures' – pepper, handkerchiefs, incense – and then he was told by one of his pupils that there was still one sentence to be written.

> 'Write it then.'
> 'It is written.'
> 'Good. It is finished.'

He sat upon the floor of his cell, singing, until he died.

So ended a life of incessant labour and prodigious learning. His reputation was unrivalled in Europe as well as in his own country. 'It seems right to me', a monk from Jarrow wrote, 'that the whole race of the English in all provinces wherever they are found, should give thanks to God that he has granted to them so wonderful a man in their nation.'

The seventh and eighth centuries were, perhaps, the most learned period in the nation's history. Bede was one of a number of scholars and clerics of impeccable if somewhat insular Latin scholarship. There was, in fact, such a literary phenomenon as 'Anglo-Latin' characterised 'by a lavish display of vocabulary designed to impress by the arcane nature of its learning . . . in obscure, learned-sounding words, such as archaisms, grecisms and neologisms',[4] a style which haunts English prose in the work of such writers as Robert Burton and Thomas Browne. The sixteenth-century term was 'euphuism' but there has always been an affection for it within the English imagination; it represents almost a deliberate parody of learning or, rather, a delight in ornate language and pattern rather than in profound scholarship for its own sake.

One of its principal Anglo-Saxon exponents was Bede's contemporary, Aldhelm, who composed epistles and treatises in an elaborate and sometimes obscure prose; he also wrote Latin verse in continuous octosyllables, and continued the native inheritance by writing puzzles or mysteries or *enigmata*. He had been educated in the cathedral school of Canterbury under the tutelage of an African scholar named Hadrian, this salient fact alone suggesting the range of scholarship and civilisation existing in seventh-century England. Hadrian had arrived with the Greek scholar, Theodore of Tarsus; Theodore was appointed Archbishop of Canterbury by Pope Vitalian, and together with Hadrian established a school which according to Bede 'attracted a large number of students', who studied 'poetry, astronomy and the calculation of the church calendar' as well as holy scripture. Bede testifies to the efficacy of their instruction by noting that in his time there were still Englishmen 'as proficient in Latin and Greek as in their native tongue'.[5] In the ninth century King Alfred lamented the loss of such learning, but such attainments would also be rare in the twenty-first century.

The tradition of the cathedral school never entirely died, even in the worst periods of Danish invasion, so that we can point justifiably to a continuous legacy of learning in England. It is the source, for example,

of 'flyting', or scholastic 'contest', preserved in the wisdom literature of
the Anglo-Saxons, by means of which two scholars would address each
other upon a particular theme and practise all their skills of rhetoric;
the same competitions were part of the curriculum in medieval schools
and continued within the Inns of Court of the sixteenth and
seventeenth centuries. It is a tradition which helped to create Tudor
drama – itself often performed in the halls of the Inns – and thus the
theatrical renaissance of the late sixteenth century.

The texts of the Anglo-Saxon schools included the *Evangelia* of
Juvencus, the *Carmen* and *Opus Paschale* of Sedulius and Arator's *De
Actibus apostolorum* together with other works from the corpus of
Christian Latin literature. Virgil's *Aeneid* was also widely known and
quoted, as well as the work of other classical writers such as Lucian and
Persius; it is an impressive list for scholars of any period, but it provides
direct evidence for the beginning of 'classics' in the English educational
system. It is often remarked, with some surprise, that the administrators and politicians of the nineteenth century were accustomed to
take quotations from, or make allusions to, the authors of classical
antiquity. Yet as early as the seventh century the English bishops and
abbots, who were the true administrators of the nation, were equally
capable of making reference to Ovid, Virgil, Cicero, Pliny and others.
There is, again, a continuity.

Bede's library was itself formidable. It contained more than 130 texts,
of which we may assume that a preponderant amount came from the
collections of Monkwearmouth and Jarrow; the range of his reading
was wide indeed, but his principal sources remain Ambrose, Augustine,
Jerome and Gregory. In other words Bede was placing himself directly
and deliberately in the tradition of European Christian exegesis. The
example of Bede and his successors provides clear evidence that the
English nation was an inalienable part of European culture and society,
as much a beacon of Western Christendom as Rome or Seville. English
learning affected scholars upon the European mainland, but in turn
European art and literature came to Canterbury and Jarrow,
Winchester and Ely, London and St Albans. It was always thus. From
the time of the Roman occupation, and perhaps earlier, England was
an integral part of the culture and texture of Europe. In 314 the bishops
of London, York and Lincoln attended a general council in Arles, while
French ecclesiastics came to England to combat the English heresies of
Pelagius. When Pope Gregory sent Augustine on his mission to England

in 597, a connection was established that was not severed until the 'submission of the clergy' to Henry VIII in the spring of 1532. The enterprise of the Greek Theodore and the African Hadrian has already been outlined; as Archbishop of Canterbury, Theodore also reorganised the administration of the English Church. When we consider 'Englishness', therefore, it is best to understand from what sources it springs.

The traffic was not in one direction only. It has been said that Boniface, a native of Crediton in Devon, 'had a deeper influence on the history of Europe than any other Englishman who ever lived'.[6] His missionary work in Hesse and Thuringia led to his veneration as the 'Apostle of Germany'; his was a cultural as well as a spiritual enterprise, and Anglo-Saxon texts or illuminations were deposited in the cathedrals and monastic foundations that he established in Germany. There was a common culture. When the founder of Monkwearmouth and Jarrow, Benedict Biscop, travelled back to Northumbria after a period in Rome he brought with him many rare books as well as silks and panel paintings from Italy; he created a library at Wearmouth which became the most important centre of learning in northern England. Bede could not have undertaken the tasks of his scholarship without the early benefactions of Biscop. Bede himself, in his *Lives of the Abbots*, describes the 'great mass of books of every sort' with which Biscop returned, as well as sacred relics, 'many holy pictures of the saints' and illustrations from the gospels which were placed around the basilica at Wearmouth. Biscop also brought back glaziers and masons from the continent and a 'chief cantor' or singing master who taught the monks of England the rules of Roman plainchant. So at the same time as Bede was composing his ecclesiastical history of England, the joint monasteries of Wearmouth and Jarrow were being furnished and ornamented in the most modern European style.

At the celebrated Synod of Whitby in 664 when the Celtic and Roman variants of Christianity were engaged in fierce debate, particularly over the dating of Easter and the nature of the 'tonsure' or shaved head of the monk, the proponents of the Roman dispensation were successful; among them Wilfrid, a nobleman from Northumbria who had travelled extensively through the regions of the late Roman Empire, delivered the following rebuke to the old Celtic or British cause. 'Do you think', he said, 'that a handful of people in one corner of the remotest of islands is to be preferred to the universal Church of Christ which is spread throughout the world?'[7] It was a defining moment and, under the aegis of the Abbess Hilda, the convocation of Whitby turned England firmly in the direction of Rome. Wilfrid's message was in fact characteristic of English Catholicism, and its sentiments were repeated by Sir Thomas More during his trial for treason in Westminster Hall. 'This realme, being but one member and smale parte of the Church, might not make a particuler lawe disagreable with the generall lawe of Christes Universall Catholike Churche.' Wilfrid and More, separated by almost nine hundred years, represent an authentic English sensibility. Both men were identified with a local area – Wilfrid was a native of Northumbria whose ministry was attended by 'the goodwill of the whole Northumbrian people, high and low'[8] while More was a quintessential Londoner admired and honoured by his fellow citizens – and yet both men considered their national identity within a larger force. Both men, incidentally, were beatified and canonised.

The history of cross-fertilisation is a long one, and further examples may be adduced. In the eighth century 'books actually made in the British Isles appear to have been taken to the continent in quite large quantities, and they were copied locally as far afield as Italy and Spain';[9] the same may be said of Anglo-Saxon sculpture. In Rome there was a special Saxon quarter, known as the *Schola Saxonum*. In the ninth century King Alfred imported both craftsmen and scholars from the continent of Europe, and his successors continued his example. The monastic reforms of the tenth century, springing from the Benedictine foundations of France and enjoining clear distinctions between the secular and spiritual life, in turn engendered a revival of monastic culture in England; monks were invited from Fleury and Cluny to encourage those of native birth. The tenth and eleventh centuries, as a result, were a period of vigorous activity; it is not surprising, therefore, that 'the presence in England of foreign scholars was perhaps never so marked as during the eleventh century'.[10]

Yet one caveat may be entered here. In the 'Regularis Concordia' of the late tenth-century Council of Winchester, effectively promulgating the monastic restoration of that period, the emphasis rests upon 'one Rule and one country'.[11] There always was a recognition of native or national values. Anglo-Saxon scribes continued to use and develop a specifically English script while employing the Carolingian minuscule for Latin texts, a development which is paralleled by the expansion of Old English prose and by the continuing life of the ancient alliterative patterns of verse. It has likewise been supposed that there was 'a fairly reluctant acceptance of some styles and fashions; except in a number of more or less isolated cases, there was no wholesale adoption of continental modes'.[12] So there is, on the face of it, a paradox or at least a disparity between England as part of European civilisation and England as the burgeoning source of a native culture.

The same conditions will present themselves throughout this book. There is at this early stage no need to reconcile them, except to notice the degree of absorption or assimilation present within the English sensibility. It has often been described as a mixed or mongrel kind, a hybrid like the people from which it derives, but it is distinctive precisely because of its willingness to adapt and to adopt other influences. The sensibility is as heterogeneous as its literature, as varied and various as the grand houses or cathedrals which were constructed piece by piece. It has been said that its uniqueness lies in the sum of its differences, but the real process is one of adoption and transformation where two hitherto incompatible influences – in the period under review they may be named as the Celtic and the Classical – are somehow amalgamated and thereby enlarged within a common sensibility. There is conflation and elaboration, not division or reduction. Thus the architecture of the Normans was incorporated and transcended by the English Romanesque, a transformation described by one historian as occurring 'on the foundations . . . established by Alfred, Dunstan, Aethelwold, and others in Wessex'.[13] The origins of the English sensibility are once again traced far back.

CHAPTER 6

The song of the past

Bede was the true begetter of English history, precisely because of his innate antiquarianism and his obsession with past times. In his *Historia Ecclesiastica Gentis Anglorum* he 'likes to speak of relics of the past, of British defences, of Roman earthworks and walls, of ruined churches, of Horsa's tomb, and so forth'.[1] Like Stukeley and Aubrey, almost a thousand years later, he was already possessed by a vision of English antiquity among old stones and broken monuments; like other Anglo-Saxons before him he wondered at the spectacle of dilapidated temples or ruined towns. Antiquarianism, in England, has always been compounded by a vision of Englishness itself; it is not a question of nationalism, which is often mistakenly introduced as an explanation or an easy device, but rather of the sentiment that in the relics of the past there is some inkling of what England is 'really like'. Antiquarians are in this respect often political radicals appealing, for example, to Saxon liberties as opposed to a corrupt Hanoverian polity.

Bede also possessed this indigenous fervour; his introduction of Old English place-names is one example, but he also elucidates the figures of English myth and folklore. He gives the names of the months according to '*antiqui Anglorum populi*', and gives English annotations of Latin terms. His national instincts – one might almost describe them as an unacknowledged atavism – resemble those of the church builders and scribes who persisted with a recognisably insular tradition despite the presence and influence of continental models. So Bede charted the movements of the English sea and of the English seasons; he prepared an English translation of the Creed and the Lord's Prayer; he sang native songs. And yet his greatest contribution to national historiography was undoubtedly the *History* which he composed in Latin; he has been described as 'the first Englishman who understood the past and could view it as a whole'.[2] In similar spirit he was the first Englishman to render the past intelligible and accessible, not only to his contemporaries but to all the generations of historians who have succeeded him. Some of those historians, like Gibbon and Trevelyan, have paid tribute to his powers, principally because he lent English history the coherence and consistency of art. His sources included calendars and chronicles, hagiographies and commentaries, annals and compilations, histories and even oral testimony, all of them purified and elevated by his rigorous style.

Bede's *History* is in five books, commencing with the topography of Britain and its earliest inhabitants but ending with a brief prayer to Jesus after its conclusion in 731. The 'matter of Britain' is seen within the context of the Roman Empire and of European history, but this does not distract Bede's attention from the manifold details of his own country; he alludes to Orosius and Pliny and Solinus but then mentions the defensive stakes along the Thames, 'which can still be seen' seven hundred years after Caesar's invasion, or interjects: 'I heard this from a man still living.' He narrates the life and death of Alban, and relates them to the town of St Albans where miraculous healings occur 'to this day'; he refers to the 'cities, forts, bridges and paved roads' of England and to the violent dynastic struggles of its rulers. There are dreams and battles, invasions and miracles, all manifested within the history of the salvation of a barbaric people.

Like the monastic illuminators of his period he was always glimpsing the numinous background of human events; he seems obsessed with the precise date of Easter, the subject of one of the most perplexing debates of the period, but only because that day prefigures the resurrection and final judgement. In his narrative the human figures are seen in outline or in rhetorical attitudes, and the events are often couched in the form of allegory; the purpose of his book is moral and eschatological, for the English are the race chosen by God. This was one of Bede's most enduring themes, and one of his most persuasive legacies. John Milton declared that England was the 'Elect Nation', a prophecy that William Blake endorsed in *Jerusalem*; the oratorios of Handel were celebrated in part because the history of the Hebrews was seen as a template of English history; in the psalm settings of William Byrd 'Jerusalem' is also a synonym of England, while the dedication to the King James Bible refers to 'our Sion'.

The legacy of Bede, therefore, was a long one; a religious view of history prevailed until the end of the seventeenth century, while nineteenth-century historians such as Acton and Macaulay employed the secular religion of Whiggism to fashion their narratives. Bede promulgated the important lesson that only a defining vision can properly order an historical narrative, and that good histories can be formulated only by good writers. History is an art, in other words, and cannot be finally distinguished from drama or from fiction.

Bede in part took his account of early Britain from the narratives of an earlier historian, Gildas, whose writing is suffused with biblical imagery and Christian lamentation. The works of Bede and Gildas may not be 'true' histories, any more than Gibbon's *The History of the Decline and Fall of the Roman Empire* or Carlyle's *History of the French Revolution* are 'true' histories, but the power of their writing commanded assent for many years.

Gildas was a Briton whose sixth-century *De Excidio et Conquestu Britanniae* (a history of England from the Roman conquest to his own time, with a lament on the evils of his day) was composed in Latin for a European audience, but it has its touches of native poetry. England is an island 'stiff with icy cold', whose faithlessness may cause it to be 'totally enveloped in thick darkness of black night'. The nation, invaded by Picts and Scots, lies like a fallen warrior 'stunned and groaning' in the very mouths of enemies who resemble 'wolves rabid with deepest hunger'. The defeated Britons flee 'to mountainous regions, overhanging hills, fortified crags, and to most dense forests and marine rocks'.[3] As in Saxon poetry, the landscape is always bleak. Gildas employs a deliberately plangent and embellished style, with exclamations and rhetorical questions, designed as much to edify and admonish as to inform. He was not above invention either, since he saw no point in spoiling a good story or ruining an interesting moral. But he was so powerful a writer that many of his more notable mis-representations were accepted until recent times. It was Gildas who promulgated the myth that the Romans and the British Celts were thoroughly at odds with each other, distinct and separate races, whereas the archaeological evidence suggests prolonged intermingling. And yet Gildas's spiritual fervour was so great that he was revered as a saint and prophet as well as an historian, while at the same time he created an historical myth or model which survived for five hundred years.

Certainly it was maintained by the ninth-century historian Nennius, who borrowed from both Bede and Gildas, thus continuing the tradition of religio-historical writing which dominated English historiography at least until the publication in 1670 of Milton's *History of England*.

Nennius collected 'The Matter of Britain' from many sources, but not the least of his virtues lies in his account of King Arthur. The Arthurian legends came to dominate the concept of Englishness, but Nennius obtains the prize as the first 'historian' to describe this notorious if ultimately elusive king. He also lists a number of 'marvels' to be seen in England – among them a hot pool in Bath which changes its temperature according to the wishes of the bather, and wells of salt near Droitwich. The love of the marvellous may again be a national trait.

The Anglo-Saxon Chronicle, which recorded events in England from the beginning of the Christian era to 1154, is filled with wonders – the sign of the cross is seen upon the face of the moon, dragons fly through the air, fiery flashes light up the landscape – while its unadorned transcript of events is interlaced with cadences and images that might have been taken out of contemporaneous epic poetry. Its narrative of the Mercian or Northumbrian poet, Cynewulf, and his rivalry with Cyneheard, dated 757, 'has often been called the first story in English' and is closely related 'to a completely lost oral-prose tradition' in the manner of 'Icelandic saga',[4] which suggests that the island was once full of sounds and sweet airs. The first story in English may have seemed like a song.

CHAPTER 7

The lives of others

If Bede fashioned a history for England, he also populated it with characters; as well as an historian he was a biographer who helped to create a form that has exercised a peculiar fascination over the English imagination ever since. There had been earlier 'lives of the saints'. There were lives of Cuthbert and of Columba, of Wilfrid and of Guthlac, all of them related to the same essential hagiographic pattern, beginning with a miraculous birth and ending with a calm or visionary death. It has been estimated that, before 900, some six hundred different lives were being read throughout the country.

The popularity of English biography can be dated quite accurately, therefore, particularly in the lives of saints associated with a specific locality or region. St Cuthbert dwelled upon Farne Island, a desolate spot close to Lindisfarne, while St Guthlac withdrew to Crowland in the Lincolnshire fens; here by prayer and miracle they were able to control their environment, as if their attachment to a certain area lent them special powers. It was another way of asserting the spirit of place.

These first English lives borrow themes and techniques from the secular poetry of their period, suggesting once more that the concept of form is a fluid one. Biography is as much an aspect of literature as epic verse. The landscape of the Guthlac biographies (there are two separate texts) is that of a 'wide wilderness' populated by fantastic demons and is not dissimilar to that of *Beowulf*; Guthlac himself is 'steadfast in truth' just like the hero of the epic poem, and is deemed to be a warrior for Christ of the same heroic temper as those who fight in secular verse. This mingling of biography and fiction seems to spring naturally from English writing; a survey of sixteenth-century literature, for example, has recently concluded that a 'notable feature of later English experiments with form' is 'the blurring of the boundaries between legend and history'.[1]

Once more we may see the hand of Bede behind a formative development in English letters. He composed a life of St Cuthbert in Latin hexameter verse before he completed one in prose, once more emphasising that there is no necessary disparity between the two genres. He was the first English writer to give historical substantiality to the accounts of the martyrs of the early Church, and began the tradition of what might be called secular as opposed to saintly biography with his *Lives of the Abbots of Wearmouth and Jarrow*. These lives are as short as those written by Johnson or Strachey, and they manifest what has become the customary English interest in character and circumstance; they dwell upon the practical details of living, too, albeit succinctly described.

Another life might be ventured in this context, since it is the first example of 'travel literature' in English and as such represents one of the true origins of the English imagination. *The Voyage of St Brendan* has been described as one of the great mythological narratives of the Christian West, but it has also been interpreted as an actual account of a sea journey to Newfoundland or Iceland; the Elizabethan magus, John Dee, included the text in his argument that England held original dominion over America itself. It has also been described as 'one of the most famous and enduring stories of Western Christendom'.[2]

Brendan and fourteen brethren set out to sea in a coracle of wood and tanned oxhide; after forty days they land upon a rocky island where a great hall and miraculous feast appear to comfort them; yet here the devil, in the shape of 'a little Ethiopian boy holding out a silver necklace and juggling with it',[3] comes to tempt them. On another island they discover herds of giant sheep, and afterwards build their camp upon the back of a great whale; in another place they encounter flocks of speaking birds who explain to Brendan that they are fallen angels. At the time of Vespers, the birds sing a hymn in praise of God and beat their wings against their sides 'as sweet and moving as a plaintive song of lament'.[4] On a yet more distant island they visit an enchanted monastery and on another they converse with a man, crouching upon a rock, who announces himself as Judas Iscariot. It is a delightful story, which can be seen as the harbinger of *Utopia*, *Robinson Crusoe* and *Gulliver's Travels*; it contains the close detail of a journey, complete with leather water-bottles and preservative salt, combined with the most extraordinary allegorical intent. It may have been the work of a British or Irish, rather than a Saxon, monk but it introduces that line of fanciful or fantastic travel-writing which has become so much part of the English genius.

*

There is one other enduring contribution which the now forgotten genre of saints' lives may be said to establish. Their stories spilled over into drama, and by the early twelfth century saints' plays were a recognised element of the 'miracle plays' and had become a popular form of theatre. The appetite for biography, especially of the more sensational kind, was satisfied with plays upon St Katherine, St George, St Thomas the martyr, St Swithin, St Andrew and many others. The drama was elicited by the confrontation between pagan and Christian, these spirited dialogues complemented by details of torture or martyrdom and by the manifestations of signs and wonders. There was comedy as well as tragedy, with Jews or pagan rulers as stock comic characters, but more significantly it has been suggested that 'the Elizabethan history plays . . . seem most likely to be descended' from these saints' plays 'in terms of character, structure and thematic development'.[5] Just as the Tudor drama derived in part from Anglo-Saxon scholastic debate, so the sequence of Shakespeare's history plays owes many of its themes and much of its symbolism to this genre of Anglo-Saxon prose. The noble origins of St Guthlac, a man whose eminence sprang out of a wayward youth, bear some relation to Shakespeare's *Henry the Fifth*; the saint's musings upon the death of kings, and the transitory nature of all human power, provide the context for *Richard the Second*.

It has been suggested that the first English tragedy was not *Gorboduc*, as the text-books insist, but a play entitled *Life of St Thomas A' Becket* otherwise known as *St Thomas of London*. It was performed as early as 1182, twelve years after Becket's death, and was still being dramatised as late as 1539. The extant prose lives of the saint emphasise the historical context of his career and the specific circumstances of his death as ordered by Henry II; the theme is one of conscience, of spiritual determination, and murder for the sake of them both. It is difficult to believe that the dramatic versions differed very greatly in content or intent, so there is a distinct possibility that 'we have a tradition of English tragedy existing over a period of 360 years and to within fifteen years of the first recorded tragedy in 1554 . . . a continuously developing form from the twelfth century all the way through the Renaissance'.[6]

Nothing can come out of nothing; *King Lear* has its roots in mummers' plays, which are themselves derived from Anglo-Saxon saints' lives. T. S. Eliot's *Murder in the Cathedral*, a verse drama on the death of Thomas Becket, is a manifest sign of continuities stretching back a thousand years. They may occur in specific, as well as general, contexts. One collection of lives, *Sawles Warde*, contains the words '*the derne beoth ant deopre then ani sea dingle*'; they are co-opted by W. H. Auden in his opening line, 'Doom is dark and deeper than any sea-dingle'.

CHAPTER 8

A land of dreams

One scholar of early English civilisation, J. R. R. Tolkien, came upon a line of Cynewulf's poetry – '*Eala earendel, engla beorhtost!*', 'Hail Earendel, most bright angel' – and was consumed by it.

Tolkien himself was a Catholic born in South Africa but brought up in Birmingham and its environs, part of the old Mercian kingdom from which Cynewulf himself is supposed to have sprung. Was there some consonance which led directly to *The Lord of the Rings*? When Tolkien read the invocation to Earendel, the star of the morning known to us as Venus, 'I felt an unconscious thrill, as if something had stirred me, half-wakened, from sleep. There was something very remote and strange and beautiful behind those words, if I could grasp it, far beyond Ancient English.'[1] It was his imagination which was awakening, stirred by ancient voices.

There was a star of the morning already risen in the seventh century; his name was Caedmon, the first Christian poet in the English language. The legend of his origin comes from the pages of Bede's *Historia Ecclesiastica Gentis Anglorum*. Caedmon was a herdsman at the monastery of Whitby, known then as Streones Healh or Streanaeshalch. He was of a modest nature, and had no pretensions to poetical skill; when the harp was handed from guest to guest at a feast, no doubt to recite episodes from a native poetry which is now entirely lost, Caedmon would leave the table and return to his hut. One evening he had retired to the stable, where he had been posted that night to care for the animals, and had slept; then in dream he saw a man standing beside him.

'Caedmon, sing me a song.'
'I have no skill in singing. That is the reason I left the feast and retired here.'
'But you will sing to me.'
'What shall I sing?'
'Sing the song of creation.'

Then at once, in his dream, Caedmon chanted a hymn of nine lines which opens, '*Nu scylun hergan, haefaenricaes uard*' – 'Now shall we praise the maker of the heavenly kingdom.' It is significant that, at this point in his narrative, Bede chose to translate the poem into Latin rather than render it in its Old English original; he may have considered the pagan implications of Caedmon's strong alliterative verse to be still too potent.

On awakening, Caedmon added more verses, and then visited the reeve of the monastery to tell his story of the night and the vision. The reeve then took him before the Abbess of Whitby, Hilda, a great religious leader of the era. She asked him to repeat his story, and his song, to a group of learned clerics who deemed his vision to be the work of God. Caedmon was admitted as a brother to the monastery and, on being educated in the scriptures, composed many verses on such sacred themes as the Incarnation, the Passion, the Resurrection, and the Last Judgement.

The miraculous event heralded a great change in the nature of the English imagination, since for the first time the old songs of the tribe were redeployed to state the truths of the Christian faith. From the testimony of Bede these poems were written down. Only the transcription of Caedmon's hymn, however, survives in eighth-century manuscripts; its popularity is attested by the fact that there are no fewer than twenty-one extant versions, so that it can truly be said that Caedmon's hymn originates the great sequence of religious poetry in the English language. It is in fact the earliest survival of all English poetry; as an epigraph to the poem is written: 'Caedmon first sang this song.'

There are certain suggestive details. The name of Caedmon itself is deemed to be of Celtic origin, intimating in turn that he was of native British descent working originally as an agricultural labourer for the ruling Anglo-Saxon tribe. So it might be said that the poetry of England rises naturally from the common stock like a melody of the land. The seventh-century dream of Caedmon is also uncannily reminiscent of William Blake's late eighteenth-century vision in the 'Introduction' to *Songs of Innocence*:

> Piper pipe that song again –
> So I piped, he wept to hear

Pipe that song, and sing that song to me; it represents the same injunction to the rapt poet. Whether it be dream or vision, it represents an inspiration which has not yet died.

*

England is a land of dreams. A letter from a French cleric to Nicholas of St Albans, written c.1178, rehearsed what was already a familiar perception:

> Your island is surrounded by water, and not unnaturally its inhabitants are affected by the nature of the element in which they live. Unsubstantial fantasies slide easily into their minds. They think their dreams to be visions, and their visions to be divine. We cannot blame them, for such is the nature of their land. I have often noticed that the English are greater dreamers than the French.[2]

For several centuries the English were characterised as 'seers of visions', and it cannot be said that the tradition has materially diminished in the work of Herbert, Traherne, Bunyan, Blake, Spenser and Keats. Whether it resembles a Celtic inheritance is open to enquiry; the Druidic priests were believed to harbour visionary powers. And how could it be otherwise on an island which, in the earliest histories, was itself established upon a vision? The goddess Diana appeared before Brutus with the news that: 'Beyond the realm of Gaul, a land there lies, sea-girt it lies, where giants dwelt of old. Now void it fits thy people . . . And kings be born of thee, whose dreaded might shall awe the world and conquer nations bold.'

In his history of England, published in 1670, John Milton recounts the narrative of Brutus and Albion in a plain and sober manner as if no willing suspension of disbelief were required. The earliest historical records are filled with manifold visions. Bede's *History* recounts the vision of King Edwin when 'he saw a man approaching whose face and appearance were strange to him';[3] the unexpected visitor laid his right hand upon Edwin's head, and disappeared. A monk named Fursey, who established a monastery among the East Angles, was taken up by angels to witness the life after death. One of the brothers in Bede's own monastery had heard the story from Fursey's own lips: 'He added that it was a frosty and bitter winter's day when Fursey told his story; and yet, though he wore only a thin garment, he was sweating profusely.'[4] Visions, then, were taken as serious and earnest tokens of divine providence, even and perhaps especially by intelligent and learned men such as Bede. Chad, the Bishop of the Mercians, was greeted by angelic spirits who promised to return within a week and carry his soul with them to heaven; there are many accounts of lights descending from the sky upon the earth, usually taken to be the bright trail of angels. A nun in the community of Barking saw a vision of a departed abbess,

Ethelburga, to whom she spoke in the following terms: 'I am so glad that you have come; you are most welcome. . . . This is not happy news. . . . If it cannot be today, I beg that it may not be long delayed.' She was addressing the spirit of her own approaching death.

Bede spoke to those who had seen visions, or spirits, in order to verify their stories because it may be that they had suffered from 'delusion'. One seemed to him wholly genuine, a vision like those that had occurred in the 'old days' of Celtic Britain. A monk named Drylhelm, from the country of the Northumbrians, was escorted by an angel to a 'very broad and deep valley of infinite length' where the condemned souls of the departed were tossed in fire 'dreadful with burning flames'.[5] It is unlikely that John Bunyan read this account, but his own image of the 'Valley of the Shadow of Death' with 'the flame and the smoke', envisioned a thousand years later in *The Pilgrim's Progress*, is part of a continuous tradition. Drylhelm was taken back to the living world, where he spoke only to a few devout contemporaries about his experience. When bathing in a freezing river, with the blocks of ice floating around him, he was engaged in conversation.

> 'It's wonderful how you can manage to bear such bitter cold.'
> 'I have known it colder.'

When urged to alleviate his own watchful self-discipline, he similarly replied: 'I have seen greater suffering.'[6] It has often been suggested that understatement is a national characteristic.

In Bede's *Life of St Cuthbert* the historian describes how the saint was visited by blessed spirits: 'Angels would often appear and talk with him and when he was hungry he was refreshed with food by the special gift of God.'[7] Eleven hundred years later William Blake was in a similar fashion visited by angels; perhaps they were the same ones. Blake had been reading Edward Young's *Night Thoughts*, a volume of mid-eighteenth-century verse in the English melancholy tradition, when a voice spoke to him; he looked across his chamber but saw nothing 'save a greater light than usual'. Blake 'looked whence the voice came', and was then aware of a shining shape, with bright wings, who diffused much light. 'As I looked the shape dilated more and more: he waved his hands; the roof of my study opened; he ascended into Heaven; he stood in the sun and, beckoning to me, moved the universe.'

It was not the first, or only, vision vouchsafed to William Blake. He had seen angels in the mulberry trees of Peckham Rye; he saw God and Ezekiel. Throughout his life he was surrounded by visionary companions, many of whom he sketched or painted. He saw a vision of his departed brother, Robert, as the spirit left the body 'clapping its hands for joy'; this closely resembles the visions reported by Bede, including that of the Abbess Hilda who upon her death was 'borne up to Heaven in the midst of the light'. Blake also drew visionary heads – those, for example, of Herod, Socrates and Voltaire – which have the hypnagogic quality of faces hovering or dissolving in a dream and are not at all dissimilar to those depicted by English painters of the thirteenth century. In fact Blake, who called himself 'English Blake', is a significant example of an artist who instinctively aligns himself with an ancient English tradition which then, as it were, reassembles itself all around him. Thus he wrote in the first chapter of his epic poem, *Jerusalem*,

> . . . Amen! Huzza! Selah!
> "All things Begin & End in Albion's Ancient Druid Rocky Shore"

Is it, then, any wonder that like his predecessors in Mercia and Northumbria Blake saw visions of angels?

Out of this land of visions emerges a poetry of the dream-world. *Beowulf* is in part a dream-poem; the strange elegies of the Anglo-Saxon spirit are enacted in unreal landscapes compounded of dream and vision. Beowulf himself follows Grendel's mother through '*frecne fen-gelad*', a terrifying fen path, towards a tarn or mere where flickers '*fyr on flode*' hiding an ancient terror. Perhaps only the Anglo-Saxons were capable of such horror, although the persistent taste for Gothic in English literature suggests that their influence has lingered.

Dreams themselves were not necessarily to be distinguished from visions; there was a class of 'dream-readers' who could distinguish between '*visio*' or '*osculum*' and mere '*insomnium*'. The dreamers of the tribe were highly praised because in their state of charmed sleep they were able to unite heaven and earth. The knights of Arthur pursued a vision of the Holy Grail, while the king himself was subject to many and disturbing dreams which prophesied devastation and ruin; the more historically established King Alfred, according to his first biographer, dreamed of St Neot of Cornwall who guided him to victory over the Viking army at Edington.

Medieval literature is filled with dream-visions. The great poem of hope and penitence, *Pearl*, unfolds within a landscape of dream where the dreamer declares that his soul or '*goste*' is '*gon in Godez Grace*'. In the prologue of *Piers the Plowman*, Langland confesses how he wandered upon Malvern Hills, went astray and fell asleep beside a stream where *'thanne gan I to meten a merueilouse sweuene'*, a marvellous dream. Within that same Malvern landscape, as exemplified in *The Dream of Gerontius*, Elgar awoke in 1900 and found Langland's dream to be true. It is reminiscent of the opening line of the Old English poem *The Dream of the Rood*, *'Hwaet, ic swefna cyst secgan wylle'*, 'Listen, I will speak to you of a wonderful dream.' Langland sleeps and wakes, yet always finds himself enclosed within a further dream so that the reader or listener becomes involved in the wilderness of the dreamscape until the last line of the 'B' text, *'til I gan awake'*. *Wynnere and Wastour* opens in dream and Chaucer perfected the art of the dream-vision in *The Parliament of Fowls*, *The House of Fame* and *The Book of the Duchess*. In each of them he falls asleep over a book, which then lingers within his dream, as if there were some deep connection between individual silent reading and sleeping. The earliest English readers must have seemed withdrawn into themselves in quite an unusual way; like the dreamer, they were somewhere between sleep and death.

Yet the dream of England spread further. The site of the second Salisbury Cathedral, laid in 1221, was found in a dream; that great late fourteenth-century masterpiece known as the 'Wilton Diptych' has been described by one scholar of the period as displaying 'the mystical dreaminess of mood' which was characteristic of 'the English version of the International Style'.[8] The same spirit animated Edward Burne-Jones when, in the late nineteenth century, he remarked: 'I mean by a picture a beautiful romantic dream of something that never was, never will be . . .' This is the dream of Edmund Spenser who, in as high and artificial a poetic language as that of the Anglo-Saxon bards, creates the enchanted landscape of *The Faerie Queene*. His melody, with each stanza prolonged to melting point, lies beyond time and the waking reality of consciousness:

> Then ouer them Change doth not rule and raigne;
> But they raigne ouer change, and doe their states maintaine

Keats described Spenser's verse as 'charmed sleep', with which state the young poet was himself familiar, and William Hazlitt extolled his 'lulling the senses into a deep oblivion of the jarring noise of the world, from which we have no wish to be ever recalled'. Those who study the nature of contemporary dreams, with their condensations and elisions,

have found in the latent and manifest content of Spenser's epic all the
workings of oneiric drama. It is a form of sleep.

Dreams float freely through the English imagination. John Milton
described even the history of his country as one of 'smooth or idle
Dreams'. In *Paradise Lost* Adam is despatched into a divine trance:

> Mine eyes he clos'd, but op'n left the Cell
> Of Fancie my internal sight . . .

Whereupon his rib is turned into Eve. Sir Thomas Browne, in *Religio
Medici*, confesses: 'I am as happy in a dreame, and as content to enjoy
happiness in a fancie, as others in a more apparent truth and reality.'
The Pilgrim's Progress is an encyclopaedia of dreams, not least the
dream-literature of the medieval poets. Its first sentence, concluding
'and, as I slept, I dreamed a dream', might have emerged from *Piers the
Plowman* or *The Dream of the Rood*. John Bunyan's dream is couched
in the same vein as that of William Langland. The pilgrim meets
Mistrust and Timorous, Hypocrisy and Civility, while Langland
encounters Fraud and Flattery, Hunger and Imagination; the three
hundred years between them pass in a moment, as if their dreams were
truly outside time. Yet *The Pilgrim's Progress* is associated, too, with a
dream of another kind. The concluding verse of its first part –

> But if thou shalt cast all away as vain,
> I know not but 'twill make me dream again

– bears a more than fleeting resemblance to the final poem of *Through
the Looking Glass*:

> Ever drifting down the stream –
> Lingering in the golden gleam –
> Life, what is it but a dream?

The notion of embarrassment will emerge in the course of this
narrative as a peculiar if elusive aspect of the English imagination. But
in this potent mood may lie one of the uses of dream. The dream may
conceal damaging or subversive themes without endangering the
psychic health of the language; it may act as a diversion or cover by
means of which potentially explosive material is smuggled into
discourse. Langland can thus assault the established order, and Carroll
advertise his sexual proclivities, without the least danger of being
'found out'. It is a feature of English understatement that it is literally
under the statement.

That is also why the great moral and social satires have employed a landscape at once intense and unreal, thus approaching the condition of dream: More's *Utopia*, and Orwell's *Animal Farm*, Swift's *Gulliver's Travels* and Samuel Butler's *Erewhon*, are among these oneiric tracts which must be interpreted as carefully as Langland's first allegory.

John Keats dreamed Adam's dream on 22 November 1817, as if he were 'surprised with an old Melody'. The young poet's *The Fall of Hyperion* is called 'A Dream' –

> For Poesy alone can tell her dreams –

and the murmur of the dream resounds throughout the unfinished cantos. In 'The English Mail-Coach', De Quincey evokes 'something of the grandeur which belongs potentially to human dreams'. And at the close of this majestic essay he composes a 'dream-fugue' like the pavane executed by John Dowland and entitled 'Lachrimae Pavin', or like some wild addicted vision enshrined in his *Confessions of an English Opium Eater*. 'In dreams', De Quincey writes in the same essay, 'perhaps under some secret conflict of the midnight sleeper, lighted up to the consciousness at the time, but darkened to the memory as soon as all is finished, each several child of our mysterious race completes for himself the treason of the aboriginal fall.' In the fifth book of Wordsworth's *The Prelude* a friend of the poet is seized by sleep 'and he pass'd into a dream' of a 'drowning world' from which he 'wak'd in terror'. How strongly the English poets have been drawn to that state of dreaming, suspended between two worlds, is manifested in a letter which Coleridge wrote in the same period – 'I should much wish . . . to float about along an infinite ocean . . . & wake once in a million years for a few minutes – just to know I was going to sleep a million years more.'

So dreams are interwoven within the fabric of the English imagination. One of Keats's first poems, 'Sleep and Poetry', takes its epigraph from Chaucer and expresses a desire to 'die a death / Of luxury'; in the face of that death he must struggle to awake, to free himself from what Byron dismissed as Keats's 'Bedlam Vision'. The image of Frankenstein appeared to Mary Shelley in a dream where 'My imagination, unbidden, possessed and guided me' towards the 'hideous phantasm of a man'. Browning's fearful 'Childe Roland to the Dark Tower Came' emerged within 'a kind of dream' invoking the earlier dream-landscape of *Beowulf*:

> This was the place! Those two hills on the right
> Crouched like two bulls locked horn in horn in fight –

Sometimes it seems that these English dreamers are all within the same dream, the dream of origin, from which they are trying desperately to awake. We need not invoke the names of Freud or Jung in order to understand these ancient images. Charles Dickens believed that he always lived partly in a dream, and his Richard Carstone at the close of his fitful life in the dream-world of *Bleak House* asks whether 'it was all a troubled dream'? At the end of his own life Charles Dickens was found 'in dreamland with *Edwin Drood*'.

There is also a continuity of another kind, as the ghosts of dead poets appear to the living in dream or vision. Robert Herrick saw Anacreon in vision. Homer appeared to Chapman, while Milton manifested himself to William Blake. Francis Thompson saw Chatterton, and the dead poet saved the living from an attempt at suicide. Chaucer and Gower appeared to Robert Greene, consoling Shakespeare's rival, while Thomas Hardy saw the ghost of Wordsworth 'lingering and wandering on somewhere alone in the fan-traceried Vaulting' of King's College Chapel, Cambridge. In that same university Wordsworth was himself moved by the invisible presence of Milton and of Spenser: 'I call'd him Brother, Englishman, and Friend.'

At the end of his great epic of the night, *The Four Zoas*, Blake wrote in triumph: 'End of the Dream'. But it has not ended yet.

Photograph of Charles Dickens dreaming, 1861, by John and Charles Watkins

CHAPTER 9

A note on English melancholy

There is a word in Old English which belongs wholly to that civilisation – '*dustsceawung*', meaning contemplation of dust. It is a true image of the Anglo-Saxon mind, or at least an echo of that consciousness which considered transience and loss to be part of the human estate; it was a world in which life was uncertain and the principal deity was fate or destiny or '*wyrd*'.

There are six extant poems in Old English which are governed by this vision of decay and desolation; they have been given titles, where none existed before, and they have been called 'elegies' for the reason that they anticipate and indeed help to fashion a body of subsequent English poetry. The laments of 'The Wanderer' and 'The Seafarer' are filled with the sorrows of exile and isolation; the singers have left the warm halls and contemplate the '*hrimcealde sae*', the rime-cold sea. 'The Seafarer' recalls his life upon the wilderness of the waters, and it becomes clear how the cold waste of the ocean has entered the Anglo-Saxon soul. Everything '*toglideth*', glides away like the waters; nothing endures; I depart while friends are left weeping by the shore's edge; the music of harps and the sound of horses must fade; I am alone, but I must endure, this is my '*wyrd*'. '*Wyrd*' in its literal sense signifies 'what will be' and this covers the accomplishment of all destinies; the judgement is executed, or the dream fulfilled. Many scholars have considered such works to harbour the keening of Celtic lament, but embedded within them are elements of endurance and reticence which arise from the Old English tradition. The poetry has an impersonal force, eschewing place-names or personal names, guided by litotes and understatement towards a powerful compression of feeling.

There is another poem, entitled 'The Ruin', which throws a curious light upon the elegiac tendencies of the Anglo-Saxons. It is a topographical poem – a much loved genre in the eighteenth century – concerning a ruined city; written in the eighth century it is some fifty lines in length and is itself a ruin or, rather, a fragment. It describes an ancient city where now the walls have fallen, the roofs decayed and the pillars crumbled into heaps of stone. Once it contained bright halls and majestic houses, but a hundred generations have passed leaving only silence and decay. These ruins represent '*enta geweorc*', the work of giants. It is a familiar phrase in Anglo-Saxon poetry appearing in both sacred and secular contexts; it is alike a tribute to the past inhabitants of this island and a homage to transience itself. It does not reflect any vainglory of the victorious invader but, rather, a genuine and sophisticated awareness of passing civilisations.

The critical and technical term 'elegy' did not enter the language until the early years of the sixteenth century but it quickly acquired a peculiarly English tone; the lament is part of the tradition, with Milton's *Lycidas* and Tennyson's *In Memoriam*, Spenser's 'Astrophel' and Shelley's *Adonais* as quite different and unusual demonstrations of its power. The 'graveyard' school of Anglo-Saxon poetry also has its own specific lineage. The homiletic sequence known as *Soul and Body*, in which the spirit addresses the decayed or decaying corpse, rehearses what one scholar has called the 'macabre emotionalism' and 'unmitigated pessimism'[1] that are associated with Anglo-Saxon poetry. That tone dominates much medieval English poetry, also, and continues well into the eighteenth century.

It would also be possible to elaborate, in this context, upon the argument which Bishop Percy advanced in one of the editorial comments in his collection of *Reliques of Ancient English Poetry* published in 1765. 'It is worth attention,' he wrote, 'that the English have more songs and ballads on the subject of madness than any of their neighbours.' This might be connected with the madness portrayed upon the Jacobean stage, and the popularity of the eighteenth-century 'graveyard' school of English poetry; but there are more elusive associations. In the nineteenth century London became known as the 'suicide capital' of the world but, even before that date, there was a more general belief that the English were a race subject to melancholia. The prevailing gloom was variously ascribed to the damp climate of the island or to the diet of beef, but we need only turn to the prevalence of elegies in the English tongue to suggest that melancholy may have found its local habitation.

It has always been there. That long sweet note of pathos can be heard equally in the music of Delius and the poetry of Keats, in the plangent harmonies of Purcell and the stately threnodies of Spenser, in the funereal meditations of Donne and the lachrymose comedy of Sterne. When the Anglo-Saxon poet of 'Judgement Day' uttered a complaint against 'this gloomy world', he was the harbinger of a powerful and sustained emotion. It has often been remarked that Gray's 'Elegy

Written in a Country Church-Yard', composed fitfully between 1746 and 1750, was the most popular English poem for some two hundred years. What other nation would cherish such mournful music?

The earliest English lyrics are suffused with melancholy. 'Ey! Ey! What this night is long!' comes from the early thirteenth century, so that the transition from Old to Middle English is not without its continuities. The songbook, of which it is a part, survives still and a scholar of English music has noted that 'its sense of weary desolation'[2] resounds across the centuries. In similar fashion another early song, with its complaint *'Blidful biryd on me thou rewe'*, is indeed a 'highly pessimistic' fragment[3] with its own successors. The woefulness of Chaucer's Reeve has all the sad music of seasonal change which seems so integral to the English genius:

> Deeth drough the tappe of lyf and leet it gon,
> And ever sithe hath so the tappe yronne
> Til that almoost al empty is the tonne

There have been periods in which melancholy became the prevailing mood or the spirit of the age. The first surviving English morality play takes as its theme the advent of death. It is an abiding preoccupation, this terror of mortality, aligned with a yearning towards transcendence. As one fifteenth-century writer expresses it,

> Me thynk thys world is wonder wery
> And fadyth as ye brymbyll bery

The great national epic of that century, Malory's *Le Morte Darthur* (as its printer, William Caxton, named it), is charged with intimations of transience and filled with plaintive passages of nostalgia. 'Then there was wepyng and dolour out of mesure.' One medievalist has spoken of its 'haunting elegiac undertone',[4] which is in part related to the simplicity of a prose which has not divested itself of its Anglo-Saxon origins: 'And syr Lancelot awok, and went and took his hors, and rode al that day and al nyght in a forest, wepyng. And atte last he was ware of an ermytage and a chappel stode betwyxte two clyffes, and than he harde a lytel belle rynge to masse.'

There is something within the language itself which propels the writer towards plangency; if we were to compare one of Macbeth's soliloquies with the Anglo-Saxon monologues of 'The Wanderer' or 'The Seafarer', we would notice the same open vowel sounds which create the syllabic equivalent of a long protracted 'oh' – *'geond lagulade longe sceolde*', 'To morrow, and to morrow, and to morrow'. In Edmund Spenser, too, the melody engages the themes of loss and decay, as if the words themselves were tokens of transience; perhaps it represents the nostalgia for Adam's unfallen language, before the babble of other voices. There is nothing more splendid, however, than Spenser's 'Two Cantos of Mutabilitie' which are appended to *The Faerie Queene*, where the old alliterative line is charged with the awareness of frailty and loss: 'What man that sees the euer-whirling wheele . . .' The alliteration of Old English may indeed be the 'pure well head of Poesie', to which Spenser alludes in the same poem. The language that speaks of decay falls back into its original patterns, like the countenances of those about to die.

For the melodic expression of grief, however, John Dowland bears the palm. His first songbook of 1597, containing compositions for the accompaniment of the lute, expresses what one musical historian has called his 'disposition to melancholy', his 'feelings of isolation' and his 'emotional sensitivity'.[5] In songs such as 'Go Crystal Tears', 'In Darkness Let Me Dwell', 'Forlorn Hope' and 'Sorrow Stay', the full flood of English melancholia can be experienced, with all the sonorous languour of its pathos and all the chromatic range of its grief. In an air published in the third volume – 'Time can abate the terror of every pain / But common grief is error, true grief will still remain' – the ' "dropping" refrain seems . . . to annihilate time itself'.[6]

It is the strangest coincidence that Dowland was for some time resident musician at the court of Elsinore, upon whose walls Hamlet walked; melancholy indeed was so favoured and so familiar a theme that in the late sixteenth century it became an English device for which only the barest signification was necessary. The melancholic was a stock figure of tragedy and even, sometimes, of comedy. He could be a malcontent, a rebel, or a scholar; he would be dressed in black, with solemn visage, his arms folded and his eyes cast down. There was the melancholic of love, like Orsino sighing for music in Shakespeare's *Twelfth Night*, or the melancholic of learning who like Hamlet enters reading a book. That book might be one of many learned English tomes written in the period, such as George Gascoigne's *The Droomme of Doome's Day*, John Moore's *A Mappe of Man's Mortalitie*, or George Strode's *The Anatomie of Mortalitie*. Childhood is foolish, youth vain; maturity a cause of pain, and old age a cause of mourning. Thus Hamlet becomes one of the central figures of English drama.

Yet melancholy served many purposes in the sixteenth century; the melancholic was often a man of learning, and could serve as a target for the predominant bias towards anti-intellectualism in England. The sick man could also be the epitome of a sick world, and the matter of satire. Those who feigned melancholy could also adopt a number of 'mad' poses, as did Hamlet, and thus play the chameleon. As Edmund expresses it in *King Lear*: 'My cue is villainous melancholy, with a sigh like Tom O' Bedlam.' It was also often an excuse for that morbid sensationalism so close to the English imagination. This delight in what has been called 'English Gothic' suffuses the work of Robert Burton whose *The Anatomy of Melancholy*, published in 1621, is a formidable digest on the pleasures and perils of that condition. Samuel Johnson declared that 'it was the only book that ever took him out of bed two hours sooner than he wished to rise', and Charles Lamb referred to Burton himself as 'that fantastic great old man'. Byron acquired all his classical learning from it, and thus became the melancholy Manfred; Keats used the book as a form of personal diary, and thereupon composed an 'Ode on Melancholy'. In this compendious volume, too, is the story of Lamia which directly inspired Keats to write his long poem of the same name. The treatise is indeed fantastic. Although Burton disclaims 'big words, fustian phrases, jingling terms, tropes, strong lines, that like Alcestes' arrows caught fire as they flew, strains of wit . . . elogies, hyperbolical exornations, elegancies etc. which many so much affect', he employs all of these devices in a great phantas-magoria of prose. It is an *opéra bouffe* of paraphrase and quotation, as Burton whispers to the great authors across the centuries or overhears them murmuring in his Oxford library. His own book is 'a rhapsody of rags gathered together from several dung-hills, excrement of authors, toys and fopperies confusedly tumbled out . . . thou canst not think worse of me than I do of myself'. So it is that 'we weave the same web still, twist the same rope again and again'. It is a line and a sentiment which more than a hundred years later, in the mid-eighteenth century, Laurence Sterne borrowed for the pages of *Tristram Shandy*, thus proving the truth of the dictum in an eminently witty manner. But it is also one of the sources of Burton's melancholy, this belief that the fine lines of the imagination may become a web or a prison – 'we skim off the cream of other men's wits, pick the choice flowers of their tilled gardens to set out our own sterile plots'. We can write nothing that has not already been written, only rearrange the inheritance in a pleasing pattern.

Burton wrote one book for the rest of his life, expanding it in the course of several editions, and it came to a conclusion only at his death. Yet this melancholy Englishman did not believe that mortality broke the charmed circle of his melancholic imagination. 'We keep our madness still, play the fools still . . . we are of the same humours and inclinations as our predecessors were, you shall find us all alike, much at one, we and our sons.' That is why the melancholy man understands the great globe itself:

> thou shalt soon perceive that all the world is mad, that is melancholy, doting: that it is (which *Epicthonius Cosmopolites* expressed not many years since in a map) made like a fool's head (with that motto, *Caput helliboro dignum*) a crazed head, *cavea stultorum*, a fool's Paradise or, as Apollonius, a common prison of gulls, cheaters, flatterers, etcetera.

This is the closest English prose reaches to abstract learning, this wistful, pedantic, digressive, solicitous and magniloquent style not untouched by irony or condescension. Like John Donne and Francis Bacon, Burton is interested in the 'new' philosophy only when it affords him fresh metaphors; but he still prefers the ancient wisdom of '*Robin Goodfellows*' or '*Puck* in the Night' as well as the knowledge contained in biographical anecdote. This tendency, too, he inherits from the native genius. Is it a peculiar disposition, also, to feel compelled to include no less than everything – just as Dickens filled his novels with crowds and Shakespeare filled the world with his characters – before concluding that all is vanity and empty striving? Even in the act of reaching out to grasp the world, English writers are troubled by melancholy contemplations.

There is a native strain, too, in Burton's false learning and in his concocted quotations, designed to confuse or tease the reader. Like the notebooks of Coleridge, his narrative endlessly repeats and anticipates itself. He quotes Chaucer and, like the poet, creates a strange embarrassed and understated persona – 'But where am I? Into what subject have I rushed? What have I to do with Nuns, Maids, Virgins, Widows? I am a bachelor myself, and lead a Monastick life in a college.' But then, in the synopses of his books or 'partitions', he parodies the continental learning of the logician Ramus. Burton refers to Malory, Marlowe, Sidney, Spenser, and alludes to melancholy Hamlet. He copies the ecclesiastical histories of the medievals and the Anglo-Saxons with his accounts of visions and miracles. So 'our Melancholy ' is demonstrated by 'that which *Matthew Paris* relates of the Man of Ersham who saw heaven and hell in a vision; of Sir *Owen*, that went down into St Patrick's Purgatory in King *Stephen's* days, and saw as much; Walsingham of him that was showed as much by St *Julian*'. Burton, having been raised in Leicestershire and educated at Brasenose College, Oxford, spent his life as a student of Christ Church, Oxford. He pored over the books of the Bodleian Library in order to write his treatise, with the purpose of relieving or reliving his own melancholy; yet it increased to the point that, according to an old account, 'nothing could make him laugh but going to the bridge-foot and hearing the ribaldry of the bargemen, which rarely failed to throw him into a violent fit of laughter'. It is rumoured that he committed suicide, and on his epitaph in Christ Church it is recorded that 'Melancholia' gave him both life and death.

Hobbes was afflicted with melancholy; in *Leviathan* he created a vision of the world born out of fearfulness and nourished by desperation. Sir Godfrey Kneller's portraits of Hobbes's noble contemporaries are distinguished by 'sensitive penetration of character and melancholy'.[7] The portrait of Charles I at his trial depicts him dressed in 'the uniform of Melancholy' with black coat and broad-brimmed black hat. Yet melancholy was as much at home among the Puritans as the defeated Royalists, leading one historian of the seventeenth century to suggest that it was 'a cultural mode available to the whole "educated" class'.[8] We know also of Milton's 'Il Penseroso'. When John Donne sat for a painting towards the end of his life, he chose to drape himself in a shroud and stand upon an urn. When he mounted the pulpit of St Paul's Cathedral he carried with him an hour-glass to remind the congregation that 'from the first minute that thou beganst to live, thou beganst to die too'. He desired to die in the pulpit. It was indeed in the pulpit that he preached his funeral sermon known as 'Death's Duell'; a few days later, at the end of March 1631, he expired. He was killed by the power of his own oration.

He mused upon 'a handfull of dust' and truly became, in the Anglo-Saxon term, an avower of '*dustsceawung*'. He was a disciple of death and a voluptuary of decay. His was a fantastic melancholy, dwelling upon the surcease of breath with morbid and fascinated relish; he created an elaborate patterning of graveyard themes, an embroidery, an *opus anglicanum*. Like Burton, he proceeds by association and paradox, the whole panoply of words determined by consonance and contrast; it is a syllabic rhetoric in which tone and colour play as much part as argument. We are approaching once more the *genius loci*. And the familiar cry goes up. 'They tell me it is my *Melancholly*; Did I infuse, did I drinke in *Melancholly* into my selfe? It is my *thought-fulnesse*; was I not made to *thinke*?' As with so many other English artists and writers, his taste for the macabre and for the grotesque encouraged theatricality of various kinds. One of his predecessors as Dean of St Paul's, John Colet, insisted upon wearing mournful black rather than the required scarlet; the image of Donne wrapped in his winding sheet, facing east to greet the rising Christ, is perhaps sufficiently theatrical. There is sensationalism, too, within the melancholia of his sermons. 'Between that excrementall jelly', he wrote, 'that thy body is made of at first, and that jelly which thy body dissolves to at last; there is not so noysome, so putrid a thing in nature.'

It is all of a piece with Jacobean tragedy, and the sensational Gothic drama of the eighteenth-century London patent theatres. With such a distinguished ancestry it is perhaps not surprising that the most successful exhibition of contemporary English art was entitled, simply, 'Sensation'.

When John Donne stood upon his urn, the knots of the winding sheet clutched in his hand, he might have been anticipating Thomas Browne's *Hydriotaphia, or Urne-Buriall* in which, as Browne intimates elsewhere, 'I perceive I doe Anticipate the vices of age, the world to mee is but a dreame or mockshow, and wee all therein but Pantalones and Antickes to my severer contemplations'. Thus "'tis all one to lie in St Innocent's Church-yard, as in the Sands of Aegypt: Ready to be anything, in the extasie of being ever, and as content with six foot as the Moles of Adrianus'. And so 'The Iniquity of Oblivion blindly scattereth her poppy'. Browne was born in 1605, but he continued his life apparently undisturbed by the vagaries of civil war, Commonwealth and Restoration. He was educated at Winchester and at Oxford, where he learned six languages, but he pursued his real studies in anatomy and medicine. He practised as a doctor in Halifax but most notably in Norwich, during which period he completed his most celebrated and erudite work. He was an expert in witchcraft and delighted in scientific experiments of any kind. 'All places, all airs, make unto me one Country,' he once wrote, 'I am in England everywhere and under any Meridian.'

Here, then, are the makings of a wholly English measure – this gravity, this grandiloquence, this sombre rhetoric always in peril of decay and dissolution into its component parts. The melancholy imagination has of course also been associated with the movement of German romanticism but, under English skies, it takes on a wholly native hue. In particular the delight in demonstration, the vast expenditure of energy into words, characterises this prose; there is no ontology, or metaphysic, but rather the plangent chords of a dying fall. From the discovery of Anglo-Saxon urns at Old Walsingham in Norfolk Browne divagates widely into burial rites and obsequies in a style at once gay and learned, comic and erudite. He digresses, and follows an argument fitfully through imperfect logic; he adduces many examples and enlists many anecdotes so that the effect, like that of Burton and of Donne, is of a garishly lit stage with too many scenes and too many characters. Yet there is nobility even within the stage-fire. 'Life is a pure flame, and we live by an invisible Sun within us. . . . Time which antiquates Antiquities . . . that duration, which maketh Pyramids pillars of snow, and all that's past in a moment.' It is a great triumph of English literature, more substantial and enduring than 'the heaviest stone that melancholy can throw at a man'.

Samuel Johnson admired Browne's prose, despite its tendency to prolixity; the haunted, shambling, melancholic figure of Johnson swallowed great draughts of such recondite learning in the attempt to sublimate his own disturbed genius. It might be otiose to place him within 'the strains of sentiment, gloomy sublimity and melancholia that became a feature of British cultural life from the mid-century'[9] but in his company we can also see Laurence Sterne and Oliver Goldsmith. Johnson believed that he was growing melancholy mad and William Adams found him 'in a desperate state, sighing, groaning, talking to himself and restlessly walking' up and down his chamber. In his diary for 18 September 1768 he wrote: 'This day it came into my mind to write the history of my melancholy. On this purpose to deliberate. I know not whether it may not too much disturb me.' Like Cowper he believed himself to be in danger of being damned perpetually. He administered large doses of opium to himself in order to alleviate his mental and physical miseries. He wished to be confined and to be whipped, a predilection known upon the European continent as 'the English disease'.

We may mark here the 'melancholy poetry' of Richard Wilson's eighteenth-century landscapes,[10] which are not unconnected with that current of nostalgia which plays so large a part in English painting; it is as if the English were born looking backwards. Melancholy lies within Tennyson and Swinburne, A. E. Housman and Christina Rossetti:

> God strengthen me to bear myself;
> That heaviest weight of all to bear,
> Inalienable weight of care

We hear it, too, within the music of Emily Brontë:

> O for the time when I shall sleep
> Without identity,
> And never care how rain may steep
> Or snow may cover me!

In twentieth-century poetry it can be glimpsed within the mournful embarrassment of Philip Larkin and the bleakness of Ted Hughes. And yet from what does it spring? Many historians and scholars have favoured the English landscape as the *fons et origo* of melancholy.

Stone portrait of John Donne in his shroud, St Paul's Cathedral, London

CHAPTER 10

The rolling hills

Much of that landscape still rises and declines in ancient patterns, which hold their own stories of lives laboriously led. The lines of ditches and hedgerows represent an ancient order; even densely built urban areas can reflect an older reality. Nineteenth-century Nottingham, for example, was 'largely determined by the medieval footpaths and furlongs of the open fields'.[1] It is an open secret that the topography of the City of London is established upon Roman and Saxon divisions.

These affinities are not simply material for nostalgia, however. It is sometimes supposed that landscape shapes human perception and that the power of the earth, the ground upon which we stand and move, is greater than that of the heavens in determining human destiny. Milton himself suggested that climate and topography nourish wit and consciousness as well as fruit, and more recent studies have confirmed the associations between locality and behaviour. It is of course a piece of ancient wisdom, but the present author has noticed its workings in various districts of twenty-first-century London.

It is the wisdom D. H. Lawrence gathered, and used, from the novels of Thomas Hardy in which 'there exists a great background, vital and wild, which matters more than the people who move upon it'. Lawrence also said that Hardy's understanding of the world derived from his recognition of the territorial imperative and that 'putting aside his metaphysic, which must always obtrude when he thinks of people, and turning to the earth, to landscape, then he is true to himself'. It can be a source of power, too, as well as vision. As John Constable said of another country, 'the Dutch were stay-at-home people. Hence their originality.' But in England itself the source of that originality, or genius, may lie far back. The spires of thirteenth- and fourteenth-century parish churches, an example of a line of beauty in the English landscape, follow a geological stratum from Lincoln to north Somerset and seem ineluctably to rise out of oolite stone. Wordsworth pursues a similar course of enquiry when in his *Guide Through the District of the Lakes* he asks his reader to imagine a primitive landscape. 'He may see or hear in fancy the winds sweeping over the lakes, or piping with a

64

loud voice among the mountain peaks and, lastly, may think of the primaeval woods shedding and renewing their leaves with no human eye to notice, or human heart to regret or welcome the change.' In the north-west region Wordsworth experienced 'low breathings coming after him'; in that same territory, five hundred years before, Sir Gawain felt '*etins aneleden him*', or giants blowing after him. The faint shudder of disquiet may be part of the landscape.

The coming of the Anglo-Saxons scarcely altered the vista of 'primaeval woods', with the ash and oak upon the claylands and beech upon the chalk. Part of the country possessed a settled agrarian regime, inherited from Romano-British or prehistoric famers. And many of the great forests had already been cut back or burned down. But much of England was still a wilderness covered with thick woods or with cold moorlands broken by outcrops of stone, marshlands, fens and heaths; log huts with thatched roofs betrayed their presence with thin plumes of smoke rising into the vast English sky, while in certain places the ruins left by earlier settlers were visible among the weeds and scrubland. Here, except for the wind sighing among the trees and the rain falling upon the damp soil, was silence – silence together with the calls of the natural world. Earnwood in Shropshire signifies 'eagle's wood', Yarnscombe in Devon means 'eagles' valley' and Arncliff in West Yorkshire 'eagles' cliff'. In these fastnesses we are not so far removed from the conclusion of *Wuthering Heights* with Heathcliff's head-stone 'still bare' upon the moor. 'I lingered round them, under that benign sky; watched the moths fluttering among the heath and hare-bells; listened to the soft wind breathing through the grass; and wondered how anyone could ever imagine unquiet slumbers, for the sleepers in that quiet earth.' Here the protagonists have returned to the earth from which they came; after their fitful sojourn in the human world they have folded back into the landscape of which they were always a part.

This odd, silent and empty England in its earliest manifestations was one that haunted the Anglo-Saxon imagination. The opening encomia in the histories of Britain describe a landscape of springs and snow-white gravelled streams, of plains and hills and various flowers; but the imaginative work of the Saxons is possessed by cold and isolation and darkness. The female persona within one short poem laments her state of houselessness; she dwells within an ancient barrow among dark hills and dales. Guthlac finds a resting place upon a primeval mound or 'hill' within the wilderness. Everywhere there are references to steep and rugged places, to black waters and ice-cold streams, to crags and mountain caves. When Bede describes Ely as 'an island surrounded by watery marshes' and Grantchester as 'a small ruined city', he is describing a waste land scarcely populated and meagrely cultivated, a darkly tangled landscape of wolves and boars. So it appears in *Beowulf*, too; the home of the monster race was the '*mor*' and the '*faestnes*', the moor and the fastness where there is frost and darkness. It is the landscape of *King Lear* where 'the wrathfull skies / Gallow the very wanderers of the darke' and the setting of *Sir Gawain and the Green Knight*:

> Thay clomben bi clyffez ther clengez the colde . . .
> Mist muged on the mor, malt on the mountez

Wild England is the context of the opening dream within *Piers the Plowman*: 'That I was in a wildernesse, wist I never where'. It is couched in Hardy's *Far From the Madding Crowd* where 'the general aspect of the swamp was malignant. From its moist and poisonous coat seemed to be exhaled the essences of evil things in the earth, and in the waters under the earth.' It is the landscape that haunts the English imagination. Thus Egdon Heath, in Hardy's *Return of the Native*, 'had a lonely face, suggesting tragical possibilities', while in 'The Palace of Art' Alfred Tennyson depicts an equally bleak vista with

> a foreground black with stones and slags,
> Beyond, a line of heights, and higher
> All barred with long white cloud the scornful crags

It is the internal landscape of T. S. Eliot's *The Waste Land*.

Within the English landscape there are hallowed places, sacred by event or by association. There is a path that leads through English literature; it is the path of human agency and human settlement, a pact with the earth leading the traveller forward. It is the forest path, the *wald-swathu*, in *Beowulf*; it is the trackway along which Jude Fawley walks, weeping, in *Jude the Obscure*. John Clare rejoiced in 'those crooked shreds / Of footpaths', of which Edward Thomas remarked that 'the more they are downtrodden, the more they flourish'; they are themselves a sign or token of national feeling, like that long serpentine line which in *The Analysis of Beauty* William Hogarth named as the line of beauty. It is the line as curved or curling, in the sinuous grace of a reclining body or in a line drawn upwards around a cone. Hogarth simply called it 'VARIETY'. Stanley Spencer's *The Bridlepath at Cookham* has the same irregular beauty as Paul Nash's *The Field Path*, both paintings showing narrow ways turning among fields and trees. The journey of Bunyan's Pilgrim, of Spenser's Red Crosse Knight, of Dickens's Little Nell, all take on the allegory of the winding path.

Since these are immemorial ways a sense of custom is strongest; their presence may linger even after all outward marks have disappeared. The pathways of the Iceni lie beneath the crossroads of the Angel, Islington, in North London. These green lanes and narrow paths flourish in obscurity, sharing that privacy and inward shelter which are so much part of the English vision; they harbour, too, the sacredness of past associations which is also part of the vision. In E. M. Forster's *The Longest Journey* the path moves towards a circle of standing stones, suggesting the primal thread linking past and present times. Yet how quickly, too, that track can degenerate from a lane into an overgrown footpath as if it longed to return to desuetude and forgetfulness; it is a return to origins, to the field-dung and to the ditch-mud which make up its being. John Cowper Powys, in the twentieth century, invoked the sensations of walking in such a secluded place where 'the spirit of the earth called out to him from the green shoots beneath his feet' so that he was filled with the *genius loci* and sustained by it. Here also he experienced 'the innumerable personalities of all the men and women who for generations have gone up and down' these tracks across the earth. So the path may encourage moments of vision. Thus, in Tennyson's *In Memoriam*:

> I know that this was Life, – the track
> Whereon with equal feet we fared

Keats knew in turn that 'The poetry of earth is never dead'. To be surrounded by the melody of landscape is to be blessed, to rest in the sleep of origins in which there is no difference between humankind and the natural world.

The poetry and prose of the Anglo-Saxons are filled with the wonders of symbiosis. Bede, in his life of Cuthbert, relates how the saint walked down from his monastery to the adjacent sea; he knelt down upon the sand in prayer, whereupon two otters 'bounded out of the water, stretched themselves out before him, warmed his feet with their breath, and tried to dry him on their fur'.[2] On another occasion some ravens pulled the straw from a hut which Cuthbert had built upon Farne Island, beside Lindisfarne; he reproved them and soon after one bird returned 'with feathers outspread and head bowed low to its feet in sign of grief'.[3] The bird inhabited the small island also, and in the legends of English life power may reside in the most local circumstances. The site of the stream or '*borne*' beside which Langland slumbered has been identified as the fountain of Malvern water which springs out of the west slope of the Herefordshire Beacon; the '*toure on the toft*' is then the Norman castle immediately above it. The scene of Constable's *Autumn Sunset* is the footpath from East Bergholt Post Office to Stratford St Mary Church, via Vale Farm. The 'dark Satanic Mills' of Blake's *Milton* can readily be identified with the ruins of the Albion Mills along the Blackfriars Road, a short distance from Blake's house in Lambeth; he was the poet of eternity, but he identified himself with a local topography. These sites are irradiated by vision, but half their power derives from their particularity. Even the earth strewn across the bones of the saints was considered sacred, and believed to contain miraculous properties.

On a larger scale, too, the country of England was considered to be charged with power. Saxton's county maps, published in 1579, provided the first complete set of visual images as fresh and illuminating to his first audience as photographs of the outer universe to a more recent generation. His work was complemented by Camden's *Britannia,* published seven years later, of which the purpose was 'to restore Britain to its Antiquities, and its Antiquities to Britain'. This was sacred soil indeed, hallowed by age and sanctified by association. Michael Drayton's *Poly-Olbion,* completed in 1622, is a poetic exercise in chorography, a great choral epic composed from 'the sundry Musiques of England'. In the twentieth century Edmund Blunden compared the English landscape to a symphony. But by whom? By Vaughan Williams? Or Havergal Brian? For Drayton the music flows from the streams and rivers, such as the Severn and the Isis, while echoing among its hills and valleys. In the twelve maps which accompanied the first edition of *Poly-Olbion*, various shepherds, fairies and deities consecrate the land with 'every mountain, forest, river, and valley, expressing in their sundry postures their loves, delights and natural situations'; the song of the earth is divinely ordered, and supplants the authority of the monarch or the newly emerging state. The four thousand names inscribed upon Saxton's wall-map of England are a holy litany; as Drayton puts it, the 'varying vein' of his poetical celebration registers the nature of 'the varying earth'. It is, once more, a highly localised vision like that of Blake or Langland.

Landscape began to emerge, in English painting, in the latter years of the sixteenth century and the beginning of the seventeenth century when various significant personages were placed in specific settings; the *Wedding at Horsleydown in Bermondsey* is one such. Milton wrote about landscape as 'lantskip'; and at the beginning of the seventeenth century Edward Norgate described it as 'an Art soe new in England, and soe lately come a shore'. Yet this new imported form took so great a hold on the English imagination that it has ever since shared pre-eminence with portraiture as the great art of the nation. In a very English study of ruins Christopher Woodward has suggested that the 'picturesque way of seeing is arguably England's greatest contribution to European visual culture',[4] which has dominated metaphors of sight in areas as diverse as Versailles and Central Park. Yet the 'picturesque remains an inseparable element of English taste',[5] dependent upon individual memory and association rather than a theoretical aesthetic or codified practice.

In Jane Austen's *Emma* is depicted a view of gardens and meadows and avenues possessing 'all the old neglect of prospect' – by which Austen means that the landscape had not yet suffered from the late eighteenth-century cult of the picturesque – but it still represented 'English verdure, English culture, English comfort'.

John Ruskin, with his acute sense of place, remarked that with the emergence of the landscape painter Richard Wilson in the eighteenth century 'the history of sincere landscape art founded on a meditative love of nature begins in England'. Yet love of nature is too crude or capacious a term to encompass the specific passion for the English countryside which animates the work of eighteenth- and nineteenth-century artists. There had been an attempt to translate the tenebrous mythologies of the French painters, Claude and Poussin, into the native English scene, but the indigenous taste for irregularity and contrast modified their lights and shades. William Gilpin's *Observations* on English scenery, published over a period of some twenty years at the end of the eighteenth century, digressed upon tones of air and earth 'rarely permanent – always in motion – always in harmony – and playing with a thousand changeable varieties into each other'. A contemporary, Uvedale Price, in turn advanced the beauties 'of roughness and of sudden variation, joined to that of irregularity'.

It cannot be the merest chance that these were also the qualities originally associated with English drama; it is as if national identity may be preserved in a thousand different guises. The emphasis is upon fluidity rather than formality, upon the manifestations of organic process rather than of any fixed design. All arts may in that sense concur. When Gainsborough turned his eyes away from the Suffolk landscape, his second passion was for music; Turner adored the poetry of James Thomson whose *The Seasons* materially affected his art among 'the bright enchantment' and 'the radiant fields', the 'dew-bright earth' and 'coloured air'. The painter also reflected that 'painting and poetry, flowing from the same fount mutually by vision . . . improve, reflect and heighten one another's beauties'. Hardy's vision of landscape was profoundly influenced by Turner's paintings, which the novelist described as 'light modified by objects'. Constable, too, believed that 'could the histories of all the fine arts be compared, we should find in them many striking analogies'. It is customary to ignore or neglect the sentiments of artists themselves, and to brook no association between poetry and painting, yet there is a connection and a continuity which have their origin in a distinctive English sensibility. Samuel Palmer was decisively influenced by the poetry of John Milton, and with his etchings illustrated 'L'Allegro' and 'Il Penseroso'; all his life he tried to re-create the 'Valley of Vision' filled with the shadows cast by moonlight and the dark foliage of overhanging trees. And why should that sensibility not be nourished from childhood, or from memories beyond infancy itself? Constable confessed that 'all that lies on the banks of the *Stour* . . . made me a painter' and that he painted 'my own places best'. It is what Charlotte Brontë meant when she called her sister Emily 'a native and nursling of the moors'.

Only the presence of some *genius loci* will explain the pre-eminence of the water-colour, for example, which has been described by one art historian as the 'medium peculiarly belonging to and expressive of the English spirit in art'[6] with its velleities of atmosphere and moist air, with its almost melancholy sense of transience and of passage, with its evocation of broken light and fleeting shadow.

The frontispiece of *Poly-Olbion* displays England draped across the image of a woman's body. In a similar spirit the American essayist, Washington Irving, once observed that the 'pastoral writers of other countries appear as if they had paid nature an occasional visit and had become acquainted with her general charms; but the British poets have lived and revelled with her – they have wooed her in her most secret haunts – they have watched her minutest caprices'. Not for the first time has the English landscape been compared to a human body. It is no allegory or personification, but a recognition of the landscape as an organic being with its own laws of growth and change.

It rained all night

In the writing of the Anglo-Saxons it is always winter; it is cold there, in a culture where the natural world is commonly considered to be an enemy. Winter, and darkness, were the prevailing conditions in a land of frost and snow falling. Storms of rain and hail pass through the night and touch 'the dank earth, wondrously cold'.[1] Endurance is all. Here 'The land was frozen with cold icicles; the water's torrent shrank in the rivers and ice bridged the dark ocean road'.[2] The Anglo-Saxon translations of the Bible import an insular weather, and in *Genesis* 'with the dawn comes an east wind and frost intensely cold'.[3] Adam is awakened from his dream of bliss to find himself, fallen, in England. 'How shall we now survive or exist in this land if wind comes here from west or east, south or north? Dark cloud will loom up, a hailstorm will come pelting from the sky and frost will set in.'[4] It becomes the weather of the world, primal weather, the storm of life. Thus Cynewulf, in *Elene*, having inscribed his name in ancient runes, compares the transitory wealth of the world to the roaring wind as it 'roves in the clouds, and travels raging'[5] until suddenly becoming still; this is a poet who watched the skies of Mercia and Northumbria.

King Alfred knew the coldness of the wind as it blew through the partitions of doors and the cracks in windows, through walls and wall-panels and the thin covering of tents; the candles were blown out by the sudden draughts, and so the king devised a lantern made of wood and translucent ox-horn in order to protect these frail sources of light. The solitary and abandoned wife, in the Anglo-Saxon fragment 'Wulf and Eadwacer', had no such comfort when 'it was rainy weather and I sat weeping'.

What kind of literature will emerge from such inclemency? One of the most haunting images in all English writing derives from this experience of cold and rain falling. It is taken from Bede's *Historia Ecclesiastica Gentis Anglorum,* at that part when the venerable historian reports the discussions of King Edwin of Northumbria and his councillors, in 627, on the wisdom of accepting the Christian faith.

Your Majesty, when we compare the present life of man on earth with

72

that time of which we have no knowledge, it seems to me like the swift flight of a single sparrow through the banqueting hall where you are sitting at dinner on a winter's day with your thegns and counsellors. In the midst there is a comforting fire to warm the hall; outside, the storms of winter rain or snow are raging. This sparrow flies swiftly in through one door of the hall, and out through another. While he is inside, he is safe from the winter storms; but after a few moments of comfort, he vanishes from sight into the wintry world from which he came.[6]

So it is the fate of humankind, to linger for a moment in the warm hall before tumbling into the cold and darkness. We may imagine the fire and smoke of a central hearth, with seats of stone or benches of wood in a circle around it; this is the image of felicity, to be contrasted with the mist and darkness of the outside world. It is the sombre weather of the imagination, this 'wintertide' of 'rine and sniwe and styrme', with the persistence of the words for snow and storm through time a true emblem of imaginative continuity. The vision reappears in *The Eve of St Agnes* by Keats when

> meantime the frost-wind blows
> Like Love's alarum pattering the sharp sleet
> Against the window-panes . . .

For Hippolyte Taine this 'troubled notion of the shadowy beyond' is national in its intensity and fearfulness; it may be compared with the unexplored vastness of the ocean and the obscurity of the wild places of the island. It releases the eloquence of melancholy and the restless intimations of ghosts and spirits which are indigenous within the literature; it awakens that vague appetite for, or aspiration towards, the supernatural in English poetry and drama. It is the fear in *Macbeth*. It is the dreadful night of nineteenth-century fiction. Images of light and darkness cast a deep shadow out of Anglo-Saxon literature into all subsequent English writing. The sparrow flies everywhere.

The significant episodes of *Sir Gawain and the Green Knight* occur in the dead of winter, as if that season disclosed the true nature of the English imagination. But there are other climatic possibilities, especially 'When the colde cler water fro the cloudez schadde'. Constable and Coleridge were preoccupied with the form and nature of clouds, particularly those of the nimbus or cumulo-nimbus bearing rain. The Anglo-Saxon word '*wolcen*' means both cloud and sky as if they were synonyms.

English fiction is itself drenched in rain, from the first sentence of

Charlotte Brontë's *Jane Eyre* to the last chapter of George Eliot's *The Mill on the Floss*. 'There was no possibility of taking a walk that day' is the opening of *Jane Eyre*, with 'a rain so penetrating' on a dark November day. Here 'with ceaseless rain sweeping away wildly before a long and lamentable blast', Jane dreams of desolate shores with 'the rock standing up alone in a sea of billow and spray'. An Anglo-Saxon vision has come upon her. In the last chapter of *The Mill on the Floss* Maggie Tulliver sits in her old room as 'the rain was beating heavily against the window, driven with fitful force by the rushing, loud-moaning wind'. The prospect of rain, and the horror of cold weather, play a large part in the management of Jane Austen's novels, also:

> 'A walk before breakfast does me good.'
> 'Not a walk in the rain, I should imagine.'
> 'No, but it did not absolutely rain when I set out.'

As one accomplished historian of English literature, Peter Conrad, has remarked, 'All Jane Austen's novels are weather-wise'.[7]

As early as 1712 Addison suggested that a guest sensitive to climate should be used 'as a weather-glass'. A Worcester gentleman, Thomas Appletree, kept a weather diary for the year 1703 in which he formulated a close connection between inner and outer weather. A clouded October day was a 'temper of weather that exactly corresponds to my saturnine and quiet melancholy genius'; rain and mist 'strikes unison to my constitution' and the rain-bearing clouds of a November day entrance him with the sensation of 'returning to my womb'. It is an English preoccupation which bears all the tokens of atavistic remembrance.

When there is no rain, the mist or fog provides the climatic echo-chamber of the imagination; mist upon the moors or open heathland, fog over Manchester and the Potteries, the smokes of London, are all equally suggestive. Tacitus, in the first century, reflected upon the 'frequent mists' of England which were as much an aspect of its reputation as that of a dreaming isle or an island filled with ghosts; mist lingered in the nineteenth century, and was particularly fruitful in the work of urban novelists. Charles Dickens's *Bleak House* is instinct with fog; his is a decaying landscape of crumbling dwellings, where the fog or 'London particular' lowered a dark veil of secrecy and obscurity over the streets of the city. The weather becomes a primitive force, taking the human imagination back to the earliest stages of existence when 'it would not be wonderful to meet a Megalosaurus' walking within the capital; then, in the countryside of Lincolnshire, 'low-lying ground, for half a mile in breadth, is a stagnant river, with melancholy trees for islands in it, and a surface punctured all over, all day long, with falling rain'. Once more it is a primeval landscape, the landscape of origin, one which arouses a native inspiration.

There is a poetry of mist, as the paintings of Turner may suggest. The twentieth-century art historian Kenneth Clark has described how by 'one of those atavistic complications which are often at the root of genius' Turner loved the sea and the sea's mist, entranced by 'the opalescent mists and lights which are found in this country alone and which have coloured so effectively the English vision'.[8] Charles Lamb testified that the fog of London was the medium through which he perfected his own vision. Just as Tacitus emphasised the mists, so painters as diverse as Monet and Whistler have extolled the fog of London as a truly native beauty. For Whistler the fog clothed the ancient river, the Thames, 'with poetry, as with a veil, and the poor buildings lose themselves in the dim sky'; for Monet 'in London, above all what I love is the fog. . . . It is the fog that gives it its magnificent breadth. Those massive regular blocks become grandiose within that mysterious cloak.' So the artists travel to England in order to savour its unique atmosphere.

Among the favoured words of Tennyson are 'damp', 'swollen', 'sodden', 'drenched', 'dewy' and, as Margaret Drabble has put it, the plangent movement of his verse 'is the long, liquid, even line of the contours of the landscape'.[9] Gerard Manley Hopkins evoked primeval darkness:

> What would the world be, once bereft
> Of wet and of wildness? Let them be left,
> O let them be left, wildness and wet;
> Long live the weeds and the wilderness yet

It is remarkable over how long a period the alliterative line has survived and remarkable, too, how it can express the oldest longings.

Certain modern painters never lost this preoccupation with the native climate and landscape. In the twentieth century Graham Sutherland became, in his word, 'obsessed' with the ancient landscape of 'narrow lanes, rounded hills, woodlands and gorse, cromlechs and ancient stones';[10] for him they provoked a sense of longing, or belonging. Paul

Nash wrote of certain English landscapes glimmering within the visible world that 'they are unseen merely because they are not perceived'. He has written of a field near the prehistoric stone monuments of Avebury where

> two rough monoliths stood up sixteen feet high, miraculously patterned with black and orange lichen, remnants of the avenue of stones which led to the Great Circle. A mile away, a green pyramid casts a giant shadow. In the hedge, at hand, the white trumpet of the convolvulus turns from its spiral stem, following the sun. In my art I would solve such an equation.[11]

It is the equation of England itself; on his seeing the stones the asthma of Paul Nash was temporarily healed, and he could breathe easily in the ancient landscape.

John Piper, entranced by the work of Blake and of Turner, was moved to depict 'the whole pattern and structure of thousands of English sites' and noted that 'each rock lying in the grass had a positive personality, for the first time I saw the bones and structure, and the lie of mountains'. He writes, too, of 'getting soaked in their cloud cover and enclosed in their private rock-world in fog'.[12] There is a curious consonance here of climate and territory which seems to have maintained itself over many generations; it is not susceptible to rational analysis, perhaps, at least not in terms which are readily understood. Nevertheless, it is there.

CHAPTER 12

The prose of the world

The earliest known examples of Anglo-Saxon prose are codes of law, confirming the supposition of administrative historians that England was always an intensely organised country; it is even possible that the administration of rural areas, like the pattern of land-holding, is derived from prehistoric practice. This context of governance, para-doxically, maintained the individual 'liberty' which was the rallying cry of eighteenth-century patriots. The laws of Aethelbert and Ine, which survive from the seventh century, are composed in the vernacular. In Europe they would, invariably, have been written in Latin. The English tongue was already seen as a noble and persuasive medium; it shares with Irish the distinction of being pre-eminent among the vernaculars of the western world.

The status of Old English was then confirmed by the policies of King Alfred who, in the second half of the ninth century, instituted a great programme of translation and transmission. The king had been so dismayed by the decay of Latin learning and of general scholarship that he determined on a course of instruction and exhortation. The diminish-ment of Latin, and the possibilities of English, could become part of the same formula of change. In the prefatory letter to his own translation of Gregory's *Pastoral Care* Alfred declared that on his accession there were so few able to understand 'their Divine Services . . . or translate a letter from Latin into English . . . that I cannot remember a single one south of the Thames'.[1] He recalled the happier times of the seventh century when foreigners sought 'wisdom and learning' in England, and lamented that all the treasure of the books of the world was lying unused; the English 'could not understand anything of them, because they were not written in their own language'. He therefore deemed it his duty 'to translate some books which are necessary for all men to know into the language which we can all understand'. He also exhorted his bishops – the magnates who were his principal audience – that 'if we have peace enough' from the incursions of the Vikings 'all the youth now in England born of free men, who are rich enough to be able to devote themselves to it, be sent to learn as long as they are not fit for any other occupation, until they are well able to read English writing'.[2]

Alfred was 'Angelonde's deorling', according to Layamon in the twelfth century, and in the letter of entreaty and advice the king established the claims of the vernacular in an unprecedented way. From the ninth to the eleventh centuries the English language became the proper and appropriate medium both for literature and for learning, and that tradition of native composition was never afterwards lost or forsaken. Alfred's wish to set up schools for the children of freemen, where the learning of English would be compulsory, is acknowledgement that the vernacular could also become the language of government as well as literature; there is evidence to suggest that from the middle of the tenth century there was an Anglo-Saxon chancery producing and distributing charters, diplomas and writs. This is of utmost significance in explaining the power and continuity of English prose for more than a thousand years. One scholar has suggested a connection 'between the two facts that England is the world's oldest continually functioning state, and that English is now its most widely spoken language'.[3]

Alfred himself has earned the title of 'the father of English prose' no less for his compositions than for his exhortations. He himself translated into English Gregory's *Pastoral Care*, the *Consolation of Philosophy* by Boethius and Augustine's *Soliloquies*; it is probable that he dictated his words to a scribe or group of scribes but, even so, it is extraordinary that a king beset by all the cares of ninth-century warfare and administration should accomplish so much. He caused to be translated Bede's *Historia Ecclesiastica Gentis Anglorum*, written in Latin more than 250 years before, as well as the *Seven Books of Histories against the Pagans* by Orosius, and the *Dialogues* of Pope Gregory. He also instituted work on that great historical compilation known as *The Anglo-Saxon Chronicle*, which in its early stages 'was essentially designed to glorify him and his royal house'.[4] In the *Consolation* and *Soliloquies* he affirmed the power of the Christian vision; he translated the desire of Augustine 'to understand God and to know my own soul', and in Boethius translated a philosophical disquisition on the contempt of the world and the consolations of wisdom; there are passages, also, on the nature of evil and the existence of free will not untouched by Alfred's own meditations and anecdotes. In the process of translation the king was compelled to accommodate these reflections within an English sensibility; he omitted long passages of Boethian autobiography as of no relevance, for example, but more importantly he was compelled to turn a relatively abstract Latin vocabulary into a plainer, simpler, more concrete language. He relied much more heavily upon detail and practical or particular instances, in a manner which we will discover to be typical or symptomatic of the English imagination. The general laws within Augustine's *Soliloquies* are matched by descriptions of trees and grasses, as well as intimations of the turbulent sea. A discussion by Boethius on the nature of fate is supplemented by Alfred with a description of the axles and wheels of a wagon. Where the Latin is complex and sonorous, the English maintains the rising and falling rhythms of speech.

The earnest practicality of the king is best adduced, however, in his translation of Pope Gregory's *Pastoral Care*, which he despatched to the bishops of Wessex, Mercia and Kent. One extant manuscript has the legend '*Deos boc sceal to wiogora Ceastre*', or 'This book to go to Worcester'. It may also have reached the courts of the principal thegns, since the themes were those of good governance and the need for administrative ability – 'What kind of man he is to be who is to rule . . . Concerning the burden of government . . . How discreet the ruler is to be in his blaming and flattering.'[5] He was not preoccupied with administration at the expense of everything else, however, and other elements of his translation programme suggest that he was possessed by a vision of Englishness and of English history in the context of the spiritual history of the world. It has been well said that he caused Bede's *Historia Ecclesiastica Gentis Anglorum* to be translated into Old English because of that historian's grasp of a national chronology; Bede's awareness and description of '*gens Anglorum*', or the English people, have been described as 'giving a strong sense of ethnic unity to the diverse tribal and provincial kingdoms of England'.[6] Alfred wished to impart that awareness to his spiritual and secular counsellors, drawing the sense of a tradition from the strength of a common language and inheritance. That same urgent wish – in his own prose Alfred uses the injunction 'now . . . now . . . now' – was formulated in *The Anglo-Saxon Chronicle*, a set of annals distributed throughout the kingdom which preserve local variations and interpolations; despite these differences in the extant versions, however, the work is all of a piece in the sense that 'English nationalism comes to the fore'.[7]

The continuation of *The Anglo-Saxon Chronicle* to 1154 suggests the persistence of a prose tradition which lasted well beyond the reign of Alfred in the late ninth century, but there is perhaps a more impressive continuity. In one of the footnotes to Matthew Arnold's endlessly fascinating lectures on Celtic literature, occurs the remark that 'Our modern English prose in plain matters is often all just the same as the prose of King Alfred and the Chronicle. Ohthere's North Sea Voyage and Wulfstan's Baltic Voyage is the sort of thing which is sent in every day, one may say, to the Geographical or Ethnological Society in the whole style and turn of phrase and thought.' If this is correct, then it is a very remarkable phenomenon. The scholar R. W. Chambers wrote a study entitled *On the Continuity of English Prose from Alfred to More and His School*; since that 'school' can be taken to include John Milton and the great historians of the eighteenth and nineteenth centuries then the influence of Alfred has been wide indeed. In the words of Chambers himself, 'it became part of the inheritance of every educated Englishman'.

Much Anglo-Saxon prose has been lost; the middle years of the tenth century, from the reign of Athelstan to that of Edgar, are scant of testimony. The final entry in *The Anglo-Saxon Chronicle*, dated 1154, marks the abeyance of English historical prose, which did not become glorious again until the early sixteenth century. Yet Alfred's own works were copied as late as the twelfth and thirteenth centuries, while his enterprise and example materially assisted the growth of a various and complex vernacular. By the latter part of the tenth century the range of Anglo-Saxon prose includes saints' lives and grammatical treatises, fictional narratives and gospel translations, medical texts and oriental legends, herbals and lapidaries, geographical texts and philosophical speculations, dialogues and astronomical works, theses on government and on ancient history, wills and laws, charters and natural history. The wealth and variety of these prose writings were not equalled in English until the fifteenth century, and in their own period they were unrivalled in Europe. Theirs was an ascendancy matched by achievements in stone-carving, metal-working and manuscript illumination.

One of the finest phases in English prose, from the late tenth to the early eleventh centuries, is most readily characterised by the works of Aelfric and Wulfstan. It has been said of Aelfric that he was 'the great master of prose in all its forms' and that he 'works on principles that would have been approved by Dryden'.[8] Just as King Alfred looks back to Bede, so Aelfric turns back towards Alfred for inspiration; thus a tradition is formed, a line of beauty and harmony stretching for as long an interval as that between Purcell and Britten, between Dowland and Elgar. We may imagine an audience gathering for the recitation of a law or charter, just as we know that the *scop* 'told the tale' of heroism ancient and modern in open spaces and in dining-halls.

But writing itself, with its roots in the folklore of runes, was considered to be a spiritual or sacred activity. It was the mark of continuity for the tribe, but it also called to the inward conscience of the silent and solitary reader. When those who were illiterate were asked to witness a written document, they simply touched a cross inscribed beside their name, but the power of writing was formulated in actual practice. 'Bookland' was the name of territory granted by 'book' or charter, while written charms were considered to be more efficacious than those merely spoken.

All this lies behind the prose of Aelfric, who himself was nervous of the power of the written word. In his preface to the translation of Genesis he remarks that '*Ic ondraede*': I fear that some foolish man, reading this book or hearing it read, will think that he can live as if he were still under the tutelage of Moses. His Old English is perhaps more lucid and elegant than any contemporary translation, but it bears the same syntax and structure as modern English. Thus the phrase 'reading this book, or hearing it read' is derived from '*thas boc raet othe raedan gehyrth*' which is simple and limpid; it is the simplicity of native speech preserved in a more enduring form.

George Eliot said of Shakespeare's prose that it remains 'intensely colloquial even in his loftiest tragedies', and it can fairly be asserted that this is a direct inheritance from the best Anglo-Saxon prose. Of course Shakespeare had encountered no writing of that period, but the English language itself had incorporated and maintained its salient characteristics; it is almost as if the language itself were as much the originator of certain texts as the writer. Certainly, in Shakespeare, the language seems to lead him forward into fresh perceptions as if it were speaking through him; he comes upon felicities in the most sublime combinations of words. Aelfric was also a literary artist, and one of great intellectual range, but the high rhythms of his prose rise and fall with the distinctive emphasis and momentum of the spoken language.

He was a monk in the late tenth century at Cerne Abbas in Dorset, close to the great chalk figure of the giant delineated upon a hill with erect penis and club in hand. He composed homilies and lives of the saints in 'the usual English speech, desiring to profit others' in 'that noble nation'; he also translated certain books from the Bible and wrote a text concerning grammar. He was part of a great monastic reform programme, in which he became an educator whose books were transcribed and distributed all over the kingdom. One other feature of his prose is instructive in this context; it follows the natural beat of English in more than one sense since it incorporates an alliterative rhythm which is all the more persuasive for being partly submerged. If the work of Aelfric is read aloud, as surely it must have been in monastic halls as well as in pulpits, it falls naturally into the cadences of oral poetry. Since English poetry is syllabic rather than accentual it will quite naturally follow the line of instinctive utterance; whatever patterns of elaboration are imposed upon it, the native breath will emerge. That is why there is within English literature a great consonance between prose and poetry, since they both spring from the same source; this is the inheritance which was bestowed upon Aelfric and which in turn he bequeathed to others.

Aelfric's contemporary, Wulfstan, evokes those qualities in a much more idiosyncratic manner. He was the first English writer to suggest the possibilities of a deliberately rhetorical prose, and his 'Sermon of the Wolf to the English' is the most famous example in Old English of the ornate and vivid sermons which have since become characteristic of England's religious literature. He ends laconically: 'God ure helpe. Amen.' Curiously, the word 'God' is of Celtic rather than Germanic provenance, related to the Erse word 'Guth' or voice. So God help us – but in this fiery address, delivered in 1014 when Ethelred was hesitant before the Danish intruders and settlers, the warnings and imprecations are expressed with an eloquence heightened by ancient echoes. Wulfstan invokes *'stric ond steorfa'*, plague and pestilence, *'wiccan ond waelcyrian'*, witches and wizards, *'bryne ond blodgite'*, burning and bloodshed, *'here ond hunger'*, war and famine. He recalls how the 'Britta' were conquered by the 'Engla' because they had fallen from God; now the 'Engla' in turn are likely to be destroyed by foreign invaders. It may seem unnecessary to sift the details of forgotten polemic, but it is important to understand that, a thousand years ago, English prose was as elaborate and as rigorous as in any of its contemporary manifestations.

There is, however, one distinction. There were effectively two languages in England since Wulfstan, archbishop of York and bishop of London, wrote and spoke Latin as fluently as English. Latin was still the preferred medium for scholars and ecclesiastics, who communicated with their peers on the continent in that tongue. Here again it is unwise to underestimate the powers and possibilities of early utterance. It has been confirmed that at the time of the Roman occupation 'British Vulgar Latin', the language of the Romano-Britons, was considerably purer than that of France or Spain. It was more 'conservative', more 'archaic', and thus closer to classical sources.[9] Its usage tends 'to agree with the pronunciations recommended by the grammarians as distinct from those of ordinary colloquial Vulgar Latin'.[10] This throws a distinctive light upon the qualities of life in Roman Britain but, significantly, seven centuries later – by the time of William's invasion in 1066 – the Latin culture of the English was still considerably more advanced and more sophisticated than that of their Norman conquerors. There were other spheres, too, in which the Anglo-Saxons excelled.

CHAPTER 13

The first initials

The art of manuscript illumination is the glory of the Anglo-Saxon period. From the strange abstract wildness of the Book of Durrow, completed in Northumbria in the middle of the seventh century, to the richness and vitality of the Grimbald gospels ornamented at Winchester in the early eleventh century, there emerge features that will become intrinsic to English art itself. And how could it not be so? A tradition of four hunded years does not pass in a night, if it can be said to pass at all.

There is much here in these early manuscript pages to excite contemplation in the twenty-first century. A bull in a field becomes an abstract shape invested in spiritual mystery, as if formed by Henry Moore; a hieratic full-length figure is decorated in radiant detail like some Pre-Raphaelite model; the ornamentation of a sacred chalice is strong and precise, as richly coloured as a tapestry by William Morris or a miniature by Nicholas Hilliard. Wandering through the intricate and elaborate mysteries of the Lindisfarne gospels we catch glimpses of William Hogarth's 'line of beauty', that long serpentine line which the artist considered to be characteristic of English art; discerning the sinuous outlines of the figures within the Lindisfarne gospels, we may be inclined to agree with Roger Fry's remark at the beginning of the twentieth century that the art of recent English painters is 'primarily linear . . . and not plastic', the only difference being that we are obliged to date this linearity back to the eighth and ninth centuries.

Other attributes may be seen as English in inspiration and in execution. The fascination for detail, and the obsession with the riddle or the puzzle, have already been discussed. But latent within them is the art of the miniature. Its apotheosis lies perhaps with the work of Nicholas Hilliard, who flourished at the Elizabethan court, but its most striking realisation may be in the art of the 'historiated initial' – by which is meant the small scenes painted within the initials of manuscript texts. These initials may be an English invention and, according to one historian of medieval art, 'this might partly account for their persistent popularity during the whole later history of English illumination'.[1] The predominance of pattern and border over figure has also been characterised as English in style. The body is represented as flat, as part of the detail, rather than an object formed in volumetric space.

In his *The Englishness of English Art* published in 1956, the German art historian, Nikolaus Pevsner, noted this denial of the body in English art, quite unlike the typical art of the Mediterranean. Pevsner associated it with the English tendency towards embarrassment and understatement. And yet it might be interpreted as an aspect of a fundamentally non-human art; it is significant that the decorations of the Lindisfarne texts are borrowed from, or related to, the abstract patterns inscribed upon weaponry and jewellery of the same epoch. In the same way the Christian poetry of *Beowulf* is striated with ancient and pagan myths. If there is some wildness here in the obsession with spirals, whorls and lines rather than human figures, one historian of Anglo-Saxon art has a possible explanation: 'It is a spiritual mystery; something eerily intangible, as though in secret shrines honour was still paid to older art, and dim traditions of prehistoric and later British aesthetic sensibility lived on to guide the artist's hand.'[2] It has been described as 'tense abstraction', and is precisely the quality that may be recognised in the art of William Blake. When Anglo-Saxon illuminators from the tenth and eleventh centuries are placed against the engravings and tempera paintings of Blake, the resemblance becomes extraordinarily clear; there is the same figural grace, the same flowing linear pattern. The drawings of the Winchester school, in particular, have a delicacy within the outline, of which Blake's instinctive movement with the brush or engraver is reminiscent. This is not, however, a matter of chance. Blake had seen the ancient wall-paintings in Westminster Abbey, as well as the funereal monuments of a later date, and had imbibed the Saxon art of outline and linear decoration.

The art of the Winchester monks and of William Blake is a wholly English achievement. One historian of medieval painting has remarked upon 'the growth of a new and strongly marked national idiom', with 'the exquisite delicacy of line and proportion in the decorative detail' as of 'a particularly English character'.[3] The 'light, agitated style of drawing', characterised by the Winchester school and amplified by William Blake, was 'intrinsically English' and a 'national idiom'[4] as English as the decorated stone crosses of the north and the elaborate embroidery of the south. Linearity and abstract pattern have already been deemed to be native characteristics. It is what Pevsner described in another context as 'the anti-corporeal intricacies of line'[5] to be traced in English architecture. It is why the English 'developed an enthusiasm for brasses – that is not sculpture at all but engraving'.[6] It can be seen in what Reynolds called the 'marks and scratches' of Gainsborough and 'the formalised linear portrait' only to be found in England.[7] It is the single line of melody in English music, where, for example, Tudor songs are 'linear in conception'.[8] It is to be observed in the length of the naves, and of the long galleries, in English buildings; after all, 'the long house was traditional in England'.[9] It is evinced in the Queen's House at Greenwich by Inigo Jones, in the straight progression of the Georgian terrace, and in 'the calm rectilinear uniformity' of York Minster.[10]

The flowing linear pattern is central to the English imagination. The line drawings of Beardsley and Gillray exemplify this tendency, and it has been said that 'line and tone rather than colour were on the whole characteristics of English painting at the end of the nineteenth century'.[11] These examples might be multiplied indefinitely, but they all lead back to the mysterious limpidity and simple outlines of Anglo-Saxon illuminators. It is what Blake called the 'bounding' outline as if it exemplified all the vigour and animation of his own 'illuminated books', in which word and image are as indissolubly connected as any on the page of a tenth-century psalter.

The Anglo-Saxons had in a sense anticipated that energy in their own preoccupation with leaping figures. Among the foliated initials of illuminated manuscripts are to be seen human figures 'climbing and jumping among the branches';[12] one illuminator from Winchester Cathedral has become known as 'the Master of the Leaping Figures' since his figures 'sway and "leap", with swinging drapery and wide-flung arms';[13] animals 'jump' with them in scenes of overflowing energy which seem so characteristic of the Anglo-Saxon world. A curious image which testifies to this delight in motion comes in an early eleventh-century psalter illuminating the Ascension of Our Lord; as is so often the case in presentations of this dramatic scene 'the subject is indicated by the feet of the ascending figure only, at the top of the picture'.[14] Four hundred years before, in the Echternach gospels of Northumbria, the 'Lion of St Mark' is shown in a bounding leap of joy. The same image occurs frequently in the literature of the medieval period, when, for example, the heart *maketh moni liht lupe* in *Ancrene Wisse*. Christ is often described as 'leaping' in the womb, while at an earlier date Bede describes the cripple healed by the apostles 'walking, and leaping, and praising God'. We may leap forward to the middle of the fourteenth century when, in a poem of London, 'lads left their labour and leaped to the place'.[15] Then we can return once more to Blake's vision where

> The little ones leaped & shouted & laugh'd

Ornamental page with the monogram 'Chr(ist) autem'. Beginning of the Christmas story, *Matthew* 1, 18. From the Lindisfarne Gospels

CHAPTER 14

Anglo-Saxon attitudes

In 1882 Gerard Manley Hopkins wrote, 'I am learning Anglo-Saxon and it is a vastly superior thing to what we have now' and, at a later date, W. H. Auden described his introduction to Anglo-Saxon literature at Oxford: 'I was spellbound. This poetry, I knew, was going to be my dish.' He also confirmed that 'Anglo-Saxon and Middle English poetry have been one of my strongest, most lasting influences'. He added that 'often some piece of technique thus learnt really unchains one's own Daimon quite suddenly'. In the Anglo-Saxon phrase, it unlocks the word-hoard. William Morris translated *Beowulf* in the last years of his life, and there have been many attempts by other poets culminating in the translation of the epic by the Irish poet, Seamus Heaney, in 2000. It is as if it represented some kind of primal memory.

The Anglo-Saxon inheritance can work in different ways, and one poem can act as the unacknowledged instigator or inspiration for a different form of perception. The theme of lonely pilgrimage in the short poem 'The Seafarer' – one of the 'elegies' in the Exeter Book – is the first evocation in the language of a metaphor which haunts the English imagination. The image of the voyager alone upon the ice-cold and raging sea is like some scene from the beginning of the world; '*stormas*' and '*flodwegas*' have surged through English poetry ever since, while sighs of transitoriness and exile have been exhaled for a thousand years. The expatriate American poet, Ezra Pound, was living in London when he translated 'The Seafarer':

> On flood-ways to be far departing

His is a spirited and sonorous re-enactment of the original, and exemplified his attempt to connect himself with an English tradition in order both to reinvent himself and to renew his own language. It is one of the great strengths of the English imagination that it does not represent an exclusive or proprietorial gift; like the language itself, it is open to anyone.

Milton's poetry bears some relation to 'The Seafarer', too. In the Anglo-Saxon poem there is a description of those who live in cities 'wingal', or flushed with wine; in *Paradise Lost* the sons of Belial dwell in 'luxurious cities' where they are 'flown with insolence and wine'. It has often been suggested that the poet of Bread Street and Aldersgate was here memorialising the street brawlers, the Hectors and Scourers, of his native city; but as he sits by his window, the candle glimmering in the dusk, an image of Anglo-Saxon brawlers also emerges. The English imagination has many mansions, and many rooms. There is another Miltonic connection with these English originals. Passages in *Paradise Lost*, completed by Milton in 1663, concerning the fall of the angels into darkness and the subsequent soliloquy by Satan, bear a startling resemblance to an Anglo-Saxon poem entitled 'Genesis B' by scholars and tentatively dated to the mid-ninth century. In that early poem Satan's first words, for example,

> *Is thes aenga stede ungelic swithe . . .*

are close in cadence and meaning to

> Is this the Region, this the Soil, the Clime . . .

An early nineteenth-century scholar, in reviewing both poems, wrote of 'a resemblance to Milton so remarkable that much of this portion of "Genesis B" might be almost literally translated'; the biographer of Milton, David Masson, describes 'striking coincidences between notions and phrases'.[1] This might be construed as no more than scholarly supposition or source-hunting; if such a resemblance exists, then it may arise simply from the consonance or, one may say, consanguinity within the English imagination itself. There are many examples of poets, or dramatists, who seem to have lifted material from their predecessors but who have in reality only been led forward by the pressures and contours of the language itself. Once a sequence of words enters the vast sphere of language, it is always a potential line of expression for any later writer; the first one or two words will activate the entire sequence.

But the case of Milton and 'Genesis B' is more interesting. The manuscript was discovered by a seventeenth-century scholar, Junius, who was in fact a close acquaintance of Milton's. Previously Milton had pored over Anglo-Saxon sources, and had written an enthusiastic note upon the divine inspiration of Caedmon; he evinced a 'long preoccupation with the old English past'.[2] What is more natural and inevitable than that his friend, Junius, should read out to him and translate the Creation poem which he had recently discovered? Satan's great speech of pride and bitterness might then find its way into the blind poet's consciousness. It offers at least a plausible explanation for continuities between Anglo-Saxon poetry and the poetry of the mid-seventeenth century.

In the seventh chapter of *Through the Looking-Glass* the messenger Haigha appears 'wriggling like an eel . . . with his great hands spread out like fans on each side'. 'He's an Anglo-Saxon Messenger', the White King explains to Alice, 'and those are Anglo-Saxon attitudes.' The posture is indeed Anglo-Saxon, and can be seen in the late ninth-century cross of Codford St Peter and in the figure of King Edgar in the foundation charter for the new minster at Winchester; the position has in fact been described as 'in essence completely English'.[3] Carroll parodies it successfully, just as he parodies Old English poetry in his lyric 'Jabberwocky':

> 'Twas brillig, and the slithy toves
> Did gyre and gimble in the wabe.

Anglo-Saxon attitudes emerge almost everywhere. The fable in Old English translation, *Apollonius of Tyre*, appears in the poetry of John Gower as well as in Shakespeare's *Pericles*. The Old English antiphons of the Advent season were known as the 'great O's' because they began with 'O' or 'Eala', and are echoed in the 1608 text of *King Lear* 'O, o, o, o'. The satire upon greedy and wastrel priests, in *Guthlac* and in other Anglo-Saxon originals, is taken up by Langland and Wycliff; the sweet breath of St Guthlac just before his demise issues from the mouth of Thomas More before his execution. The panther in the Exeter Book, who shines brightly and is the image of Christ, re-emerges as the 'tyger' of Blake's lyric; in T. S. Eliot's *Gerontion* there appears in turn 'Christ the tiger'. The spiritual narrative of *The Dream of the Rood*, a devotional poem of the late seventh century with its focus upon the material image of the cross, prefigures the seventeenth-century meditations of George Herbert and Henry Vaughan. The *wyrd* or doom of Anglo-Saxon poetry is matched by Chaucer's 'executrice of wyrdes' in *Troilus and Criseyde* before being resurrected as 'Life's Doom' in Thomas Hardy's epic poem *The Dynasts*. The conflict between tribal loyalties of revenge and the Christian pieties of forgiveness and redemption, so central to the Anglo-Saxon imagination, was reinterpreted again and again in Elizabethan and Jacobean tragedy; the great preoccupations of ninth- and tenth-century England were flourishing in the sixteenth and seventeenth centuries. 'Periods' of a literary or historical nature do not succeed each other in neat chronology; they overlap and intermingle, fade and then flare up, so that we might call the history of the last two thousand years 'the Anglo-Saxon Period'. Instead of asking what is 'modern' about the Anglo-Saxons, enquire instead what is Anglo-Saxon about 'the modern'.

Middle English

'Sir Bedivere throws the sword Excalibur into the water.'
Manuscript illustration, early 14th century

CHAPTER 15

The alteration

Linguistic change is the principal arbiter of imaginative transition. A passage from the gospel of St Matthew may illustrate the point. '*Arise and nim thaet cild and his modor, and fleoh on Egypta land*' becomes 'Rise up and take the child and his modir, and fle in to Egipt'. In the same passage '*swefnum*' becomes 'sleep', and '*forspillene*' is changed to 'destrie'. These are neither the most marked nor the most remarkable variations between Old English and Middle English but they manifest a sea-change, rich and powerful, in the English imagination.

The dating of Middle English is of course imprecise, like all linguistic phenomena, but it is generally accepted as spanning the period 1066 to 1485 and thus conveniently covers the years from the battle of Hastings and Norman domination to the battle of Bosworth and Tudor domination. It is not quite as easy as that.

The old Anglo-Saxon culture, for example, did not wholly die. The great monasteries, particularly those which were not reorganised by the Norman clergy, preserved the inheritance of Anglo-Saxon learning; that learning represented a vigorous and sophisticated culture which could not altogether fade from the memory of man. The alliterative line, the signature of Anglo-Saxon verse, survived in ways which are not yet fully understood. But it seems likely that it was maintained by public recitation or the pressures of native tradition. It emerges fully armed, for example, in an early mystery play:

> I shall make the still as stone, begynnar of blunder!
> I shall bete the bak and bone, and breke all in sonder.

The salient feature about traditional or customary speech is that it was not written down or transcribed by monkish chroniclers, so its latter-day silence in the written record does not testify to its absence.

That there continued a popular tradition, of heroic myth or folklore, can hardly be in doubt. When in the eleventh century the people of Christchurch rebuffed an attempt by monks to raise money, a great fiery dragon is supposed to have visited its wrath upon the town. Dragons and beasts continued to appear in the twelfth and thirteenth centuries, as a direct inheritance of the previous civilisation when the Anglo-Saxon world was, according to J. R. R. Tolkien, 'a world of dragons'. The Old English '*draca*' gave its name to Drakelaw or 'Dragon's Hill' in both Derbyshire and Worcestershire, and on the Sutton Hoo shield perched a winged dragon. To see dragons in the thirteenth century, therefore, is to see with Anglo-Saxon eyes. Celtic perceptions lingered, also; the Welsh poems and tales, the latter collected in the *White Book of Rhydderch*, were known in England and France and 'had a liberating effect on the European imagination'.[1] From them springs King Arthur, whose national exploits will soon be surveyed.

A specifically English spirit was maintained long after the Conquest in the transcription of Alfredian writings. The late twelfth-century poem *The Owl and the Nightingale* is in part based upon French models, and is satirical at the expense of the primitive inhabitants of Britain as covered in black and blue 'woad', but on three occasions the poet quotes the apophthegms and maxims of Alfred who is called 'the wise'. The poet himself may not have perused the king's Old English translation of Boethius' *De Consolatione Philosophiae*, but the memory and indeed the living presence of Alfred's learning, quoted in this courtly poem as if it were the most natural thing in the world, testify to the continuing influence of Anglo-Saxon scholarship in Middle English.

These allusions are further proof of one of the most significant and salient aspects of the English imagination: its sentimental and almost pious attachment to the past, as exemplified by the large number of scriptoria at Canterbury, Malmesbury, Thorney, Ely, Rochester, Worcester, Evesham, Durham and Abingdon, all producing 'historical work which ensured the survival of the Old English past'.[2] For the monks of these institutions, the centuries before the Conquest were a 'golden age' of art and scholarship in which Saxon liberties joined with Saxon genius to create a miraculous civilisation. Bishop Wulfstan, of Worcester, was in particular 'a dedicated preserver of the past' who instituted the Worcester Chronicle and jealously guarded the ancient documents of his foundation. The writings of Aelfric, too, were copied throughout the twelfth century.

Anglo-Saxon culture was not necessarily scorned by its Norman conquerors. William was a ruthless and violent man whose principal purpose was to stamp his authority upon the country; effectively he achieved this by extirpating the old secular and sacred leaders, the thegns and some of the abbots, while at the same time importing the members of an Anglo-Norman administration. But once that power had been successfully imposed, currents and cross-currents may be seen stirring underneath. Just as the delicate liquidity of the Anglo-Saxon 'line' survived in thirteenth- and fourteenth-century psalters, so native artists and sculptors 'found employment and favour with the Normans'.[3] The patrons of the Bayeux Tapestry itself employed Anglo-Saxon embroiderers as well as Anglo-Saxon techniques, and indeed the Normans 'found some good reasons to regard themselves as the inheritors of Anglo-Saxon tradition'.[4] It is always wise to look for evidence of continuity rather than of violent change, because in persistence and permanence lie the true strengths of human nature.

Yet human expression does change and, after the Conquest, Anglo-Saxon was effectively marginalised as the vehicle of law and governance. The native language gave place to Latin and to Norman French, suffering in the process a devaluation from which it never fully recovered. Old English – or, to be more precise, West Saxon – had in any case become a highly artificial dialect, far removed from the vernacular, and so its demise as an 'official' writing was no difficult matter. The last poem composed in the old language was an encomium upon Durham, whose cathedral was the long home of Bede and of St Cuthbert; in its final line that saint is said to be waiting for 'Doomsday', like the language and the civilisation themselves.

The technical developments are easily ascertained from the written records, although the history of almost two centuries must thereby be abbreviated. The inflections of Old English faded away, together with its more difficult diphthongs; an archaic or at least artificial language, as it slipped from official use, was thereby brought much closer to the sound and cadence of speech in a natural process of simplification. Prepositional structures became standardised and the now conventional syntactical order of subject–verb–object emerged. Very few texts of what can loosely be described as Early Middle English survive from the eleventh and twelfth centuries, and it can be surmised that it was predominantly a spoken language; it was perhaps *the* spoken language, even during the period of West Saxon or Old English dominance as the medium for writing. It must also have been an amorphous and variable language, therefore, changing according to region or even local district. There is a dialect of the central midlands and another of the east midlands, one of London and another of Durham. It was, as a result, immensely susceptible to influence. Many French words entered the vocabulary, among them 'mercy' and 'war', 'fruit' and 'grace', but the evolving tongue also adopted Scandinavian words from the Danish settlers who had arrived before the Conquest, among them 'law' and 'die', 'husband' and 'knife'. No other phase in English history has witnessed so profound a change in its language, and the glotto-chronological picture is rendered even more obscure by the fact that Latin and French were also being written and spoken; England was a multilingual, or at least trilingual, nation for the first and last time in its history.

Much speculation has been devoted to the exact status of each of these three languages, and it can be surmised that Latin was employed for administrative and ecclesiastical records, French for law and business, and English for more mundane or practical purposes. It has been suggested that French was spoken as a mark of social status, and that even artisans or tradesmen might use it in order to seem 'superior'. There is a sprinkling of French words or phrases, as well as Latin 'tags', in the demotic of native Londoners. Yet so much is guesswork, and so little corroborated, that the truth is very deeply concealed in the well of history. One suggestive detail, however, has survived. There is a fourteenth-century chronicle on the life and death of Thomas Becket; it is written in Latin, but at one moment the anonymous historian breaks into English with '*Hugh de Morevile, ware! ware! ware! Lithulf heth his swerde adrege!*', warning one of the murderers that Lithulf – an English name – has drawn his sword. Interestingly enough the speaker here is a Norman lady, but this interjection suggests that English was the language of instinctive feeling or emotive expression. It was the language of impulse even for those who might ordinarily write in Latin or in French. Common sense would also suggest that the vast mass of the native population customarily expressed themselves in their local dialect of English. In that sense it may also be surmised that the language itself represented the breath, or spirit, of the people. It was varied and amorphous because the inhabitants were themselves of hybrid breed; there are Celtic, Scandinavian, Norse and French elements in the language to the same extent that they also existed in the general population.

It was a heterogeneous language, absorbing and assimilating external influences, but is that not a model or metaphor for the English imagination itself? In the course of this narrative it will be demonstrated that English literature, in particular, borrowed elements and themes from continental texts only to redefine them in the native style; it might even be said that it is in the nature of English literature precisely to reside at this nodal point where two languages or

98

perceptions meet. It is only to be expected, therefore, that the language itself will embody this perpetual tendency.

There were some after the Conquest who lamented the loss of the old learning. A fragment from Worcester Cathedral is written in the famous hand known to scholars somewhat eerily as 'the Tremulous Hand of Worcester'. He can be forgiven his incapacity, however, since in the fragment he sighs over the demise of old '*englisc*'. In translation he declares that 'These taught our people in English. . . . Now those teachings are all forgotten, the people lost and helpless; now our people are taught in other languages, and many of the teachers are damned, and the people with them.'[5] The supposition must be that the people, or '*folc*', were being taught in Anglo-French, although of course only a small proportion of the population would attend any of the cathedral schools. There was in any case little vernacular literature in the eleventh and early twelfth centuries, although the evidence of the first religious lyrics in Middle English suggests that there was some kind of popular or oral tradition of verse-making. By the end of the twelfth century, however, can be found English compositions which testify to a developed or at least developing prose. Many of these English texts were in fact translations, from Latin or from French, and were written 'for lewed men that luitel connen / On Englisch hit is thus bigonnen' or 'For him that con not iknowen / Nouther French ne Latyn'.

So the vernacular, the language of the 'lewed', could not be artificially depressed. It sprang up at the end of the twelfth century – from Portesham in Dorset with Nicholas of Guildford's *The Owl and the Nightingale*, from Arley Kings in Worcestershire with Layamon's *Brut*, and from the north with *Cursor Mundi*. It is for all practical purposes inconceivable that these three fully achieved poems came out of darkness and silence; they may have been derived from French and Latin originals but they are in no sense apologetic about their employment of the vernacular. As the poet of *Cursor Mundi* puts it:

> This ilk bok is es translate
> In to Inglis tong to rede
> For the loue of Inglis lede,
> Inglis lede of Ingland,
> For the commun at understand

This love of the English people is complemented by the introductory verses of Layamon's *Brut* when he declares 'thet he wolde of Engle tha aethelaen tellen'. The use of alliteration in *Brut* suggests some form of continuity with the archaic past, even if it may be an artificial and deliberately imposed connection. Both *Cursor Mundi* and *The Owl and the Nightingale* are conducted in rhymed octosyllabic couplets which come out of French, Anglo-Norman and Latin verse, and represent what has been described as a European or international art-form, but the very tone and sprightliness of the verse are already recognisably English in sympathy and feeling:

> The nightingale bigon the speche . . .
> In ore vaste thicke hegge
> Imeind mid spire and grene segge

It must be admitted that at this relatively early date it is not a particularly illustrious or noble language, but it has the freshness and vivacity of all newly awakened things. The resurgence of English has been somewhat tendentiously linked with the loss of Normandy in 1204, at which point the Anglo-Norman aristocracy were forced to choose between homelands, but there is without doubt a new emphasis upon Englishness as a defining term. In the thirteenth century, too, various historical chronicles were written in English verse in order to identify 'the national community of the English' and thus 'to provide a history of the land in its distinctive language'.[6] Layamon's *Brut*, which first narrates the life and career of Arthur in the vernacular, is similarly preoccupied with this singular 'land' as the focus of endeavour.

In the fourteenth century the language once more became an instrument of power and force, in one of those explosions of range and energy which occur in the interaction of various elements that on their own would precipitate no great movement; the next such galvanic charge would take place in the last two decades of the sixteenth century. At the parliament of 1337 a French ambassador spoke 'in English, in order to be understood of all folk'. When Thomas Usk composed a *Testament of Love* in 1385 he wrote that 'Treuly, the understanding of Englishmen wol not strecche to the privy termes in Frenche, what-so-ever we bosten of straunge language . . . let us shewe our fantasyes in such wordes as we lerneden of our dames tonge.' The invocation of 'dames' here may suggest the matrilinear bonds of native English, but again it has recourse to the notion of the maternal land itself. That sense of identity is reassembled in another verse history of the period where

> Here may men rede whoso can
> Hu Inglond first bigan

> Men mow it finde in Englische
> As the Brout it telleth ywis

It is important to recognise that the spread of the language was itself acompanied by, and cannot be distinguished from, the extension of historical consciousness. There also came with it a strong sense of exclusiveness:

> Selden was for ani chance
> Praised Inglis tong in France

writes the anonymous author of *Cursor Mundi* with a suspicion of wounded pride. In 1352 a history in Latin by Ranulph Higden, a monk of Chester, complained that English children felt obliged to 'leave their own language, and to learn their lessons . . . in French, as they have since the Normans first came to England. Also gentlemen's children are forced to speak French from the time they are rocked in their cradles . . . and rustic men wish to liken themselves to gentlemen, and seek with great eagerness to speak French, in order to be more respected.'[7] No more than thirty years later Higden's history was translated by a Cornishman, John of Trevisa, who appended the following remarks: 'Thys manner was moch y-used tofore the furste moreyne, an ys sith then somdel ychanged . . . so that now, the yer of oure Lord a thousand three hundred foure score and fyue . . . in al the gramer scoles of Engelond children leveth Frensch and construeth and lurneth an Englysch. . . . Also gentil men habbeth now moche yleft for to teche here childern Frensch.' The only unusual word in this passage, 'moreyne', signifies plague and refers to the Black Death of 1349 which dramatically reduced the native population. A sense of mortality, or of dwindling numbers, may also encourage a sense of identity, threatened or otherwise. It is nevertheless true that by the last year of the fourteenth century English had more or less supplanted French. A book of *Travels* has a prologue which explains that it is translated 'out of Frensch into Englyssch, that every man of my nacioun may understonde it'. There is also an intimation here of a democratic and egalitarian temper which the use of the old language – one might say, the liberties of the native language – might encourage. Thus Robert Mannyng, in his *Chronicle*, declares that he has written in 'symple speeche':

> Bot for the luf of symple men
> That strange Inglis can not ken

The author of *Of Arthour and of Merlin* vouchsafes similar sentiments when he admits that:

> Of Freynsch no Latin nil-y tel more
> Ac on Inglisch ichil tel ther-fore;
> Riyt is that Inglische understond
> That was born in Inglond

Even when writing poetry in French, John Gower dedicated his work to the English nation of the fourteenth century: '*O gentile Engletere, a toi j'escrits.*' The public events of the period confirm this new dispensation. In 1356 the mayor and aldermen of London decided that the proceedings in the sheriff's courts were to be conducted in English; it is both the context of Chaucer and the explanation for the fact that eleven out of the twenty-five extant Arthurian manuscripts were copied or distributed in the capital. From a very early period London was a centre of national consciousness. The oldest legal document written in the vernacular is dated 1376, and the first parliamentary document in English survives from 1378; the Lord Chancellor opened the parliamentary session of 1363 in his native tongue, and from that session emerged the Statute of Pleadings in which the king ordained that all pleas 'shall be pleaded, shown, defended, answered, debated and judged in the English tongue'.[8] The same latitude was not advanced to the students of Oxford, however, where Latin remained the common language; any scholar heard to converse in English was, on a second offence, to be exiled to a corner of the room where he was obliged to eat alone. Yet we can say that by the fourteenth century a body of work had emerged, written in the English language and celebrating English tradition. Thus Robert of Gloucester, in his chronicle of 1300, sets out to assert that 'Engelond is ryght a mery lond, of all others on west the best'.

Henry IV was the first English king since the eleventh century who returned to English as his native speech. He claimed the throne before the 1399 parliament in English – 'he chalenged in Englyssh tunge', as a chronicle puts it – and nine years later composed his testament in the vernacular. By the end of the fourteenth century, in fact, 'English had invaded the realms of lyric and romance, of comedy and tragedy, of allegory and drama, of religion and education' so that it had become 'the language, not of a conquered, but of a conquering people'.[9] One musical historian has noted that 'this change of orientation coincides with a renaissance in the setting of English words to music';[10] there was in court circles a resurgence of interest in English songs and carols, although their popularity in the wider country is never likely to have diminished.

The English language was also being strengthened by the new technology. In 1474 William Caxton printed a narrative of Trojan history because he had 'never seen hit in our englissh tonge'. Having been born in the Weald of Kent, however, he was familiar with the 'brode and rude' language of his compatriots; he also recognised how much it had changed in his own lifetime. So he decided to regularise it, and to avoid 'curios' or excessively simple speech; he did not print any alliterative works, either, because they varied too much from the standard. The drive and animating force within the language was the pressure towards uniformity; only then would it acquire the strength and significance of Latin or French. It is perhaps not surprising that London, the seat of 'documentary culture'[11] and the common home of poets as diverse as Langland and Chaucer, should provide the conditions and the aspirations towards such a standard. We read of the 'imposition of normative discourse' from the examples of monarchy and parliament, of a shift 'to heavily authorised texts and stylistic uniformity' as well as 'a rise in the status of literate professionals'; by 1450 there emerge 'intensified ritualisations and an obsession with codes of conduct',[12] some of them literary. Caxton himself was part of the merchant class of London but, perhaps more significantly, the offices of the government were settled in London and in adjacent Westminster; while the spoken dialect of London was a bewildering argot of English and foreign influences, the standard of writing became that of London heavily influenced by the central midlands. The clerkly standard, or 'Chancery standard', then became the basis of what is now known as 'modern literary standard English'. There is, again, a recognisable continuity within the English imagination.

Arthur, Prince of Wales. Henry VII named his eldest son after the legendary
King Arthur, in an attempt to win over the people in the west and to
legitimise the Tudors' dubious claims to the throne

Queen Victoria and Prince Albert dressed as Queen Guinevere and King Arthur,
at a fancy dress ball on 12 May 1842

'Figure of Guinevere' circa 1858. By William Morris, who was described as possessing a 'medievalised mind and turn of thought', like so many of his contemporaries

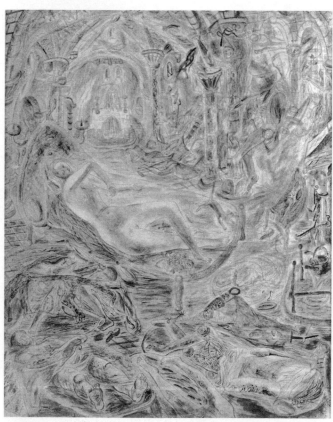

'Guenever.' David Jones's illustration to the Arthurian legend takes the obsession into the 20th century

CHAPTER 16

He is not dead

There may have been a British warrior-king named Arthur – the name itself is of Roman provenance – who flourished in the late fifth century, and who may conceivably have won a victory against the English invaders at a place known only as Mons Badonicus, but the evidence is so slight as to be practically non-existent. But how is it, then, that this spectral and fugitive tribal warrior became the central figure or figment of the English imagination whose creative life has stretched into the twenty-first century with no sign of abatement?

Those who engage in a conspiratorial theory of history believe that the legend of King Arthur was predominantly Norman in inspiration, and was designed to obscure the true and real achievements of the genuinely English King Alfred. But the stories of Arthur lie much further back. He has been equated with the primeval legends of the sun god, and compared with Hercules and Adonis. In Otranto Cathedral there is a mosaic of 'Rex Arturus' in which the king rides upon a goat while wielding a phallic club; he is encircled by a zodiac, in which shape the landscape of Glastonbury itself is purported to be formed. This is suggestive but by no means conclusive; it may simply imply that, in taking over the figures of an ancient myth, the English were trying to borrow or assimilate the features of an older British earth-worship. The sleep of Arthur in the unknown region of Avalon has also been related to Plutarch's invocation of the old British belief that the great god Cronos still sleeps upon an island surrounded by waters. This in turn has been related to the myth of the original Albion, which has been associated with the legend of Atlantis; the Druids were supposed to believe that Albion, the spirit or embodiment of the English, was an original portion of the lost continent. It is a very rich, not to say heady, brew. Any attempt to drink it will inevitably lead to numbness and disorientation.

The extant fragments of the Arthurian legend are themselves of sufficient interest. It seems most likely that the story of Arthur was originally Celtic in inspiration; Welsh poems of the ninth and tenth centuries already invoke Arthur as a figure of the remote past, and the *Black Book of Carmarthen* mentions the names of his knights or retinue while mysteriously suggesting that *'anoeth bit bed i Arthur'*, 'the world's wonder is the grave of Arthur'.[1] This is the first surviving reference to the occluded demise of the ancient king. It suggests also the extent to which Celtic elements inform what are believed to be characteristically 'English' legends. Another Celt, the historian Nennius who wrote in Latin, refers to Arthur as 'a commander in the battles' of Britons against the Saxon invaders; there are references also in the *Annales Cambriae* compiled in the seventh or eighth centuries, which seem to confirm the hypothesis that Arthur was an historic if remote figure. It records, of 'Year 72', the battle of Badon in which 'Arthur bore the Cross of our Lord Jesus Christ on his shoulders for three days and three nights, and the Britons were the victors'.[2] It is of passing interest that Avalon, the island to which Arthur is taken in death, is a transliteration of Attalon, apple trees, or Afalxon, apples; the apple tree was also one of the sacred trees of England, and the object of ceremonial worship known as 'apple-wassailing' which may have been influenced by earlier insular cults. In account books as late as the 1670s and 1680s we read of boys paid to 'howl away' disease from the apple trees. It would seem that once more an ancient English rite has arcane origins.

The provenance of Arthurian stories and legends then moves to Cornwall, and to Brittany, which suggests that an oral tradition concerning the king existed among the Brythonic Celts of these regions. His fame, and the exploits increasingly attached to his name, spread across Europe perhaps because of the very generality of his achievement. One Welsh poem of the thirteenth century exemplifies his ambivalent status: 'And then, lo and behold bards coming to chant song to Arthur, but no one could understand that song . . . except that it was in praise of Arthur!'[3] He hunts a boar; he fights a hag; he slays a giant; he searches for a magic cauldron; he sets tasks for his knights by which they will obtain their suit. The mosaic in Otranto Cathedral is complemented by another figure of Arthur above the north doorway of Modena Cathedral; a similar version adorns Bari Cathedral, also in Italy. Ailred of Rievaulx confessed in 1141 that the exploits of Arthur moved him to tears, while in 1113 certain canons of Laon in northern France fell into dispute with a Bodmin man who asserted that Arthur still lived. He had already become a folk memory.

In the light of Arthur's Celtic origin it is perhaps not surprising that the first definitive or coherent account of the king should spring from the pen of Geoffrey of Monmouth, who has been described variously as of Welsh, Cornish or Breton stock. Geoffrey's *Historia Regum Britanniae* was completed by 1138; the author was canon of St George's, Oxford, but his ambitions were literary rather than spiritual. He had already composed a text entitled *Prophetiae Merlini*, so it can fairly be asserted that he had an abiding passion for the earliest history of the island. Two English chroniclers, William of Malmesbury and Henry of Huntingdon, had in fact recently provided an historical digest of the Anglo-Saxons; it seems likely that Geoffrey wished to furnish a chronology of the earlier Celtic or British people, in which the Saxons would play less prominent a role. Geoffrey himself said that much of his material had been derived from 'an ancient book in the British language', but no appropriate Welsh or Celtic text has yet been discovered. The fact that no such book has been found does not preclude its existence, although many scholars believe that few documents from this early period could have provided the detail and circumstance of Geoffrey's account. *Historia Regum Britanniae* is a more secular account of national history than most previous Latin originals, largely because the writer has chosen to emphasise the cycle of fortune rather than the providence of God. Significantly, therefore, the story of King Arthur is thereby placed in the context of an apparently authentic chronicle rather than in fable or romance.

The audience for *Historia Regum Britanniae* could scarcely have been the scattered Celtic communities in the west of the country but, rather, Anglo-Norman aristocrats and ecclesiastics as well as those few Anglo-Saxon thegns or abbots who had survived the ascendancy. The emphasis was not upon the race of Arthur, but upon the land he administered and defended; if it was a national epic, in part inspired by the cleric Geoffrey's reading of Virgil's *Aeneid*, it was the epic of a sacred earth or territory. It is important once more to suggest the Englishness of this sensibility. Celtic source material and Celtic longings, as well as the texture of Geoffrey's Latin prose, are subdued by it; it is a field of force that creates its own lines of energy. One of the first pagan spells to be transmitted in Anglo-Saxon was that summoning the goddess of the earth; the earliest race of the English, from Angeln in the south of Denmark, was described by Tacitus as uniquely worshipping 'Nerthus, that is Terra Mater'.

It is of particular interest, too, that the histories of Arthur are implicated in decline and failure; at the highest point of the king's power, after he has conquered the Romans in continental Europe and is about to march on Rome itself, he is undone by the treachery of

Mordred and dies in battle against him at Camblam in Cornwall. The story of Arthur has always been striated with sensations of loss and of transitoriness, which may well account for its central place within the English imagination; the native sensibility is touched with melancholy, as we have seen, and the sad fate of Arthur and his kingdom corresponds to that national mood. There is something, too, of determination and endurance within this dominant sensation. Some men say that Arthur will rise again; we must endure our going hence. It is the kind of stoicism which has been seen as characteristic of Anglo-Saxon poetry, perhaps nowhere better expressed than in 'The Battle of Maldon' where the most famous Saxon or English cry has been rendered – 'Courage must be the firmer, heart the bolder, spirit must be the greater, as our strength grows less.' That combination of bravery and fatalism, endurance and understatement, is the defining mood of Arthurian legend.

So Geoffrey's narrative became the representative national epic; it was immediately popular, with more than two hundred Latin manuscripts still extant, and was employed as source material until well into the eighteenth century. Here, too, in lucid and readily accessible form are national myths of another kind; Geoffrey relates the history of King Lear and his three daughters, of Cymbeline, of Merlin and the removal of Stonehenge from Ireland to Salisbury Plain.

Within seventy years *Historia Regum Britanniae* was translated into French verse by a monk from Jersey, Robert Wace, whose *Roman de Brut* first introduced the 'Round Table' as an image of true chivalry. A French narrative poem, *Erec et Eride* by Chrétien de Troyes, which has been described by an historian of French literature as the 'first Arthurian romance'[4] was written soon afterwards. The poem was adapted into shorter verses or *lais* by Marie de France who, paradoxically, lived in England and 'was writing for a French-speaking Norman audience'.[5] Once more it is the land or territory, and only by indirection the race or tribe, which is being celebrated.

Certainly this is the concept introduced by Layamon's *Brut*, the first translation into English of Wace and the first work in the English language to describe King Arthur himself. In the opening lines Layamon declares that '*Layamon gon lithen, wide yond thas leode*', Layamon travelled widely through this land, and would tell of the leaders of England. This has led some scholars to suggest that 'the true hero of the *Brut* is the land itself'.[6] It may be of some significance, therefore, that it is also the first surviving long poem in Middle English and that it uses what seems to be a deliberately ornate and 'poetic' alliterative line as an echo of old song. The use of a long accentual line and the employment of alliteration suggest, in other words, that one of Layamon's principal models was the verse of the English past.

Layamon himself was a twelfth-century priest at Areley Regis in Worcestershire, not far removed from the great monastic libraries of the west midlands. In this colder climate the romance of the Anglo-Norman poets does not intrude, and there have been many attempts to distinguish Wace's *Roman de Brut* in French from Layamon's *Brut* in Middle English. That great literary scholar, C. S. Lewis, who was himself half in love with the Anglo-Saxon past of this country, has described Layamon's work as graver and more sombre than that of Wace. It possesses the hardness and gravity of the Old English sensibility, which we may perhaps now term the English sensibility itself. A light-hearted description of a spiral staircase in a tower, in the French of Wace's poem, is transformed by Layamon's interpolation so that it becomes '*An ald stanene weorc; stithe men hit wurhten*', 'it was an old stone work; hard men made it.' Old stone elicits a strong response in the poetry of the English; it is perhaps part of the antiquarian persuasion, and it suggests the presence of the past which is so much an aspect of the native inheritance.

Layamon, too, is more susceptible to wonders and supernatural events than his French counterpart; he introduces '*aelvene*' or '*ylfes*', or the 'little people' of British provenance. Engravings from the sixteenth century show men walking into the caves of the 'brownies' as they were known on account of their swarthy complexions; as late as the seventeenth century people could be suspected of witchery merely for having had dealings with these strange prehistoric folk of the moors. Here once more we may see one of the sources, and earliest examples, of that later English taste for ghost stories and for 'horror'; as Bacon once concluded, 'the thing is ancient but the word is late'. The native tendency is indeed as ancient as *Beowulf*, as enduring as the Gothic novel, and has not faded yet.

Another element of Layamon's *Brut*, quite distinct from any French version, dwells in the elusive English notion of reticence or embarrassment. When Merlin reveals the secret of transporting the monoliths of Stonehenge:

> Thus seiden Maerlin and seoththen he saet stille
> alse theh he wolde of worlden iwiten

'Thus said Merlin and then he sat still, as though he would go out of the world.' Similarly, when young Arthur is acclaimed as king:

Arthur saet ful stille

and then spoke a few cryptic words. This brevity or understatement, fading into silence, seems characteristic; it is present also in English medieval illumination where the pomp and circumstance of the continental courts are quite missing.

Layamon's *Brut*, a poem of some sixteen thousand lines, was composed at some point between 1185 and 1225. The loss of Normandy in 1204 has already been noted, so that Layamon's 'sense of "England" is made all the more relevant'.[7] His preoccupation with the land is matched only by his emphasis upon 'continuity' and his interest in 'ordinary people'.[8] It is possible, therefore, that Layamon's use of English and his adoption of the alliterative line were methods of evoking or even creating a natural and national community of English speakers. This emphasis may also account for the direct and dramatic use of dialogue within the narrative, the comparative lack of subtlety in the exposition, the interest in supernatural strangeness, and the weight placed upon historical associations or references. It was as if a lost past were being revived, and this first version of Arthur's exploits in English provided 'a unifying account of national origins and a focus for patriotic spirit'.[9]

Other dynastic chronicles, written in the vernacular, followed. An alliterative version of *Morte Arthure* had been transcribed by the beginning of the fifteenth century; it is the product of a highly literate and sophisticated culture, to which has been appended in an unknown hand '*Hic jacet Arturus rex quondam rexque futurus*', 'Here lies Arthur, the once and future king'.

It is a legend of origin combined with the myth of revival; part of the power of the Arthurian saga lies in its uncertain significance so that the very absence of meaning, particularly in the ambiguous death of Arthur, has encouraged a hundred different meanings – national, social, tribal, cultural – to rush into the available space. Arthur himself lies suspended between heaven and earth, the significance of his equivocal posture matched by the sense of suspended significance in the texts devoted to him.

There are many other chronicles, romances and fables to be found in the eight compendious volumes of the French 'Vulgate Cycle', of which the authorship is unknown; they include no less than everything, the romance of Launcelot and Guinevere, the story of Merlin, the adventures of Bors and Gawain, the death of Arthur, their chronology 'spanning the entire history of the Grail quest from its origin in the Passion of Christ to its successful accomplishment by the chosen Arthurian hero'.[10] But the chivalric fictions and spiritual allegories of the French writers were not necessarily to English taste, and the native English chronicles were prone to emphasise the violence and suffering of heroism while turning spiritual meaning into a vague sense of superstitious dread; the environment is local and detailed, blessed with any number of historical associations in order to lend the adventures a wholly English context.

There is an accompanying desire 'to create a tradition of secular English literature to rival that in French'.[11] By native instinct or literary fortune the reign of Arthur was intimately attached to the national linguistic enterprise, so that his name and fame will live as long as the English language itself.

The English tales flourished for almost three hundred years, from 1250 to 1550, and we may reach tentative conclusions about the nature of early English sensibility in a comparison with their French counterparts. The stories tend to be narrated in a shorter and simplified form, with the vocabulary of love and courtesy excised; the 'linear' English mind seemed to prefer an adventure complete with heroic and violent special effects. Great debates are foreshortened and reduced to practical discussion of pragmatic import. Psychological intimacy and interior drama are eschewed in favour of 'the exaggerated and the grotesque' with 'a marked preference for combats with giants and monsters rather than mere human opponents'.[12] This taste for sensation and horror has endured as long as the Arthurian legends themselves.

The inscrutability or ambiguity of those legends – the ever elusive 'Holy Grail' is in that sense emblematic – has in turn meant that countless political allegories and historical associations have been cast upon them. In England the stories of knightly grandeur and chivalric honour, in the service of a strong central court, created a glorious past to which less glorious contemporaries might wish to attach themselves. In the late twelfth century the exhumation of Arthur in the grounds of Glastonbury, at the behest of Henry II, was meant to assure the disaffected Welsh that their great chieftain was well and truly dead. It is believed that a hasty reading of Geoffrey of Monmouth by the monks of Glastonbury had originally led to the rapid insertion of other bodies into the supposed Arthurian graves, together with various relics quickly inscribed with appropriate material; at first Arthur and Guinevere were found in the same tomb, but a more thorough reading of the text led to her being silently removed. Mordred, the treacherous nephew, also vanished from the grave site.

In the context of English history itself, however, the extent to which a powerful imagination or a passage of significant writing can affect external events – can in a real sense 'create' history – is of absorbing interest.

The antiquarian concerns of the English encourage, also, a brooding over the past as if it harboured some secret message or inspiration. Thus in 1278 Edward I and Queen Eleanor visited Glastonbury and, having inspected the remains of the once and future king, ordered that he be taken in pomp and reverence to the high altar of the abbey there. Edward was at that moment facing an insurrection of the Welsh, advancing under the inspiration of Arthur, and the king wished to claim Arthur as his own with the manifest suggestion that Edward was the chosen and legitimate successor. An historical figment, at best an obscure war-lord, was so honoured by historians and chroniclers that he became a potent force in thirteenth-century dynastic politics. It is a signal example of the power of historical writing. In the fourteenth century it was affirmed that the object of the knights' quest, the Holy Grail, was in fact the chalice used by Christ at the Last Supper which had been brought to Glastonbury by Joseph of Arimathea. Thus the cultic status of this spot of English earth grew and grew; it has often been surmised that fact and fiction strangely mingle in English biography and historiography, so the story of Arthur may be adduced as the harbinger of a great national tradition.

In 1344 Edward III decided to establish a fellowship of the Round Table, which pledge was modified four years later into the Order of the Garter. So the recipients of this honour have to thank an Oxford cleric named Geoffrey for their advancement. Henry V wrote to the Abbot of Glastonbury, in 1421, demanding that the remains of Joseph of Arimathea should also be miraculously recovered; but the king died before any exhumation could take place, and the site of Joseph's supposed burial has never been revealed.

Then in 1486 Henry VII named his first son Arthur as a way both of reuniting the English nation after the dynastic 'Wars of the Roses' and of affirming his own legitimacy as sovereign. There were jousts and banquets in medieval style, while the image of a young King Arthur was delineated on the walls of Richmond Palace. The 'image of King Arthur riding a golden triumphal chariot through the sphere of the sun . . . was to have enormous significance for the development of the Tudor Arthurian myth'.[13] In fact the only two prospective heirs to the throne of England, who were given the name of Arthur, both died young. Would the myth of Arthur have survived so long without the untimely deaths of his later avatars?

In the year before the christening of Henry VII's heir, the young Prince Arthur, a yet more splendid addition to the Arthurian legend emerged in the shape of Malory's prose epic in eight books, under the title of *Le Morte Darthur*.

Little is known of Thomas Malory himself; he was a soldier of an old Warwickshire family and was present at the siege of Calais in 1436. He inherited an estate at Newbold Revell but quickly lapsed into a career of violence, theft and extortion. He broke out of several prisons, on one occasion swimming across the moat, and he fought with Warwick against Edward IV. He died on 14 March 1471 in or near Newgate prison, in which gaol he is likely to have written the entire epic of Arthur which closes 'Praye for me while I am on lyve that God sende me good delyveraunce'. It is fortunate that we do not expect our greatest authors to live virtuous lives, since this thief, blackmailer and ruffian has produced what his editor has called 'the one work of real poetic value in the whole field of modern Arthurian fiction'.[14] ' "What?" seyde Sir Launcelot. "Is he a theff and a knyht? And a ravyssher of women? He doth shame unto the Order of Knyghthode and contrary unto his oth. Hit is pyte that he lyvyth" '. These words must be the finest evidence for an embarrassed author in the entire history of English literature.

Thomas Malory first began the enterprise by adapting an alliterative *Morte Arthur* which, at a later date, Caxton considerably modified; that strange archaising mode did not fit naturally with the printer's idea of 'standard' English. Then Malory turned to the vast corpus of French romances, together with some English additions, and radically shortened their rambling theses on courtly love and other speculative matters; he cut the theology, while at the same time condensing certain of the stories. He introduced these stories one after the other as if they were organic accretions of some total design, in the manner of an English cathedral of the same period. Malory is also of a decidedly pragmatic turn. As an Arthurian scholar has put it, 'he exalts the practical over the ethereal and spiritual';[15] this will be seen to be a characteristically English response. Malory's brevity is in fact an essential engine of the plot which turns upon sudden crises and arbitrary adventures; there are dramatic speeches rather than interior monologues, incidents rather than characters. This sensibility, deriving in part from the fierce reticence of the Saxons, runs very deeply through the English imagination.

The prose of *Le Morte Darthur* has the simplicity and vividness derived from great originals, while at moments of violence and high drama Malory reaches out for the alliterative tradition once more. The prose indeed generally registers that vernacular straightforwardness which Professor Chambers traced from *Beowulf* to the works of Sir Thomas More.

Sir Dynadan is dressed in 'a womans garmente', one of the earliest examples of that English taste for cross-dressing, 'and when quene Gwenyver sawe sir Dynadan ibrought in so amonge them all, then she lowghe [laughed] that she fell downe; and so dede all that there was'. There are other examples of this colloquial register – 'And there he lay lyke a fole grennynge and wolde nat speke' – which remains half the strength of written English prose.

There are certain principal themes in *Le Morte Darthur*, not the least of them being that great reverence for a distant past which is so much a part of national literature. But there are also certain key words which define this heroic world, among them 'sothe', 'custom', 'aventure', 'worship', 'body', 'hole', 'felyship', 'marvayles', 'secretness', all of them creating a charmed landscape of confrontation and of peril. The narrator makes mistakes, loses his sources, or refuses to endorse a certain section of the narrative; these are characteristically English manoeuvres, brought most delicately to life by Geoffrey Chaucer in his role as the embarrassed narrator. Malory is not an expert on 'psycho-logical individuality, and realistic time-schemes', let alone causality,[16] but many later English novelists have suffered from these minor failings. The slightly surrealistic air of his prose is suggestive in another sense, however, because it contributes to 'the strangeness of Arthur's kingdom'.[17] It consorts, too, with the dominant note of the book, that 'haunting elegiac tone or undertone . . . its sad suggestions of the vanity and transience of all things, of the passing away of pomp and splendour, of the falls of princes'.[18] It reflects the mysterious and arbitrary workings of providence, doom foretold and prophetic dream. It has always been noticed that Sir Lancelot is the real hero of Malory's narrative, but the central brooding figure is that of Arthur, the once and future king whose connection with the Holy Grail was to excite the attention of Blake and Tennyson, Scott and Rossetti, Steinbeck and Eliot.

In Malory's account, 'The Day of Destiny', Arthur's sword is thrown into a lake. 'And there cam an arme and an honde above the watir, and toke hit and cleyght hit, and shoke hit thryse and braundysshed, and then vanysshed with the swerde into the watir.' When Arthur is told of this he replies, 'Alas, help me hens, for I drede me I have tarryed over longe.' He is placed in a barge, with fair ladies in black hoods; all of them 'wepte and shryked'. As he is guided away Sir Bedyvere cries out to him, 'A, my lorde Arthur, what shall becom of me, now ye go frome me, and leve me here alone amonge myne enemyes?' 'Comforte thyselff,' said the king, 'and do as well as thou mayste, for in me ys no truste for to truste in. For I muste into the vale of Avylon to hele me of my grevous wounde. And if thou here nevermore of me, pray for my soule!' Arthur never was heard of again, in this life, and Malory adds a final paragraph:

> Yet som men say in many partys of Inglonde that kynge Arthur ys nat dede, but had by the wyll of oure Lorde Jesu into another place; and men say that he shall com agayne, and he shall wynne the Holy Crosse. Yet I woll not say that hit shall be so, but rather I wolde sey: here in thys worlde he chaunged hys lyff. And many men say that there ys wrytten uppon the tombe thys: Hic Jacet Arthurus, Rex Quondam Rexque Futurus.

Here is 'the peace that passes all understanding'. Yet in this account of dolorous departing, we seem to have mislaid the actual British warrior king who fought against the English. What is the spell of this enchantment thrown over a thousand years of English literature and English art? It lies in its unknowability; the probability that Arthur was British rather than Anglo-Saxon serves only to emphasise his otherness. He is the other who is being continually sought, even if the encounter may destroy you. He represents blood kinship and tribal fealty for the heterogeneous and muddled race of the English; he represents sanctified leadership, uniting England and the Holy Grail. Yet at the same time he is an image of transience and of loss, the unendurable loss of one who just slipped away. He is the shadow on the page. John Milton invoked 'Arturumque sub terris bella moventum', Arthur under the earth fomenting wars, and Dryden wished to compose an epic concerning 'King Arthur, conquering the Saxons'. Both of them are images of ferocious national identity, not untouched by melancholy and decay.

His memory was kept alive in folk-tale or oral tradition, and in the early eighteenth century it was recorded that 'King Arthur's story in English' was 'often sold by the ballad-singers, with the like Authentic Records of *Guy of Warwick* and *Bevis of Southampton*'.[19] Arthur slept in popular superstition, therefore, and he was not dead.

He was recovered for literary purposes in the nineteenth century, after suffering more than two centuries of relative neglect. He was restored in Tennyson's early Arthurian poems, composed in the 1830s and 1840s, and in that poet's *Idylls of the King*; Hallam Tennyson has written of his father that 'what he called "the greatest of all poetical subjects" perpetually haunted him'. William Morris wrote *The Defence of Guenevere*, and Swinburne composed *Tristram of Lyonesse*. There were scores of other revisions and redactions of Arthurian material, and they are still being issued. It was Tennyson, however, who 'created a taste for Arthurian poetry unprecedented since the Middle Ages'.[20] He began with 'The Lady of Shalott' and ended with *Idylls of the King* which 'occupied the poet for more than fifty years and came closer than any other work of the age to being an epic and a national poem'.[21] The advantage of English historicism is that it allows contemporary events and preoccupations to be observed in the context of a transcendent past; so the reader of *Idylls of the King* may draw conclusions about Victorian attitudes to women and nineteenth-century science. Medievalism did not preclude modernity, but actively encouraged it, with the unspoken assumption that 'the Victorian world may profit from the patterns of the past'.[22] Thus Hallam Tennyson noted of his father's Arthurian poems that he 'infused into them a spirit of modern thought and an ethical significance' which revived an entire literary tradition.

This is the true significance of Arthur: by not dying, by being perpetually reborn, he represents the idea of the English imagination. By creating a national epic, Tennyson also reasserted the power and efficacy of English literature itself. That epic, envisaged by Milton and Wordsworth alike, embodied the realisation 'that the Arthurian legend was more than legend, was in fact the great national fount of myth and symbol'.[23] Tennyson had discovered Arthur in childhood. 'The vision of an ideal Arthur as I have drawn him', he wrote, 'had come upon me when, little more than a boy, I first lighted upon Malory.' So in tracing that king's doleful life he was returning to his own beginnings, and in the conflation of mood and memory he was also touching upon the source of national literature itself.

Tennyson told Caroline Fox that he believed Arthur to have been an 'historical personage',[24] yet it is the music of Tennyson that lingers, that swelling cadence which is the movement of the language itself; it is a solemn music which always seems to anticipate its own dying fall, and so is consonant with the theme of Arthur and of Avalon. Yet, somehow, it exists too outside the rhythm of human time in a perpetual exequy to its own nature. Merlin, the great riddler, understood this:

> For an ye heard a music, like enow
> They are building still, seeing the city is built
> To music, therefore never built at all,
> And therefore built for ever

That is what is meant by the suspension of meaning in the English epic of Arthur, which itself allows so many allusions and changing identifications. As Tennyson said of certain interpretations of his Arthurian characters, 'They are right, and they are not right. They mean that and they do not.' Yet the meaning lies in the melody itself, in the music of transmission and inheritance which has no ultimate meaning except its survival through time. It is the search for pattern – pattern for its own sake – and for sacred order. That is why Arthur has survived.

It has been said that 'Wilfred Owen saw the remnants of Arthur's knights' in the carnage of the Western Front and heard the music 'in the screaming funnel of a hospital barge'.[25]

> And that long lamentation made him wise
> How unto Avalon, in agony,
> Kings passed in the dark barge, which Merlin dreamed

These lines were influenced by Tennyson's 'The Passing of Arthur' where is evinced

> . . . an agony
> Of lamentation, like a wind that shrills
> All night in a waste land

The lamentation was taken up by T. S. Eliot, too, who so wished to unite himself with the English tradition that his poetry clustered around the music of Malory. 'Therefore men calle hit – the londys of the two marchys – the Waste Londe, for that dolerous stroke.'

The piety of England

CHAPTER 17

Faith of our fathers

In 'the Tale of the Sankgreal', as related by Thomas Malory, Sir Galahad witnesses the miracle of transubstantiation during the holy communion of the Catholic Mass. The bishop took up a wafer 'which was made in lyknesse of brede. And at the lyfftyng up there cam a figoure in lyknesse of a chylde, and the vysage was as rede and as bryght os ony fyre, and smote hymselff into the brede, that all they saw hit that the brede was fourmed of a fleyshely man. And than he put hit into the holy vessell agayne.' It is a strange scene, as the wafer of bread is transformed into a child and man before being dipped into the chalice, but it is fully consistent with the belief of Malory's contemporaries that in the miracle of the Mass the Word does indeed become flesh. There are many stories, or legends, of the eucharist turning into a burning babe, just as the miraculous properties of the consecrated host were endlessly attested. It is at the heart of Catholic England and, as a matter of instinctive practice and natural belief, at the centre of the culture which Catholic England manifested. The material world was relished with as much fullness as spiritual truths were venerated. It has been said of London customs of the fourteenth century that 'the drinking bouts and rough games had once been religious ceremonies in themselves: and the two ideas were still confused in the popular imagination'.[1] The remark is of the utmost significance for any understanding of medieval England.

From the reports of foreign observers it becomes clear that in the fourteenth and fifteenth centuries the English were notable for their piety; they rivalled the Romans in their love of ceremony, and the Spanish in their devotion to the Virgin. The bells of the London churches deafened those who were unfamiliar with them, and a continental observer noted of the citizens that 'they all attend Mass every day, and say many Paternosters in public, the women carrying large rosaries in their hands'. This was the dispensation and condition of England until the time of Henry VIII, and it is open to question whether the legacy of the last five hundred years will outweigh or outlast a previous tradition of fifteen hundred years.

*

We may begin by saying that England then was at the centre of Catholic Europe. It was a shared civilisation of ceremony and spectacle, of drama, of ritual and display; life was only the beginning, not the end, of existence and thus could be celebrated or scorned as one station along the holy way. It was a world in which irony and parody of all kinds flourished, where excremental truth and holy vision were considered fundamentally compatible, where Aquinas could mount towards heaven with his divine dialectic and Rabelais stoop towards the earth with his gargantuan corporeality. It was a world of symbolic ceremony, with the processions of Palm Sunday, the rending of the veil in Holy Week and the washing of the feet on Maundy Thursday. Doves were released at Pentecost in St Paul's Cathedral, and the Resurrection dramatised on Easter Day in Lichfield Cathedral. It was a world also deeply imbued with symbolic numerology; this lies behind the pre-occupation with form and ritual, as well as the fascination with pattern. There were the five wounds of Christ and the five joys of the Virgin, the five wits of the human self and the five principal social virtues of fraunchise, felawship, cleanness, cortaysye and pite. This concern for pattern is embodied in the form of the pentangle, otherwise known as 'David's Foot' and created by the wooden swords of early folk-dancers with the cry of 'A Nut! A Nut!' or a Knott –

> . . . the English call it,
> In all the land, I hear, the Endless Knot[2]

There are seven sins, seven sacraments, and seven works of mercy, all of them part of the passage of humankind through earthly existence; the importance of allegory may here be glimpsed, with the allegorical 'reading' of texts and illuminations as a fundamental prerequisite for the understanding of *Piers the Plowman*, *Pearl* or the 'General Prologue' of *The Canterbury Tales*. We might suggest in turn that the history plays of Shakespeare, and the symbolic fictions of Charles Dickens, owe something to this now buried or disregarded tradition.

The day itself was the medium of ritual. The canonical hours of the Church – with the 'Great Hours' of Lauds and Vespers mingled with the 'Little Hours' of Prime, Tierce, Sext, None and Compline – materially altered the shape of time in medieval discourse. The hours were connected with the narrative of Christ's Passion, with Sext representing the crucifixion and entombment, but there was also a further litany of time with the hours of the Virgin as intercessor and intermediary for mankind. The sequence of hours then represents the passage of sacred events which are beyond the claims of time; linear duration is replaced by cyclical commemoration so that the elusive present moment is always hallowed by the presence of spiritual truth. Thus the drama of the medieval period is at once eternal and starkly contemporary, the shepherds both local men and emblems of wandering mankind. When in one of the nativity plays a sheep, stolen from a field near Bethlehem, is disguised as an infant child in a cradle the allusion to Christ as the Lamb of God might seem crude and even shocking; but, for the Yorkshire audience of 'The Second Shepherd's Play' in 1440, it would have seemed natural if decidedly comic. There was no aversion to things of the flesh but, rather, an understanding of them as tokens of the divine order. A prayer at the end of the Mass celebrates the fact that God blesses 'oure brede & oure ayl', where the bread of holy communion is seen to be equivalent to the bread upon the table of kitchen or tavern.

In a drama of the Crucifixion the 'pinners' or nail-makers re-enact all the physical details of Christ's suffering – 'He weyes a wikkid weght' – in comic corporeal re-enactment of the mystery. It will often be remarked, in this study, how the most ostensibly tragic and comic episodes are thoroughly intermingled in English drama and English fiction; here lies one of the explanations. When the fifteenth-century recluse, Julian of Norwich, saw the face of the devil, 'the color was rede like the tilestone whan it is new brent . . . his here was rode as rust'. Red was also the colour conventionally attributed to the hair of Herod and of Judas. So the more vivid the material of physical description, the more intense becomes the spiritual experience. Thus again in Julian's revelations, 'the blewhede [blue] of the clothing betokinith his stedfastnes'.

This equivalence between the material and the ideal can lead to irony as well as pathos, parody as much as melancholy; in a world where certain sacred truths are accepted without question, then parody and irony themselves become necessary devices. The great historian of the Middle Ages, Johan Huizinga, remarked 'that the line of demarcation between seriousness and pretence was never less clear than in the medieval period';[3] it is a temperamental characteristic which has never entirely deserted what might be called the Catholic imagination. It has been said that Chaucer's fabliaux, in *The Canterbury Tales*, suggest that 'men's lives are seen as burlesque re-enactments of sacred prototypes'.[4] But this equivalence might also encourage a sense of completeness or wholeness. In the ceremonies of Corpus Christi, when the sacrament was carried down the principal streets with banners and crosses in attendance, wreathed in smoke and attended by joyful chanters, the physical communion of the faithful was joined in spirit to the heavenly community. The ritual then became a social and cultural performance, a form of outdoor theatre not unlike the mystery plays when the crucifix rather than the eucharist was carried through the streets of England's towns. This had been the message of St Augustine: the religion of the urban centres demanded an audience, just like that of the theatre, where a 'secret sympathy' is shared.

There is another connection with the English imagination, also, in the context of 'the rhetoric of performance and the performance of rhetoric',[5] whether in the debate poems of Chaucer or the declamations of Tudor drama. We cannot at this date, in other words, separate an English sensibility from a Catholic sensibility. The world of miracles and marvels is still alive in Shakespeare's late plays.

What else might be expected from a Catholic sensibility? The delight in splendour is of course related to the intoxication with the marvellous, but resplendent pomp and display were also the means of celebrating the hierarchy and order of the universe. If the people of England gazed heavenward, and looked up at the night sky filled with light and harmony, they believed that they were looking inward not outward; the pattern of the heavens then became a paradigm for the orders of significance upon the earth, whether orders of interpretation, orders of human rank, orders of dream, or orders of perception. This is of some importance to the writer and artist, since the concept of personality was not far advanced; just as the personal sinfulness of a priest made no difference to his power upon the altar, so unique or individual perception was less important than the corpus of approved and acquired knowledge. Authenticity was more significant than individuality or originality, so we may expect an art or a literature that rests upon things already known and understood. It is the essential reason why Pope translated Homer and William Morris translated *Beowulf*, why Tennyson modelled his verse upon Arthurian epic and why Alfred translated Boethius and Augustine. If in one aspect we describe the English imagination as antiquarian in instinct, animated by the delight in the past, then it is important to see how a predominantly Catholic culture and sensibility may still dwell within it.

It is a nice point indeed to settle rival instincts and rival claims. There was an English Catholicism, with its rituals and its own local saints, but the Roman declarations at the Synod of Whitby and the arrival of

Norman abbots steadily diminished its power; the names of its saints linger in Cornwall and Northumbria, but their shrines and relics have long gone. Nevertheless ecclesiastical historians have outlined a particular form of English spirituality which renders it distinct. It has been described as one of earnest practicality combined with a certain strain of optimism; it also manifests a native common sense and instinct for compromise. Its hermits and anchorites, so much a part of medieval life, illustrate both a tendency towards individualism and a distaste for regimentation or excessive display. The spiritual pragmatism may have begun with Alcuin who, at the court of Charlemagne, wrote out manuals of practical conduct for the Christian layman; but it was perhaps best summarised by Robert of Bridlington who wrote that priests ought also 'to plough, sow, reap, mow hay with a sickle, and make a haystack'.[6] It has been called the *via media* of English spirituality. As William of Malmesbury put it, 'Best is ever mete', or moderation in all things. This, too, has been described as a 'distinctively English manifestation'[7] of 'saving sanity and discretion'. It is perhaps the reason for the relative failure of the Carthusians in England, with their obsessive dedication to silence and penance. There had also been a movement away from excessive clericalism, and the medieval English priest was characteristically a comic figure lambasted for greed, drunkenness and lechery.

There has never been in England a tradition of theological specu- lation, in the manner of an Augustine or an Aquinas, or of devotional concepts divorced from practice; the nearest equivalent to the great '*summa theologica*' of European Catholicism are the short handbooks for English contemplatives or anchorites. It is of some significance that these treatises were always directed towards individuals and were concerned with the exigencies of the solitary life; they were not monastic productions or authoritarian edicts. They were instruments of personal direction, in other words, and were 'intensely English in that they combine unimpeachable orthodoxy with individualism'.[8] The piety of the English was by no means a morbid piety; there has been no Savonarola or Luther but instead Wycliff and Tyndale. Pelagius refused to countenance the orthodox belief that humankind had inherited the primal guilt of Adam and that 'original sin' thereby damned the world to perdition without the intervention of divine grace; he was a thoroughly English heretic. The affective devotion of the English has also been free of lachrymose or penitential excesses; the manuals of prayer consistently invoke the Incarnation rather than the Passion. It is an aspect of what has been called English optimism which, in native tragi-comic fashion, runs beside English melancholy. It is manifested in the benevolent expression upon the statues in Wells Cathedral and in the belief of Julian of Norwich that 'al manner of thyng shal be wele'. In the images of Spain and Italy the Holy Virgin is seen as a figure in tears; in England she is characteristically represented as the loving mother of the divine babe. It has been described as the difference of 'the clear lines of English perpendicular against both the baroque and the whitewashed shed'.[9]

It would be wrong to suggest, however, that English Catholicism represents an independent version of European Catholicism; the fact that the great monastic orders, the Benedictines and the Cistercians, flourished all over England would disprove any such simple statement. The Dominican and Franciscan friars also helped to create the large body of English lyric, both sacred and secular, as well as a variety of English texts; among the great Franciscans can be numbered, in the thirteenth and fourteenth centuries respectively, Roger Bacon and William of Ockham. All of them, too, wrote in Latin for a European community of scholars. Nevertheless, it has often been maintained that their sensibility was of a distinct and distinctive English kind. Thus Ockham believed that 'all knowledge is derived from experience',[10] an argument which anticipates in an uncanny way the English predilection for empiricism, or logical positivism, or whatever term is used for a principled but pragmatic attitude towards all metaphysical speculation. Roger Bacon, too, has often been seen as the forerunner of his more famous namesake, Francis Bacon, in his emphasis on the importance of scientific method in intellectual enquiry. So we have the paradox of a distinctively English sensibility working within, and gaining strength from, a European and Latin tradition of learning. When we read also that, in the twelfth century, English architecture and painting represented 'a great, at moments supreme, exponent of a European style'[11] the question of influence and identity becomes a difficult one.

If there is such a thing as a native cast of thought it can properly be understood only in the context of a broadly European sensibility. There was a great movement of 'humanism' in the twelfth century, for example, but the most significant contribution which England made to the new learning was historical and practical in nature. Has this not become a familiar theme? The great strength of English learning was of course monastic learning, but from the English religious houses came tens of thousands of charters, annals and chronicles. Matthew Paris, who died in the middle of the thirteenth century, wrote a history of his monastery as well as a universal history entitled *Chronica Majora*. There is no English Aquinas, whose scholasticism rose into the empyrean, but rather John of Salisbury whose books were concerned with the art of government. The English writers were well versed in patristic texts and in classical literature but they applied their learning to administrative and diplomatic affairs. As R. W. Southern wrote in his *Medieval Humanism*, this 'mixture of philosophical interest and practical familiarity'[12] was unique to twelfth-century England. He compares their work to that of Jeremy Bentham and Walter Bagehot in the late eighteenth and nineteenth centuries, and traces a distinct native sensibility in this preoccupation with the art of government. We may draw a similar conclusion about the career of Sir Thomas More, a great humanist and companion of Erasmus who became a courtier and a statesman rather than a philosopher or a theologian. He was an English European. The English imagination, and the English sensibility, emerged out of both collusion and collision with European exempla.

The Chapter House of Wells Cathedral

CHAPTER 18

Old stone

The new rulers of England knew that there was power in stone. The cathedrals of Worcester, Canterbury, Winchester and Norwich were all completed or at least consecrated by the end of the eleventh century; St Paul's, Durham and Chichester were in the process of being built, as were Ely and Gloucester. The cathedral of Old Sarum had been completed by 1092. In the twelfth century the cathedral of Lincoln was being erected, and Wells begun. But this was also the century of the monastic foundations, many of them with abbeys as large and as grand as any cathedral. It has been estimated that there were approximately six hundred of these communities in England, with sixty-nine in Yorkshire and fifty-one in Lincolnshire. These monastic foundations colonised the land about them, with pastures and sheep-walks, so it can truly be said that they helped to create the landscape of England. Of the thousands of parish churches, many acquired spires so that the glory of faith aspired from the land to the sky. In the thirteenth century Salisbury and Westminster were raised in the Gothic style, while the great west front of Wells Cathedral was fashioned with its painted tableaux and gilded statuary gleaming like the gate of heaven itself.

When Julian of Norwich believed that she was dying her parish priest held a cross before her face saying, 'I have browte thee the image of thy maker and saviour. Louke thereupon and comfort thee therewith.' It is a characteristic medieval scene, but the abbeys and cathedrals of England fulfilled the same purpose as the crucifix before the dying woman. The faithful saw them and were comforted.

Over four centuries the styles altered according to different modes of perception, with the broad movement of change from Romanesque to Gothic classified into the somewhat arbitrary divisions of Early English, Decorated and Perpendicular; but the statement of power and glory remained the same. Perpendicular has been described as a purely native architecture, without parallel in continental Europe, but in truth the central characteristics of English churches persist through time. The native predilection for patterning, and the delight in flat wall surfaces, have already been suggested as aspects of English taste; the combination of ingenious or elaborate surface decoration with blankness and evenness might offer interesting material to those who study the pathology of nations. But the English cathedrals are also noticeable for their emphasis upon the horizontal rather than the vertical; their naves tend to be longer than their counterparts elsewhere, and their vaults lower, thus giving the impression of 'common-sense stability'[1] which might otherwise be interpreted as solidity or dignity. They might have been fashioned by the architects of Stonehenge, so massively do they dwell and endure upon the land. Another historian has noted that 'the English national style is not elegantly Gothic . . . but sturdily plain and matter of fact'.[2]

They are a complete statement of artistic intent, therefore, and as a result the architecture of England has been used as a metaphor for its music and literature. Fifteenth-century English music, for example, has been characterised as 'the distribution of masses of sound in order to provide effective contrasts, the development of harmonic thinking, and the cultivation of a highly decorative superstructure'[3] in the manner of Perpendicular building. C. S. Lewis compared the model of certain medieval books to that of 'cathedrals where work of many different periods mixed'.[4] He names Chaucer and Malory in this context, both of them creating narratives which seem to grow incrementally and to expand according to some organic principle rather than to a well-defined logic of organisation. It has often been remarked how the structure of English cathedrals is comprised of discrete parts; presbyteries and chapels and transepts are added without any attempt at uniformity in their arrangement, so that different styles and different periods can be observed side by side. Lincoln Cathedral, for example, has been described as 'a building with a series of projections stepping out at right angles to the principal axis'. This strangely fluent and harmonious development 'is characteristic not only of Lincoln but of the English Gothic in general' and is 'in sharp contrast to the French Gothic cathedrals'.[5] There is no logic or authoritarian code evinced here, but a kind of inspired practicality; it might be called the aesthetics of pragmatism, if indeed any aesthetic can be adduced from it. The conservatism of English architecture has often been discussed, but it is the conservatism of organic form – literally the need to conserve itself as it develops according to its own laws of being. That is why it is also such a natural expression of native aptitude and sensibility.

If these churches are instinct with the spirit of place, then they may come alive. One thirteenth-century poet wrote of the 'head' and 'eyes' of the church while the roof rears up 'as if it were conversing with the winged birds, spreading out broad wings, and like a flying creature striking against the clouds'.[6] The cathedral may also adopt the shape of other organic forms. The beginning of this history was concerned with the tree worship of the ancient Britons, and it is perhaps appropriate that the long naves of the English cathedrals have been compared to avenues of trees. Sculpted out of stone are the leaves of vine and ivy, oak and wild apple, hawthorn and maple. At Southwell, Canterbury and Christ Church Cathedral in Oxford, among other sacred places, are to be found carved effigies of the Green Man or 'Jack in the Green' with foliage curling out of his mouth and head; Jack is the tree spirit invoked in ancient ritual.

The green men are in fact only one of a number of pagan devices fashioned out of stone in the corners and recesses of cathedrals, like old spirits banished into the darkness. You cannot see them until you venture almost too close to them. Then you may notice fauns and satyrs, goats and dragons, carved upon bosses; there are capitals filled with the wild gaiety which seems to characterise one aspect of the medieval spirit. There are also scenes of matchless detail; a man with toothache holds open his mouth in pain, in Wells Cathedral, and a farmer belabours a thief with a pitchfork. In Beverley a man carries his scolding wife in a wheelbarrow, and a fox is hanged by geese; in Manchester a hare grills a huntsman over a fire, and at Blackburn a fox preaches to a congregation of hens. These scenes are conceived in a native spirit of mockery; if humour and pathos can be effortlessly mingled in English drama and fiction, so the sacred and the profane are deemed to be natural companions. It is a question of not adopting any one emotion, or manner, too seriously or for too long.

This is nowhere more evident than in the grotesque miniatures which obtrude in the margins of sacred books; they are known as 'babooneries' and according to Nikolaus Pevsner in *The Englishness of English Art* they represent a wholly native convention – 'if one tries to trace the baboonery to its source,' he wrote, 'one finds that it originated in England'.[7] It is a remarkable, but not unexpected, fact. In 1383 Wycliff denounced 'peyntings and babwyneries', and in *The House of Fame* Chaucer celebrated 'subtil compassinges . . . Babewynnes and pynacles'. There are monkeys disporting themselves in the margins of illuminated psalters, and on the top of a page illustrating the Passion of Christ are two medieval wrestlers; villagers are fighting 'pick-a-back' among a Jesse Tree, while on the Beatus page of the Gorleston psalter ten rabbits solemnly and decorously conduct a funeral complete with candles and crucifix. A duck is taken off by a fox, with the word 'queck' issuing from its beak, and there was a vogue for depicting men with wooden legs (a vogue which Charles Dickens would adopt at a later date). These 'grotesques', often described as 'hideous', appeared at the end of the twelfth century but spread rapidly in the thirteenth and fourteenth centuries. The secular mind may even be tempted to conclude that the real artistic interest is to be found in the margins rather than in the illuminations themselves. They are marked by bizarre medieval humour, the visual equivalent of Thomas More's verses on farting and eating excrement, but they are also characterised by an informality and liveliness that seem decidedly English in spirit; the love of fantastic detail, too, animates them as well as a passion for fine or delicate outline. This celebration of the grotesque and the ridiculous of course resides in what one art historian has described as the 'strangely English spirit that sets comic relief even in a tragedy',[8] but perhaps it also represents defiance of a divine order which consigns humankind to misery in this world and possible damnation in the next. In a world of illness, pain and epidemic plague, what other response is there but mad laughter?

The provenance of many babooneries is taken to be London, and that locality emphasises the fact that illumination was now a secular rather than monastic art; part of the craft guild was reserved for 'lymenours', professional artists pursuing their trade in workshops or as part of itinerant groups which toured the country. Three or four artists gathered together, like masons, and set up shop wherever they were required; it is likely, also, that each individual contributed a different skill to the enterprise so that the illuminated page was the product of several hands. This may in turn account in part for the secular appearance of the babooneries themselves, not the least of which depict scenes of ordinary medieval life with that attention to intimate and familiar domestic detail which plays so large a part in the English imagination. Henry Fielding described it well when he extolled the 'exactest copying of Nature' in his fiction, and John Dryden expressed an admiration or affection for the 'distorted face and antic gestures'. Hume remarked that 'if we copy life the strokes must be strong and remarkable.'[9] So in medieval miniatures we see workmen clambering up ladders, farmers ploughing, boys leaping and women dancing.

A great deal of attention is paid to foxes and geese, hens and rabbits; this might be ascribed to the notorious English fondness for animals (which is perhaps a means of displacing fondness for each other), but there may be other sources. Human senses and familiar sins were often given animal shape or 'bestiarized', where the sow becomes gluttony and the fox covetousness, and this form of caricature has left a lasting inheritance. In eighteenth-century satirical prints the Duke of Cumberland was depicted as an ox, and the Duke of Newcastle became a goose; Henry Fox was necessarily portrayed as a fox, and James Boswell as a lecherous monkey. In masquerades in the early decades of that century, also, guests were dressed 'some, in the shape of Monkeys and Baboons, others, of Bears, Asses, Cormorants, and Owls'. There seems to be some primitive force at work.

There are other medieval patterns implicit in later English productions. One historian has noted that in the manuscript illuminations there is no essential concern with 'human experience, human drama and emotion'.[10] There may be spectacle and crowded action, but there is no interiority of feeling; the outline, rather than the three-dimensional figure, is presented only. But these are precisely the criticisms aimed by contemporaries at Fielding and Dickens, at Smollett and Sterne. It seems to be a native fault, if fault it be, that attention is often reserved for the surface.

'Babooneries' or miniature domestic scenes arrayed in the margins of the illuminations often act as a kind of frame around the sacred text. A Chaucerian critic has in turn concluded that 'the frame' of *The Canterbury Tales* 'gives us that strong sense of real life that the poem affords'.[11] In a fifteenth-century Book of Hours the central figures, of Virgin and Child and worshipper, are depicted in grandiose but stiff formal attitudes; the frame around it, however, is replete with human life and activity as a pilgrimage makes its way.

The transpositions from illumination to text are natural and inevitable. In 1250 the artists working upon the murals in the queen's 'low room' at Westminster requested a copy of the *Gests of Antioch* in order to illustrate scenes from it. In turn the devisers or creators of the medieval drama directly copied scenes and images from wall-paintings, stained-glass windows and roof-bosses. In a Catholic culture certain visual icons or exempla are universally recognised, and can inform every mode of art. The illustration of a royal pageant, dated 1514, shows the principal guests with costumes and attitudes taken from the stages of the 'cycle drama' of Chester or York. In a culture of spectacle, the appropriate costume or uniform will be displayed. The scene of 'Christ among the Doctors' is depicted in manuscript and stained glass, with the child in a seat raised higher than the doctors themselves; there is a stage direction to the same effect in a miracle play, where 'they lead Jesus into their midst and make him sit in a higher seat, while they themselves sit in lower ones'. It is possible that after this movement the players remained still for a moment, forming a silent tableau as if they had become carved or painted figures. English Catholic culture was mediated through these images. In the roof-bosses of the English churches Herod 'is shown contorted with rage, his legs grotesquely crossed',[12] while the same character is depicted in the Coventry mysteries in the same posture as a sign of 'crossed' or thwarted human energy. These cycle plays conducted their audience through the history of the universe, from Creation to Doom, but that sacred chronology was also depicted in the wall-paintings and stained glass of the churches. It was the unifying myth, the grand context for the creation of art and literature alike. And it survives still. Stanley Spencer's twentieth-century paintings, *The Resurrection in Cookham Churchyard* and *The Resurrection of the Soldiers*, where all emerge at the sound of the final trumpet, seem to derive from medieval images of the Apocalypse; the same artist's *Christ delivered to the People* and *The Crucifixion*, with the leering faces of the workmen putting the hammer to Christ's nails, might be a detailed transcription of a scene from one of the medieval mysteries. Spencer was an English artist filled both with a mysterious sense of place and with an encompassing vision that accommodates a medieval as well as a modern sensibility. 'When I see anything', he once wrote, 'I see everything.' In this context it is perhaps interesting to note that 'he found it very important to paint what is in the extreme foreground. . . . It seemed to him all wrong to start at an arbitrary plane say 10 feet distance rather than at the nearest plane in one's line of vision.'[13] He recaptures, or retrieves, an essentially medieval painterly vision.

CHAPTER 19

Part of the territory

'It is not surprising', Walter Oakeshott wrote in *The Sequence of Medieval Art*, 'that East Anglia should in the fourteenth century have been the centre of artistic production in England.'[1] Another historian emphasised 'the predominance of East Anglia over all other regional theatrical traditions in late medieval England'.[2] A unique form of 'tail-rhyme stanza' has been located in romances derived from that region. The two greatest female writers of the fourteenth century, Julian of Norwich and Margery Kempe, both came from East Anglia. So there exists a pattern of activity, which at a later date manifested itself in the 'Norwich School' of painting.

Its two principal counties, Norfolk and Suffolk, are named after the North Folk and South Folk of the Anglo-Saxons but the topographical boundaries of those tribes are uncertain; we may also include parts of Cambridgeshire and Essex in what was the most fertile and, excluding London, the most densely populated region of the country. East Anglia was to a certain extent isolated from the rest of England by its fens. Its commerce with Europe flourished, however, since it was open to all the trade routes of northern Europe and the Netherlands; the wool trade prospered, in particular, as the emergence of the great 'wool churches' of Long Melford and Lavenham may testify. Another topographical aspect lent a particular tone to the area. There were few great 'manors' but instead a large number of villages and towns filled with merchants and a farming population. In turn this seems to have created, or helped to create, what has been described as an 'economically precocious and religiously radical area'.[3] The area was radical in more than one sense, however; anti-monarchical in tendency, it gravitated towards parliament or the barons rather than to the king. It possessed a flourishing merchant economy, 'involved in a capitalist and cash-marketing system',[4] and out of it sprang a distinctively local art and literature.

The illuminations of what has come to be known as the 'East Anglian School' are of an unmatched liveliness of outline. Whether the subject-matter is taken from bestiaries or literary romances, Bibles or lives of the saints, they are all domesticated within a native idiom which combines naturalism with grotesquerie. There are East Anglian daisies in abundance and, in the Luttrell psalter, domestic scenes which might almost illustrate a novel by Samuel Richardson. The influences of northern Europe have been assimilated, but they have also been coarsened and simplified. They have turned native, in other words.

The burgeoning of religious theatre in East Anglia was primarily due to the commercial success of the region. There were many monasteries and many great churches but, equally significantly, there were more than one hundred East Anglian areas where dramatic performances were conducted. Just as the illuminations of the 'East Anglian School' were characterised by a diversity of influences and sources, so one historian of medieval theatre has described East Anglian drama as possessing 'a richness and diversity of theatrical practices unmatched in any other region of the country'.[5] On the basis of vocabulary and dialect several individual plays can be traced to their source in East Anglia, among them *The Castle of Perseverance* and *The Killing of the Children*. Characteristically these dramas were highly local affairs, run by individual parishes and performed for local profit. (One of them, at Snettisham, was known as a 'Rockefeste' in anticipation of later festivals.) Just as grotesques and writhing figures play so large a part in East Anglian books, so East Anglian drama can be recognised by its emphasis on spectacle and by its general theatrical effectiveness; the characteristics are those of ribaldry, grotesquerie and 'shameless manipulation of audience sympathy'.[6] It is a local art within an international context.

Julian of Norwich can also be placed in this unique setting. She was known as 'the Recluse atte Norwyche', and was born towards the close of 1342. It seems likely that she inhabited a cell outside the church of St Julian, near the centre of Norwich, which belonged to the Benedictine nuns of Carrow. The rest of her life is known only through her own words. In her thirty-fourth year, at her mother's house, she lay close to death; on the seventh night of her agony, after the priest had placed the crucifix before her face, she was granted sixteen 'shewings' or revelations within two nights. It is believed that, after this pilgrimage of the spirit, she entered the Benedictine community as a recluse or devoted laywoman. Then, out of her epiphanies, came her reflections in *Revelations of Divine Love*. She wrote in an East Anglian dialect, with northern additions, and her writing possesses a local savour. She vividly describes the drops of blood upon Christ's face, which 'were like to the scale of heryng in the spreadeing on the forehead'; his dying body was 'lyke a dry borde' and he was hanging 'in the eyr as men hang a cloth to drye'. When the devil appears to her 'anon a lyte smoke came in the dore with a grete hete and a foule stinke'. These powerful images might have come directly out of East Anglian drama; when Julian declares, 'Methought I would have beene that time with Mary Magdalene', at the Crucifixion, she may be recalling her experience of watching the dramatic and sensational Passion plays of her neighbourhood. When she describes how 'halfe the face' was covered with 'drie blode', she might have been watching a theatrical scene. She is granted a vision of a very English St John of Beverley as if he were 'an hende neybor', a dear neighbour, and of course the actors in the liturgical drama were in a literal sense neighbours and acquaintances.

The spiritual dimension of life on earth could not be better exemplified. When she confirms that she studied the pains of Christ as they were depicted in painting or in stained glass, a particular quality of art or theatre can be seen to inform a particular kind of devotion; indeed, in any just analysis, art and devotion cannot be separated. This, also, is part of the Catholic inheritance of England.

Just as the art of East Anglia is derived from many different sources, English and European, so in turn the lineaments of Julian of Norwich's piety have been traced to European spiritual mentors such as St Bernard and St Catherine of Siena, St Thomas Aquinas and William of St Thierry. Yet it has been said that 'Julian perfectly expresses the English spiritual tradition' because 'she combines all the strands of our patristic lineage into something new'.[7] It is the characteristic English procedure of assimilation and change, expressing itself in what has been described as Julian's native cheerfulness and common sense; her 'optimism' and her 'prudence' are 'inherent in all English spirituality'. Her methods are practical and her metaphors pragmatic; the penitent must labour as does the gardener, 'delvyn and dykyn, swinkin and sweten, and turne the earth upsodowne'. Thus she rejects 'the tight juridical categories of scholastic moral theology, and the exaggerated penitential rigours of the Franciscans',[8] arriving at a wholly English and East Anglian compromise.

Another native of that region has added significantly to England's religious history. Margery Kempe came from Bishop's Lynn in Norfolk, and was a contemporary of Julian of Norwich whom she once visited for spiritual consolation. Her father had five times been mayor of this prosperous 'wool' town, and her husband was elected its chamberlain in 1394. She was an East Anglian woman of wealth and competence, who tried her hand at both brewing and milling; yet *The Book of Margery Kempe* is primarily concerned with her spiritual and visionary experiences in which she encountered, and conversed with, Christ himself. The experience of the Passion would overwhelm her 'sumtyme in the cherch, sumtyme in the strete, sumtyme in the chaumbre, sumtyme in the felde', so that East Anglia becomes the site of eternity. But if Julian of Norwich was influenced by continental theology, Margery Kempe was in more literal fashion affected by continental travellers. Lynn was the port to which pilgrims came from Scandinavia and Europe, on their way to the sacred sites of England. Hers is again a local, and universal, story; Margery Kempe, very much the literal-minded daughter of East Anglian devotion, was able also to witness the details and forms of continental piety and, within certain limits, to adopt them. She knew the people of 'Deuchlond' and a friend, Alan of Lynn, had already indexed the works of St Bridget of Sweden. Yet once more, in native fashion, she mingles the ideal with the real, the sacred with the profane, with an almost Chaucerian eye for significant detail. Her career as a brewer did not flourish 'for, whan the ale was as fayr standyng undyr berm as any man mygth se, sodenly the berm wold fallyn down'; the froth, in other and more modern terms, would go flat. When she asked a man to have sexual intercourse with her he replied that 'he had levar ben hewyn as smal as flesch to the pott!' This matter-of-fact dialect could be effortlessly turned to spiritual matters. Jesus came to her in vision and informed her that she would be 'etyn and knawen of the pepul of the world as any raton knawyth the stokfysch'. Sometimes the voices of those people of the world can be heard. 'I wold thu wer in Smythfeld,' one London woman told her, 'and I wold beryn a fagot to bren the wyth.' The same vivid detail, seen in the margins of the psalteries or on the scaffolds of liturgical plays, animates Margery Kempe's East Anglian account of her visionary experiences.

Out of that native soil sprang other writers and artists, among them John Skelton of Diss whose rough and exuberant 'Skeltonics' became once more influential in the twentieth century:

> To wryte or to indyte,
> Eyther for delyte
> Or elles for despite

John Lydgate of Suffolk was the most prolific and popular poet of the fifteenth century; there are writers such as John Bale, Gabriel Harvey and Nicholas Udall who together emphasise the fact that no other region of the country 'could boast of so many prominent, identifiable, bookish figures'.[9]

So in the fourteenth, fifteenth and early sixteenth centuries the seal had been set on the prolificity and variety of East Anglia in illumination, drama and literature. Some may interpret that superiority in terms of wealth; where mercantile profit leads, the arts will follow. Yet others have discerned a local passion. One historian of art has concluded that the 'flat expanses' and 'rolling outlines' and 'wide skies' of East Anglia 'have had a curiously powerful hold on the English creative intellect and have been a striking stimulus to it'.[10] It might even be remarked here that 'flatness' of surface and the bounding outline have also been the defining characteristics of English art; it is as if the landscape itself adopted the form of the English imagination.

The poetry of England

'Sir Jeffery Chaucer and the Nine and Twenty Pilgrims on
their Journey to Canterbury.' By William Blake

CHAPTER 20

A song and a dance

The English have always excelled at popular song, untouched by any conscious literary art. Dance songs, and part songs, and ballads, and processional chants, were once as much part of communal life as the social and religious ceremonies which decorated existence in a more formal way. Several thousand lyrics from the eleventh to fifteenth centuries survive; most of them are anonymous and, therefore, the unnamed songs of the land. There are religious lyrics in the vernacular dating from the eleventh century, although we know from other testimony that 'English' songs were being performed by travelling singers or wandering minstrels in earlier centuries. It has to be remembered that sung verse was a more direct, and indeed easier, form of communication than prose. Sermons were turned into rhyme and moral homilies also acquired the natural dimensions of verse; even the hermit in his cave or simple thatched dwelling might proclaim that 'the songe of louyng & of life es commen'. Just as Caedmon, the herdsman from Whitby Abbey, was the first to sing naturally in Anglo-Saxon, so the first medieval lyrics to survive sprang from the mouth of St Godric. Yet it is perhaps characteristic that sacred and profane material became thoroughly intermingled; the addresses to Christ became those of a human lover, while the lyrics of courtly love were permeated with spiritual allegory. There are songs of love from 1300:

> Nou sprinkes the sprai,
> All for love icche am so seeke
> That slepen I ne mai

These are matched by songs of sacred woe as Mary laments the death of her son:

> Sodenly afraide,
> Half wakyng, half slepyng,
> And gretly dismayde,
> A wooman sate wepyng

The monks (here 'muneches') of Ely are celebrated with a dance measure, at a date put in the eleventh century:

> Merye sungen the muneches binnen Ely
> Tha Cnut King rew ther by;
> Roweth, knites, noer the land
> And here we thes muneches saeng

It is perhaps significant that dance songs were never prohibited by English ecclesiastics, unlike their counterparts on the continent; indigenous tradition was stronger than religious caveats. As Layamon wrote in 1189, 'Tha weoren in thissen lande blissfulle songs'.

The most blissful are those wrapped in mystery and enchantment. Some lines on the conception of Jesus, for example, emphasise the delicacy and simplicity of medieval English:

> He cam also stille
> Ther his moder was,
> As dew in Aprille
> That falleth on the grass.
> He cam also still
> To his moderes bowr,
> As dew in Aprille
> That falleth on the flowr

There is the strange ballad scribbled down in the early fifteenth century:

> She sente me the cherye
> Withouten ony ston . . .

It is matched by the enchanting carol of Corpus Christi which begins:

> Lully, lulley, lully, lulley,
> The fawcon hath born my mak away

in which a series of still images, as vivid as hallucinations, ends with:

> And by that bedes side there stondeth a ston,
> 'Corpus Christi' wreten theron

It is the simplicity of these verses that is most arresting and significant, as if they came from a pure well of speech undefiled. The same lucidity and clarity are to be found in ballads, originally of oral provenance and later turned into 'broadsides' to be distributed throughout the country. As Philip Sidney wrote in *A Defence of Poesy*, composed in the early 1580s, 'I never heard the olde song of *Percy* and *Douglas* that I found not my heart mooued more than with a Trumpet . . .' The same simplicity occurs in dance songs, the extant fragments of which are to be found jotted down in the margins of manuscript books:

> Trippe a lutel with thy fot
> And let thy body go

They are described as possessing a 'peculiarly English strength',[1] which in certain circumstances may simply be marked by the resonance of key words. 'Drinke to him derly of full god bous' or 'To revele with this birdes bright' are salient examples, where 'booze' and 'birds' make up a significant line of English music. A short poem on the Passion, dated to the early fifteenth century, has a strange affiliation with the later verse of George Herbert:

> O! Mankinde,
> Have in thy minde
> My Passion smert,
> And thou shall finde
> Me full kinde –
> Lo! Here my hert

In part it is the ancient pattern of four stresses which fulfils a native cadence, and can easily be turned into the octosyllabic couplet which is also one of the mainstays of English verse:

> For many ben of swyche manere,
> That talys and rymys wyl blethly here

This movement has as its counterpart the process of alliteration, which seems to represent a national or instinctive tendency in the language. Much has been written about the 'alliterative revival', of the fourteenth century, when poems such as *Sir Gawain and the Green Knight*, *Pearl* and *Piers the Plowman* were written. These are all works of highly conscious literary art, and were by no means the issue of some 'popular' or 'buried' tradition of Old English speech, but their alliterative form is entirely consonant with their English origin. It is remarkable how much alliterative verse is concerned with the incidents and examples of English history, for example, so that the native preoccupation with the past seems to clothe itself in significant and appropriate form. Alliteration is also widely employed for the purposes of translation from the French and Latin, as if the Englishness of the new versions could then be most effectively conveyed. The Latin prose of the Church fathers was translated into heavily marked cadence and ingenious alliterative prose, as a way of creating an informal English rhetoric in compensation for classical stylistics. Alliteration was also a means of assimilating foreign learning into the vernacular, so that historical as well as theological texts could be transmitted to 'lewed' men. It was once believed that the 'alliterative revival' sprang out of the north or the north midlands, and there is some evidence of northern inflexions or dialect forms, but provenance is less important than purpose.

Language may fashion as well as convey meaning, and the alliterative style, in particular, seems to guide its exponents towards moral and social complaint; this political or didactic tradition is normally accompanied by the use of Old English words, as if it truly were the dialect of the tribe. The alliterative line is marked by concreteness and specificity also and, in poems like *Piers the Plowman* or *Wynnere and Wastour*, it carries the moral weight of balance and parallelism. That is why sermons and homiletic pieces made extensive use of alliteration, and why a poem on London's guardian saint, Erkenwald, concludes with 'Meche mournyng and myrthe . . . mellyd together'; it is the reason why a moral treatise of Richard Rolle reminds the reader that 'Al perisshethe and passeth that we with eigh see'. It may be that alliteration is implicated in the natural English tendency to compromise, since it balances opposing forces with equal strength. There is no doubt, however, that the alliterative voice was accommodating and encompassing; it could harbour a range of what anachronistically might be termed 'populist' sentiment as well as the refined narratives of courtly adventure. That again is a token of Englishness or, as one critic has written of the alliterative *Sir Gawain and the Green Knight*, that 'combination of the romantic and the real, of humour and high tone, of lyrical delicacy and verbal wit'.[2]

If it is a genuine native utterance, then, it may be profitable to identify other of its characteristics. Alliterative English verse is not a particularly subtle medium for the expression of human feeling. Of the English lyrics it has been claimed that they are 'almost entirely wanting in "romance" resonances';[3] the 'cloying sentiment' of French originals has been 'stripped away . . . as if not acceptable to English audiences'.[4] This refusal to sentimentalise, or express strong feeling, is extended to the author who tends in general to adopt the role of embarrassed narrator excusing a lack of artistry. In similar spirit the alliterative poems tend to address serious topics with a certain lightness of touch or what has been described as 'laconic presentation';[5] the quality of understatement is directly inherited from Old English poetry but it preserves its stern life in Middle English and beyond. In translations from the French, also, 'a dramatic pattern of events, vividly conveyed, often seems preferred to subtle thematic undercurrents', and the ambiguous or complicated knights and ladies of Gallic provenance 'tend to take on the clearly defined outlines of folk-tale types'.[6] This is a very significant observation because it emphasises a profound tendency in the English imagination – to eschew dramatic complexities for dramatic incident, to avoid intimate or interior character development in favour of the broad outlines of popular tradition, to abandon the messy complications of love or sentiment in favour of action or spectacle. The tendency always is towards simplification. The stanzaic *Morte Arthur* takes a pencil to the French *Mort Artu* and 'the English poet, as the English habit was, has compressed and simplified the French story'.[7] Four centuries later French dramatists were complaining that their English adaptors shortened their plays out of all recognition, and even mingled the plots together in order to provide 'variety'.

The English author of *Ywain and Gawain* took the romances of Chrétien de Troyes and removed 'the web of psychological generalisation and paradoxical ratiocination in which he emmeshes his characters';[8] in addition the 'long passages of emotional and intellectual intricacy are much reduced by the English poet'.[9] Therefore, 'formality and intellectual reasoning vanish to be replaced by sweetness of tone and dramatic immediacy'.[10]

It is the difference between those two icons of their respective national cultures, Racine and Shakespeare; it is also the distinction between Dickens and Balzac. Even when the English poets borrow from French lyric originals, they still manage to excise the paradoxes and the abstractions, the conflicts and the contradictions, in favour of a 'harmonious and optimistic' construction of the world of love. It is the same optimism and gaiety to be found in Julian of Norwich. Shakespeare suggested that the truest poetry is the most feigning but on this occasion the borrowed words burn brighter than the originals. Indeed this aspect of the English imagination is of some significance. Is the national genius, after all, simply a collection of borrowings?

The English vision tends towards the local and the circumstantial. The prose and poetry of the fourteenth century are filled with material imagery, and with specific, almost humble, detail. The interest is once more in shared or common feeling, with the alliterative line elucidating and eliciting a popular voice; many of the alliterative romances were indeed aimed at a public assembly which would have welcomed local allusions and enjoyed the narration of physical adventure in homely language. That is why there is a great emphasis on visual detail, so that the audience might *see* the scenes being presented to them. Here once more we recognise the tutelary presence of the illuminations and the wall-paintings, the liturgical plays and the stained-glass windows.

The apparent resurgence of alliterative poetry in the fourteenth century is matched by textual evidence of an increase in all forms of English writing, again complemented by an increased confidence in the national sensibility. There are many now forgotten names and forgotten poems; *Cursor Mundi* is a scriptural history of some thirty thousand lines in rhymed octosyllabics, matched only by Robert of Brunne's *Handlyng Synne* in the same measure and *The Prick of Conscience* similarly rhymed. Dan Michel's *Ayenbite of Inwit* is a penitential work in prose, which provides the context for the visionary works of the fourteenth century. John of Trevisa's translations of Higden's *Polychronicon* and of Bartholomew the Englishman's *De Proprietatibus Rerum* were part of the same urgent desire to 'Englisch' every aspect of the world. Robert of Gloucester's *Chronicle* and Gower's *Confessio Amantis* fulfilled the same cultural project. Gower himself brought to the English world the received tales of Dido and Ulysses, Orestes and Penelope; he was avidly read by Ben Jonson and introduced by Shakespeare into *Pericles*. He lived and died in the borough of Southwark – where his tomb rests in the cathedral – but his renown and influence have now been far surpassed by a much more illustrious friend and contemporary.

'Longways Dance.' By Thomas Rowlandson

CHAPTER 21

Fathers and sons

William Caxton was the first to call Chaucer 'the worshipful father' of 'our englissh', who is then celebrated as 'first auctor'. Dryden in turn described him as 'the Father of *English* poetry' who fructified the 'Mother-Tongue', and from this union issued 'the various manners and Humours (as we now call them) of the whole *English* Nation'; there emerged 'God's Plenty', in other words, and Dryden continued the familial metaphor by remarking that 'we have our Fore-Fathers and Grand-Dames all before us'. The sexual element of this linguistic commingling is emphasised by Matthew Arnold's delight in Chaucer's 'free . . . licentious dealing with language'. The perception is compounded in the fifteenth century by the poet Thomas Hoccleve's lament that upon the death of Chaucer 'al this lond it smertith', as if he were some kind of mythical father whose demise created a waste land.

There are many suggestive details here. The mingling of poet and language, father and mother, is seen as a potent sexual act which has mythical associations; it is a mystery indeed since, with the inseminating power of the poet, language gives birth to language. It is the source and womb of itself, with the poet only as temporary agent or begetter. This deeply held metaphor may in part be responsible for the 'sexist' interpretation of literary history, where the author is implicitly deemed to be male. The idea of the father is important in another English context, however, since the familial or domestic sensibility is a very powerful one in national literature; it may have its origins in the Anglo-Saxon image of the lighted hall or in the Chaucerian vision of a collocation of pilgrims, but the idea of a close-knit community (generally withstanding the depredations of a cold and hostile natural world) is central to the English imagination. We have traced it back to *Beowulf* and beyond.

Chaucer was a Londoner, the son of a vintner or wine-merchant; he was born in a grand house in Thames Street at some time between 1340 and 1345, grew up in the streets of London and has in fact become typically associated with them – or, rather, with the men and women of the fourteenth century whom he loved so much that they will live for ever in his verse. Yet he was not a 'man of the people' in any modern sense. He came from a wealthy oligarchy of city merchants, and spent all his life in royal or administrative service. He was closely associated with the family and 'affinity' of John of Gaunt, and as a result retained a number of highly lucrative sinecures. He was the poet of the court, too, with his verses being distributed among the nobility. It has also been argued that he found another audience for his poetry among the wealthy city merchants and their families.

He was sent on diplomatic business to both France and Italy but, despite his involvement in affairs of state, he rarely alludes to contemporary events in his published work. There is only one reference to the Peasants' Revolt of 1381, for example, but the absence of comment upon such events is only to be expected in his bookish and aureate art. It was courtly poetry in every sense; it was crowded with minute and realistic detail, suffused with emotional symbolism, concerned with individual portraiture, and filled with classical learning. The courtly sensibility of the period was at once bejewelled and highly emotive; it is embodied in the sad if majestic reign of Richard II who, in 1400, died of starvation after his enforced abdication. It was the year in which Chaucer himself died.

Yet of course there is also great humour in the poetry of Chaucer; it is the comedy of a shrewd and practical man of affairs who mocks pretension, false learning and false sentiment and who also delights in the low 'humour' of the fabliau. His is the comedy of the mystery plays raised to a much higher and more sophisticated level. G. K. Chesterton considered it extraordinary 'that Chaucer should have been so unmistakably English almost before the existence of England'; but it is perhaps not so surprising in a poet whose personal modesty and broadness of feeling, whose respect for tradition and inventive diversity, make him indeed the fountain of English poetry.

The metaphor of language as a spring, or stream, is equally important to the critical understanding of Chaucer's work. Any discussion of his poetry will notice its prolonged and fluent cadences, which can be termed its musicality; the images attendant upon it, however, have interesting fluctuations. One of the earliest references appears in a poem by Chaucer's contemporary, Eustache Deschamps, who writes of Chaucer's 'fontaine' from which he desires 'avoir un buvraige'; Chaucer provides 'la doys', or stream, which will refresh him in Gaul. Lydgate, lamenting Chaucer's death, announces that

> The welle is drie, with the lycoure swete

and then again regrets the absence of those

> golde dewe dropes of speche and eloquence

In a climate of rain and mist, the immediate metaphors are those of streams, and wells, and dew. Spenser considered himself to be the successor of Chaucer and prayed:

> But if on me some little drops would flowe,
> Of that the spring was in his learned hedde

It is as if the English language were indeed a course of flowing water. In *The Faerie Queene* Chaucer is depicted as the 'well of English vndefiled' and the 'pure well head of Poesie'. 'Well' itself is an Old English word, so that the idea of a spring issuing from the deep earth is also a metaphor for the presence of the ancient language.

Dryden described Chaucer as 'a perpetual Fountain' so that the stream is always fresh and ever renewed; implicitly Dryden is placing himself within the same movement, and declares that 'I found I had a Soul congenial to his'. This suggestion of broad continuity appears in Dryden's preface to *Fables Ancient and Modern* in which his own translations of Chaucer into 'modern *English*' are gathered; in that same place he states that '*Spenser* more than once insinuates, that the Soul of *Chaucer* was transfus'd into his body; and that he was begotten by him Two Hundred years after his Decease. *Milton* has acknowledged to me that *Spenser* was his original . . .' So the image of the well, or fountain, or stream, has remarkable connotations, not the least of which is a doctrine concerning the transmigration of souls. Dryden continues with a remark, on the subject of translation, that 'Another Poet, in another Age, may take the same liberty with my Writings'; Dryden places himself within the stream or, as Hazlitt has put it, 'water from a crystal spring'.

To this may be added the recognition of the springs hidden within Chaucer's poetry, as, for example, when William Empson notes in *Troilus and Criseyde* the presence of 'a stream . . . cleansing and refreshing'.[1] There is another stream, too, which is to be found within what Matthew Arnold termed 'the liquid diction, the fluid movement' of Chaucer's line; we may imagine the cadence flowing through Spenser, Milton and Dryden. It is a form of English music. It is also a matter of what was termed 'sweetness', as of sweet water, and is implicit in Wordsworth's reverie of laughing with Chaucer by the mill-

stream of Trumpington near Cambridge. It is implicit in the first line of
The Canterbury Tales 'Whan that Aprill with his shoures soote',
although the music is lent a deeper resonance in the first line of T. S.
Eliot's *The Waste Land* when April becomes 'the cruellest month'
whose showers produce only the disturbed movement of memory.

The natural metaphors applied to Chaucer's verse are in one sense
incongruous, since the poet's own language is a literary compound of
different sources and heterogeneous borrowings. It is as if his successors,
and indeed his contemporaries, wished to naturalise the artificial
process of becoming English; they heard the music, too, but wanted to
claim it as a native melody, indigenous as the stream which issues from
the rocks. Chaucer's poetry, however, is elaborately and deliberately
rhetorical with all the devices of *exclamatio*, *interrogatio* and
interpretatio. By his own account the narrator of the poems is a bookish
and reticent creature, half in love with words and old literature, who
seems to advance or represent the claims of learning over experience. In
The Book of the Duchess the narrator, suffering from insomnia, asks for
'a book . . . To rede and drive the night away'; it was a 'romaunce . . .
in olde tyme', but eventually he sleeps and dreams. On awaking he finds
the old romance still in his hands, and decides then to put his own dream
'in ryme'. So literature is here the beginning and end of the process,
aroused by a book and manifested in a book. In *The House of Fame* the
classical myths and stories take on emblematic and pictorial form as if
they were manuscript illuminations. The opening of *The Parliament of
Fowls* reveals 'a bok . . . write with lettres olde' which acts as a
commentary upon Cicero's *Somnium Scipionis*; once more words and
dreams are thoroughly intermingled, as if only in sleep could the
narrator speak freely. But again this is a device to disguise all of
Chaucer's calculation and consideration, so that the words might
somehow seem to be natural or inspired. Once more it represents a
desire to naturalise – to ground, in almost a literal sense – a highly
complex and various language. The English predilection for dreams has
already been discussed, and it is perhaps appropriate that Chaucer 'is
the first European writer to use this formula'.[2]

This emphasis upon books or literature is of vital significance to
Chaucer in more than one sense, however, since like all English writers
of the period he relies upon borrowings and adaptations in order to
forge an English sensibility. In his prologue to *The Legend of Good
Women* he declares that 'On bokes for to rede I me delyte', with the
further argument that

> And yf that olde bokes were aweye,
> Yloren were of remembraunce the keye

'Remembraunce' here is the term for historical memory, in the sense that Chaucer's own histories of 'good women' such as Dido or Thisbe are made up out of other histories; just as language springs out of language in the perpetual stream or fountain of words, so books spring out of other books. In *The Parliament of Fowls* he puts this mysterious arrangement thus:

> For out of olde feldes, as men seyth,
> Cometh al this newe corn from yer to yere,
> And out of olde bokes, in good feyth,
> Cometh al this newe science that men lere

'Science' here has its original meaning of the state of knowing itself, so that the parameters of knowledge and understanding are fashioned by the learning of old books. This may not be an immediately familiar or even intelligible concept, but it is of the utmost importance in any understanding of the medieval imagination and, in particular, of the peculiarly English genius of Chaucer's work. It can be said that knowledge, or truth, was a collective and communal enterprise; the individual author might enlarge or increase the store, but the principal act was not of creation but of assimilation and reinvention. Rhetoric was the means of reordering, in delightful or graceful form, already available materials and themes. The truth lay in authority, not in individual fabrication; hence Chaucer's reticence and parodic portrayal of himself as silent and preoccupied. 'For evere upon the ground,' the Host of the Canterbury pilgrims complains, 'I se thee stare.' Chaucer's narrator is 'domb as any ston' because his inability or unwillingness to speak is a token of his incapacity. Of course this is also a rhetorical device, disguising his novelty and inventiveness, but it does illuminate the essential truth of Chaucer's art; it is comprised of borrowed materials, and his genius lay in his ability to reorder and juxtapose already existing parts of poetic invention. He built a new dwelling out of old stones, and his talent for synthesis was matched only by his powers of assimilation. This will help to explain what have been called the encyclopaedic tendencies of his work, by which means he will supply lists of exempla within the course of a narrative poem or will simply copy out highly orthodox material as in his sermon upon penitence which ends *The Canterbury Tales*. An event or an adventure will be briefly narrated, as the preface to a fervent litany of sources and authorities; poetry becomes a means of adducing learning. He will write *A Treatise on the Astrolabe*, or translate the *Consolation of Philosophy* by Boethius, with the same attention as that which he gives to the vivid portrayal of the Wife of Bath; they are all intrinsic parts of his literary endeavour to refurbish 'science' and human scholarship. No one exercise is to be preferred to another, because they all pertain to the arts of rhetoric. He considered himself to be part of a tradition, although it was his destiny fundamentally to alter the nature of that tradition.

He was writing no more than the truth, however, when he remarked that the new science came 'out of olde bokes'. He will sometimes signal his source material in manifest ways.

> The remenant of the tale if ye wol heere
> Redeth Ovyde, and ther ye may it leere

is the advice given by the Wife of Bath. *The House of Fame* makes reference to no less than nineteen books or authors within its 2,158 lines. *The Book of the Duchess* alludes to Ovid, Macrobius, Livy, Dares, Phrygius, the *Romance of the Rose* and the Bible; in order to assert its authority it must name its authorities. Chaucer, more than any other European poet of the period, employed this device. When one critic describes 'his slightly ridiculous pedantry and bookish exaggeration',[3] he is in fact alluding to an English characteristic which has been maintained by many writers over several centuries.

But of course the influence of earlier written work upon Chaucer runs deeper than any overt reference, since the act of translation was the single most important aspect of his art; in this, if in no other, respect he manifests a quintessentially English genius. It has been suggested that he wrote French verse before he began composition in English but, even if this hypothesis is dismissed, it serves to emphasise the fact that Chaucer was educated in a trilingual court where the principal literary vernacular was still French. It is perhaps not surprising, therefore, that his first full-scale enterprise in English, *The Book of the Duchess*, is an adaptation of various French 'dits' or stories. His general French affiliations are numerous and extensive, and in fact Eustache Deschamps remarked in particular upon Chaucer's great merit as a 'grant translateur' of the French tongue into English. Certainly one of his earliest exercises was the translation of the *Roman de la Rose* which converted a whole range of European sensibility into English; his abiding preoccupation rests precisely here, in his diligent efforts to accommodate continental styles and models within the vernacular. And, until the nineteenth century, this was an enterprise which all English poets wished to share. The process of adaptation and assimilation is instinctive.

Chaucer had read Deschamps himself, but he had also studied Machaut and Froissart; he read French translations of Ovid and Boccaccio, while various other sources have been located for elements of *The Canterbury Tales* as well as *Troilus and Criseyde*. The essential matter lies, however, in Chaucer's wish to incorporate the fluency and seemliness of French verse within his own vernacular; Middle English was in any case an absorbent medium and had incorporated a great number of French words, but Chaucer's purpose was to elevate that mixed and various speech into a literature. His debt to Italy, to Dante and Boccaccio in particular, then became of paramount importance; it was Dante who, after all, had single-handedly created an Italian vernacular poetry to rival that of Latin and Greek. Boccaccio declared that before Dante 'there was none who . . . had the feeling or the courage to make it the instrument of any matter dealt with by the rules of art. But he showed by the effect that every lofty matter may be treated in it; and made our vernacular glorious above every other.' This was precisely the intent and ambition of Chaucer himself – to create an English literature or, rather, to create out of English a literature. Far from being baffled or defeated by the essentially hybrid nature of the language, with elements of Latin, French, Norse and Anglo-Saxon all compounded, he decided to exploit and celebrate its variety. It did not have the purity of Italian, or the grace of French, or the unchanging sonority of Latin; but, rather, it possessed all these attributes together with many more. When Chaucer first experimented with Dante's *terza rima* in English it was a way of proving, both to himself and to his audience, that the language was already capable of masterly expression.

At the close of *Troilus and Criseyde*, which itself is supposed to derive ultimately from Boccaccio's *Il Filostrato*, Chaucer appends a verse which demonstrates his literary ambition:

> Go, litel bok, go, litel myn tragedye . . .
> And kis the steppes where as thow seest pace
> Virgile, Ovide, Omer, Lucan, and Stace

Virgil, Ovid, Homer, Lucan and Statius were the classical authors most celebrated and most widely read in the medieval world, and Chaucer is placing himself in their company. But there is also another context. Three of the great European poets – Jean de Meun, Dante and Boccaccio – had also composed such self-regarding tributes associating themselves with Homer, Ovid, Virgil, Horace, Tibullus and others; so, in imitating their device, Chaucer is also representing himself as part of a European literary tradition. Here, then, is the importance of Chaucer to the English imagination. He was the first poet self-consciously to create the idea of an English literature worthy to rival that of the classical past. He also implicitly establishes himself at the beginning of that tradition, and so all subsequent myths of source and origin spring from him.

In the same poem Chaucer prays that God send him the power to write a 'comedye' as well as a 'tragedye', but then addresses his 'litel bok' with the words 'But subgit be to all poesye'. It is interesting, perhaps, that *The Oxford English Dictionary* believes this to be the first occasion on which tragedy and comedy appear as English words. Chaucer may have derived 'comedye' from Dante's *Divina Commedia* but, whatever the exact provenance, the status of his remarks is clear; it is worth re-emphasising the fact that he was fashioning the idea of literature out of English itself. In his own arduous and continual practice he had learned its capacity, or its capaciousness, and in a preface to his prose treatise on the astrolabe he places his trust in 'trewe conclusions in English, as well as sufficith to these noble clerkes Grekes these same conclusiouns in Grek, and to Arabiens in Arabik, and to Jewes in Ebrew, and to Latyn folk in Latyn'. The English language is therefore placed upon the same level as Greek, Latin and Hebrew as a medium for truths both sacred and profane.

His resourcefulness is far-reaching, too, since in order to create the idea of an English literature he was obliged to celebrate the native propensities of the language; we might even say that the largeness of his aim was such that the language spoke through him. It had steadily been speeding up, with the alliterative line in particular moving in a much freer and more fluid cadence, but Chaucer expanded its range so successfully that it gained infinitely more freedom and elasticity. He invented the decasyllabic couplet, otherwise known as the 'heroic couplet', but more significantly he treated the various forms of verse with a fluency that brought them closer to the native intonations of speech. From this derive later critical remarks about his 'sweet numbers' and 'smoothly flowing diction'; it elucidates those comments upon his employment of a 'rhythmical tradition' and a 'native tradition' so successfully that the rhythm of native speech is attached to his own music. The pattern is one of variety and purposefulness, heterogeneity within the cadences of significant form.

The variety is itself exemplary. His greatest if most incomplete achievement, *The Canterbury Tales*, is a consummation and celebration of all previous English literature. Its 'general prologue', and twenty-four separate tales, cover every form from sermon to farce, from saint's life to animal fable, from heroic adventure to full-scale parody. Its twenty-eight characters (including Chaucer himself) furnish an assembly of fourteenth-century people in a medley of occupations and professions. *The Divine Comedy* has come to earth; *The Romance of the Rose* has been humanised. Chaucer's is an inclusive art, in other words. He understands and reflects every aspect of human society, spiritual and natural. That is why his characters are at once fully naturalistic and archetypal. He creates stories as well as allegories. The Wife of Bath is both a realistic fourteenth-century woman, in a period when women were often very powerful, and a compendium of medieval attitudes towards her sex.

The Canterbury Tales is, then, a conflation of narratives written in different styles and upon different themes; the metrical changes are extraordinary and even within the boundaries of one narrative the language is mixed and various. The appearance is one of perpetual novelty, like the surface of a swiftly running stream, mixed with elements of wonder and surprise. This in no way mitigates the central truth that Chaucer would not have considered himself an 'original' writer in any modern sense. The fact that he borrowed themes, stories and characters from a variety of sources is testimony to his deep traditionalism; yet he was obliged to invigorate and intensify this familiar material with such arts of rhetoric as variation and display. He creates the impression of diversity, of 'newness', as a way of reaching an audience which itself desired novelty and surprise. The demand is noticed by Chaucer himself in *The Canterbury Tales* – 'Diverse folke diversely they seyde . . . Diverse men diverse thinges seyden . . . Diverse men diversely hym told . . . Diverse folk diversely they demed'.

Hence the extraordinary interaction in his verse between French and Latinate idioms, between the low English of the fabliau and the aureate diction of the saints' tales. Chaucer is constantly employing new words, but often uses them once only so that the process is one of continuous novelty. He employs another device, too, whereby he can align ancient and modern. He will juxtapose old stories with new framing devices, so that a preface or prologue can set an unfamiliar context for a familiar tale. Thus 'there is no paradox in the fact that Chaucer invents so few stories yet is so inventive a story teller'.[4] To be thoroughly traditional yet novel: this was the great demand, and was Chaucer's great achievement. By bringing together these various sources and conflicting styles, Chaucer established a literature and helped to stabilise a language capable of accommodating it.

It has been argued that in the process he created the idea of England and the notion of 'Englishness' – that the characters of *The Canterbury Tales* prefigure those of Fielding or of Smollett and that the poet's humour is itself a profoundly native affair. At a later stage in this volume we will be discussing the nature of a specifically London vision, but the argument may be anticipated by quoting some of Chaucer's words on his native city. He is said to have celebrated 'the citye of London that is to me so dere and sweete, on which I was forth growen; and more kindly love have I to that place than to any other in yerth'. The notion of Chaucer's 'Englishness' must also be set beside his attachment to a more local territory. He was born in the parish of St Martin in the Vintry; although he travelled throughout Europe in the course of his official duties, he returned to his dwelling above the city gate at Aldgate. It has often been said that, the more local and locally identifiable a writer, the more universal may be his or her vision. But what are we to make of the vision of Chaucer's Englishness? His diversity and variety are in this context significant, particularly in his ability to mingle pathos and parody, tragedy and irony. Another London visionary, Charles Dickens, called the mixed style, 'streaky well-cured bacon', and it has become a defining characteristic of the English imagination. The fellowship of the pilgrimage itself provides a variety of characters and humours, the miller and the knight, the parson and the pardoner, all of them adding to the image of a disparate nation. Where in Boccaccio only the aristocrats speak, in Chaucer the voices of the servants and the churls can plainly be heard. The romantic tale of Palamon and Arcite, spoken by the knight, is followed by the miller's tale of lechery and buffoonery:

> And up the wyndowe dide he hastily,
> And out his ers he putteth pryvely
> Over the buttok, to the haunche-bon;
> And therwith spak this clerk, this Absolon,
> 'Spek, sweete bryd, I noot nat where thou art.'
> This Nicholas anon leet fle a fart . . .

The lyrical dignity of 'The Man of Law's Tale' is immediately followed by the pantomime bravura of 'The Wife of Bath's Prologue'. The editors of *The Riverside Chaucer* have noted 'Chaucer's attempts . . . to forestall, even undercut, high pathos'[5] and, in 'The Merchant's Tale', the 'mixing of genres, styles, voices, and tones, of pagan and Christian elements, even of narrative levels'.[6] This was the style of London, and of England. It may also reflect Chaucer's own social being and his 'somewhat ambiguous position poised somewhere between the court . . . and the city and shifting in relation to those two poles'.[7] It may be that Chaucer's decision to combine 'high' and 'low' was a way of deliberately enhancing his claim for the novelty of English literature; nevertheless it was precisely this decision to mingle sacred and secular, romantic and real, which animated his English genius.

There is also the question of embarrassment. It is partly a matter of reticence. It lies in Chaucer's self-effacement, and in his oblique portrayal of himself as a bookish innocent abroad. It lies also in his detachment from his work. Of one unusually obscene narrative Chaucer writes:

> And therfore, whoso list it nat yheere,
> Turne over the leef and chese another tale . . .

Nikolaus Pevsner noted the same quality in the work of Hogarth and suggested that this 'oddly detached attitude in an artist to his own creation, this seeming lack of compulsion, is English'.[8] It partly represents the risk of seeming superior, or of expressing too much enthusiasm for one's work, but for Pevsner it was deeply implicated in a deliberately self-conscious method of working. It is present in Chaucer's highly sophisticated employment of various and different styles for each of the Canterbury narratives. This has been termed the 'commonwealth of style' at once 'eclectic and low-key'.[9] It is present, too, in what one biographer has called the 'apparent tentativeness' of Chaucerian style 'like an embarrassed giggle, that response to grandeur which takes refuge in off-handed irony and levity'.[10] The detachment of William Shakespeare from his own creation, as well as his consistent note of scepticism, has been well documented; there can really be no better evidence of the dramatist's detachment than in his willingness to allow his work to remain unexamined and uncollected until after his death. It has also been noticed in the 'detachment of the English eighteenth-century portrait',[11] characterised by restraint and understatement. In the twelfth chapter of *Emma* Jane Austen anatomises 'the true English style' as one 'burying under a calmness that seemed all but indifference, the real attachment'.

That is perhaps why the American essayist Ralph Waldo Emerson described English taciturnity as endemic for 'six or seven hundred years'. Pevsner lists other observations of a similar nature. Muralt, a Swiss traveller, described the English in the late seventeenth century as 'taciturn, obstinate' while in 1740 the Abbé Leblanc noted them to be 'naturally inclined to silence'. It lies in that absence of overpowering feeling which is so noticeable in *The Canterbury Tales* where the very mixture of 'high' and 'low', reverential truth and domestic detail, militates against any grand or noble statement. William Morris recognised it in the English landscape, too, where there is 'not much space for swelling into hugeness . . . no great wastes overwhelming in their dreariness . . . all is measured, mingled, varied, gliding easily one thing into another' like Chaucer's language itself where its various elements commingle and flow together.

This reticence may of course have its origins in the fierce protectiveness and self-defensiveness of the Anglo-Saxons, combining fatalism and fortitude equally, but in Chaucer it is not unmixed with friendly irony. When he is accused of questioning female faithfulness in love, Alcestis defends him by saying that Chaucer's works were only translations and that in any case he wrote 'Of innocence and nyste what he seyde'. He did not understand what he was saying, in other words, and this native reluctance openly to profess sentiments of love appears in *Troilus and Criseyde* where he declines any authorial role in the developing love-tragedy: 'Men seyn – I not – that she yaf hym hir herte.' But this calculated naivety can work its own enchantment, so that, for example, the pilgrims on the road to Canterbury are larger than life or, rather, larger than the narrator's own life. It has been described as 'a yielding to the essential humanity of his companions, a sense of being overwhelmed by their worth, and success, and obvious talents'.[12]

Chaucer is not alone among his contemporaries in consistently underestimating or understating his own artistry. The poet of *Cursor Mundi* asks apologetically, 'Quat sal I sai yu lang sermoune?' The author of *The Prick of Conscience* pleads:

> . . . haf me excused at this tyme
> If yhe fynde defaut in the rhyme

Thomas Usk, a London scrivener executed for high treason in 1388, apologises that 'bycause that in conninge I am yong, and can yet but crepe, this leude A.B.C have I set in-to lerning', while of John Gower it has been written that 'in this unemphatic understatement he is typically English'.[13] The same attitude emerges in the most unexpected places; thus the state of instrumental music in England has plausibly been related to 'the continuing failure of the English to make their own contribution to virtuoso display',[14] which in turn is associated with the dislike of novelty and the pleasure taken in invisibility. All these forces work together, for good or ill. That most confessional of authors, Thomas De Quincey, himself professes to embarrassment at 'breaking through that delicate and honourable reserve which, for the most part, restrains us from the public exposure of our own errors and infirmities'. His tone is redolent of his first meeting with William Wordsworth which, he stated, was marked by 'a peculiar embarrassment and penury of words'. There is the murmured voice of Sir Philip Sidney in *A Defence of Poesy*: 'I coniure you all, that have had the eville lucke to read this incke-wasting toy of mine . . .' When a critic writes of Sidney's contemporary, George Gascoigne, as exercising 'an almost perverse delight in self-effacement',[15] we recognise that the irony is very deeply embedded. One literary historian has noted that in 'the English discursive tradition . . . irony is pervasive'.[16] It is a central fact.

CHAPTER 22

The foolish giant

The 'popular tradition of English religion', wrote Christopher Dawson in *The English Way*, a study of English piety, '. . . exists in its purest and most unadulterated form in the work of Langland'. *Piers the Plowman*, therefore, 'embodies the spiritual unity of the English people'. In the early twentieth century it was remarked of that poem, 'therein is to be found the key to the Englishness of today, with the same strength and weakness, the same humour, immutable'. Yet the vision of Langland is wholly Catholic in its range and intensity, wholly medieval in its preoccupations and implications. If it is essential to the nature of Englishness, of what precisely does that Englishness consist?

Piers the Plowman survives in a variety of extant versions, with three large clusters of significant composition known as the 'A', 'B' and 'C' texts. A dream-work manifesting ten dreams, two of which are dreams within dreams, it is an allegorical poem, in which the allegories are so filled with the living power of the imagination that they take on a pre-eminently human shape. In that respect they are tokens of the mystery of the Incarnation which is at the heart of fourteenth-century Catholicism. Piers the Plowman, the labouring farmer who becomes the type of Christ, is one of a number of active agents engaged in the redemption of humankind; yet he is so powerful a figure that on hearing his name 'Longe Wille' faints with joy. Long Will, or the narrator, is of course Langland himself who is the dreamer of dreams.

The poem contains all that is known about Langland, except for a stray memorandum. He was born in the early 1330s, possibly at Cleobury Mortimer in Shropshire, and was sent to a monastic school in Great Malvern; he became a 'clerk' or scholar there, and wrote one of the first versions of the poem while walking among the Malvern Hills. But then he travelled to London, where he was married; in that city he earned a precarious living as a chantry singer for men's souls and as a part-time copyist of legal documents. Like Blake and Dickens, More and Milton, he trod the streets of London and saw visions. He lived with his wife, Kit, and his daughter in a mean tenement along Cornhill; he must have been a noticeable figure, with his shaved head and his long tattered coat like that of a beggar. He was extremely tall and thus known to his neighbours by the nickname of 'Long Will'. He mentions Cock Lane and East Cheap, Tyburn and Shoreditch and Southwark, where he was often 'lost in daydreams of times past'; he was so distracted that he was held to be 'a fool' or 'a lorel', a good-for-nothing. He paid no respect to 'lordes or ladies' and refused to pay the customary obeisance, 'God loke yow, lordes!', to those in authority. He himself lived in extreme poverty, and in one of the versions of *Piers the Plowman* he dwells with unremitting clarity and charity upon the lives of the poor around him. He was also a dreamer, a visionary, who spent most of his life in working and reworking his one great poem of existence. Out of the wretchedness and violence of London came this great paean to love and grace. In this, too, he may become representative of the English imagination.

Piers the Plowman is an odd, sometimes awkward, poem packed with the accumulation of suffered experience and yet at the same time open and expansive; it seems to have been created out of some organic process, over a period of thirty years, and once more we may apply the architectural metaphor of a medieval cathedral. Like a cathedral, too, it harbours sacred symbol and grotesque or realistic detail, placing them so closely together that they are perhaps not to be distinguished. Subliminally, perhaps, they represent the same life. Here again is a mark of Langland's Englishness when 'Clarice of cokkeslane, and the clerke of the cherche', along with other frequenters of a tavern, 'grete sire glotoun, with a galoun ale. There was laughyng and louryng, and "let go the cuppe".' In this context William Langland has also been compared to William Hogarth, since he has the London artist's enthusiasm for the significant detail of urban life.

What Langland understood, he shared. He attacked rapacious clerics and mendacious friars; he spoke out for the ordinary people of England. All the laughter and savagery, all the intense emotionalism, of the old Catholic civilisation are contained within his poem. *Piers the Plowman* is written in the alliterative measure; it is as if Langland were adopting a common voice, an intensely vivid and dramatic cadence with effects not unlike those of the ribald or divine dialogues of the mystery plays which were performed along the same streets of London in which he walked. His style has been described as 'rude', or 'quaint', or 'homely', but its stubborn veracity is part of its imaginative strength.

Langland was dismissed as an eccentric, but much of the English genius resides in quixotic or quirky individuals who insist upon the truth of their independent vision in the face of almost universal derision. Langland rambles; he wanders into theological speculation and effortlessly mixes the comic and the sublime; he will list the various foodstuffs of the poor, and then has a vision of the crucified Christ. He will portray himself as a dazed and helpless narrator but will then introduce the characters of Do-well, Do-bet and Do-best, who migrated into the imagination of John Bunyan. His genius was in fact of such a thoroughly English kind that his work was immediately recognised for what it was; it has the deep momentum of the English imagination.

John Ball, 'the crazy priest of Kent' and incipient Leveller, was hanged, drawn and quartered in the summer of 1381 for writing a letter which contained these words: 'biddeth *Peres Plouyman* go his werke, and chastise well Hobbe the robber' which was taken as a signal for popular rebellion. Langland himself was no insurrectionary; he was thoroughly medieval in his inclinations, and believed in the theory if not in the practice of hierarchy. But his visionary spirit continued to dwell in the language and was, for example, a potent influence upon William Tyndale. To a learned scholar, Tyndale declared of his own English translation of the Bible, 'I will cause a boy that driveth the plough, shall know more of the scripture than thou dost'; the image of the ploughman, then, remains central to the idea of Englishness and the use of the English language. It may be appropriate to note here the presence in Tyndale's translation of his native Gloucestershire dialect, which was spoken only a few miles south of the Malvern Hills where Langland had once walked. These are local variations upon a common and overwhelming theme.

An analogy might be drawn between Langland and William Blake, or 'English Blake' as he called himself, who laboured upon his visionary allegories with as much stubborn assiduity as did Langland. When 'Long Will' questions Abraham, the dialogue is couched in words that might have been employed by Blake himself. '"In a somer ich seye hym", quath he, "as ich sat in my porche, where god cam goynge thre, ryght by my gate".' God came by my gate as I was sitting in my porch. And Blake said, 'I have conversed with the spiritual sun. I saw him on Primrose Hill.' He saw the devil climbing the staircase of his house in Hercules Street, Lambeth. Both poets shared a domestic, almost neighbourly, attitude towards eternity.

There are other resemblances which are significant in themselves but are also tokens of a greater continuity. The allegorical personages in *Piers the Plowman*, like the four Daughters of God and the 'loveli ladi' who is 'Holicherche', have the same strangeness and mystery as the Daughters of Albion or Vala in the prophetic books of Blake; great spiritual forces are clothed in human shape, eschewing all philosophical or abstract exegesis, and their actions are given dramatic expression. Blake, like Langland, was taken for a fool or a madman; but both were engaged in crafting a vision of the eternal world. There is, however, one significant difference. Langland created his vision in the context of Catholic England where all the associations and meanings were immediately comprehensible; Blake laboured in the post-Catholic world of the eighteenth century where allegory and spiritual meaning were devoid of any context at all. Hence his obscurity and his apparent irrelevance to the life around him. Yet both men possessed a pure lyric gift which flares out from time to time in passages of incomparable beauty, many of them associated with the sudden emergence of the natural world. 'By a wide wildernesse and by a wode side' walks Langland, where Blake avers that 'Thou hearest the Nightingale begin the Song of Spring'.

The two men are together in the landscape of the English imagination.

Solitaries and recusants

The great composers of the 16th century, Thomas Tallis and
William Byrd, were both unrepentant Roman Catholics

CHAPTER 23

The mysterious voice

The mystical tradition in England is of mysterious origin. It must in some way be associated with those early intimations of the supernatural in the land of mist and ghosts; English is the language of vision. In its fourteenth-century sense 'mystick' denotes spiritual allegory or symbolism, generally of a recondite nature, and is not directly related to the visionary imagination except as the token of a secret or hidden god. In the seventeenth century the term was applied to the nature of ancient or occult wisdom. 'Mysticism', in its now orthodox meaning, is also a seventeenth-century term. It is so powerful and persistent a force, however, that the medieval mystic Richard Rolle, among whose works belong *The Fire of Love* and *The Form of Life*, has been described as 'the true father of English literature' and worthy of a 'supreme place in the history of English prose'.[1] He died when Chaucer was a child and Wycliff a student at Oxford, but chronology is less important than ontology. What Rolle invokes is 'longis inspiracion of godd, vndirstandynge, wysdome and syghynge'. Rolle turned from Latin to English in the last ten years of his life, as if he were returning to the source of his inspiration; at the end he was travelling back to the beginning, and in his native speech celebrating the longings and aspirations that made him both hermit and visionary. If we cannot use the term 'mystic' for Rolle, as an anachronism, then we may at least reintroduce the word 'solitari' for his condition. It is certainly appropriate that his English meditative works were addressed to contemplatives like himself, who sought in silence and solitude the presence of God. Here again is one of the curious features of the English imagination: all the great religious works of the medieval period were written by and for 'solitaries', where we see a native individualism in its most poignant and persuasive form. These were no monastic productions, only the work of individual recluses. Theirs is the unheard melody within English music.

There had been Anglo-Saxon hermits, celebrated in saints' lives and in popular legend, who were so characteristic of English Catholicism that in the sixteenth century Holinshed remarked: 'The heremeticall profession was onely allowed of in Britaine.' This is a pious exaggeration but it contains an important truth. One of the first prose works in Middle English, written in the late twelfth century, is known as the *Ancrene Riwle* or *Ancrene Wisse*; it is a manual of living for three female recluses who lived in 'cells' a few miles from Wigmore Abbey in Herefordshire.

It is an interesting work in many respects, not least for its erudition and for its incorporation of French 'romance' elements within an overwhelmingly pious treatise. Like burgeoning Middle English itself, which in its exuberance manifests Latin and French influences as well as Anglo-Saxon repetition and alliteration, the narrative is of mixed tone. Female recluses were considered to be no longer of this world; the Mass for the Dead was celebrated before the anchorite was led in procession to her cell, whereupon all the ceremonies of the Burial Office were performed including the scattering of earth. She then lay prostrate upon her 'bier' before being pronounced dead to the world. Yet the *Ancrene Wisse* is a moderate and gentle text, filled with the 'sweetness' which has always been considered characteristic of English spirituality. It contains no ostentation or regimentation, and it is quite without extravagant piety; it is factual, intimate and domestic. There is an account of a child being comforted when his parent whips the object that hurt him, and of the way a man will tie a knot in his belt to remind him of a service he has promised to perform. Moderation is to be observed in penitential exercises, since the law of love is more important than the rigours of penance; you must pray, but you must also eat and dress properly. This shrewdness or practicality is wholly consistent with the great themes of English spirituality, and may even be said to characterise it.

So it is that 'moderation' and 'a robust note of common sense' can be attributed to the mystical writings of Richard Rolle,[2] who in his solitary state chanted the song of divine love. He was in many respects eccentric, and at the beginning of his devotional life was considered by many to be mad, but the workings of the English imagination are to be found in lives as well as in letters. He was born at Thornton Dale near Pickering in Yorkshire, around the year 1300, and at the age of thirteen or fourteen was enrolled at Oxford University. He did not complete the course of seven years' study but instead, in his own words translated from the Latin, 'longed for the sweet delights of eternity'. He returned home, where above all else he desired the life of a hermit. So he asked his sister to meet him in an adjacent wood and bring with her two of her 'over-dresses', one white and one grey, as well as their father's rain-

(*Top left*) 'Carpet' page, from the Lindisfarne Gospel; (*right*) King David with musicians. The art of manuscript illumination is the glory of the Anglo-Saxon period, while the geometric intricacy of its lines, borders and patterns is also exemplified by such artefacts as the shoulder clasp found in the Sutton Hoo burial site (*below*).

(*Left*) Anglo-Saxon attitudes: King Edgar, illuminated manuscript of the 10th century; and (*below*) 'Driven by the Spirit into Wilderness', panel from the 20th-century Christ in the Wilderness series by Stanley Spencer.

(*Below left*) 'Twas brillig, and the slithy toves did gyre and gimble in the wabe.' Lewis Carroll's lyric *Jabberwocky* (*Through the Looking Glass*) is a parody of Old English verse. (*Below right*) Sir Ian McKellen in the 2001 film of 'Lord of the Rings'. J. R. R. Tolkien's imagination was first stirred by the strange beauty of 'Ancient English' poetry.

(*Above*) 'Event on the Downs' by Paul Nash.
'There is a path that leads through English literature.'
(*Below*) 'Seascape Study with Rainclouds' by John Constable.
'English fiction is drenched in rain.'

The nave of Durham Cathedral.
'The rulers of Britain knew that there was power in stone.'

'The Wilton Diptych':
an example of typically English
'mystical dreaminess of mood'.

'Canterbury Tales': illuminated initial,
with a portrait of Geoffrey Chaucer,
'the worshipful father' of 'our englissh'.

In medieval times,
the English were noted
for their piety: St
Leonard with crozier
and manacles, St
Agnes or St Catherine
with sword and book,
two saints, from a
screen in St John's
Maddermarket,
Norwich.

An insular art: the English love of
the miniature. Nicholas Hilliard's
portrait of Elizabeth I (*left*) measures
two inches by one and seven-eighths
of an inch, while in Richard Dadd's
visionary painting, 'The Fairy Feller's
Master-Stroke' (*right*), the little
figures are grouped among hazel nuts.

The English visionary sensibility:
William Blake and Samuel Palmer were,
in their different ways, intent upon
discovering the spiritual lineaments of
the world. (*Facing page*) 'Daniel Delivered
out of Many Waters' by Blake and (*left*)
'A Hilly Scene' by Palmer.

The enduring magic of the legends of the Knights of the Round Table: 'Sir Galahad, Sir Bors and Sir Percival', romantic 19th-century painting by Dante Gabriel Rossetti, and 'Gawain', dramatic 20th-century opera by Harrison Birtwistle, in which a severed head continues to sing.

hood; on their encounter he clothed himself in the white dress, cut off the sleeves of the grey dress and donned that before putting on his father's hood. It says much for the power of the visual and dramatic imagination that he instantly became the 'figure' or 'type' of the hermit. The sister cried out, 'My brother is mad! My brother is mad!' – whereupon, according to one hagiographical account, 'he drove her from him with threats, and fled at once without delay'. He eventually found refuge in the house of a local landowner where he became hermit in residence with his own 'cell' in the grounds. His patrons would bring visitors to him, for their gratification or edification, and on one occasion 'he proceeded to give them excellent exhortations while at the same time never ceasing his writing – and all the while what he was writing was not the same as what he was speaking'. He eventually left this refuge and began a wandering ministry, before settling down as a recluse in the county of Richmond where he acquired a reputation for sanctity and for the power of healing. One commentator has suggested that he was always possessed by the landscape of his childhood, that of the North Yorkshire moors and marshes, and has compared him with the Brontë sisters.[3] There is indeed the same fervour, the same expansive longings, and the same musical cadence within his writing.

He wrote originally in Latin, but his prose is imbued with a powerful native and alliterative spirit: *'fervebunt fetentes formidine futura; formosus et fortis in feno falluntur . . .'* When he returned to writing in English in the latter years of his life, he employed an idiom no less powerful and idiosyncratic. 'To me it semys', he wrote, 'that contemplacion is Ioyfull songe of godis lufe takyn in mynde, with swetnes of aungell louynge.' The words 'sweetness' and 'song' are never far from his lips in a prose filled with polyphony, so that his readers may feel a 'swetnes in thaire hert of the lufe withouten ende'. In his solitude he finds a language of praise and joyfulness, as if in the silence he could hear English music. His metaphor and his practice are of speech becoming song, the spoken words turning into poetry, as the soul is irradiated so strongly by the fire of love that 'he or scho that feles it, that has it, and that loves God, syngand tharwyth'. Once more the 'sweetness' of English spirituality is celebrated, in a delicate line which hovers between poetry and prose. The line of English melody runs continually so that when Richard Rolle writes, 'My hert, when sal it brest for lufe? Than languyst I na mare', he anticipates the tone and cadence of George Herbert's 'You must sit down, sayes Love, and taste my meat: So I did sit and eat'. In *The Oxford Book of English Mystical*

Verse only four pages separate Richard Rolle from John Donne and the great seventeenth-century religious poets, providing textual evidence of continuity. When Rolle writes 'I stand in still mowrnyng', in motionless sorrow, he anticipates T. S. Eliot's 'still and still moving', as if the cadence of English music were itself motionless and continuous.

If the music of Rolle is characteristic, it simply reflects his spirituality. It has been described as affective individualism, marked by a 'resolutely anti-intellectual character'.[4] Thus, in his addresses to other solitaries, he avoids scholastic dogma and formal theology; he avoids, too, the penitential rigours of extreme pietism in favour of modest and moderate admonitions. His tendency is, if anything, towards dramatic re-enactment as if the spirit of the mystery play were abroad. With 'the cros heuy & huge & so hard trust upon thi bak, that thou art cruyschid to hepe & schrinkist ther-vndir' we are led into the scene of the Crucifixion as by a guide. The practical event is more important than theological speculation, since 'luf es hard as hel'.

There are hundreds of extant manuscripts of Rolle's spiritual writings; he was venerated as a saint, although he was never canonised, and his cell in Pickering became the object of pilgrimage. Yet if his holiness has faded, his importance has not. He established a tradition, and a tone, which encompasses the work of Traherne and of Herbert, of Crashaw and of Donne, of Vaughan and of Eliot.

Continuity is also to be found with the work of another medieval solitary, Walter Hilton, whose treatise on the stages of contemplative union with God has an image of music which is close to that of Rolle. The physical body is 'bot as an instrument and a trumpe of the soule, in the whilke the sowle blowith swete notes of gostly louynges to Iesu'. It is an English music located beyond time in the mystic's experience of eternity. Yet if there is one more significant image within the work of Walter Hilton, it is that of the journey or pilgrimage. It is an ancient topos, of course, but Hilton is the first to employ it extensively in English as a metaphor for spiritual enlightenment. He describes the dangerous and laborious journey of a pilgrim to Jerusalem, talking to others along the way, beset by evil spirits, resisting temptations, until he reaches his destination. It is hard not to recognise the resemblances between Hilton's account and that of Bunyan in *The Pilgrim's Progress*. In Hilton's narrative the soul or pilgrim glimpses his destination in 'smale sodeyn liytinges that glideren out thurgh smale caues fro that citee', while Bunyan's Pilgrim is greeted outside the same city by 'Shining Men' or 'Shining Ones'; the space of three hundred years, between Hilton and Bunyan, vanishes in a moment. It is the moment, as small as a nut or a grain of sand, that according to Blake 'Satan cannot find'. It contains the living imagination.

It has sometimes been suggested that Walter Hilton also composed the mystical treatise known as *The Cloud of Unknowing*, although the attribution is in dispute. Yet that treatise shares, with the texts of other English mystics, a distaste for the formal organisation of the devotional life; the narrator believes that he writes childishly and, like Chaucer, casts himself as the simpleton. It is a very English device. His style is direct and practical with the emphasis upon plain speaking. 'Bot now thou askest me what is that thing. I schal telle thee what I mene that it is.' His exhortations use domestic and familiar images which, together with his 'humorously shrewd observations',[5] allow a great intimacy of address. The 'good gracyous God' is as healthful and as 'plat & pleyn as a plastre'. There are occasions, however, when the author strikes a more plangent note; we might then be in the company of John Donne or Gerard Manley Hopkins. 'Look up now,' he demands, 'weike wreche, & see what thou arte. What arte thou, & what has thou deserved . . .' It is the same music.

CHAPTER 24

The inheritance

The term 'medieval' was not coined until the early nineteenth century, anticipating the strong affinities between Victorian sensibilities and the earlier Catholic civilisation, but the presence of the 'old faith' never did wholly fade. How could its spirit be exorcised when the language itself was formed in the eleventh and twelfth centuries? If we wish to follow the traces of a Catholic culture, we need only examine the words and cadences of written literature. The metric variations in medieval religious verse such as 'Conduct of Life' and 'The Whole Duty of Man', from the twelfth century, were described by Samuel Johnson as containing 'the rudiments of our present lyrick'. The prosody of versified saints' lives in *The South English Legendary* employs 'verse patterns later found in [Coleridge's] *The Ancient Mariner*'[1] so that the theme of spiritual redemption in the late eighteenth-century poem is maintained by the ancient cadence itself. The consonance is also a form of resonance, whereby the old spiritual life of the language is harboured in contemporary settings. That inheritance may work in more elusive ways, also, with the physical horrors associated with the legends of martyred saints 'providing the authentic frisson that Gothic novels later developed'.[2]

It is difficult to know whether an interest in the medieval period represents an interest in medieval Catholicism also. There is evidence of a deep spiritual continuity, but that must be balanced against the fervour of Nonconformism and the moderate compromises of the Anglican settlement; one of the consequences of that moderation, for example, lay in the end of affective piety in favour of a more measured devotion to Christ the Redeemer rather than to Christ the Sufferer. The mysteries of the Passion, and the annual celebration of it, were replaced by the individual exigencies of conscience and the private path towards salvation. The dramas of popular faith were gradually displaced by the plainness of orthodox worship; just as the churches were stripped of their paintings and images, so the cults of the Virgin and the saints were abandoned in favour of attention to the translated words of the New Testament.

Shakespeare does invoke, however, the Catholic doctrine of

purgatorial fires in *Hamlet*. Thomas Carlyle, the great intuitive historical mind of the nineteenth century, described Shakespeare's work, and the civilisation that sustained it, 'as the outcome and flowerage of all which had preceded it . . . attributable to the Catholicism of the Middle Ages'. It could not be otherwise; the chronology allows no other conclusion. A more dramatic example, if the phrase may be allowed in this context, can be found in the life of one of Shakespeare's contemporaries. John Donne, who preached at St Paul's Cross as dean of the cathedral, was a convert from Roman Catholicism. His own brother, a more steady Catholic, was imprisoned in 1593 and died in incarceration; the priest discovered with him was given the ritual execution of disembowelling and hanging. The nature of that death emphasises the mortal peril in which many Catholics found themselves after the Reformation; they were deemed to be traitors as well as heretics, servants of a foreign power and corrupters of the state. They were to be hunted down, imprisoned or executed – just as the Catholic authorities had hunted down Lutherans or 'new men' before the Reformation.

The penalties imposed upon Donne's clandestine faith must have deeply oppressed his childhood and youth – he remained a Catholic until his early twenties – and this may help to account for the anxiety and uncertainty infused within his poems. One critic has suggested that Donne's 'habits of thought remain Catholic when he feels himself threatened'[3] and that his *Holy Sonnets* are striated by Catholic devotion culled especially from the Advent Offices and the Hours of the Blessed Virgin. The conclusion may be, then, that his poems are 'the work of a man who has renounced a religion to some manifestations of which he is still, at a profound level, attached'.[4] That might almost be translated into a description of early seventeenth-century English culture in general.

Donne's theatricality, and his metaphors of power, might be adduced here as further evidence of his attachment. His conflation of sacred and secular love recalls the mingling of courtly love and religious fervour in Catholic England. When De Quincey refers to Donne as a rhetorician rather than a poet, he is referring to that earlier tradition. Donne's antitheses, when two opposed ideas are yoked violently together, may in turn be a token of his own divided and divisive religious sensibility. They are part of the morbid intensity of his nature. It is perhaps not unexpected, therefore, that his poems circulated only in manuscript until after his death.

The author of *English Spirituality* has remarked that between the fifteenth and seventeenth centuries, despite the fissure of the Reformation, a spiritual tradition was maintained. Between Margery Kempe and John Donne, between Julian of Norwich and George Herbert, there was 'the same living stream, the same lineage';[5] the religious prose and poetry of the seventeenth century 'grew directly from fourteenth-century doctrine' so that the 'Caroline divines continue and develop this tradition'.[6] George Herbert's work, albeit expressive of a life of ill health and retirement, has all the serenity of the early mystics. It may seem curious that Protestant devotion and expression should spring directly from medieval Catholicism, but it is part of a larger continuity. One of the arguments of this book is that a native spirit persists through time and circumstance, all the more powerful for being generally unacknowledged.

Anecdotal evidence in any case suggests that a Catholic sensibility did not wholly disappear in the centuries subsequent to the Reformation; John Milton's family were Catholic, and it has been supposed that William Shakespeare's father was a Catholic recusant. The great composers of the sixteenth century, William Byrd and Thomas Tallis, were both unreformed Roman Catholics. In turn their plangent English music of loss affected twentieth-century English composers such as Frederick Delius, Ralph Vaughan Williams and Peter Warlock; Vaughan Williams's *Job* and Warlock's *Corpus Christi Carol* are, in particular, evidence of a strong religious sensibility even if it is expressed as 'a plaintive liquescent chromatic harmony of unutterable desolation'.[7] Is it advancing too incautiously to suggest that the chromatic harmonies attendant upon transition and loss, so central to the genius of English music, are affected by the work of those sixteenth-century English composers languishing in internal exile?

Here may be mentioned the Roman Catholicism of Edward Elgar whose declaration of faith in *The Dream of Gerontius*, 'Sanctus Fortis', is one of the most memorable and moving passages of twentieth-century music. All the yearning and nostalgia of Elgar's passionate nature lie somewhere within it, and the best commentary upon the entire oratorio comes from William Byrd's preface to his *Psalms, Sonnets, and Songs of Sadness and Piety* published in 1588; 'To sacred words . . . there is such a profound and hidden power that, to one thinking upon things divine and diligently and earnestly pondering upon them, all the fittest numbers occur and freely offer themselves to the world.'

In twentieth-century music, also, there has been an abiding interest in the nature of Catholic drama. Britten's opera, *Noye's Fludde,* was based upon a Chester mystery play and was first performed in a parish church in the summer of 1958; his canticle, *Abraham and Isaac,* was a setting of a miracle play from the same area. Peter Maxwell Davies's *Worldes Blis* was inspired by a thirteenth-century song. This consummation of modern and medieval may be found in Harrison Birtwistle's opera *Gawain,* based on the story of *Sir Gawain and the Green Knight,* which like its medieval counterpart renders the scenes of physical dismemberment, in one of which a severed head sings, 'comic . . . by their sheer theatricality'.[8]

John Dryden described the Catholic communion as the 'milkwhite hind, immortal and unchanged', but it is perhaps more significant that in *The Hind and the Panther* he chose to write a beast fable established upon medieval models. The real continuity lies in theme, cadence and form rather than in public professions of devotion. The Catholicism of Alexander Pope emerges forcibly in his self-created role as a social and political satirist, but more apposite is the fact that he chose to translate the poetry of Chaucer. As Hippolyte Taine attested of Pope's verse, 'the old imagination exists . . . nourished, as before, by oddities and contrasts . . . it needs a succession of expressive figures, unexpected and grinning, to pass before it . . . it prefers this coarse carnival to delicate insinuation'. The author of *The Dunciad,* in other words, possessed a Catholic imagination.

Thomas Chatterton's school in Bristol was built upon the ruins of a Carmelite convent, and so it is not inappropriate that in his Rowley poems he resurrected the world of medieval Catholicism. William Morris was described as possessing a 'medievalised mind and turn of thought', like so many of his contemporaries. From where else did Tennyson's *The Idylls of the King* emerge? It is a question of affinity.

Throughout this study there will be signs and tokens of what Hippolyte Taine called 'the old imagination' – whether in the music-hall or in the pantomime, in the writings of Tolkien or the novels of Anthony Burgess, in the tradition of 'magic realism' in English fiction or in the paintings of Graham Sutherland. The allegories and bestiaries of the medieval English imagination re-emerge some centuries later in George Orwell's *Animal Farm* as well as in the beast fables of Beatrix Potter and A. A. Milne. In similar fashion, the comic transvestism of the mystery plays continues to flourish in the contemporary pantomime.

Mummers' plays continued into the modern era, while the dancing of the mystery dramas was sustained in the 'jig' at the close of Tudor plays and the more ceremonial steps of the seventeenth-century masque.

No study of the English imagination can ignore the fact that the medieval English theatre was revived to striking effect in the twentieth century. A study of this curious phenomenon has suggested that 'more medieval drama has been produced in the twentieth century than in its own time' and in the closing decades of the last century there was 'a performance of almost every extant medieval text'.[9] The lacuna of five hundred years might as well not exist. The Catholic culture of fifteen hundred years could not wholly die. Its inheritance is buried just below the surface of our own time.

Women and silence

Mary Herbert, Countess of Pembroke, sister of Philip Sidney,
circa 1590. Miniature by Nicholas Hilliard

CHAPTER 25

The female religion

In 1907 Elizabeth Robins, an American-born novelist, declared: 'If I were a man, and cared to know the world I lived in, I almost think it would make me a shade uneasy – the weight of that long silence of one-half of the world.' The silence is that of the female.

In England, as in the rest of Europe, women were instructed in silence by the Church; by biblical dictate, they could not preach. Even after that Church had been reformed, the relationship between public speech and public obloquy was continually reaffirmed. In 1675 Richard Allestree composed a treatise entitled *The Ladies Calling* in which he remarked that 'this great indecency of loquacity in women' is 'a symptom of a loose, impotent soul, a kind of incontinence of the mind'. Thus it has been suggested that 'female silence' was a sign of 'female chastity'.[1] Female speech is by its very nature dangerous and lubricious. It partakes of the body, and indeed draws the lineaments of the body into language; that is why male novelists and dramatists enact female speech as a continuous flow of words which, in the mouths of Mistress Quickly and Mrs Malaprop and Mrs Nickleby and a thousand successors, has its rational elements subverted and discomposed. There were a thousand images, too, of prattling women in medieval and sixteenth-century drama. Female gossip, in English law, connoted subversion and wantonness; if a man called a woman a 'whore' he could defend himself by professing that he implied 'whore of her tongue' rather than 'whore of her body'. As one tract put it, 'More shall we see fall into sinne by speech than silence'. There was every reason, then, 'for construing a woman's closed mouth as a sign for that vaginal closure'[2] which rendered a woman's body the private property of her male partner.

Yet the silence itself is interesting; as Elizabeth Robins intimates, it might even be threatening. Silence might be the token of anger; it might be filled with resentment. It might be the silence of oblivion and of disregard, or what Virginia Woolf in an essay upon women's writing described as 'the accumulation of unrecorded life' as if the silence represented a negative energy. The silence might be fruitful, like the silence of the mystic or the visionary. It might be filled with the explored riches of the interior life. Yet more often than not silence was a token of exile and isolation.

The first Anglo-Saxon poems composed by a woman dwell upon these solitary themes. Tentatively entitled 'The Wife's Lament' and 'Wulf and Eadwacer', these poems might provide a suggestive introduction to subsequent women's writing in English. The female narrator in 'Wulf and Eadwacer' laments her separation from her lover in lines of plangent loss:

> *Thaet mon eathe tosliteth   thaette naefre gesomnad waes*
> *uncer giedd geador*

Or, in a contemporary version, 'that can easily be sundered which was never united, our mutual song'. 'The Wife's Lament' is similarly suffused with suffering experience:

> *Ich this giedd wrece   bi me ful geomorre*
> *mirre sylfe sith*

'I make this song of my deep unhappiness, of my own fate.' There has been much speculation about the male authorship of these poems, as if somehow there were no possibility of female Anglo-Saxon poets with access to scriptoria or writing materials. In fact the history and condition of Anglo-Saxon women, at least those of high birth, suggests precisely the opposite. 'The Wife' identifies herself as a woman and writes in the Old English feminine gender; it takes a peculiar illogic to ascribe the poem to a monk or male *scop*. If we enter the 'earth-hall' in which the Wife is compelled to dwell, we may find in the dust of that place a ring inscribed in the Anglo-Saxon manner 'A lady owns me. May he be cursed who steals me from her.'

The Wife laments the loss of her 'husband' or 'man' or 'friend' who has been forced by his kinsfolk to leave her; she is now living in a strange land, and has been banished to a 'barrow' or 'earth-cave' in a barren landscape. Throughout she emphasises her private circum-stances – 'I tell this story . . . I tell of my own experience' – where the pattern of feeling determines the formal shape of the elegy. As its editors have stated, events are narrated 'in an order which subordinates them to the dramatic expression of the woman's lament' as 'appro-priate to the flux of her feelings';[3] the use of parallelism and contrast, so much part of the Anglo-Saxon imagination, 'emphasises focal points in the woman's orientation of her feelings'.[4] One exemplary study of the subject, Christine Fell's *Women in Anglo-Saxon England*, has noticed 'the evidence of emotional effect' in both poems and has remarked that 'there is little enough of this kind of poetry in Old English',[5] which suggests a defining mood or tone. One literary historian has suggested that 'The Wife's Lament' indicates 'an exile from the centre of power',[6] which can be construed as masculine power; could not the whole threnody of desire and separation be part, then, of a more general anger and desolation?

It is not necessary to repeat the old commonplace of the female writer as the medium for 'feeling' rather than 'thought' (as if there were any true distinction between them), but the dramatic rendition of sorrow and the emphasis upon suffered experience in these two Old English poems are at least suggestive. The 'Wife' is also a traveller, albeit a reluctant one, who has settled in a strange land; subsequent narratives will confirm that the theme of exile and travel, whether mental or physical, is a constant feature of English women's writing.

The role and nature of women in Anglo-Saxon society were far more secure and far more powerful than in subsequent cultures. Before the Conquest of 1066, the pattern of female virtue consisted of wisdom, liberality and nobility; under the Anglo-Norman dispensation her qualities consisted principally of beauty and coquettishness. The Old English word 'hlaford' or lord could equally apply to a woman, and all the available evidence from Anglo-Saxon England suggests that 'women were then more nearly the equal companions of their husbands and brothers than at any other period before the modern age'.[7] The status of the female had more practical applications, also. Within a marriage 'the finances are held to be the property of husband and wife, not of the husband only' and in the codes of Aethelbert 'a woman had the right to walk out of a marriage that did not please her'.[8] The penalty for fondling a woman's breasts was the large fine of sixpence.

It is not too difficult to find, therefore, the context for a female bard. In Old English, 'mann' could be used of both sexes. The word for fate in that language, 'wyrd', is a feminine noun which in a fragment of poetry is deemed to 'weave' the events of the world. It has its place within the two principal elements which determine Old English descriptions of the female, that of the 'peace-weaver' and that of the 'shield-maiden'. This is not some piece of antique lore merely. A central theme of this study has been one of unacknowledged continuity with the Anglo-Saxon past; this ancient dichotomy in the description of women, maintained by females as well as males, has deeply imbued the English sensibility. It is perhaps worth remarking, also, that one Old

English charm invokes the powers of '*eorthan modor*' or mother earth.

One of the 'shield-maidens' was Aethelflaed, '*famosissima regina Saxonum*', who according to William of Malmesbury 'protected her kinfolk and terrified aliens'; one of the 'peace-weavers' was Abbess Hilda who encouraged learning and devotion in her foundations at both Hartlepool and Whitby. It was customary for an abbess to administer the 'mixed' or 'double' houses of monks and nuns, perhaps as an atavistic remembrance of the period when the Germanic tribes worshipped a principal goddess. The nuns themselves, in foundations such as that of Barking, were widely noted for their learning and for their assiduous work in the areas of grammar, metrics and the holy scriptures. They were known, too, for their study 'of the historians and the entries of chroniclers'.[9] Their importance now lies, however, in an exemplary historical role connecting female identity and indeed female power with religion. It is a matter of historical resonance, echoing through the later careers of Margery Kempe and Christina Rossetti. One of the great students of the scriptures, albeit from a secular perspective, was Mary Ann Evans alias George Eliot; she translated David Friedrich Strauss's *Das Leben Jesu* into English as well as Feuerbach's disquisition upon Christianity. There is a real affinity between her and the Anglo-Saxon nuns who can be presumed to have been engaged in similar works of translation.

The extant manuscripts cannot now be distinguished by gender, but the work of an English nun named Hygebury has been identified. Two other nuns, Leoba and Berhtgyth, composed religious poetry and were equally renowned for their learning '*in liberali scientia*'.[10] Yet Berhtgyth's letters also 'reveal intense loneliness and a sense of isolation',[11] while on missionary work in Germany, which may suggest that the nuns were more willing or better prepared to evoke their private experience as well. The association between poetry and the life of the nun is in any case a potent one. Thus in the sixteenth century Aemilia Lanyer depicts herself 'as defender and celebrant of an imagined community of good women, sharply distinguished from male society and its evils'.[12]

The hagiographical tradition of female saints and martyrs is significant in this context; the first books about women, often written by women, emphasised their preternatural power of courage and endurance in the face of otherwise unendurable pain. These devotional lives were also read by women; the power of this communal activity may then be said to have coloured the later status of women as besieged and afflicted victims of predominantly male power. The visionary fervour of Mary Wollstonecraft, or of Emmeline and Sylvia Pankhurst, was perhaps in part inspired by latent folk-memories from the time of the Anglo-Saxons; it was a period, after all, when 'the inclination to hold women in reverence remained, and found expression in the readiness with which they revered women as saints'.[13] It is an invisible power of suggestion and association, comparable with the persistence of legend; it was reported that Hilda transformed the snakes along the Whitby coast into ammonites, and those same minerals are to this day popularly known by local people as 'snake stones'. The images persist.

The changed and inferior status of women in England after the Conquest materially affected their literary expression, and scholars have long noticed the paucity of women's writing in Middle English; what literature there is, is of a devotional nature. Two or three lives of saints, in Anglo-Norman, can be attributed to nuns; certain hagiographies are also dedicated to female patrons, whether sacred or secular. Two of these lives are of St Audrey and of St Catherine, and we may place them within the context of an audience of 'noble' women who journeyed easily from a lay state to a spiritual vocation. The narratives define what has been described as 'career virginity', where the refusal of marriage or of an inheritance leads ineluctably to a religious commitment and to a life among other women; it was a way of eschewing male power and of avoiding the network of male associations and references that characterised a feudal state. The theme of rejection, however carefully veiled (in more than one sense), is of enormous consequence in the continual struggle of the female voice to be heard.

We may note here the formidable presence of Marie de France who, despite the evidence of her name, was an Anglo-Norman poet living in England. She is best known for her *lais*, over half of which concern the plight of women married to men whom they do not admire or reverence; they are caught 'in unhappy and unpromising marriages', while also restrained by 'chivalric demands and ambitions'.[14] In other circumstances they might have become anchorites or nuns, sustained by a diet of hagiographical literature, but Marie de France's characters are filled with passionate sentiment. She is concerned 'with the inner life of the emotions',[15] exemplified in her own case with the words of the prologue in the *lais*:

Who ever has received knowledge
and eloquence in speech from God
should not be silent or conceal it,
but demonstrate it willingly[16]

In the context of the late twelfth century, this is a bold declaration. Marie's themes are equally significant, of course, dwelling upon 'women's need to free themselves, by the mind and will, from oppressive situations'.[17] She might almost be anticipating Jane Austen and Charlotte Brontë who, despite their diverging genius, would surely have recognised a common maternity. Marie de France is concerned, too, with 'problems of daily reality' and with 'the truth that is revealed by experience'[18] rather than that relayed by authoritative tradition or masculine chivalric ideals. In that sense her work may be deemed characteristic.

One scholar of the early medieval period has suggested that the relative dearth of material is the result of the fact 'that each woman writer has to wield her pen as an experimenting individual rather than as the fully official inheritor of a tradition'.[19] This is not in itself a local problem; there never was a recognised or recognisable female 'tradition', so that individual female writers have had to discover it within themselves. They have always been isolated. Aphra Behn and Virginia Woolf are in that sense the true inheritors of a medieval dispensation. The absence of any imaginative line or bond – the fact that most female writers of the sixteenth and seventeenth centuries did not know the works that preceded them – may in part explain that recourse to living experience and to individual feeling which is characteristic of many later English women writers. It is not a question of female sensibility as opposed to male sense, but rather a necessary compensation for the absence of a written tradition.

Only in this context, therefore, can we comprehend the literature of female piety in the medieval period; it is predominantly a record of spiritual experience. The writings of Julian of Norwich and Margery Kempe are in that sense emblematic, particularly in their determination to celebrate the claims of bodily experience and physical sensation over doctrinal matters. The Wife of Bath, in Chaucer's poem, declares, 'By God! If wommen hadde writen stories'; to which Julian of Norwich replies, 'Botte for I am a woman, schulde I therfor leve that I schulde nought telle yow of the goodenesse of God?' When Julian explains to her readers, no doubt themselves predominantly female, that 'I am a womann, leued, febille and freylle', it ought to be recalled that her most notable contribution to medieval religious writing is her revival of the concept of God as the Mother and Christ as the mother of humankind. She invokes 'Mother Jesus' vouchsafed in 'tendernes of love'. It has been suggested that 'she developed the theology of divine motherhood far beyond any previous writer' in terms of initial creation, redemption and spiritual nourishment with the milk of grace.[20] The emphasis is once more upon the experience of loving and even, by implication, upon the experience of childbirth as the feminine version of Genesis. Private revelation and personal experience may thus be a substitute for the authority of the Church. In the case of Julian these more private sources of authority are extended and amplified by her own knowledge of the scriptures and of patristic literature; it has been demonstrated that she used her own translations of the Vulgate, and was well acquainted with all relevant Latin and vernacular writing. It has also been concluded that she was well versed in all the devices of rhetoric, and employed its *colores* to embellish her argument. Her favourite expedients include rhyme and alliteration, which in turn raise an interesting matter of inheritance.

It could be argued that the Anglo-Saxon respect and reverence for women are somehow emmeshed in Old English itself, and that by instinct or intuition certain female writers have recourse to alliteration as a measure of their original pre-eminence. What might be termed 'philogyny' can thus be seen as a measure of cadence as well as of sensibility. In her influential essay on women's literature, 'A Room of One's Own', Virginia Woolf has recourse to alliteration in her impassioned moments of meditation – 'that spot the size of a shilling'[21] which the sexes can discern in each other, a moment of stillness when a 'single leaf detached itself from the plane tree at the end of the street, and in that pause and suspension fell', and how sexist writing is 'doomed to death'. Alliteration is a formidable textual feature of *Wuthering Heights*, also, as, for example, in Cathy's invocation of 'woods and sounding water, and the whole world awake and wild with joy'. There is also a stern tactility in Emily Brontë's language which may not be unconnected to Anglo-Saxon origins. The name of Heathcliff itself is suggestive; Hareton and Catherine incorporate 'heart' and 'earth', which itself is the last word of the novel.[22] Woolf speculates upon 'the rhythmical order' of her perceptions, but it may represent some atavistic longing to be part of an earlier and more benign dispensation.

*

Another aspect of medieval women's literature may offer suggestive analogies. Julian of Norwich dictated her narrative to a willing amanuensis, and the pressure of speech lies behind her insistent cadences; in similar fashion the autobiography of Margery Kempe is conceived as an oral feat, with plentiful references to women's speech throughout it. She explains, for example, how the Abbess of Denny 'oftyntymys sent for the said creatur that sche xulde come to speke wyth hir and wyth hir sisterys'; Margery Kempe and Julian of Norwich spent several days in converse, 'for the ankres was expert in swech thyngys and good cownsel cowd yeuyn'. Julian's revelations were couched in the form of speech. In her desolation she was vouchsafed a vision of Jesus 'syttyng upon hir beddys syde' in the shape of a man clad in purple silk. 'Dowtyr,' he said, 'why hast thou forsakyn me, and I forsoke neuer the?' Once more the intimacy of address, and homeliness of detail, mark out a characteristic native spirituality; in Margery Kempe's spiritual journal there is none of the brooding plangency of Thomas à Kempis's *Imitatio Christi*, for example, but rather the unaffected and somewhat rambling narrative of a Norfolk gentle-woman. When she began to describe her experiences of spiritual love, her neighbours asked her: 'Why speke ye so of the myrth that is in Heuyn; ye know it not & ye have not be ther ne mor than we.' But from this time forward she became a loquacious pilgrim towards eternity; she spoke so volubly that certain preachers would not allow her in their churches. Others would not eat with her because she spoke of nothing but the gospels, and many accused her of being a charlatan too ostentatious in her avowals.

The Book of Margery Kempe, one of the first autobiographies in English, is devoted to the 'forme of her leuyng' or the form of her living in the world, where the circumstantial detail of the fourteenth century is manifested. The reader can hear the voices. When she left Canterbury Cathedral she was harassed by cat-calls – 'Thou xalt be brent, fals lollare!' You will be burned! On her devotional visit to Julian of Norwich, the recluse imparted to her these final words: 'I pray God grawnt you perseuerawns.' There are many 'Chaucerian' moments, by which is meant that strange but exhilarating conflation of the sacred and the secular, of piety and farce. She was, after all, both garrulous wife and mystic visionary, and in that respect she seems to have been as thoroughly English as Noah's Wife in the mystery plays. She held acerbic conversations with monks and bishops. She 'spak boldly and mytily' but saw Our Lord in all humbled and wounded creatures. She sat weeping in a poor woman's house, until the woman herself begged Margery to stop; at which moment Jesus whispered to her, 'Thys place is holy.' In the work of the female mystics, speech is revelation.

A scholar of the Paston letters largely composed in the fifteenth century has noted, of the female members of that family, 'even those who could not write were thoroughly articulate . . . for the most part the language is manifestly the speech of the time, only organised and sometimes heightened a little'.[23] The description might equally well be applied to the novels of Fanny Burney, who was unique among writers of the late eighteenth century in creating a conversational argot. Her novels rely 'heavily on the power of speech to reveal character and class' and contain 'long stretches of dialogue'.[24] *The Oxford English Dictionary* lists no less than 114 additions first cited in her works – including 'dabble', 'gay-looking', 'unappeasable', 'undemurringly', 'unamusing', 'showable' and 'plain-sailing', all of which might be described as elements of eighteenth-century demotic. Her preoccupation with speech, therefore, manifests a concern for the texture and process of daily life.

The writings of Margery Kempe and Julian of Norwich are characterised by one great sustaining voice. The visionary experience allows occasion and place for the manifestation of a female sensibility; it is a sacred area where the privileges of the male hierarchy do not apply, and where female authority can plausibly be asserted. It is the context for the succession of female mystics and prophets, from Jane Lead to Joanna Southcott, who oppose themselves to the dispensations of male power. Jane Lead, the seventeenth-century Protestant mystic, was vouchsafed the sight of 'a Woman Cloathed with the Sun' who proclaimed, 'Behold me as thy Mother' – an apparition not unrelated to Julian's insistent invocations of God as the Mother. Lead gave precedence to the 'exploration of her inner life',[25] where the emphasis rests again upon the power of experience rather than upon the stages or levels of visionary meditation outlined by male mystics.

It has been estimated that in the period from 1649 to 1688 'well over half the texts published by women . . . were prophecies',[26] and there were very many female radicals or polemicists caught up in the religious controversies of that period. One of them, Margaret Fell Fox, reiterated one of the central claims – 'the Church of Christ is a Woman' – which springs directly from the texts of Julian. In historical and scholarly accounts of this female activity the name and example of

medieval women visionaries are continually invoked to suggest a line
of influence or inheritance. We are not far removed from the poetry of
Emily Brontë –

> God within my breast
> Almighty ever-present Deity!
> Life, that in me has rest
> As I undying Life, have power in Thee!

– where mystical experience has gone through the refining fire of her
fervent imagination. Or, as Jane Eyre puts it, 'As I saw them with my
spiritual eye, before I attempted to embody them . . .' The somewhat
patronising assumptions about female 'intuition' find their origin in the
visionary acts and writings of medieval and seventeenth-century
women. It was the claim of Dorothy Richardson, the great exponent of
a language formed by female perception, that women possessed the
faculty of prophecy. 'It's because they see the relation of things which
don't change,' she wrote, 'more than things which are always
changing.' It is a suggestive remark, implying a commitment to the
ground of being rather than the busyness of becoming, and is
complemented by Virginia Woolf's description of life as 'a luminous
halo, a semi-transparent envelope surrounding us from the beginning
of consciousness to the end'. This uterine light is not far removed from
Jane Lead's vision of the 'Woman Cloathed with the Sun' and suggests
a profound affinity between these otherwise quite different writers. It is
the vision of glowing maternity which Julian of Norwich also saw.

In this light we may return to the manifestations of religious verse
among female writers. In the fifteenth century is noted a hymn to the
Virgin written by 'an holy anchoress of Mansfield' and another hymn
attributed to Eleanor Percy, Duchess of Buckingham. It has been
speculated that certain other poems concerning the Mother of God,
particularly those in which she laments the death of her son, are
composed by women because they emphasise those inward themes of
loss and isolation which have been discovered in the female poetry
of the Anglo-Saxon period. It will become clear that the Reformation,
with its emphasis upon the guiding light of inner experience, lent
legitimacy and authority to the religious works of women, but of
course the connection between gender and piety was already well
established. The daughter of Thomas More, Margaret Roper, had been
thoroughly educated in the classical disciplines; yet her devotion was
such that she translated Erasmus's treatise upon the *Pater Noster* and

composed a devotional manual upon the *Four Last Things*. Fifteen such devotional works were written by women in the sixty years after 1545; it may not seem a considerable number but, in the context of the time, it is prolific and 'established the literary presence of women'[27] throughout the sixteenth century.

Many female prose-writers and poets from that period have been rescued from time's oblivion by recent scholarship, among them Katherine Parr, Anne Locke the martyr, Anne Askew who was sustained by the direct and powerful utterances of forebears such as Margery Kempe, and Anne Wheathill who is tentatively supposed to have possessed a 'feminine consciousness'[28] and who wrote: 'I cannot but lament, mourne and crie for helpe, as dooth a woman, whose time draweth neere to be delivered of hir child; for she can take no rest, till she be discharged of hir burthen.' It has been suggested that religious piety is 'the principal subject-matter of women's verse, the principal justification for women's writing and the best guarantee of a poetess's success for two hundred years'.[29] It is not a question of a 'feminine' sensibility, as promulgated in the nineteenth century and sustained by various scholarly guises into the present century; 'intuition' and 'sentiment' are not at odds with reason or doctrine, nor is religious devotion necessarily a displacement of 'emotion' and 'passion'. Women were as capable of writing treatises and sermons as were men. It is simply that for social and historical reasons their imaginative competence was deemed to be within the sphere of affective piety – in things unchanged, to use Dorothy Richardson's account, rather than in the changing world.

At this point we may embark upon a short journey. A medieval prelate was visiting the isolated cell of a female anchorite when he remarked that her great compassion and understanding were unusual in one who had no contact with the world. 'On the contrary,' she replied, 'I am always travelling.' She was indeed a mental traveller, with the same facility for venturing into distant places as the contemporaneous female mystics. Travel itself was a reality, rather than a metaphor, for other medieval women. If Julian of Norwich wandered through time and space in search of the divine vision, Margery Kempe engaged in more earthly pilgrimages to Jerusalem, Rome, Constantinople and Danzig. In that sense she is the forerunner of eminent women travellers who include Lady Hester Stanhope and Gertrude Bell. The journeys were fuelled by attitudes of discontent and sentiments of exclusion; the only way to escape a masculine world was, literally, to get away. The fervent contemplations of Julian of Norwich can be deemed modes of withdrawal, just as Margery Kempe's extensive travels are a sure token of her resentment at an English ecclesiastical polity which seemed designed to exclude or marginalise her.

There is another aspect to these journeys, however, which lies in the affirmation of individuality and individual experience. Many English women travellers have been noted for their apparent eccentricity of demeanour, Margery Kempe and Lady Hester Stanhope being practically indistinguishable in that respect. But this is only a sign both of their evident difference and of their desire not to be chastened or modified by male preconceptions. When Mary Wollstonecraft decided to travel within continental Europe she remarked: 'You know I am not born to tread in the beaten track'; when Lady Hester Stanhope embarked upon a journey which would lead her to a flamboyant exile in Turkey, she concluded: 'Go out of England I am determined.' Both of them derided the idea of feminine 'weakness' or powerlessness, and in a literal way demanded their liberty. The Wife of Bath was only one of the women who in Chaucer's narrative 'longen . . . to goon on pilgrimage'. It is appropriate, then, that Dorothy Richardson should entitle her twentieth-century fictional sequence *Pilgrimage*.

The most important female poet of the sixteenth century was undoubtedly Mary Sidney, Countess of Pembroke and sister of the more famous Philip. She created a space beside her illustrious sibling, and her growing mastery of English verse implied an assiduous pursuit of a literary career. It has been suggested that her goal was 'to extend the formal range of English lyric and to demonstrate the capacity of Elizabethan poetry to match the variety and flexibility of the French',[30] but it is important to note that she established her mastery in poetry of a Calvinist persuasion. This coincidence of female expression and religious devotion is further adumbrated by Aemilia Lanyer, perhaps best known as the putative 'dark lady' of Shakespeare's sonnets but with a more lasting claim upon the attention of posterity as the first English female poet to publish a substantial collection of her verse. In *Salve Deus Rex Judaeorum* she invokes an imagined community of good women and remarks upon what is

> . . . seldome seene
> A Womans writing of divinest things

The association between female creativity and 'divinest things' is clearly an assertion of worth rather than of incapacity before the more scholarly male. The various divisions within her completed work are entitled '1. The Passion of Christ. 2. Eves Apologie in defence of Women. 3. The Teares of the Daughters of Jerusalem. 4. The Salutation and Sorrow of the Virgine Marie'; the emphasis upon female virtuosity and piety can hardly be overlooked. Lanyer also composed nine dedicatory poems to various royal and noble women, thus confirming the volume's status as a female document. She asserts that 'it pleased our Lord and Saviour Jesus Christ, without the assistance of man . . . to be begotten of a woman, borne of a woman, nourished of a woman, obedient to a woman; and that he healed women, pardoned women, comforted women'. In her poem upon a community of women at 'the *Paradice* of Cookham', the estate belonging to the Countess of Cumberland, Lanyer seems in some instinctive manner to have been looking back at the communities of Anglo-Saxon nuns who were located in the same region of Berkshire. Cookham of course became the enchanted place of Stanley Spencer's imagination, where he envisioned both *The Nativity* and *Bridesmaids at Cana*. The connections run deep.

In sixteenth- and early seventeenth-century drama composed by women such as Joanna Lumley and Elizabeth Cary, the emphasis rests upon 'the spiritual heroism of their female characters, exalting the feminine archetype of the Christian soul'.[31] The same preoccupation exists among female pamphleteers and female autobiographers who explicitly aligned their sex with their religious experience; the standard comparisons are once again made with Margery Kempe, as the original of what has been called the 'forthright' woman. As Margaret Fell Fox puts it, in *Womens Speaking Justified* published in the calamitous year 1666, 'the Church of Christ is a Woman, and those that speak against the Womans speaking, speak against the Church of Christ, and the Seed of the Woman, which Seed is Christ'. The woeful events of 1666, together with the ferocious civil conflict which preceded them, may in fact have materially assisted the enterprise and pugnacity of female writers with an unstated presumption concerning the ills of the masculine world. We will notice a tone of barely restrained anger and frustration, not unconnected with subversion, in women's writing of this and a later date. Certainly the imperatives of silence and obedience, once enjoined upon women, were now scarcely honoured by those females whose formidable piety forced them into expression.

Mary Sidney's *Psalmes* is of course a translated work. Translation itself has been deemed to be an intrinsic feature of the English imagination, but the connection between translation and female literature is a peculiarly close one. It was generally considered to be a secondary activity, appropriate to women who could not be considered to have 'authored' a text without some prior fertilisation. It is inevitable that earlier literate nuns, under the direction of their abbess, would have translated portions of the sacred scriptures and passages of prayer for their less educated sisters. That is why Chaucer characterised his Second Nun as a translator. There was indeed in the medieval period an efflorescence of female translators who in their submissive role towards the authoritarian text may be said to have followed the injunctions of silence and obedience in a literary context. Their self-effacement may have disguised the fact that they were surreptitiously appropriating the authority of these texts, but in the period their activity was seen as akin to that of embroidery. In the sixteenth century, too, there was a 'great outpouring of translation'.[32] It has been estimated that one-third of the extant works by women are couched in this form. John Florio felt compelled to apologise for his translation of Montaigne on the presumption that 'all translations are reputed femall', but the remark obscures the real achievement. Mary Sidney's great task was to re-create the sacred literature of the psalms in the vernacular, thus asserting the capability and strength of the English language itself. The mode of translation was also an indirect means of establishing a tradition or at least a continuity of women's writing.

A renaissance

Edmund Spenser. Engraving by George Vertue, 1727

CHAPTER 26

But newly translated

Only half the story of the English imagination resides in England itself; the rest derives from continental sources. Allusions to the 'Renaissance' began to appear only in the 1840s, having been borrowed from the French, and from the historian Michelet in particular; it would be unwise, in any case, to set any specific date for the cultivation of continental European learning in England. It began in the years of the Roman settlement, and was considerably enlarged by the Anglo-Saxons. There has never been a time, in fact, when European scholarship and cultivation did not materially affect the fabric of English life. Boccaccio described the English as tardy in classical studies – '*studiis tardi*' – but by the fifteenth century the introduction of the 'new learning', largely based upon Latin translations of Greek originals, was effected by Humphrey, Duke of Gloucester and brother of Henry V. The assertion of national sovereignty did not impede the development of an international movement in letters.

London became a centre of learning, catholic in every sense, and even in the early fourteenth century there are records of St Paul's almonry school holding volumes of Ovid, Horace and Virgil. The central pathway of learning, therefore, was between England and Italy; from Rome and Florence and Ferrara came newly discovered or newly translated classical texts. There were English scholars and theologians, also, who studied Greek in an effort to reclaim the learning of Europe. An analogy might be made with English domestic architecture when, in the middle of the fifteenth century, the number of windows increased so that 'almost for the first time sunlight is allowed to pour into the house'.[1]

And so the first English humanists – among them William Grocyn, Thomas Linacre and John Colet – travelled abroad in search of the purer light of learning. They read Aristotle and Plato in the original, in an effort to imbibe the language of the ancients without the intermediaries of medieval scholastic or encyclopaedic commentaries. Colet established a new school in the precincts of St Paul's, and there instituted a curriculum largely under the influence of the Dutch humanist Erasmus; Erasmus himself visited London, claiming that it harboured more genuine scholars than Italy itself, and took up a post as Professor of Greek at Cambridge. Just as the proponents of the 'new learning' wished to restore classical texts to their original purity, by a more rigorous approach to matters of grammar, so they wished to renovate the Catholic Church by removing its scholastic and super-stitious accretions. Erasmus and Colet in turn were the mentors and companions of Thomas More who was the first man to translate the work of the Greek satirist, Lucian, into English and who wrote his treatise, *Utopia*, in Latin for the benefit of a European community of scholars.

England was therefore in the advance guard of a new European civilisation. By introducing Greek and Latin authors as models for imitation and composition the proponents of the new learning, whether at St Paul's School or at Cambridge University, were shaping English sensibility along the lines of classical European scholarship. This in turn was to have a profound effect upon many generations of English pupils and undergraduates, who became aware of ancient Greek and Roman history before they were acquainted with its English variant, and who learned how to write verse in those ancient tongues before they ever ventured into the English language. When Erasmus suggested that the English schoolmaster should instruct his pupils in Cicero and in Ovid, and that his 'themes be selected from Homer, Sophocles, Euripides, Virgil or even sometimes from histories', we may observe that what became a peculiarly English education was in fact based upon the precepts of a classical European civilisation. Milton may have considered the English to be the chosen nation, but he believed Europe to be his home. He denounced a king in Latin, so that Europe might hear. When we remember, too, that Spenser and Sidney imbibed their neo-Platonism from its sources in fifteenth-century Italy, and that Spenser in particular derived his style from Erasmus's lessons upon *copia* or rich and abundant style, then we may recognise that the origins of the English imagination are not wholly to be found in England itself. Christopher Wren remarked in 1694 'that our English Artists are dull enough at Inventions but when once a foreigne patterne is sett, they imitate so well that commonly they exceed the originall'. It is a shrewd observation, and may explain why the great English poets have excelled at translation. A German art historian, Hans Swarzenski, has in turn noted that 'English art needed repeated stimulation from abroad to remain productive and creatively alive', as if the national genius were not strong enough to exist upon its own resources. This may account for the intrinsic tone of melancholy noticed by others. Yet it may also be the cause of humour. In *The Unfortunate Traveller*, Thomas Nashe remarks that 'I, being a youth of the English cut . . . imitated four or five sundry nations in my attire at once'. In *The Merchant of Venice* a 'young baron of England' is depicted thus: 'I think he bought his doublet in Italy, his round hose in France, his bonnet in Germany, and his behaviour everywhere'.

England has in fact relied upon translation to nourish its native genius. The Anglo-Saxon renderings of Augustine and Boethius are only the beginnings of a process which included Chaucer and Malory and Wycliff. Ezra Pound, a writer whose own true gift lay not in self-expression but in translation, remarked that after the Anglo-Saxon example 'English literature lives on translation, it is fed by translation; every new exuberance, every new heave is stimulated by translations, every allegedly great age is an age of translations, beginning with Geoffrey Chaucer . . .'[2] Here is an important truth. For many centuries, in fact, translation itself was the characteristic activity of the English imagination. In John Donne's meditations it even becomes a metaphor for the sacred world. 'All mankind is of one *Author*, and is one *volume*; when one Man dies, one *Chapter* is not *torne* out of the *booke*, but *translated* into a better *language* . . . *God's* hand is in every *translation*; and his hand shall binde up all our scattered leaves againe, for that *Librarie* where every *booke* shall lie open to one another.' Before the twentieth century every serious poet, or at least every poet who wished to be considered as serious, attempted translation as a significant and necessary art. These poets were, in truth, creating new works of art. It might even be claimed that the English imagination most successfully conveyed itself through the medium of translation; it stimulated fresh creation and brought renewed life into the language. Thomas Wyatt translated Petrarch and Marlowe translated Ovid, Jonson translated Catullus and Milton translated Horace, Dryden translated Virgil and Pope translated Homer, Congreve translated from the Greek and Johnson from the Latin, Shelley translated Plato and Tennyson translated Homer. The references could be multiplied indefinitely.

The practitioners of this art argued over the relative merits of metaphrase (direct word-for-word translation), paraphrase (a freer rendition) and imitation (a looser transcription in a modern setting). Of the last John Denham wrote, in 1667: 'If Virgil must needs speak English, it were fit he should speake not only as a man of this Nation, but as a Man of this Age.' Perhaps the greatest artist of translation,

John Dryden, believed that imitation consisted in 'taking only some general hints from the original, to run division on the ground work as he pleases'. That is why Dryden himself preferred paraphrase, where the translator remained faithful to the purport and sense of the original without exact copying. The technique is suggested by Ben Jonson in *The Poetaster* when he describes the ability of the true poet 'to convert the substance, ór riches of another poet, to his own use . . . to draw forth out of the best and choicest flowers with the bee, and turn all into honey, work it into one relish and savour: make our imitation sweet: observe how the best writers have imitated, and follow them'. In one sense this practice continued the medieval traditions of authorship, when the individual maker bowed in humility and reverence before the established authorities and where *imitatio*, in the Platonic sense, was the condition of poetry itself.

Yet the art of translation has been modified over the centuries. In the sixteenth and seventeenth centuries there was a progressive loosening of texture, so that a certain awkward novelty in Elizabethan translation was replaced by smoothness and fluency. In the first wave of sixteenth-century translation, however, the whole wealth of antique learning flooded into the language. Among the histories, for example, were those of Sallust, Livy, Thucydides, Plutarch, Herodotus, Tacitus, Pliny, Xenophon and Suetonius; they remained the staple of classical scholarship into the twenty-first century. Among the poets were Ovid, Virgil, Homer, Juvenal, Lucretius, Seneca, Martial, Sappho, Horace, Lucian and Propertius. But if this activity represented an Elizabethan voyage of discovery, to use a metaphor current at the time, it was also a voyage of expropriation and colonisation. Of the Romans one translator, Philemon Holland, wrote: 'They conquered us by the dent of their sword, we have to conquer them by the dint of our pen.'

Translation also replicated splendour. Even in the middle of the sixteenth century it was possible for Roger Ascham to conclude that 'as for the Latin or greke tonge, every thynge is so excellentlly done in them that none could do better. In the Englysh tonge contrary every thinge in a maner so meanly, both for the matter and handelynge, that no man can do worse.' The opinion of Ascham may be over-emphatic, but it can at least be affirmed that the absorption of the Latin and Greek tongues did indeed modify whatever was 'meanly' in the native language. When Marlowe translated Ovid's *Elegies* he experimented with the abrupt tone and declamatory style of the dramatic monologue, with suggestive consequences for the rest of Tudor drama. The introduction of new forms, and an unfamiliar range of feeling, meant that the possibilities of the language were infinitely extended. Blank verse, that measure which more than any other seems to have moved with the English imagination, was introduced by the Earl of Surrey for his translation of the second and fourth books of Virgil's *Aeneid*; the unrhymed iambic pentameters represented a deliberate attempt to imitate the plangency and gravity of Virgil's hexameters, and in turn they were deployed by Marlowe who scorned the 'jigging veins of rhyming mother-wits'.

Some of these forms, newly translated, were wholly unfamiliar. Wyatt intoduced the epistolary satire into English, for example, through his translations of Horace; then, in his translations of Italian poetry, he deliberately introduced what the Italians knew as the 'magnificent' style. At a later date Milton adapted it within his graver and more sonorous music. Cowley encountered quite by chance the Greek odes of Pindar and 'having considered at leisure the height of his invention and the majesty of his style, he tried immediately to imitate it in English'. It is this urgency, this excitement, which characterised the role of the translator. In *The Shepheardes Calender* Spenser modelled his poetry on that of Virgil's *Eclogues* and the 'new poet', as Spenser was known, thus created 'a new vernacular language'.[3] From Ovid and Martial, through the medium of Nicholas Grimald and Christopher Marlowe, came the closed decasyllabic couplet which was to exert a powerful hold upon eighteenth-century poetry:

> In summer's heat, and mid-time of the day,
> To rest my limbs upon a bed I lay

It wrought a change in the English language as great as anything recorded in Ovid's *Metamorphoses*. When Joseph Hall copied Juvenal and Horace he declared:

> I first adventure: follow me who list,
> And be the second English satyrist

So satire, which would become an intrinsic aspect of the English imagination, was itself borrowed from European classicism. Thus fluency and dignity are compounded with novelty. Translation had become a means of conflating the tradition and the individual talent. The music of the past, to adapt Samuel Johnson's phrase, helps to tune the tongues of the present. It is the story of English literature itself.

In an edition of his works, published in 1735, Pope offered a commentary upon his translations of Horace. 'The occasion of my publishing these *Imitations* was the clamour raised by some of my *Epistles*. An answer from Horace was both more full, and of more dignity, than I could have made in my own person.' It is an interesting claim, to have adopted or borrowed another voice with such success that it is no longer Pope who writes. It may be called pastiche or imitation, but the practice is deeply congenial to the English imagination principally because it combines the twin tendencies towards historicism and theatricality; the self-effacing narrator can hide himself in another persona while at the same time displaying all the ornamentation and complexity of an old style made new.

This curious art of reincarnation was also maintained by John Dryden who, in the preface to one translation, remarked: 'I desire the false Criticks wou'd not always think that those thoughts are wholly mine, but that either they are secretly in the Poet, or may be fairly deduc'd by him.' This of course might be used simply as a device to divert attention or criticism; contemporary satires, in particular, might be open to perilous scrutiny if they were not presented as the work of Juvenal or Horace. It affords the opportunity of what is called 'plausible denial'. With the use of allusion and quotation, for example, the political situation of the 1640s could be depicted in the convex mirror of the Roman civil wars; indeed Thomas Hobbes discovered one of the causes of the war between Charles I and Cromwell in the excessive reading of classical history.

But there are also more powerful forces at work in the adoption of a persona through translation. It offers access to an earlier world or previous civilisation, so that writer and reader are both in their own time and somewhere other. Ben Jonson's drinking songs use sixteenth-century London taverns as the doorway into the banqueting halls of first-century Rome; the cities of the second and eighteenth centuries are mingled in Samuel Johnson's 'London', modelled upon Juvenal. It is a way of understanding the past by seeing it as part of the present, affording glimpses of a larger continuity which can be vouchsafed through language itself. Much can be discovered in the process. Entirely new moral structures, or structures of feeling, can emerge from an enriched and more complex language. New verse systems can lead ineluctably to new forms of perception; the 'pagan beauty' of the classics can create a new aesthetic, and the introduction of blank verse can help to fashion a new sensibility. The importation of the essay, the epigram and the satire directly fashioned the English virtues of individualism and scepticism.

It was believed at the time that newly translated works would create new knowledge. Nicholas Udall declared, in a work published in 1549, that 'a translator travailleth not to his own private commodity, but to the benefit and public use of his country'. Ten years earlier Richard Taverner translated Erasmus 'to the furtherance and adornment' of his country and its language. The culture was 'refined' in every sense. Sir Thomas Hoby's translation of Baldassare Castiglione's *The Book of the Courtier*, in 1561, was extraordinarily influential in the social and administrative life of the nation; it had been read in the original by Thomas Wyatt, Thomas Cromwell and Thomas More, among others, and its 'Englysshing' conferred upon it instant popularity. John Florio's translation of Montaigne's *Essays* in 1601 modified the consciousness of an entire age; it altered, in particular, the language of Shakespeare's plays. Thomas North's translation of Plutarch's *Lives of Famous Greeks and Romans* assisted Shakespeare's art, also, and furnished material for *Antony and Cleopatra*, *Julius Caesar* and *Coriolanus*. Thomas Hoby, in the preface to his translation of Castiglione, had encouraged 'profound learned men in the Greek and Latin' to under-take similar work so that 'wee alone of the world may not be still counted barbarous in our tongue, as time out of mind we have beene in our maners'.

The English language was indeed strengthened and rendered more resourceful. One of the merits of translation, for example, was its encouragement of variety in both syntax and vocabulary. When John Dryden suggested that Virgil 'maintains majesty in the midst of plain-ness' he was signalling his own ambitions for his translation, and so successful was he that in the process he managed to recast the native idiom. It appeared at the time to be an experiment, but two hundred years later Dryden was celebrated by Gerard Manley Hopkins for evincing 'the native thew and sinew of the English language'. Foreign sources and idioms were so thoroughly absorbed that they became 'native'. When Dryden put Virgil's *Georgics* into English it was remarked by Addison that the Roman poet 'has so raised the natural rudeness and simplicity of his subject with such a significance of expression, such a pomp of verse, such variety of transitions and such a solemn air in his reflections'; at the same time he was complimenting Dryden on his ability to bring these qualities into English verse. It has in fact been suggested that Dryden's greatest poetry does indeed lie within his translations, but that his genius lay in his conceiving of them as 'new' poems. Dryden's prose furnishes another example, in his ability to incorporate the Latin periodic sentence within the English language and thereby to produce an Augustan prose which was admired for its copiousness and grace; it became the standard for all eighteenth-century prose so that Englishness itself, the English of Addison and Steele, of Gibbon and of Johnson, was created out of a foreign idiom.

The power of translation is nowhere more evident than on the English stage. It would hardly be overstating the case, in fact, to suggest that English comedy and English tragedy, as we now understand them, sprang directly from the imitation of classical models. Once more the native genius, or what is generally taken to be a wholly native art, was created and maintained by a broadly European culture. The Latin tragedies of Seneca were first printed in 1474, with further editions some twenty years later. They were translated in the latter half of the sixteenth century. The first known performance of Senecan tragedy in England, that of the *Troades*, took place at Trinity Hall, Cambridge, in the winter of 1551; eight years later the first English translation of the play was published. Three years after that publication, in 1562, what is generally regarded as the first English tragedy, *Gorboduc*, was staged in the hall of the Inner Temple. The important point, in this medley of dates and places, is that *Gorboduc* itself is directly based upon the plays of Seneca; the line of English tragedy then continued with *Jocasta* and *Gismond of Salerne* which are also modelled upon Seneca in their fervent rhetoric and sensational effects. These Roman plays were profoundly congenial to the sixteenth-century English imagination, filled as they were with high sentence and bloody action, impassioned meditations upon fate and melodramatic turnings of the plot. Out of *Gorboduc* and *Jocasta* come Marlowe's *Tamburlaine* and the whole panoply of English tragedy; the basic five-act structure of the drama was also copied out of Seneca, and the plangent bombast of his monologues helped to colour the blank verse of the English stage. It is a direct example of the manner in which translation becomes a creative principle.

It is appropriate, therefore, that what by common consent is Marlowe's first play, *Dido Queen of Carthage*, should be in large part a dramatic transcription of Virgil's *Aeneid*; that *Tamburlaine* relies upon a translated life of that ruler by Petrus Petrondinus; that *Doctor*

Faustus was inspired by a translation out of the German *Historia von D. Johann Fausten.*

If we look deeply enough, the great works of the English language appear to spring from mixed and muddled origins. It is well enough known that Shakespeare employed translations of Latin originals, among them North's Plutarch and Golding's version of Ovid's *Metamorphoses*; phrases from them emerge in his verse as if by some surreptitious act of magic.

It is recognised, too, that for the plot and structure of his comedies Shakespeare freely borrowed from the Roman dramatists, Terence and Plautus. But it is less readily understood that the form and texture of English comedy itself are derived from classical originals. In 1527 the pupils of St Paul's staged the *Menaechmi* of Plautus and then, in the following year, Terence's *Phormio*. The first translation of a Roman play, published in 1530, was that of Terence's *Andria*. This may be seen as part of the curriculum of the 'new learning', as promulgated by More and Erasmus, but it also had material consequences for the development of English drama. In 1533 Nicholas Udall, a schoolmaster of Eton and Westminster, published a translation entitled *Floures for Latine Spekynge Selected and Gathered oute of Terence*; it was a grammatical treatise, but four years later Udall wrote a play, *Ralph Roister Doister*, which has the merit of being the first formal English comedy. The connection, then, is clear. The five-act structure of English tragedy came out of Seneca; the five-act structure of English comedy emerged from Terence.

The debt to the classical tradition is various and profound. It created what might be called the horizon of English literature, beyond which the bright multifarious works arose. In fact by force of example it can be said to have created the English literary tradition itself. Dryden once remarked that 'Shakespeare was the Homer or father of our dramatic poets; Jonson was the Virgil, the pattern of elaborate writing' with the further analogy that 'Spenser and Milton are the nearest in English to Virgil and Horace in the Latin'. After the language had gained a fresh access of strength and power from classical sources, therefore, English itself could be seen as equivalent to Greek or Latin with its own history and traditions. The antiquarian William Camden began to compile an historical digest of the language, for example, and in the early seventeenth century Richard Verstegan wrote of 'the great Antiquitie of our ancient English toung'. In succeeding years the Old English of the

Anglo-Saxons was thoroughly examined, too, with the appearance of the 'Caedmon manuscripts' of homiletic verse. But principal attention was paid to the poetry of the medieval period. 'As Greece has three poets of great antiquity,' it was written, 'and Italy other three auncient poets: so hath England three auncient poets, Chaucer, Gower and Lydgate.' Thus a literary tradition was formed.

The passion for classical literature also engendered an image which has endured for almost five hundred years. Hopkins called it the 'Sweet especial rural scene'. It first emerges in Virgil's pastoral poetry, where the shepherd Tityrus lies beneath the shade of a spreading beech and pipes a woodland song upon his reed; generations of schoolchildren assimilated this sylvan picture of ease and gracefulness since, according to Sir Thomas Elyot, 'the pretty controversies of the simple shepherds therein contained wonderfully rejoiceth the child that heareth it well declared'. It became the inspiration for Edmund Spenser's *Shepheardes Calender* as well as for the pastoral poetry which sprang from it; it was also the context for Sir Philip Sidney's defence of poetry itself, when he declared that 'Nature never set forth the earth in so rich tapestry as diverse poets have done'. The use of this classical landscape may even represent the beginning of nature-worship itself in English, as opposed to the Anglo-Saxon wariness concerning the natural world. The contrast between city and country, and the role of the poet as a simple Orpheus murmuring:

> . . . let woods and rivers be
> My quiet though inglorious destiny

echoed through English poetry, until the pastoral vision was taken up in transcendental form by William Wordsworth. Wordsworth himself translated Catullus. So, in a sense, the cycle of influence is complete. A country parson in Mrs Gaskell's *Cousin Phillis* puts a similar point very well – 'It's wonderful how exactly Virgil has hit the enduring epithets, nearly two thousand years ago, and in Italy; and yet how it describes to a T what is now lying before us in the parish of Heathbridge, county——, England.'

Just as there are archetypal scenes and images echoing through the classicism of English literature, so there are representative passages in translation which, passing through many hands, create new forms of English music. One such is the chorus from the second act of Seneca's *Thyestes*, a passage from which was first translated by Sir Thomas Wyatt:

> For hym death greep' the right hard by the croppe
> That is moche knowen of other, and of him self alas,
> Doth dye unknowen, dazed with dreadfull face

That last phrase, in its dark magnificence, is redolent of a whole language. In the translation of Jasper Heywood it becomes:

> That knowne hee is to much to other men:
> Departeth yet unto him selfe unknowne

The lines carry the open vowel sounds that are so much part of the melody of English and, in the seventeenth-century translation of Sir Matthew Hale, they take on the dying fall of the couplet:

> To be a publick Pageant, known to All,
> But unacquainted with Himself, doth fall

They become more complex in the poetry of Abraham Cowley:

> Does not himself, when he is Dying know
> Nor what he is, nor whither he's to go

But they reappear, refreshed, in Marvell's gay perplexity:

> Into his own Heart ne'er pry's,
> Death to him's a Strange surprise

There had been much critical debate about the disabling number of monosyllables in the language, which resisted the attempts to beautify and 'benefit' that language through translation; the example of Marvell, however, suggests that the native resourcefulness of English can be carried even by its simplest words. The line continues.

CHAPTER 27

The Italian connection

In *The Arte of English Poesie* the Elizabethan critic and poetaster, George Puttenham, recorded that in the last years of the reign of Henry VIII:

> sprang up a new company of courtly makers, of whom *Sir Thomas Wyat* th'elder & *Henry* Earl of Surrey were the two chieftaines, who, hauing travailed into Italie, and there tasted the sweete and stately measures and stile of the Italian Poesie, as novices newly crept out of the schools of *Dante Arioste* and *Petrarch*, they greatly polished our rude & homely maner of vulgar Poesie from that it had bene before, and for that cause may iustly be sayed the first reformers of our English meetre and stile.

The earlier generation of More and Colet had been part of a European humanist culture and Catholic civilisation, but then the gradual process of national self-awareness after the Reformation intervened. Wyatt and Surrey were in a sense native reformers who wished to benefit and amplify the language of their country without necessarily identifying themselves with any continental dispensation. Yet their debt to Italy is clear. Another Elizabethan writer argued that 'for we are (as pretely noteth the Poet) severed from the worlde, it is thought, the common knowledges came later to us, then to other our neighbours: for our farther distance from the places where artes first sprang'.

The Italians, in particular, considered the English to be lacking in 'civilitie'. In *Volpone* Ben Jonson creates a garrulous and affected 'Lady Would-Be' – 'Which o'your poets? Petrarch? Or Tasso? Or Dante? Guarini? Ariosto? Aretine? Cieco di Hadria? I have read them all.' Italian poetry was not so much fashionable as indispensable for anyone pretending to literacy. Elizabethan literary criticism was established upon the models of Italian Renaissance criticism; the Italians gave to England the sonnet and the *terza rima*; the works of both Machiavelli and Castiglione were extraordinarily influential. Geoffrey Chaucer, himself under the spell of Italian masters, had at an earlier date experimented both with the sonnet and with *terza rima*; but the new forms fell rapidly out of use. The language was not yet ready for them, and so they lay dormant within its fabric until Sir Thomas Wyatt conjured them forth.

Wyatt's first translation had been of Plutarch's *Quyete of Mynde*; he had attempted a prose treatise by Petrarch himself, but grew tired of its prolixity and repetitiveness. Significantly, however, he blamed the tedium upon 'lacke of such diversyte in our tong', so that 'it shulde want a great dele of the grace'. This was precisely the 'grace' he wished to emulate in his poetry, specifically in his imitations of the Petrarchan sonnet, which (*pace* Chaucer) was to initiate in English the sonnet tradition which spread out from Sidney, Spenser and Shakespeare into the language of Milton and then wider still into Wordsworth and Keats. Wyatt translated sixteen sonnets from Petrarch; he gained from the Italian originals melodic strength and complexity, even as he added the reflections of troubled individual experience. But the important point is this: it was only by imitating the play of contrasts and opposites in Petrarch's poetry that Wyatt was able to discover his own ambiguous and haunted voice. His famous sonnet reputed to be cast around the image of Anne Boleyn, opening 'Whoso list to hunt, I know where is an hind', is modelled upon Petrarch's *Rime* 190 which creates a symbolic vision of a white hind. The contraries of Wyatt's love poems –

> I find no peace, and all my war is done.
> I fear and hope, I burn and freeze like ice

– are directly based upon Petrarchan conceits. They became so much part of English vocabulary and style that it is easy to forget or ignore their European origins; but they remain there none the less. The image of the spring or river occurs in Wyatt's poetry before it flowed through the melodies of subsequent poets:

> From these high hills as when a spring doth fall,
> It trilleth down with still and subtle course

But it is hard to resist the suggestion that his metaphor is charged with a recognition of his own 'high' sources. The metaphor might also be applied to Wyatt's epistolary satire, where his colloquial style and apparent plain speaking are established upon the satires of the Italian poet Alamanni. One opens abruptly with:

> Mine own John Poyntz, since ye delight to know –

where the name of Alamanni's friend, Tommaso Sertini, has been substituted. Wyatt imitates Horace and Chaucer also, conflating foreign and native sources.

Yet the paradox, as contrary as anything within Wyatt's difficult and divided poetry itself, is this. Out of these voices Wyatt has created something wholly fresh and original. Critics have often adverted to the fact that he is more concrete and particular than his Italian sources, and that he imposes the constraints of individual experience and circumstance upon the more declamatory address of the Italian originals; all this is true, and all this is characteristic of English translation. But the most extraordinary transformation lies in the mingling of old forms and old voices to create something entirely new; it is akin to the process of alchemy, that obsession of the sixteenth century, when a compound is changed into a rare element. It is the English imagination itself which has worked this miracle of transmutation. Many of the greatest poems in the language are the product of it, especially since that language is composed of borrowed tongues and purloined phrases.

Wyatt's sonnets themselves entered general circulation with the publication by Richard Tottel of *Songes and Sonnettes* in the summer of 1557. It was designed in large part to advertise 'the honorable stile of the noble earle of Surrey, and the weightinesse of the depewitted sir Thomas Wyat the elders verse'. Publication was deemed 'to the honor of the Englishe tong, and for the profit of the studious of Englishe eloquence' with a 'statelinesse of stile remoued from the rude skill of common eares. . . . And I exhort the vnlearned, by reding to learne to be more skilfull, and to purge that swinelike grossenesse.' Here eloquence bears a moral as well as a stylistic burden, and the importance of English translation is nowhere more apparent than in the dismissal of 'swinelike grossenesse' as unworthy of a national tradition. In fact the publication of what was also known as *Tottel's Miscellany* marked one of the first stages in the creation of a vernacular tradition, and the volume was of exemplary importance in the deployment of the sonnet as a fashionable English form. The pre-eminence of the book can be judged, perhaps, in the fact that the first collection of an individual poet's work – that of Barnaby Googe – was actually published six years later. The translation from manuscript to print, and thus the creation of a larger English public for poetry, was largely the work of Richard Tottel who after William Caxton can be described as the begetter of book culture in England.

Barnaby Googe's *Eglogs, Epytaphes and Sonnetes* was followed sixteen years later by Edmund Spenser's *Shepheardes Calender*, which has the distinction of being the most carefully fashioned and self-conscious literary debut up to that date. It has been said that artistic genius must create the taste by which it is to be judged, but Spenser also managed to formulate a tradition. The book was published anonymously but the editorial glosses composed by a certain 'E.K.' hailed the writer as *'the new poet'* gathering up the inheritance of Virgil and of Chaucer, of Marot and of Skelton. It is in fact a testimony to the newly acquired power of the vernacular that it could be presented in this fashion; the book itself was accompanied by woodcuts as well as textual glosses, thus enhancing its status as an art object and a permanent memorial to the importance of English verse which has, as it were, acquired a classical veneer. Spenser was more audacious, however, in his desire to reclaim the old strengths of the English language. As 'E.K.' put it, 'in my opinion it is one special prayse, of manye which are dew to this Poete, that he hath laboured to restore, as to theyre rightfull heritage such good and naturall English wordes, as have ben long time out of use and almost clene disinherited'. He adds that there are some who, upon hearing or reading 'an olde word albeit very naturall and significant', dismiss it as 'gibbrish' but such ought to be ashamed 'in their own mother tonge straungers to be ranked and alienes'. Spenser's project here is all of a piece with the rising current of nationalism and Protestantism shaping the English sensibility of the late sixteenth century, evinced also in the bloody conquest of Ireland in which Spenser himself played no insignificant role.

Spenser was a Londoner, born in 1552, who imbibed Protestant humanism at Cambridge. He became a member of the Earl of Leicester's household but, more importantly, he was acquainted with Philip Sidney; these young men started a literary club under the name of Areopagus which, according to John Aubrey, was established 'for the purpose of naturalizing the classical metres in English verse'. In 1580 Spenser became secretary to the Lord Deputy of Ireland and was a witness, if not a participant, in the English terror against that country's native inhabitants; he directly benefited from the spoliation, also, when he was awarded a castle and estates in County Cork. It was in Ireland, too, that he completed the first three books of *The Faerie Queene* – a strange jewel to emerge from the blood and mire. He was given a pension by the queen in 1589 but the affairs of state rarely remain beneficent for long. His castle in Ireland was burned down during Tyrone's rebellion of 1598, and Spenser's youngest child perished in the flames. It is said that the poet returned to England with a broken heart. He died in the following year.

In an essay of 1820, William Hazlitt first recognised the association between poetry and power. In a discussion of Shakespeare's *Coriolanus* he declared that 'the principle of poetry is a very anti-levelling principle. It aims at effect, it exists by contrast. It admits of no medium. It is every thing by excess. It rises above the ordinary standard of sufferings and crimes. It presents a dazzling appearance. It shows its head turreted, crowned and crested. Its front is gilt and blood-stained.' Hazlitt was a wonderfully astute critic, and he has here discerned an aspect of the English imagination which is manifest in writers as diverse as John Milton and Christopher Marlowe. In this passage, too, he might have been directly describing the work of Edmund Spenser. *The Shepheardes Calender* is embellished and ornamented as if it were a classical text, but this is only an acknowledgement of Spenser's debt to the Roman poetry of empire and of power. Yet there were more recent continental models. Spenser's production imitates an edition of *Arcadia*, written by the Italian poet Sannazaro and published seven years before, and there is a more general obligation to the cult of Italian neo-Platonism which had arrived in England a hundred years earlier. It is the philosophy of *The Shepheardes Calender*. A vision of divine harmony and order can be glimpsed in all created things, through the medium of which the soul aspires to spiritual revelation; the appetite for virtue and for beauty is the same, while all things work harmoniously on earth as they do in heaven. Spenser's interest in symbolism, and his obsession with numerology, are aspects of a doctrine which was by degrees assimilated into his native Protestantism. This is the paradox which reflects the nature of the English imagination itself. A highly charged European culture, of which England was really only the marginal recipient, was used by Spenser to promote the cause of the vernacular language and the native sensibility. The authors to whom Spenser alludes in his verse are Chaucer and Langland, with the implicit understanding that they represent a national spirit of reform and renovation. For example, one of the two characters in the eclogue for May is named 'Piers' which had become a token of English rootedness and sincerity.

The same conditions apply to Spenser's epic of nationhood, *The Faerie Queene*, which is fashioned after European models. There are passages literally translated from Ariosto's *Gerusalemme Liberata*, as well as more general borrowings from European epics or romance. Yet once more Spenser mingles these contemporary or near contemporary European elements with a self-conscious English antiquarianism. Thus he combines a modern vocabulary, among its words being 'fierce', 'piercing' and 'noblesse', with such Middle English borrowings as 'ydrad', 'troden' and 'brast'. He manages to be both ancient and modern at the same time, and so becomes sufficiently representative of the national tradition.

Spenser's century was obsessed by its past, just like every succeeding English century. The justification for Tudor governance lay in inheritance or continuity. The Tudor monarchs claimed to draw their lineage from Arthur, and to find their origins even further back in the story of Brutus and of the foundations of England itself. The great displays of heraldry and genealogy come from the Tudor period, as do the history plays of Shakespeare; the image of empire was to include America, the land which Henry VII 'causyd furst for to be founde', but its authenticity was based upon a supposed Arthurian empire which according to Dr Dee comprised 'twenty Kingdomes'. The Arthurian myth of 'Britaine' and 'this Brytish Monarchie' was thus linked, for example, with the sixteenth-century conquest of Ireland. In *The Faerie Queene* itself Spenser extols

> Mightie Albion, father of the bold
> And warlike people, which the Britaine Islands hold

This too became part of the national myth of Protestantism or what has been called 'the Spenserian idiom of Protestant chivalry'.[1] So everything came together, as the Tudor kings asserted power based on historical models and the English genius busily conflated past and present.

The same propensity is evident in the architectural vogue for the perpendicular Gothic, combined with modern experimentation, to produce the Elizabethan 'prodigy houses'. *The Faerie Queene* itself is a kind of 'prodigy house'. It is to be found in the jousts and tilts of the Tudor court, as well as in the bogus crenellation of Tudor castles. It is part of that fascination for lavish externals which characterises Tudor portraits as well as Tudor poetry. This predilection for the past even emerges in the new art of literary criticism. In *A Defence of Poesy* Sir Philip Sidney numbered Spenser among those 'English poets who have done good work' but then remarked of Chaucer that 'truly I know not, whether to merveile more, either that he, in that mistie time, could see so clearley, or that wee, in this cleare age, walk so stumblingly after him'. It is a characteristically English tone, revived in every generation. The best work was done in the past, and contemporary writers only 'stumble' afterward. It represents, perhaps, a way of suppressing or concealing the powerful disturbances of the present moment. It may be a form of disguise, therefore, or embarrassment. But the truism remains. Nothing excellent or distinguished can happen again. All lies in the past. It is, in truth, an intrinsic part of the English imagination.

This native tradition has been examined by one Renaissance scholar, Richard Helgerson, who in *Forms of Nationhood* created his own genealogy of books deriving from Spenser's *The Faerie Queene*. They are, in order, Camden's *Britannia* (1586), Hakluyt's *Principall Navigations, Voyages and Discoveries of the English Nation* (1589), Hooker's *Laws of Ecclesiastical Polity* (1593), Shakespeare's history plays, Speed's *Theatre of the Empire of Great Britain* (1611), Drayton's *Poly-Olbion* (1612), and Coke's *Institutes of the Laws of England* (1624). Their context may be located in a letter which Spenser wrote to Gabriel Harvey in 1580 – 'Why a' God's name, may not we, as else the Greeks, have the kingdom of our own language?' The authors named were all born between 1551 and 1564; as Helgerson remarks, 'Never before or since have so many works of such magnitude and such long-lasting effect been devoted to England by members of a single generation.'[2] With the exception of Hakluyt's *Principal Navigations* they were also all attempts to repossess or reformulate the past as an instrument of contemporary polity and understanding; they are evidence of the antiquarianism which seems endemic to the English imagination itself.

The Faerie Queene itself is a creation of great and elaborate artifice, an allegory and a romance sustained within the smooth and even line; the phrasing is perfectly attuned to the cadence, in the fullness of achieved harmony, so that Spenser seems to let the imagination speak in its own clausal melodies. This measured artifice, so well displayed in other guises by Shakespeare and Milton, is an integral part of English poetry and of the English imagination; it is the artifice of those quintessentially English spirits, Puck and Ariel, but it can also acquire the more ponderous tones of Satan in *Paradise Lost*. *The Faerie Queene* has been described by a modern scholar as 'dream-like' containing 'well-known elements of the dream process',[3] and it has haunted English poetry like a dream. Its metre is reawakened by Byron in *Childe Harold's Pilgrimage* and by Shelley in *The Revolt of Islam*, and its dream is continued by Keats in his 'Imitation of Spenser'. The analogy here is with music, the music of the reed or flute, a timeless and enchanted music which like dream can roam over the centuries.

The Faerie Queene is in Spenser's own word an epic of 'Faeryland', constructed in six books on symbolic and numerical principles. Certain books concern individual heroes and heroic adventures, such as those of the Red Cross Knight in Book One, while others are interwoven with various narratives and episodes in the manner of English embroidery. Spenser himself deemed its principal figure to be King Arthur who, in the poet's own words, becomes 'the image of a brave knight perfected in the twelve private morall vertues as Aristotle hath devised'; but in truth Arthur is only one element in the heterogeneous mixing of classicism and romance, faery and Christian lore. It is a visionary conception, and what later critics called a Gothic poem or a piece of English tapestry; it possesses its own internal laws of growth and change, so that in a sense it seems to be in the process of writing itself.

The Faerie Queene is modelled upon continental sources, so that the paradox remains of a quintessentially English production finding its provenance within a larger European culture. Yet it is still notably English in manner and inspiration. It represents a collection of incidents and episodes which emerge effortlessly from one another; it is highly decorative and scenic, eschewing intensity for the sake of variety. It proffers a European euphony and elegance, but manifests itself in the English love for surface variety and decoration. It moves from pathos to 'Gothic' horror as if they were good companions, and descends easily from melodrama into allegory. It has been said of romance itself 'that it embodied in English the same greatness which had found an alternative form of expression in Latin and Greek' epic[4] but, amidst its stylistic variation and exaggeration, is there not a hint of fulsome self-mockery? The success of *The Faerie Queene*, therefore, lies in the very nature of its Englishness. This vast and elaborate system of words might even be described as the alembic of the English language in all its mixture and variety. It then becomes time to address the question of heterogeneity itself. Its name is Shakespeare.

Mungrell tendencies

William Shakespeare. 17th century engraving by Martin Droeshout

CHAPTER 28

A short history of Shakespeare

To write about Shakespeare is to write about everything. We might adopt the opening lines of Gerard Manley Hopkins's poem 'The Blessed Virgin Compared to the Air We Breathe':

> Wild air, world-mothering air,
> Nestling me everywhere

This capacious movement opens up a vista of

> This needful, never spent,
> And nursing element . . .

And so may Shakespeare be compared to the air we breathe. The incalculable number of his phrases and aphorisms that has entered the general vocabulary testifies to a greater truth, that he is now within the fabric of our language. Such is the power and persuasiveness of his work that each day, somewhere in the world, a book is published upon his work or upon his influence.

In 1711 he was described as 'the Genius of our Isle', and the celebration of David Garrick's 'Shakespeare Jubilee' at Stratford in 1769 confirmed his status as 'the god of our idolatry'. Alexander Pope and Samuel Johnson, Samuel Taylor Coleridge and William Hazlitt, all contributed to what became known as 'bardolatry'. In the year 2000, Shakespeare was named as the dominant figure in the previous thousand years of English history. The appropriation of Shakespeare as the national genius, therefore, is a striking and significant fact; those who have never read a line of his work consider him to be a token of national consciousness. His being is so fluid that it can acquire the shape of a nation, his personality so little known or understood that it can be endlessly reinterpreted; he has become the 'affable familiar ghost' of his sonnet sequence.

The process may be said to begin with Ben Jonson's remark that 'hee was (indeed) honest, and of an open, and free nature'. The interpretation has then run as follows. Shakespeare was not overwhelmed by any sense of his own importance. Shakespeare was not self-obsessed. He was not pretentious. It is so benevolent an image that it has since become that which the English wish to form of all their writers. Elements of his biography are then adduced. The fact that he possessed 'small Latin and less Greek', falsely interpreted as an insult on Jonson's part, has been used to suggest that he was not in any sense an intellectual; this distrust of intellectualism runs very deep within the English sensibility. The evidence that he played no part in the publication of his plays has led to the supposition that he did not take his work in the theatre very 'seriously' – that he was not, in other words, in love with his own writing. The possibility that this negligence might be a token of supreme confidence has not really been considered. Shakespeare is fixed for ever in the image of modesty and self-effacement, thus embodying or representing the highest virtues to which English writers can aspire.

The evidence that he collaborated with other dramatists on an *ad hoc* basis, even at the very end of his career, has in turn lent weight to the depiction of him as supremely pragmatic; the image of the writer as workman, labouring in shifts to produce masterpieces, has great appeal to a native sensibility that always eschews the theoretical for the practical. The fact that the dramatist also earned a great deal of money, and that he was on a small scale a successful speculator, affords equivalent satisfaction.

Yet Ben Jonson's words are also open to another interpretation. 'Open' itself, as a description of Shakespeare, is infinitely interpretable. What Jonson seems to have meant by his 'open and free nature' is a sensibility alert and responsive to other temperaments. The fact that it can also imply sincerity and artlessness serves only to confirm the impression of Shakespeare as candid, straightforward and affable. Yet it ought of course to be remembered that Shakespeare was an actor before he became a dramatist, and that he remained an actor for much of his working life. It may be possible to counterfeit openness. He may have been 'free' in his nature, too, because he secretly realised that his genius was inexhaustible.

All the elements of Shakespeare's life seem to come together within his drama. The folk-tales of his Warwickshire childhood and his schoolboy reading of Latin literature, for example, combine in his creation of classical enchantments. But his biography provides other conclusions. The 'missing years', when he may have been a tutor in a recusant household, contain the mystery without which no life of a writer is complete. His journey to London and his employment as an actor prepared him for the hard and raucous business of the stage. His early success as a dramatist, far eclipsing any reputation as an actor, directly resulted from his ability to please the crowd. But even though he never stopped writing for that many-headed hydra, he had aspirations towards gentility and coveted his own coat of arms; he was also a successful businessman, who owned property in both London and Stratford. He can never be fully identified with either place, and his hovering between two worlds seems wholly appropriate in a man of such equivocal personality.

That is why there has been endless speculation about the religion which the playwright espoused; the evidence suggests that his father was a Roman Catholic, and that as a result Shakespeare was brought up in a recusant household while outwardly assenting to the creed of the reformed Protestant Church. It is perhaps worth noting that, in contrast to his contemporary Marlowe or to the Jacobean playwrights, Shakespeare never indulged in 'Catholic-baiting'. The representatives of the Roman faith are generally presented in his drama as well-meaning, if sometimes ineffectual, figures. Intriguingly, he also takes two cautious dips into the malarial marshes of dogma. In *Henry IV Part One* Falstaff jokes with Prince Hal, declaring that he will never be saved if merit be the condition for salvation; in *Love's Labour's Lost*, the Princess of France teasingly reproaches a forester for suggesting that her beauty, being a merit, will save her. Both examples clearly refer to the misconception, popular among Protestants of the time, that Catholics believed humankind was saved by its own virtues. The bantering tone, all the more remarkable given the religious tensions of the period, suggests either that Shakespeare took a light view of religious dissension, or that he was indulging in the Persian habit of *taqqiyah*, the perverse pleasure derived from colluding with one's oppressors. In any case, Shakespeare's unwillingness to invoke either anti-Roman rhetoric or Protestant theological prejudice must surely lend weight to the 'recusant' theory of his origins.

The childhood dissimulation, if such it was, may then have had a profound effect upon the burgeoning dramatist. To utter all the phrases of religious orthodoxy, and to believe none of them, would emphasise both the power and the hollowness of words. To be suspended between two worlds, between seeming and being, would enhance any vision of existence as a stage. To hold secretly to a persecuted faith would be a hard lesson in disguising; to be 'of an open and free nature' might then paradoxically become an act of concealment. It adds lustre, in any case, to the supposed mystery or impenetrability of Shakespeare's character;

it was the duty of every English Catholic to remain invisible in order to keep his or her faith inviolate.

All this may be idle supposition, however, and no more than a winter's tale to satisfy the native appetite for anecdote and biographical speculation. It is more just, and easier of proof, to suggest that the dramatist's 'open' sensibility afforded him access to the wealth of English culture before the Reformation; the mysteries and miracles were a living part of his linguistic and theatrical inheritance. In the ritual drama of his last plays he even seems to mimic, or adopt the postures of, the Catholic Mass.

Ben Jonson also suggested the extent of Shakespeare's facility in his remark that 'I remember, the Players have often mentioned it as an honour to Shakespeare that in his writing, (whatsoever he penned), hee never blotted out line'. Jonson was not necessarily impressed by this facility – 'would he had blotted a thousand' – but subsequent commentators have interpreted that easy grace as the token of genius or inspiration. Shakespeare did not know where the words came from; he knew only that they came. By a subtle transition he then became 'fancy's child' or even nature's child, warbling 'his native wood-notes wild', wherein he became aligned with the pastoral dream of England. His fluency can also be seen as an aspect of his 'open' nature, since he became susceptible to the slightest inflection of the language; rare combinations and congregations of words emerged in the process, so that Shakespeare becomes a principle of organisation. It is well known that he depended upon the plots, and even the words, of others; he lifted passages from North and borrowed images from Ovid. There is hardly a play of his which is not established upon some earlier source, historical or dramatic, so that he corresponds to the English archetype; he seems most original when he borrows most freely. Like the language and the nation itself he is altogether receptive, taking up external or foreign constituents and moulding them instinctively to his purpose. This may on occasions become a cause of ambiguity and, as the clown admits in *As You Like It*, 'the truest poetrie is the most faining'. The remark is amplified by Olivia in *Twelfth Night*:

> VIOLA: Alas, I tooke great paines to studie it, and 'tis Poeticall.
> OLIVIA: It is the more like to be feigned, I pray you keep it in.

Yet the richness and elaboration which these borrowed words disclose is all Shakespeare. Once more the alchemical analogy, in which the process of transformation is as significant as any product of it, seems appropriate. His education at the grammar school in Stratford led him towards Virgil and Erasmus, Horace and Ovid; despite Jonson's remark about his 'small Latin', he also knew Terence and Plautus and Seneca, from whose dramas he variously borrowed. It is also appropriate that, in an age of cultural transmission from Europe to England, Shakespeare should rely heavily upon a number of translations – among them North's Plutarch, Chapman's Homer and Golding's Ovid. He translated the translations, and rendered them original again.

It has been said of Shakespeare's *The Rape of Lucrece* that 'in a poem derived mainly from Livy and an annotated edition of Ovid, we have in one stanza echoes from two poems of Ovid, a Biblical parable and the marginal note on it, and possibly from Juvenal's description of the miseries of old age. It is probable that Shakespeare, here and elsewhere, consulted the *Adagia* of Erasmus.'[1] This is not to mention Shakespeare's scattered and forgotten reading. Even if the materials were not original, however, their combination was new and surprising. That was once itself the definition of great art. But Shakespeare performed a different miracle. In his act of remembering and restoration, all the resources of his imagination clustered around the words and images so that they were immeasurably strengthened and deepened; they became echoic with past and present life, instinct with powerful intuition which is the verbal equivalent of feeling, at once startlingly new and hauntingly familiar. That is why they resist interpretation or, rather, why they are open to innumerable interpretations: meaning is suspended, or exists only in the forceful interplay of difference. It is as if we were gazing upon language in the act of expressing itself.

In this process of retrieval and recapitulation, Shakespeare effortlessly and inevitably refined many English archetypes. More than any other dramatist, he is the poet of dreams and visions. In the island of ghosts and spirits, according to the ancient topographers, he summons up Ariel and Titania, Oberon and the witches of *Macbeth*; ghosts wander through his tragedies and histories and his last plays are surrounded by visionary enchantments. His characters, in extremity, see humankind as an hallucination or phantasm where 'Life's but a walking Shadow'; it is the melancholy vision of the land lost in mist, populated by what Addison described as Shakespeare's 'Ghosts, Faeries, Witches and the like imaginary Persons' and addressed to an English race which is 'naturally Fanciful' and 'disposed to Gloominess and Melancholy of Temper'. Many of his plays are crowned with melancholy endings, followed of course by the jig of the actors. The most powerful passages of Shakespearian verse flow with the music of loss or transience:

> These our actors,
> (As I foretold you) were all Spirits, and
> Are melted into Ayre, into thin Ayre . . .

The qualities of the English imagination are everywhere apparent in Shakespearian drama, but in so rare and refined a form that they often pass unrecognised or appear under the general rubric of 'Shakespearian' effects. It says much about the antiquarian persuasion of the English genius, for example, that all of the plays set in England itself are also set in the past. The early sequence of the history plays represents the first serious and prolonged attempt to introduce the English chronicles to the stage; in a nation (or city) obsessed with its past, they proved instantly popular. Shakespeare had divined the native mood, and expressed a genuine native spirit, in dramas which reflect the bloodthirstiness and disparagement of death commonly associated with the English. They are in part designed to legitimise the dynasty of the Tudors, and thus to bring a political interpretation to bear upon English history, but they are also filled with an egalitarian spirit in the exploits of Pistol and Mistress Quickly. Shakespeare is aware of the lurking and ominous 'mob', a threatening force in *Julius Caesar* and *Coriolanus*, but as a naturalised Londoner he could not help but be awed by the power of popular feeling. When the opening line of Henry V's speech, 'Once more unto the breach, deare friends, once more', is echoed or parodied by Bardolfe's 'On, on, on, on, on, to the breach, to the breach' we know that the 'low' characters may use a 'low' language but that they can still plainly be heard.

The antiquarian disposition itself is not of course unique to Shakespeare, although it has readily been associated with his name. Almost all of Charles Dickens's and George Eliot's novels, for example, are set in the past – generally some thirty or forty years before the time of their composition – and in the twenty-first century there has been a vast resurgence of interest in historical fiction. It is a constant tendency of the English imagination. In the case of Dickens his preoccupation with his own past is the source or root of his genuine interest in the historical past. Might the same be surmised of Shakespeare?

When Shakespeare reached towards the more remote past, too, he re-created the English myths of Lear and Cymbeline which had previously lingered in the pages of old romances. But there are formal, as well as thematic, associations. In the simplicity of *King Lear*, in its pure and unattenuated beat of doom, it is possible to glimpse the outlines of the medieval morality plays in which the individual man upon the earth, or Everyman, submits himself to the divine will.

The exemplary force of saints' lives, particularly those female saints who played so large a role in Anglo-Saxon spirituality, lies behind the sufferings of Isabella in *Measure for Measure*, of Marina in *Pericles*, of Hermione in *The Winter's Tale*. The history plays are themselves a secular re-enactment of the mystery plays which, with their ritual and pageantry, satisfied the public appetite for spectacle. Shakespeare's debt to medieval drama is various and profound. His clowns are latter-day lords of misrule, and Richard III a reincarnated Vice in another costume. How else may we interpret or explain the effective if crude sensationalism of the plays, early and late, except as the affirmation of a native form or spirit? The severed heads of the history plays – enter 'the Queene with Suffolkes head' in the second part of *Henry VI* – converse with the severed head of Cloten in *Cymbeline*, while Tamora feasts upon the flesh of her children in *Titus Andronicus*. It has often been remarked that there is a vast disparity between the melodrama of Shakespeare's plots and the miracle of his language. The two elements can be reconciled only in the desire of an English audience for ornate effectiveness. The equivalence of plangent lyricism and strident stage action may be repugnant to the scholar or sensitive critic, but not to anyone who understands the native appetite for variety and display. The Shakespearian tradition is part of a more general consciousness.

That is why the sea flows everywhere in his drama. It is the key image uniting the language of Shakespeare's first play, the 'wilde Ocean' in *The Two Gentlemen of Verona*, to the wilder mysteries of *The Tempest*. There are six references to the sea in *The Two Gentlemen of Verona*, but some thirty-two in *The Tempest* where the sea has an actual and mythical presence throughout the drama. The cold unruly sea of the Anglo-Saxon imagination is so pervasive in the plays of Shakespeare that it seems to break and dissolve into overwhelming mist and storm. Every play, including *The Merry Wives of Windsor* and the pastoral comedies, includes a reference to the sea; it is employed literally and metaphorically, with the 'wild sea of my conscience' and 'an Ocean of salt tears' flowing within the 'sea in a stiff tempest' and the 'sea, mounting to the welkin's cheek'. Many of Shakespeare's characters compare themselves with the sea, troubled by sighs and tears. The ocean itself is wide and wild, and within its depths many may suffer 'a sea-change'. There are tempests and howling winds upon the face of the deep; there are rocks and sands and tides to mock the purposes of men. We 'float upon a wilde and violent Sea'; with these words the Scottish thane, Ross, in *Macbeth* is united with the 'Seafarer' of the Old English poem. Shakespeare himself may never have seen the sea, but his language is permeated by its presence.

There is another aspect of Shakespeare's art which has always been considered characteristic both of him and of the native tradition from which he springs. It lies in his mingling 'high' and 'low', king and fool, prince and gravedigger, commander and soldier, scholar and buffoon. He ignores the 'unities' as described by Aristotle and other classical sources, in favour of a 'mixed' or 'mungrell' mode inherited directly from the medieval drama. Samuel Johnson expressed it well in the preface to his edition of Shakespeare: 'Shakespeare's plays are not in the rigorous and critical sense either tragedies or comedies, but compositions of a distinct kind; exhibiting the real state of sublunary nature, which partakes of good and evil, joy and sorrow, mingled with endless variety of proportion and innumerable modes of combination.' His plays are as various as consciousness itself, fluently moving from farce to pathos, comedy to tragedy, while all the time shifting form from theatrical pageant to intense soliloquy. No mood is maintained for very long; all is variety and process with a fluidity and mobility which, as Johnson suggests, resemble life itself. The apparent death of Juliet is succeeded by a conversation between three mirthful musicians eager for their dinner and unwilling to play 'some merie dump'. A conversation between Henry IV and the Earl of Warwick, on high matters of state, is quickly followed by the entrance of Justice Shallow and by a long farcical scene:

> KING: I will take your counsaile,
>   And were these inward warres once out of hand,
>   We would (deare Lords) vnto the holy land.
> SHALLOW: Come on, come on, give me your hand sir, giue me your
>   hand sir.

Here the contrast between verse and prose is an apt token of the larger contrasts within the play itself; the pressure of Shakespeare's imagination can be measured in the repetition of 'hand' in both passages, as if the elementary prose sprang naturally and inevitably from high poetry. This is one of the characteristics of Shakespeare's art – that high and tragic matters evoke low and farcical conclusions, almost as a principle of life itself. The same sudden transition occurs in the same play, the second part of *Henry IV*, where the consonance of sound between 'die' and 'pie' fashions a memorable moment:

> KING: But beare me to that chamber, there ile lie,
>   In that Ierusalem shall Harry die.
> SHALLOW: By cock and pie, you shal not away to night, what Dauy I
>   say?

Poetry must give way to prose, and kings to clowns. Language itself may bear the burden of these changes:

> IUSTICE: There is not a white haire in your face, but should haue
>   his effect of grauity.
> FALSTAFF: His effect of grauy, grauie, grauie.

In Samuel Johnson's great dictionary gravity is followed by gravy, also, with the same quotation from the second part of *Henry IV* (mistakenly marked by Johnson as from the first part). But if language performs its own tricks, of all writers Shakespeare heard them most clearly. The heterogeneity of the native tongue, compounded of so many sources and influences, seems in itself to create his heterogeneous sensibility. We cannot disinter language from consciousness, or speech from behaviour; all are of a piece. It is the imagination itself. Yet sometimes we seem to reach the limit of language:

> HAMLET: You cannot Sir take from mee any thing that I will more
>   willingly part withall: except my life, my life, my life.

Shakespeare often uses these triple repetitions to suggest distraction or emptiness; it is a way of continuing the sound without any formal sense, and finds its apotheosis when Hamlet does indeed part with his life:

> HAMLET: . . . the rest is silence.
>   O, o, o, o

It anticipates Lear's own death scene:

> Neuer, neuer, neuer, pray you vndo
> This button, thanke you sir, O, o, o, o

where language itself has a dying fall.

There are two scenes, in *Hamlet* and *King Lear* respectively, which have by common consent become representative of Shakespeare's hybrid art. One concerns the dialogue between Hamlet and the 'two Clownes' who are also sextons. One clown sings as he throws up the skulls from an open grave meant for Ophelia, and this joyfulness in the face of death becomes the occasion for Hamlet's aspersions upon human destiny. 'Why may not imagination trace the noble dust of *Alexander*, till a find it stopping a bunghole?' In an earlier passage he had complained 'that the toe of the pesant comes so neere the heele of the Courtier he galls his kybe' – he chafes his heel. This is of course precisely the effect of Shakespeare's own dramaturgy where a scene at court is swiftly succeeded by a scene among fools. Shakespeare set the context for the appreciation of his own work, where what is most artificial can be deemed natural and true.

The second example of this hybrid art concerns Lear and his Fool in the storm, where Shakespeare combines the foolishness of the once great king with the mad wisdom of his jester. Their actions and language have been blamed for their excess; Tolstoy in particular accused Shakespeare of grandiloquence and bombast. In his essay upon *King Lear* Tolstoy concluded that the play had no real meaning – or, rather, that it was devoid of religious consciousness or spiritual consolation. Tolstoy also accused Shakespeare of inelegant arbitrariness; he saw no order in the storm scene, for example. But there can be little doubt that Shakespeare would have delighted in the accusation. In the same essay Tolstoy concluded that the condition of great art was 'Sincerity, i.e. that the author should himself keenly feel what he expresses'. Yet Shakespeare 'feels' only through the medium of contrast, just as he holds no settled opinion except within the play of oppositions. Lear cannot be imagined without the Fool any more than the Fool can be conceived without the presence of Lear. Just as their language is made out of opposition, so they are significant only in terms of their differences. In the dramatic re-enactment of character, 'sincerity' is not an issue. To be merely sincere is to be incomplete. For a narrative to be animated by one passion or single theory, for a play to aspire to one form, for a novel to seek integrity and unity of design – all are in pursuit of a false principle.

We are entering here a highly charged and rarefied area of the English imagination, which can only be fully understood by example. If we turn to Matthew Arnold for guidance, we will find conclusions which were generally accepted throughout the eighteenth and nineteenth centuries:

'No people', he wrote, 'are so shy, so self-conscious, so embarrassed as the English, because two natures are mixed in them, and natures which pull them in such different ways.' He is alluding to the mingling of the Celtic and Germanic inheritance, to which he adds the observation that the English have 'no fixed, fatal, spiritual centre of gravity'. We may recall here Tolstoy's remark that Shakespeare lacked a religious sensibility; the dramatist did indeed play 'grauity' against 'grauy'. In the nineteenth century it seemed that 'we have Germanism enough to make us Philistines, and Normanism enough to make us imperious, and Celtism enough to make us self-conscious and awkward; but German fidelity to Nature, and Latin precision and clear reason, and Celtic quick-wittedness and spirituality, we fall short of'. Arnold's vocabulary may not be as persuasive in the twenty-first century as it seemed to his contemporaries, but he cannot be faulted for his generalisations upon 'this mixed constitution of our nature'. The mixture grows every day, much to the delight of those who understand the inclusive nature of Englishness itself. Its name, once more, is Shakespeare.

CHAPTER 29

And now for streaky bacon

The mixed and mongrel style of the English imagination emerges in the most disparate contexts. The alliterative line of the Anglo-Saxons encouraged 'paradox or antithesis'.[1] *Beowulf* combines heroic adventure and horror, pathos and fantasy. Chaucer can change tone from farce to tragedy in an instant. Spenser delights in his alterations of mood. Marlowe specialises in comedy and horror mixed. The fact that precisely the same descriptions have been applied both to Shakespeare and to Dickens suggests, at the very least, a certain continuity of expression.

The absence of studied or central feeling can be glimpsed in fourteenth-century English music, also, with its unique 'interactions between the popular and the learned'.[2] The upper part of one motet is an anthem to the Virgin Mary while the tenor accompaniment is a demotic and secular song entitled 'Dou way, Robin'; both are to be sung at the same time. In Worcester Cathedral the arcades of the choir are composed 'in a deliberately clashing rhythm, a technique borrowed from Lincoln'.[3] The poetry of Wyatt and Skelton is filled with 'deliberately clashing' imagery also. In one love poem or 'balet' Skelton proceeds with the conventional aureate diction:

> Of al your feturs fauorable to make tru discripcion

only to descend quickly into lewd abuse:

> Jaist ye, Jenet of Spayne, for your tayll wagges

Wyatt performs the same act of sudden transition:

> For fancy ruleth though right say nay,
> Even as the good man kissed his cow . . .

If the English language contains the elements of many other languages, Saxon and Latin among them, then paradox and incongruity will be of its very nature. It may encourage irony or scepticism, and when Samuel Johnson observed that in 'metaphysical' poetry, 'the most heterogeneous ideas are yoked violently together' he was remarking upon a native tendency. But it does not have to be a violent practice; in the archaic and artificial diction of *The Faerie Queene* all possible languages are accommodated within the music of Spenser's verse, in a poem which in the words of Shakespeare's Polonius is 'pastoral-comical, historical-pastoral, tragical-historical, tragical-comical-historical-pastoral' all at once.

The English delight in the hybrid emerges forcefully in English drama. The nature of the earliest plays, where buffoonery and death were paraded side by side, is the context for a thousand years of what Sir Philip Sidney called 'mungrell' drama which 'be neither right Tragedies, nor right Comedies, mingling Kings and Clownes'. In the great 'cycles' of York or Chester, a multitude of verse forms encompass a variety of styles and themes. Christ is surrounded by figures of fun, and the crudity of farce can sometimes be touched by intimations of eternity. So the 'mungrell' style can in a way achieve transcendence – of all the mystery cycles in Europe, only the English aspired to a complete statement of human destiny from Creation to Doom. The 'mixed' or 'mingled' style, abused and rejected by the more learned courtiers and scholars, might nevertheless afford the direct experience of extremes. Here are all the constituents of divine comedy. The rapid movement from farce to the sublime in the York plays was accompanied in 1426, according to one censorious preacher, by 'feastings, drunkenness, shouts, songs, and other insolences'.

Moralists also inveighed against sixteenth-century drama, often on the assumption that 'high' and 'low' elements were being promiscuously mingled. The drama offended decorum on every level. The 'unities' of time and place are not observed in the Elizabethan theatre, where the imperative is still that of the mystery plays; a vast inclusiveness is required, registering complexity and variety in each part of the design. There were 'medlies' which were 'part pageant, part morality play, part clowning and political cabaret'.[4] The contemporary playwright, however, did not necessarily apologise for his various genius: 'If we pretend a mingle-mangle, our fault is to be excused, because the whole world is become an hodge-podge.' Lyly can in 'hodge-podge' fashion parody himself. One soliloquy in his play, *Endymion*, is couched in a 'high' style – 'Behold my sad tears, my deep sighs, my hollow eyes, my broken sleeps, my heavy countenance' – only to be deflated by a young page who ridicules 'moonshine on the water'. All the pastoral romances of the Elizabethan stage have this double perspective, so that in characteristic English fashion love is mocked as well as celebrated. Heywood asked himself 'why among sad & grave

Histories, I have here & there inserted fabulous jeasts & tales, savouring of Lightnesse?' And he answered, simply, that 'I have therein imitated our Historical & comical Poets, that write to the Stage'.

'High' and 'low' were confused in quite another sense, too, since in the late sixteenth century the audience at the Rose or Curtain comprised courtiers and merchants, scholars and 'mechanicals', poets and pie-men:

> For as we see at all the playhouse doors,
> When ended is the play, the dance and song,
> A thousand townsmen, gentlemen and whores
> Porters and serving-men together throng

Thus wrote Sir John Davies in 1593, a time when the finest examples of English drama were being composed for this mixed and heterogeneous collection of citizens; it can even be argued that when the audiences were segregated, as they became in the latter half of the seventeenth century, great plays could no longer be written. The early 'adulterate' audience, on the other hand, came to see themselves in the hybrid drama of the stage. On the wooden scaffold the actor, considered then to be of low profession, is enunciating the highest sentiments. In the dramatic act, all order and degree are thrown into confusion. In the first part of *Henry IV* Falstaff speaks in feigned passion:

> For Gods sake Lords, conuay my tristfull Queene,
> For teares do stop the floudgates of her eyes

But then the hostess replies, 'O Iesu, he doth it as like one of these harlotrie plaiers as ever I see.' The shifting of perspective, and therefore the mixed mode, are complete when the actors remark upon their own theatrical devices.

In the early seventeenth century, through the agency of playwrights such as Marston and Beaumont, the 'tragicomedy' became 'the century's most popular dramatic form',[5] but a 'Tragicall Comedie' had already been acted before Elizabeth I in 1564. This conflation of sadness and absurdity has been the native and instinctive mode ever since drama first emerged in England, but now it acquired generic identity. In the frontispiece to Ben Jonson's *Workes* in 1616, the regal figure of 'Tragicomoedia' is flanked by 'Satyr' and 'Pastor' playing musical instruments. John Fletcher defined 'tragi-comedy . . . in respect it wants deaths, which is enough to make it no tragedy, yet brings some near it, which is enough to make it no comedy'. Dramatic conventions and theatrical 'types' were then thoroughly mingled, just as plots and themes had been. The English 'mungrell' idiom was established and defined. Or as Michael Drayton wrote at the end of his celebration of England, *Poly-Olbion*:

> My muse is rightly of the English straine
> That cannot long one Fashion intertaine

As in art, so in life itself. Dryden remarked that his play, *The Spanish Friar* (1680), was 'an unnatural mingle' devised in order to please the continuing 'Gothic' taste of the English audiences. His funeral was conducted according to the same precepts. As George Farquhar described it, 'And so much for Mr. *Dryden*, whose Burial was the same with his life; Variety, and not of a Piece. The Quality and Mob, Farce and Heroicks; the sublime and Redicule mixt in a Piece, great Cleopatra in a Hackney Coach.'

In this period there emerged 'anti-masques' celebrating disorder with parodic dance measures, and 'semi-operas' of a typically mixed form including spectacle, speech and song as well as 'heroic rant, conjuring and magical illusions, singing spirits, music as sexual temptation, political allegory, and interpolated masques'.[6] Seventeenth-century virtuosi criticised the 'medlie and motlie Designes' of contemporary artistic taste, and in English architecture of the seventeenth century there appeared an idiom which 'is neither Italian, French, nor Dutch Baroque but an increasingly interwoven mixture of the three, combined with elements borrowed from none, which are particularly English'.[7]

This mixed and motley style can also be applied to the English intelligence. Samuel Johnson wrote of Thomas Browne that 'His style is a tissue of many languages; a mixture of heterogeneous words, brought together from distant regions, with terms originally appropriated to one art, and drawn by violence into the service of another'. It recalls his criticism of the 'metaphysicals' for violent juxtaposition of imagery, but they were only mingling the sacred and the secular in the tradition of the mystery plays. Browne himself had a thoroughly English mind.

The constituents of eighteenth-century drama do not materially differ. The names change, but the reality remains the same. Thus 'monstrous medlies' became the most popular form of stage entertainment, earning the rebuke of Alexander Pope in *The Dunciad*:

Hell rises, Heav'n descends, and dance on Earth:
Gods, imps, and monsters, music, rage, and mirth,
A fire, a jigg, a battle, and a ball,
'Till one wide conflagration swallows all

The most popular and representative drama of the eighteenth century is, without any doubt, John Gay's *The Beggar's Opera* from which many imitations continue to emerge. The play, first performed in 1728, is concerned with the early eighteenth-century London 'underworld' in which a highwayman appropriately named Macheath is pursued both by Lucy, the daughter of a Newgate warder, and by the daughter of a receiver of stolen goods. It may seem simple enough, but its form is mixed and various. The *Whitehall Evening Post* 'found occasion to complain with equal tartness of *The Beggar's Opera* then running at the two main London theatres: at one house Lucy was being played as high tragedy, and at the other she was played as low comedy and "we scruple not to pronounce them both wrong" '.[8] *The Beggar's Opera* was neither farcical nor heroical, neither comic nor tragic, but all four at the same time. It was also intended as a parody of the Italian opera – hence the absurdly brazen *deus ex machina* at the end by means of which Lucy arranges Macheath's escape – and thus represents both the absorption, and rejection, of foreign influence. Gay had entitled an earlier play *The What D'Ye Call It* and labelled it as a 'Tragic-Comi-Pastoral Farce'. No one seemed to care. The audiences took naturally to it.

In the last act of *The Beggar's Opera* Macheath is in the condemned hold of Newgate when the bell of execution sounds; the gamester or gangster cries out, 'Here – tell the Sheriff's officers I am ready.' This is a pure theatrical joke, a parody of the same solemn moment in Otway's *Venice Preserv'd*, written almost fifty years earlier, when Pierre utters the immortal phrase, 'Come, now I'm ready' as the passing-bell tolls out its note of doom. It is meant to be a comic moment in *The Beggar's Opera*, yet instead it enters that enchanted English world where pathos and humour mingle effortlessly. Gay himself noted that, in this scene, 'how ludicrous soever the general character of the piece may be . . . the joke ceases'. He adds: 'I have observed the tolling of *St Pulchre's Bell* received with as much tragical attention and sympathetic terror as that in Venice Preserv'd.' Even within the parody and the burlesque the audience is plunged into pity and horror, before being immediately lifted out of it with the pastiche of a 'happy ending'. The power of the heterogeneous form is emphasised by the contemporaneous report that 'several thieves and street robbers confessed in Newgate that they raised their courage at the playhouse by the songs of their hero Macheath, before they sallied forth in their desperate nocturnal exploits'.

The Beggar's Opera was also considered to be a satire upon the thefts and depredations of Robert Walpole and his administration, so that 'high' and 'low' were conflated in a more pointed political sense; the whole of society is a highway robbery, in this account, with the face of the prime minister hidden by a scarf. In this context, therefore, we can see the 'mungrell' drama of the English as evincing that instinctive egalitarian or levelling spirit which is always present within the English imagination.

The association of Walpole and Macheath in the form of a 'monstrous medlie' was unwittingly complemented by Samuel Johnson's observation on English politics itself; he wrote in one pamphlet that governments 'are never to be tried by a regular theory. They are fabricks of dissimilar materials, raised by different architects, upon different plans.' This distrust of theory and regularity in all cultural proceedings is familiar enough; more significantly, perhaps, public administration itself is seen to partake of the 'mixed mode' so instinctive to English cultural expression. The analogy with 'different architects' serves only to confirm the native genius since, in the eighteenth century, architecture was also of the mixed and mongrel kind. It has been noted that the west front of St Martin-in-the-Fields, so incongruous a composition, was 'an attempt to re-create the effect of a Gothic spire in classical terms',[9] an odd effect by James Gibb which was immediately copied by less prominent English architects. James Wyatt designed one country house in a curious 'amalgam of Roman, Chambersian, Picturesque and Greek Revival elements'[10] and the whole mixed effect was deemed beautiful; John Nash, the architect who was most attuned to fashionable taste, built in 'Gothic, castellated, Italianate and classical styles'.[11] The garden at Kew once harboured 'an Alhambra, a mosque, a Gothic cathedral; a number of classical temples, a classical orangery, a ruined arch, a chinese pagoda and a "House of Confucius"'.[12]

The abiding tendency towards eclectic and heterogeneous ostentation is discussed by Nikolaus Pevsner in his *The Englishness of English Art*, where he notes that the mixed effect applied also to the mingling of past and present; he infers that in the sixteenth century 'funeral monuments were self-consciously made to look medieval',[13] and that eighteenth-century gentlemen's clubs were designed to resemble Renaissance palaces. He characterises it as 'this English quality, the quality that has made England the land of Follies'. He relates it to the reticence or detachment of the English artist, so that the 'mixed' mode comes naturally to those who cannot take seriously, or consider very long, one feeling or one style or one theory. He notes also that 'England was the first country to break the unity of interior and exterior and wrap buildings up in clothes not made for them but for buildings of other ages and purposes'.[14]

In nineteenth-century architecture, too, the 'mungrell' tendency is everywhere apparent in edifices which took traditional eclecticism and pastiche to even greater levels. There were four standard styles available – Greek, Italian, Tudor and Gothic – and they could be mixed in any proportion to guarantee the effects which we now call 'Victorian'. But there was also the 'Flemish Renaissance' style, and the 'Queen Anne' style; the New Scotland Yard building combined the modes of the Dutch and French Renaissance, while the Natural History Museum in South Kensington took Romanesque architecture as its model. The Brighton Pavilion was based upon 'Hindoo' originals. We may add that breaking 'the unity' has always been an English obsession. Alexander Pope thus describes, in English verse

> How Tragedy and Comedy embrace;
> How Farce and Epic get a jumbled race

These just representations of general nature begin with the beginning of life itself. In the sixteenth chapter of Laurence Sterne's *Tristram Shandy*, just after Tristram's mother has suffered a phantom pregnancy, 'my mother declared, these two stages were so truly tragicomical, that she did nothing but laugh and cry in a breath'. *Tristram Shandy* itself is a 'medley' or 'gallimaufry' taken to its widest and wildest extreme; it is a sterling example of that rambling, wayward, inconsistent and inconclusive native temper which Charles Dickens described as 'streaky well-cured bacon'.

The novels of Dickens himself have been alternately praised or blamed for their reliance upon the concatenation of farce and tragedy, pathos and romance. Dickens was much influenced by the conventions of nineteenth-century theatre, and in one speech declared that 'every writer of fiction, though he may not adopt the dramatic form, writes in effect for the stage'. The 'stage' of his period was characterised by extravagant plots and exaggerated performances, where tragedy and melodrama jostled each other for attention; he had as a child read the great works of eighteenth-century fiction, with their strange mixture of formality and farce, elegance and violence. The 'tragicall comedie' of urban life was compounded by his personal experience; he suffered violent changes in his own childhood, particularly when he was set to work in an old blacking factory. Hence the scrap of dialogue in *Nicholas Nickleby*:

> 'There were hyacinths there this last spring, blossoming in – but you'll laugh at that, of course.'
> 'At what?'
> 'At their blossoming in old blacking bottles.'

As a young man he wrote a parody of *Othello* with an Irish hero, O'Thello, and he knew already that he possessed a gift for subverting 'high' drama; in his early journalism he could mimic 'all the voices' from the judge and the beadle to the thief and the vagabond. While writing the comic and picaresque narrative of *The Pickwick Papers* he began the solemn and pathetic story of the orphan introduced to London servitude in *Oliver Twist*. But then *The Pickwick Papers* contains its own sorrowful mysteries, such as the powerful scenes set in Fleet Prison, and *Oliver Twist* is filled with a wild and hysterical humour. Once more we witness the workings of the native genius, in what Dickens described as 'the tragic and the comic scenes . . . sudden shiftings of the scene, and rapid changes of time and place'. All of his subsequent works are characterised by the violent transition of moods and themes, so that even in the description of wretchedness and despair he will find a detail which is inimitably comic.

There is another element here which is less easy of definition. Many contemporaries noticed a certain 'hardness' in Dickens's temperament and demeanour, and it may be that the heterogeneity of his style came from an unwillingness or incapacity to express wholly genuine feeling; every sentiment must be extravagant, and every emotion contrived. The mixed style, after all, was theatrical in origin. Yet it may also be aligned to a national character which, in previous centuries, was known for its violence and insensitivity to suffering.

It is difficult to express that which is amorphous. Englishness is the principle of appropriation. It relies upon constant immigration, of people or ideas or styles, in order to survive. This 'mungrell' condition was perhaps best expressed by Daniel Defoe, of all writers the most various and adaptable. In his poem, 'The True Born Englishman', the heterogeneity of the English imagination is lent its proper context:

> From this Amphibious Ill Born mob began
> That vain ill-natured thing, an Englishman . . .
> By which with easie search you may distinguish
> Your Roman-Saxon-Danish-Norman English.

Antiquarianism and English history

Britannia: frontispiece illustration to William Camden's *Britannia* (1600)

CHAPTER 30

Among the ruins

In his twenty-ninth year John Milton wrote in a letter that 'my genius is such that no delay, no rest, no care or thought almost of anything, holds me aside until I reach the end I am making for, and round off, as it were, some great period of my studies'. In Bread Street, London, he studied as if for life.

Milton is in all respects a profoundly English writer, and became an iconic representative of England for poets as diverse as Blake and Wordsworth. His first great ambition was to compose an epic upon the 'Matter of Britain'; in 1639, two years after composing the letter upon his genius, he wrote a poem in which he entreats his pastoral pipe, if *patriis mutata camoenis* (if transformed by native songs), to play a British melody. In another poem of the same period, 'Mansus', he speculates upon the commemoration of English kings in his own native verse. He was aware of his inheritance. The mystical vision surrounding *Paradise Lost* and *Paradise Regained* is conceived within the vast apparatus of the miracle plays; as one critic has put it, *Paradise Lost* is 'the last of the medieval attempts to write the history of Everyman, to survey the whole course of events from the Creation to man's final ascent into Heaven, and to relate this course to the universal plan of Divine Providence'.[1]

Paradise Lost was itself immensely influential. The resourceful and melodic verse of that poem revived, for all practical purposes, the role of blank verse in English poetry. Wordsworth's *Prelude*, for example, could not have been written without Milton's example. He became '*the* English author who could be presented as a classic to a burgeoning middle-class readership'.[2] Handel set his poetry to music, and scenes from that poetry were depicted by Blake, Fuseli and a host of other artists aspiring to the sublime. In the year of Milton's death John Dryden composed an opera of *Paradise Lost* entitled *The State of Innocence*, thus inaugurating two centuries of Miltonic imitation.

Even as Milton still wrote, his was known as an 'antiquated' style. This could be a term of celebration – 'ancient liberty recover'd to the Heroic Poem', as a 1688 edition of *Paradise Lost* asserted – or a term of mild opprobrium. One early eighteenth-century history claimed that

'Mr Milton chose to write (if the Expression may be allow'd) a hundred Years backward'. In the 1730s it was suggested by William Warburton that Milton's archaic style was 'best suited to his "English History"; his air of the antique giving a good grace to it'. Here Warburton touches upon a presiding element of Milton's genius and, by natural extension, of the English imagination itself; it lies in the nature, and nurture, of antiquarianism.

Goethe mocked the English obsession with the ruined fabric of the past. In his *Faust* Mephistopheles asks:

> Are Britons here? They go abroad, feel calls
> To trace old battle-fields and crumbling walls . . .

In the fifth act of Shakespeare's *Titus Andronicus*, a soldier remarks that:

> from our troupes I straid,
> To gaze vpon a ruinous Monasterie,
> And as I earnestly did fixe mine eye,
> Vpon the wasted building suddainely . . .

And in Webster's *The Duchess of Malfi* Antonio claims that

> I do love these ancient ruines:
> We do never tread upon them, but we sette
> Our foot upon some reverend history

The prospect of ruined walls seems to provoke some inward delight and to release some natural fervour. We are greedy for times past. Consider Byron drinking wine out of a monk's skull in the ruined quarters of his ancestral dwelling, Newstead Abbey, where 'Thy yawning arch betokens slow decay'. Shelley composed *Prometheus Unbound* among the ruins of the Baths of Caracalla and among scenes of 'sublime and lovely desolation'. Edward Gibbon conceived his *Decline and Fall* within the broken Capitol. Fatalism and melancholy are here mingled in characteristic fashion, but some pleasure may also be derived from the prospect of destruction and extinction; it is part of the curious English love affair with death itself, as if only that quietus can effectively destroy feeling. When this is conflated with an admiration for all things antique, then a rich mixture indeed is being concocted.

It may help to elucidate the mysteries of the native passion for artificial ruins, which was known throughout Europe to be a particularly English obsession. Picturesque ruins, constructed out of brick or painted on canvas, were first recommended in Batty Langley's *New*

Principles of Gardening published in 1728; the enthusiasm spread so rapidly that forty years later there were books concerned with the principles of their composition. 'In wild and romantic scenes', Thomas Whateley wrote, ' may be introduced a ruined stone bridge, of which some arches may still be left standing.' Lord Kames in *Elements of Criticism* (1762) remarked that these melancholy objects manifested 'the triumph of time over strength', which might be described as a characteristically Anglo-Saxon sentiment. Kames also suggested that their effect was picturesque since 'each of the emotions is most sensibly felt by being contrasted with the other'; this in turn might be considered a sufficiently native expression of that familiar appetite for heterogeneity and variety.

Classical ruins were agreed to be delightful, especially if adorned with ivy and judiciously arranged cracks, but it was believed that ancient British monuments were more suitable in an English landscape as 'an object to be seen at a distance, rude and large, and in character agreeable to a wide view'. There is a curious atavism at work here, manifested also in the desire to re-create thirteenth-century castles in the grounds of eighteenth-century stately homes. 'Mr Lyttleton', the poet and landscape gardener William Shenstone wrote, 'has near finish'd one side of his castle. It consists of one entire Tow'r, and three stumps of Tow'rs, with a ruin'd Wall betwixt them.' Shenstone himself assisted Bishop Percy in his collection of ancient British poetry, which demonstrates, perhaps, the ubiquity of these antiquarian restorations. Horace Walpole said of Lyttleton's edifice that 'it has the true rust of the Baron's wars' but, since its window tracings were taken from a minor thirteenth-century abbey at Halesowen, the nostalgia felt for the past was not unmixed with a certain delight in vandalism.

The Anglo-Saxon word *'aergod'* means literally 'as good as the beginning', and thus the most excellent or the very best. It is the antiquarian temper in miniature. The Anglo-Saxons themselves cultivated antiquarianism in a refined and learned spirit, and indeed the past of the Anglo-Saxon imagination was much more elaborate and more intense than any current model. To them, history was of pressing social and religious significance, and began at the moment of Creation. It was deeper and darker than our own misty sense of origin. King Alfred engaged enthusiastically in historical research, and his imagination ranged like an eagle over the kingdoms of the past. Bede loved to write of 'earthworks and walls, of ruined churches'.[3] The yearning for ruins is of long duration.

The English landscape itself seems to harbour ruins as if in an embrace, but their cultivation may also be an aspect of English melancholy. In the Anglo-Saxon poem 'The Wanderer', there is an invocation of the ruined walls which are 'standing beaten by the wind and covered with rime. . . . He then who in a spirit of meditation has pondered over this ruin and who with an understanding heart probes the mystery of our life down to its depths. . . . How that time passed away, grown shadowy under the canopy of night as though it had never been!' Another Anglo-Saxon poem is an elegy upon the same theme, and has been entitled 'The Ruin'; it is the harbinger of a flood of English writing devoted to the power of old stone.

In the early middle ages, too, there was a consciousness of what one literary historian has described as 'the fierce glory of the past';[4] it is evident in the romances as well as in the histories, in verse as well as prose chronicle. That past was seen as better and brighter than the present, furnishing examples of liberty and heroism all too manifestly absent from a contemporary England. The Arthurian romances, which many of the English imbibed as children, were a token of this lost inheritance. Yet here, too, there is an arresting connection. Is it not possible that this longing for the past was in part a longing for childhood itself? From this latent infantilism, too, may spring all the exuberance and violence of the early English character.

The conventions of antiquarianism were continued in verse history, monastic compilations, chronicles such as the *Gesta Regum Anglorum* and *Historia Novella*, as well as in the millions of charters prepared by scribes throughout the medieval period. Yet it was really only in the sixteenth century that antiquarianism became a recognised or at least recognisable pursuit, which as a result obtained institutional status. In 1586 the Society of Antiquarians was formed, with several distinguished members meeting regularly to read papers on various aspects of England's history. Tudor scholars were obsessed with genealogy and historiography, partly as a way of confirming contemporary dynastic politics within the myths and legends of the country and partly as a way of reclaiming the past in imminent danger of destruction at the hands of the religious reformers.

John Leland, who flourished in the first half of the sixteenth century, was the first Englishman to style himself an 'Antiquarian' and thus can lay claim to being the begetter of what became a significant national pursuit. He was educated at St Paul's School and at Cambridge, after which he studied for several years in Paris; the Erasmian humanism which he imbibed in his earlier years was, therefore, amplified by his studies in the texts of the ancients. But his antiquarianism itself was of specifically native growth. He became a royal librarian and, in 1533, was commissioned by Henry VIII 'to peruse and diligently to serche at the libraries of monasteries and collegies of this yowre noble reaulme, to the intente that the monuments of auncient writers as welle of other nations, as of this your owne province mighte be brought owte of deadely darkenes to lyvely lighte'. So he embarked upon a long journey across the realm, searching for ancient works which 'lay secretely yn corners' of old libraries and scriptoria. It is quite clear, from his notes and written records, that his passion for antique learning was matched only by his fascinated preoccupation both with the landscape of England and with the myths that sprang from it. In an account of the library of Glastonbury Abbey, Leland remarks that he 'paid my respects to the deity of the place'. In his *Itinerary* Leland divined the nature of English place, and bequeathed to the nation a tradition of sacred topography which has never wholly been lost; it is perhaps appropriate that, on his gravestone, his name is spelt Leyland in anticipation of the 'ley-lines' later traced across the English soil. In the words of one commentator, he became 'the forerunner of every travel writer on the subject of England from Defoe and Cobbett to H. V. Morton, Arthur Mee and Pevsner'.[5]

But the understanding of place was only one aspect of Leland's endeavours. As he makes plain in his published work, *The Laboriouse Journey and Serche for Englandes Antiquitees*, he was intent upon reclaiming and recovering the relics of the history of this island, and was in the process able 'to herald the establishment of a new kind of scholarship'.[6] He was passionately concerned with 'all the remains of most sacred antiquity', while 'the mere sight of the most ancient books took over my mind with an awe or stupor of some kind'. Among those books were the histories and chronicles compiled by the great scholars of the past. The antiquarian met his peers and colleagues in the course of his grand pursuit, and became aware of the longevity of historical enquiry in England. It was his good fortune to enter these libraries just two or three years before their destruction and dispersal at the time of the Reformation. This was a period when monasteries and convents were plundered by the agents of Thomas Cromwell, and when abbeys and other old foundations were destroyed for reasons of avarice and in order to signal the power of Henry VIII over the religious life of the nation. It was an act of wholesale devastation.

That is why ruins have always had an especial significance in England, where they are a visible token of an ancient civilisation extirpated in the early sixteenth century. The landscape of England was considered to be 'haunted with strange intimations from shadowy vanished worlds', while ruined abbeys and monasteries, abandoned chapels and hermitages, were the shipwrecks of an old storm. 'Amidst the gloom arose the ruins of an abbey,' William Gilpin wrote, '. . . a profusion of rich Gothic workmanship.' This was another meaning of 'Gothic' itself, as a synonym for a lost Catholic past. It might have sinister implications, since in 'Gothic' novels of the eighteenth century dark nuns and murderous monks pass by night, but the term was often touched with veneration and nostalgia. There has always been an organic need among the English to connect the present and the past, and the forced disassociation from a thousand years of Catholic history provoked in some a profound unease.

John Leland himself was perhaps the last man ever to touch or scrutinise *in situ* the texts of what is now a lost and forgotten inheritance. He saved some of the books, but most of the material was destroyed, 'some to serve theyr iakes [toilets], some to scoure theyr candelstyckes & some they sent over the see to the bokebynders, not in small nombre, but at tymes whole shyppes full, to the wonderynge of the foren nacyons'.

It is something of a paradox that the English, who of all nations used to pay homage to their past and to what Leland called 'examples of extraordinarily wonderful antiquity', should also be the most willing to efface and destroy that past; the vandalism of the Victorian developers in the 1880s, and of urban developers in the 1970s, testifies to that contrast. Yet it is not so difficult to elucidate. The power of the past lies beneath consciousness itself, and is so strong that the most invasive forces of destruction cannot necessarily efface it. It has also been argued that if antiquity is deeply embedded in place and in time, then extant physical memorials are not necessary.

Leland himself became insane, and was for two years in the care of his brother until he died; whether that insanity was produced by the spectacle of dissolution, and by the looting of all that he treasured, is an open question.

He was succeeded in his antiquarian zeal by a number of Tudor historians and topographers, among them John Stow, William

Camden, John Bale and Sir Henry Savile. In the sixteenth century there was a great demand for a national historiography as noble as national history itself. Bale asked for 'some learned Englishman . . . to set forth the English chronicles in their right shape'. It was recalled that Henry VII had 'complained much of our histories of England, and that the English nation, which is inferior to none in honourable actions, should be surpassed by all in leaving the memory of them to posterity'. Antiquarianism could then be associated with national pride, and with the humanist demand for a return to 'sources' and clarity of style; certain antiquarians were also concerned to revive the memory of the primitive English Church as a way of claiming spiritual legitimacy for England outside the jurisdiction of Rome. But the pure spirit of enquiry still remained the principal agent within the endless chronicles of the sixteenth century.

John Stow of London, however, can bear the title of Leland's worthy successor. He was born in 1525, the son of a tallow chandler in Threadneedle Street; although he practised as a tailor for a while, his true passions were antiquarian. His first published work was an edition of Chaucer, that great exemplar of 'ancient' English, before he embarked upon the systematic exposition of the old urban and national chronicles. In one of his earlier volumes, *A Summarie of Englyshe Chronicles*, he wrote that 'it is now eight years since I, seeing the confused order of our late English Chronicles, and the ignorant handling of ancient affairs, leaving mine own particular gains, consecrated myself to the search of our famous antiquities'. But his claim to enduring fame must lie with his comprehensive and elaborate *Survey of London*, published in 1598 as both a celebration and a memorial. It records the antiquities and monuments of the city, ward by ward, as well as local features and particular buildings. In a sense it captures the essence of English antiquarianism, which is conveyed in the notation and description of place. His *Survey* was successively edited and corrected by Munday, Dyson and Strype who themselves celebrated London as 'birthplace and breeder to us'.

This passionate attachment to one area is of the essence of antiquarianism. Stow loved London and spent much of his time wandering among its new buildings as well as its ruins which 'cost many a weary mile's travel, many a hard-earned penny and pound, and many a cold winter's night study'. Yet in this pursuit he noted buried walls and old halls, ruinated tenements and luxurious lodgings, tennis courts and warehouses, each of which he attempted to date; his was an enormous undertaking, and every English historian owes him a debt. Yet his greatest achievement, perhaps, was to lend antiquarianism a local habitation. In his reports upon areas of narrow lanes or of monuments to local worthies he divines the *genius loci* – 'now there is no such void place for willows to grow, more than the churchyard, wherein do grow some high ash trees. . . . The antiquities be these, first in Stayning Lane, of old time so called, as may be supposed, of painter-stainers dwelling there.'

His near contemporary, William Camden, had a similar reverence for the antiquity of place; his *Britannia* was published in 1568 with the purpose of restoring 'Britain to its antiquities and its antiquities to Britain' by undertaking a survey of each county. The pursuit is known as chorography – the writing of place – and seems particularly suited to the English imagination. Camden himself helped to establish the Society of Antiquarians, which lent institutional coherence to a presiding national passion. The antiquarians characteristically delivered in English rather than in Latin their papers on local topography and customs, on charters and chronicles, on tombs and monuments, on laws and genealogy. The linguistic bond between the nation and its inhabitants was thereby asserted. It has been suggested that antiquarianism itself sprang from changes in land ownership, so that new families and new gentry might be ennobled by their location in county history rather than in medieval chronicle; but the study of the society was wider ranging, embracing the interrelationship and historical interaction between the land and its people. At a later date antiquarians were generally acknowledged to be radical in intent, establishing, for example, the nature of pristine English 'liberties', but even at this early juncture there was a marked hostility to antiquarian research from the court; James I effectively closed down the society. By concentrating upon the land and its people, antiquarians were deemed to be anti-monarchical in tendency; this in turn suggests once more that the English imagination itself may be of implicitly egalitarian temper.

The antiquarian publications of the seventeenth century follow broadly in the tradition established by Leland, Stow and Camden; Elias Ashmole's *Institutions, Laws and Ceremonies of the Order of the Garter*, William Dugdale's *Origines Judicales* and Robert Plot's *Natural History of Oxfordshire* took antiquarian methods into different areas. In the 'epistle' to his *Parochial Antiquities* White Kennet remarked that 'I cannot but congratulate the present Age, that a genius to our National Antiquities seems now to invigorate a great many Lovers of their Country'. As one historian of seventeenth-century literature has remarked, 'Antiquarianism had undoubtedly become endemical in learned circles, and the utter devotion with which it was often pursued sometimes suggests that seventeenth-century fanaticism was emerging again in a new and more benign form.'[7]

Yet the rigour of such studies faded by degrees into a form of imaginative antiquarianism. Inigo Jones, on surveying the monoliths of Stonehenge, pronounced them to be of Roman origin; he was no doubt encouraged in this belief by the classical ambience of his masques for the early seventeenth-century court. John Aubrey was always of an antiquarian disposition; he studied old stones and collected evidence of folklore, all in the service of an overwhelming passion for the past. His contemporary, the antiquarian Anthony à Wood, described him as 'a pretender to antiquities . . . a shiftless person, roving and magotie-headed, and sometimes little better than crased . . . being exceedingly credulous, would stuff his many letters sent to A.W.[8] with fooleries and misinformations'. But in that sense Aubrey was the very model of an English antiquary; he was exactly the sort of person whom Goethe derided, but who has added immeasurably to the English capacity for nostalgic scholarship. His knowledge was capacious but piecemeal, and was transmitted in random notes or jottings. 'I have not leisure,' he wrote in typically English fashion, 'to heighten my Stile.' He had a native fascination for biographical detail, too, and his *Minutes of Lives* combine erudition and scandal in an unmethodical digest.

The full movement of fanciful or romantic antiquarianism, however, manifested itself in the eighteenth century as the precursor or harbinger of what has become known as 'romanticism'. The most celebrated and influential antiquarian study of the eighteenth century was undoubtedly Bishop Thomas Percy's *Reliques of Ancient English Poetry*, published in 1765; its three volumes created the 'ballad industry', which was to have so powerful an effect for the next two hundred years, and reintroduced the Arthurian myths into English discourse. The titles of many of the ballads, rescued and often 'improved' by Percy, are indicative: 'King Arthur and King Cornwall' vies with 'Robin Hood and Guy of Gisborne', while 'Hugh Spencer's Feats in France' lies alongside 'Durham Field'. Percy's collection also inaugurated a revision of English poetic history.

This tendency to look backward, in the act of historical retrieval, emerges also in the eighteenth-century rediscovery of ancient music. An

'Academy of Ancient Music' was established in 1731, and became 'the first organisation to perform old works regularly and deliberately';[9] it was joined in 1776 by the 'Concert of Ancient Music', and one historian has noticed that 'no other country rivalled it in the amount and diversity of old music performed during the eighteenth century; no other went so far in building up significant social roles for such works in public ritual, or in defining them as a canon'.[10] The antiquarian tradition had existed before; the term 'ancient music' emerged at the turn of the seventeenth century, and before that date Elizabethan 'anthems and services'[11] were performed in many English cathedrals. But in the eighteenth century 'ancient music' became a key phrase for any understanding of English culture. The academy published a series of letters upon musical subjects, addressed nominally to Italy, in one of which it was stated that 'when you cast your eyes upon those pieces [by Tallis and Byrd], you will clearly perceive that true and solid music is not in its infancy with us, and that, whatever some on your side of the Alps may imagine to the contrary, the muses have of old taken up their abode in England'. It is of some significance that, in 1728, Daniel Defoe was one of the first to propose an Academy of Music; William Hogarth, too, was one of its members. It would seem that the notion of ancient music was remarkably congenial to the English imagination. It has even been claimed that the 'tradition of ancient music was the foundation of the canon of musical classics in England',[12] where antiquarianism becomes the standard both of taste and of performance.

The same predilections are also to be found in the arts of architecture. William Kent and John Vanbrugh were enchanted and influenced by medieval architecture, and did not hesitate to reproduce ogees, quatrefoils and fan vaulting. Batty Langley published a volume entitled *Gothic Architecture Improved by Rules and Proportions* in 1747, but in fact it was the irregularity and eclecticism of Gothic which most appealed to the English imagination. Vanbrugh himself summarised this native inclination when he wrote that there 'is perhaps no one thing which the most polite part of mankind have more generally agreed on; than in the value they have set on ancient times'.

It is no paradox, therefore, that the culture of nineteenth-century England, which witnessed the development of an entirely new metropolitan civilisation, should itself have been similarly preoccupied with 'ancient times'. It is none the less curious that the Victorian age of innovation should also be the age of restoration, that a fervent belief in progress should be accompanied by a deep need for revival, and that a period of unprecedented industrial and commercial expansion should also be a period of unremitting nostalgia. Yet the vagaries of the human and social constitution are such that apparently irreconcilable forces can work together. There was some comfort to be derived, after all, from the close identification of Victorian architects and poets with medieval England; it offered a vision of permanence in the face of constant change, and a monument of faith in an age when scepticism and unbelief were everywhere apparent. The vogue for Pre-Raphaelite painting is part of the same movement of taste.

The close association with medievalism also provided an image of organic unity, of a civilisation established upon firm religious and cultural principles, in a period when every aspect of society was being called into doubt. Between 1821 and 1823 Augustus Charles Pugin published *Specimens of Gothic Architecture*, which may be seen as equivalent to Sir Walter Scott's *Kenilworth* composed in the same period. Nineteenth-century architecture itself is marked by a conflation of antique styles, from the early Gothic of Pugin himself, most thoroughly exemplified by the interiors of the Palace of Westminster, to the high Victorian Gothic of Butterfield and Burges. Even a pragmatist such as George Gilbert Scott realised that the English imagination was thoroughly backward. 'I am no medievalist,' he wrote in *Remarks on Secular and Domestic Architecture, Present and Future*,

> I do not advocate the styles of the middle ages as such. If we had a distinctive architecture of our own day worthy of the greatness of our age, I should be content to follow it; but we have not; and the middle ages having been the latest period which possessed a style of its own . . . I strongly hold that it has greater *prima facie* claims to be used as the nucleus of our developments than those of ancient Greece or Rome

Once more emerges the peculiar fact that an old style is considered more appropriate for a new civilisation; peculiar, that is, to the English imagination. Gilbert Scott's own attempts to restore the churches of medieval England were not altogether popular and prompted accusations of vandalism. His endeavours, however, led to the establishment by William Morris of the Society for the Protection of Ancient Buildings, an institution which reflected Morris's own intense medievalism, which in turn was exemplified by such writings as *The Defence of Guenevere and Other Poems*.

It was suggested, even at the time, that the language and attitudes of the past presented the best medium for understanding the forces of the present. The obliquity is always apparent in John Ruskin's writing, for example, where in *The Seven Lamps of Architecture* and *The Stones of Venice* he becomes a fiery prophet, loud in his denunciations and lavish in his celebrations, his own rich and multivalent prose levelled against the abuses of modern English culture. The same historicism was at work in Charles Lamb, albeit in milder vein, when the phantoms of an evanescent past are invoked to obscure or shade the horrors of modern civilisation. This nostalgic antiquarianism affected the work of poets also. Tennyson explained that 'It is what I have always felt even from a boy, and what as a boy I called "the passion of the past". And it is so always with me now; it is the distance that charms me in the landscape, the picture and the past, and not the immediate to-day in which I move.' Here is a clear exposition of one aspect of the English imagination which wishes to walk in the veiled distance and in remembered days. Even those writers most concerned with what in the nineteenth century was called 'the condition of England question' veiled their fictions in the subdued light of the past; Dickens is only the most obvious and formidable example. Shakespeare was never moved to address the social problems of his period and preferred, instead, to re-create a legendary English past. There are many English writers of genius who have been unwilling, or unable, to insert their work into the present moment or to sketch the outlines of the 'modern' condition. It is in part a matter of reticence and embarrassment, but it also represents a signal tendency within the national temperament.

John Stow

CHAPTER 31

The conservative tendency

Just as a medicine is 'conseruatyf of strength', there must necessarily exist a connection between antiquarianism and conservatism, in its ancient sense of preservation.

The fabric and structure of Anglo-Saxon building embody 'a clear impression of simplicity and veneration for the past: there seems to have been an unwillingness to sweep away old buildings to make way for modern innovations'.[1] In the building of the great fourteenth-century cathedrals, 'the English move was in the direction of more discipline and greater sobriety'[2] in opposition to that of her continental neighbours; in England rococo was renounced in favour of classicism, and the 'Flamboyant' style was ignored for the Perpendicular. English medieval painting consistently followed traditional principles, while the music of the thirteenth century manifested 'an inherent conservatism' principally 'by putting old techniques to new uses'.[3] Note values stayed the same for two centuries. The tradition of organ music remained unchanged from the Restoration to the late nineteenth century. Even in the twentieth century Benjamin Britten was celebrated for his ability 'to revitalise older elements in the musical language'.[4] Gerard Manley Hopkins and W. H. Auden revived the practice of alliteration in their various and different poetries.

It has been said that the 'New Towns' constructed after the Second World War represent 'extraordinary testimony to the continuities in English culture'.[5] The architectural styles of the era, particularly that known generally as 'Tudorbethan', testify to an innate conservatism or nostalgia for antiquated architectural form, where an allusion to 'the past' is supposed to convey substantiality and a measure of dignity to otherwise meretricious dwellings. The same pattern of permanence exists within other English structures; medieval halls become long galleries which in turn become picture galleries; Jacobeans copied Elizabethans who in turn copied medieval floorplans. There are certain regions of the country where 'it is impossible to date buildings even roughly on style alone', so persistent is one type of building.[6] In districts where stone can be quarried, late seventeenth-century houses are 'indistinguishable even in detail' from those of the early sixteenth century and, in the northern counties, the long and narrow houses have 'grown out of the common type of hall with upper and lower ends'[7] thus emphasising the common medieval inheritance.

But the conservative imagination is still best exemplified by the plain or common English house, a territorial interest 'unique among Europeans'.[8] English family homes, in particular, are remarkable for their conservatism and ubiquity. An observer of London has noted that 'the uniformity of the houses is a matter of course and has not been forced upon them';[9] it suggests some organic law of growth and being, as if the houses themselves reflect the spirit of their occupants. The same observer, Steen Eiler Rasmussen, has also noted that 'the common little house of which there have been thousands and thousands is only sixteen feet broad. It has probably been the ordinary size of a site since the Middle Ages.'[10]

English streets often follow ancient trackways. The lanes and alleys within the City of London were first laid at the time of the Roman settlement. 'Knight Rider Street', south of St Paul's Cathedral, is believed to contain the line of an old circus used for gladiatorial and equestrian display. The present Guildhall, in the City of London, is established on the site of the Roman amphitheatre where administrative matters were debated and which in turn the Saxons employed for their *folkmoots*. There is a continuity here of some two thousand years. The administrative units of the City of London, too, were first established in Saxon times; that air of good governance, which has always been characteristic of the City and indeed of the larger country, has ancient properties. The curve of an old field path is duplicated in the shape of West Street, beside Cambridge Circus, and the cross-roads at the Angel, Islington, are a simulacrum of the crossing of tribal paths many thousands of years before. It has often been said that London, vandalised by fire and architects equally, has lost its history. The powers and forces of past time, however, are not easily destroyed; they remain visible beneath the surface of the earth.

CHAPTER 32

A short history lesson

In England history has always been considered a manifestation of literature rather than of scholarship. There has been a blurring of formal boundaries, quite unlike the more disciplined or theoretical historical enquiries of France and Germany.

The sixteenth-century theatre, for example, witnessed the particularly English manifestation of the 'history play', and the models for nineteenth-century history painting were derived as much from fiction (Walter Scott) as from history (Lecky). No account of the English imagination is complete without an understanding of this strange yet very practical conflation in which myth or fiction is mingled with observed facts and details. It is the most expeditious way of creating a narrative, nobly exemplified by John Milton who, in his *History of England*, declared 'that which hath received approbation from so many, I have chosen not to omit. Certain or uncertain, be that upon the credit of those whom I must follow . . . I refuse not, as the due and proper subject of story.' There is so strong a consonance in the English language between story and history that no one seemed able or willing to distinguish one from another. Indeed Milton also declared: 'I have therefore determined to bestow the telling over ev'n of these reputed Tales; be it for nothing else but in favour of our English Poets, who by their Art will know, how to use them judiciously.'

Bede is the father of English historiography, but he also possesses the moral and literary intent which shapes his historical imagination. 'If history records good things of good men,' he wrote, 'the thoughtful reader is encouraged to imitate what is good . . .'[1] There is a story of a 'Briton' named Lucas who, in the twelfth century, incited an army 'to fight to avenge their fallen comrades by relating history to them';[2] this must represent one of the most practical instances of the historical imagination at work. As one historian has put it, 'History was fundamental to medieval English experience and thought',[3] whether in the form of verse or chronicle.

The verse fiction concerned with Arthur, Layamon's *Brut*, became 'the standard vernacular history text-book of late medieval England',[4] and the human past itself became a repository of stories and adventures of an exemplary nature. As C. S. Lewis has remarked in his study of the medieval period, *The Discarded Image*, 'the question of belief or disbelief' was not of paramount concern; the true significance of reading history was simply 'to learn the story'.[5] If the historical past differed from the present, it was only in the fact of its being better and more glorious. These habits of thought may change their forms, but they do not wholly die.

In the sixteenth and seventeenth centuries, for example, the resources of English history were considered material for tragedy rather than heroic fable. Sir Walter Raleigh's *History of the World* includes the passage 'Thou hast drawn together all the far-fetched greatness, all the pride, cruelty, and ambition of man, and covered it over with those two narrow words, *Hic Jacet*'; the historical imagination is united here for a moment with English melancholy. That private note, almost one of self-communing, persists in seventeenth-century historical writing, most notably in Clarendon's *The True Historical Narrative of the Rebellion and Civil Wars in England* and Gilbert Burnet's *History of My Own Times* where autobiography, biography and historical narrative are effortlessly mingled in what are truly literary texts. The historian duly recorded events that occurred, according to his discrimination and judgement, but the dry exactitude of continental accounts was singularly missing.

It has often been said that 'pure' history began to be composed in the eighteenth century, but this is to overlook the mixed nature of the enterprise. Historians of the Whiggish tendency were eager to create a history of progress and gradual enlightenment, particularly in social and governmental affairs, and were, albeit unconsciously, translating into institutional terms Bede's injunction to record 'good things of good men' so that 'the thoughtful reader is encouraged to imitate what is good'. Other historians of the period sought for general 'laws' of society and human activity, which could then be transmitted in didactic fashion; their emphasis is not so different from that of medieval saints' lives, where the exemplary patterns of history are considered of most importance. Eighteenth-century history has in fact been described as 'philosophy, teaching by example'.[6] Clarendon and Gibbon both wrote autobiography as well as history; the novelists Tobias Smollett and Oliver Goldsmith both composed histories as well as fictions. Gibbon's great work, *The History of the Decline and Fall of the Roman Empire*, shares with Johnson's *Dictionary* the general desire for moral education, to elevate and to purify the reader, but the creative impulse is as pervasive and as significant as the didactic or historical.

In eighteenth-century England history painting was considered to be the highest and most noble of painterly genres. Sir Joshua Reynolds, in his *Discourses* at the Royal Academy, defined it as the summation of all art. It was the 'Great Style' which, in its emphasis upon significant and virtuous form, covered epochs as disparate as the classical and the medieval; if the subject was in any way ancient, it was creditable. Of course the preoccupation with historical themes was not unique to England, but in this country it was taken up with most enthusiasm. As an eminent historian of English art has put it, 'historical painting was more in accord with the Anglo-Saxon temperament';[7] indeed there were many compositions upon specifically Anglo-Saxon subjects such as Alfred and Vortigern. The eighteenth-century painter, James Barry, expressed the national ideal when he suggested that history painting and sculpture 'should be the main views of any people desirous of gaining honours by the arts. These are the tests by which the national character will be tried in after-ages.' It is a broad statement but, in a period when the power of history had seized the English imagination, it was considered to be no less than truth.

The young artists of the second half of the eighteenth century were possessed by the ideas and ideals of the past; one need only look at the records of the Royal Academy exhibitions to comprehend the extraordinary confluence of taste. In 1763 Robert Edge Pine received a hundred-guinea prize for his painting of Canute, while in the same year John Hamilton Mortimer completed his portrait of the humiliation of Queen Emma. There were portraits of Edward III, Earl Godwin, Cymbeline and Ethelred; there were historical engravings executed on a subscription basis such as Boydell's *Shakespeare Gallery* and Bowyer's *Historic Gallery*. The obsession was in turn aligned to a movement in theatrical taste, with the introduction of 'period costume' upon the stage, and the production of such dramas as John Brown's *Athelstan*, Richard Glover's *Boadicea* and Thomas Arne's *Alfred*.

The lines between history and myth – or, more crudely, between fact and fable – became increasingly difficult to unravel, but so powerful was the hold of historicity upon the English imagination that no serious effort to accomplish this was even undertaken. As Jonathan Richardson put it in his *Essay on the Theory of Painting*, 'as to paint a History, a Man ought to have the main qualities of a good Historian, and something more; he must yet go higher, and have the Talents requisite to be a good poet; the rules for the conduct of a Picture being much the same with those to be observed in writing a poem'. It might be added, in parenthesis, that the rules for the composition of history were also much the same as those for poetry itself.

Gibbon's *Decline and Fall*, the first volume of which was published in 1776, anticipates by a decade or so that fascination with the mysterious and the primitive which marked the beginning of 'romanticism'; it is also the harbinger of Gothic and of the 'sensational' in literary fiction. Like all great historians, Gibbon was preoccupied with style. His mode of composition was to 'cast a long paragraph in a single mould, to try it by my ear, to deposit it in my memory, but to suspend the action of the pen 'til I had given the last polish to my work'. This was to be partly the procedure of Charles Dickens who wrote *A Child's History of England* with a thoroughly nineteenth-century emphasis upon what the Victorians termed 'the battle of life'. It was a narrative of conflict and desire, manifested in certain key words such as 'turbulent', 'relentless' and 'dreadful'. It was animated, too, by what the nineteenth-century historian J. A. Froude described as the central principle of historiography: 'One lesson, and only one, history may be said to repeat with distinctness; that the world is built somehow on moral foundations; that, in the long run, it is well with the good; in the long run, it is ill with the wicked.' This is also the message of Bede and of the other Anglo-Saxon historians who considered 'history as veiled revelation full of intimations, mutually confirmative, of an ever-present divine plan'.[8] It also repeats the methodology and purpose of the medieval chroniclers and poets.

Dickens's emphasis upon the 'battle of life' is related to other Victorian themes. There are many connections and associations between the author of *The Origin of Species by Means of Natural Selection*, for example, and the writer of *Great Expectations* and *Hard Times*. Just as Charles Darwin read Milton and Dryden, so in turn his theoretical text was read by George Eliot and Anthony Trollope. Darwin also read contemporary fiction, sent by post from the London Library, in order to mitigate the symptoms of his nervous complaints; in the process he thoroughly absorbed the mechanism of their plots. He also read Henry Buckle's *History of Civilisation in England* and Henry Mayhew's *London Labour and the London Poor*. *The Origin of Species* itself begins like a novel – 'When on board the H.M.S. *Beagle*, as naturalist, I was much struck with certain facts in the distribution of the inhabitants of South America' – and then proceeds to depict a dark world dominated by struggle and sexuality, by the necessity of labour and the appetite for power. Marx condemned *The Origin of Species* as a harsh 'satire' upon the possibilities of mankind, and that literary or generic reference is the best possible introduction to what is essentially a work of fiction, even if the fiction is concealed within Darwin's scientific transcriptions. The darkness and complexity of Darwin's world are matched by the description of London in Dickens's *Bleak House*. And why should it not be so? The blurring of boundaries and of genres, so instinct and vital an aspect of the English imagination, also reveals a profound truth. It discloses the power of language itself. To force divisions within the English language is to work against its capacious and accommodating nature. To expect a writer to produce only novels, or histories, is equivalent to demanding from a composer that he or she write only string quartets, or only piano sonatas. Music is music; writing is writing. All of them are contained within English music.

In the English tradition

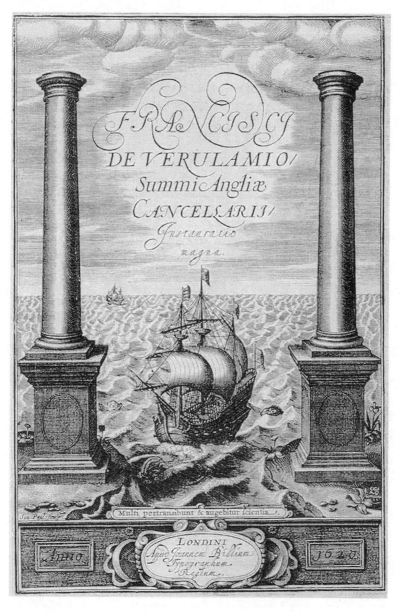

The pillars of Hercules. Title page of Francis Bacon's *Instauratio Magna*, 1620

CHAPTER 33

The song of the sea

The island is filled with the sounds of the sea. In Anglo-Saxon poetry, the metaphor of the ship was used as a token of movement and of composition itself, the narrative becoming a vessel which had to be driven across the face of the deep. The ship also became the frail form of the human being tossed on the ocean of life, with faith and hope and charity as its three anchors. King Alfred continually resorted to nautical imagery, and his own experience of the sea in peace and in war informs his writing; he declares, for example, that 'a good steersman, by the raging of the sea, is aware of a great wind ere it come. He bids furl the sail and sometimes lower the mast, and let go the cables, and by making fast before the foul wind he takes measures against the storm.'[1] He uses many compound variants for the sea – *egorstream, hronmere, laguflod, fifelstream, merestream* – as if its reality could only be understood as shifting and multitudinous. It rises, too, in other Anglo-Saxon prose: in Byrhtferth's invocation of 'the salt sea-strand', for example, and in Werferth's description of 'the person who approaches land in a frail ship'.[2] In *The Anglo-Saxon Chronicle* we read of 'the tossing waves, the gannet's bath, the tumult of waters, the homeland of the whale',[3] this fervent litany calling up the spirit of the deep. The poetry of the sea is deeply implicated in the Anglo-Saxon imagination with its '*sealte saestreamas ond swanrade*', the salt sea-currents which are the swans' path, running into all subsequent English verse. The sea is also '*cald waeter*' with lines which vary 'the emphasis on the "depths" to "space" to "terror" '[4] suggesting the English fear of the ocean. In Anglo-Saxon poetry it is as if the island of Britain were truly the home or harbour. This in turn has informed the pastoral dream of England as a calm and tranquil haven. The exile or wanderer, in contrast, is customarily depicted as surrounded by 'the sea booming – the ice-cold wave'.[5]

The depths of the sea are used as the image of privation and isolation, even of hell itself, 'that bottomless swell beneath the misty gloom'.[6] The answer to one Anglo-Saxon riddle, invoking the 'ocean bed' and 'the vast depths of the sea', is presumed to be 'submarine earthquake'.[7] In the fourteenth century Dame Julian of Norwich is taken in vision 'downe into the see-ground, and there I saw hill and dalis grene,

semand as it were mosse begrowne, with wrekke and gravel'. The same
vision was also vouchsafed to William Blake who depicted Newton on
the floor of the sea, sitting upon a moss-stained rock with his compasses
spread out before him. We can put with it Blake's lament:

> The Corse of Albion lay on the Rock the sea of Time & Space
> Beat round the Rock in mighty waves & as a Polypus
> That vegetates beneath the Sea . . .

So an image created in the eighth or ninth centuries casts a shadow for
many hundreds of years. The sea is both margin and mystery. The
historian Gildas describes how the Britons were driven to the sea's edge
by their oppressors, until the sea drove them back again. In medieval
fable there are many departures by sea, with erstwhile companions left
weeping by the shore. Layamon, in his epic poem *Brut*, changes his
French source in order to concentrate upon storm and shipwreck; the
alliterative *Morte Arthure* resonates with all the qualities of the sea, the
ancient measure of the verse summoning up some instinctive and native
response to the delights and perils of the encroaching waters. We might
even be inclined to believe that the Saxons rode over 'the sea's bath' and
'the whale's road' to the chanting of alliterative song, its measures
mingling with the beat of the waves.

English writers, employing continental models, continually enlarge
their source material with national tales of ships and of the sea. Of John
Gower, that most representative of medieval English poets, it has been
written that 'the idioms and technical terms of shipmen and the sea are
amongst the most distinctive features of his language'.[8] It is a national
preoccupation, evinced no less in painting and in music than in poetry.

The fashion for marine painting had its origins in the eighteenth
century, and the great master of the English sea was J. M. W. Turner.
He was the painter of storms, effortlessly able to convey the huge
movement of waters; he was the poet of rain-clouds and winds, tracing
on canvas the gusts of turbulent light. Once he had himself lashed to a
mast so that his own breath and the breath of the sea might be mingled
and surely here, if anywhere, there is some native or atavistic spirit at
work; it is as if this Cockney boy, who felt the romance of the ocean,
were becoming once more the seafarer of the Anglo-Saxon lament. He
painted the sea in all its manifestations and conditions, from the turbid
magnificence of *The Fighting Téméraire* to the quiescence of the
Evening Star. Of *Snow Storm*, where a steam-boat is seen in a vortex

of mist and swirling water, Ruskin wrote that it is 'one of the very grandest statements of sea-motion, mist, and light, that has ever been put on canvas, even by Turner'. In *Staffa, Fingal's Cave* all the yearning of Turner's nature is to be found in the evanescent glow of the sun setting upon the face of the deep while all around great clouds of mist and darkness cast their shadows over the heaving waters. When human figures are introduced into his sea-scapes, fishermen or mariners, they are frail things; they are bowed before the immensity. Turner has often been compared or associated with the 'romantic' poets, particularly in his understanding of natural sublimity, but in truth his instinct and inspiration lie much farther back in a physical or physiological response to the movement of great waters.

In *The Enchafed Flood* W. H. Auden, who had himself been so mightily stirred by the Anglo-Saxon imagination, remarked that the sea represents 'that state of barbaric vagueness and disorder out of which civilisation has emerged'. In similar spirit, some trace memory of original Saxon migrations lies, perhaps, within the fascination and horror of Turner's seas. For Auden the sea represented the true condition of humankind, the setting of all great choices and decisions, so that even in this twentieth-century poet there is the residue of some strange atavistic passion.

But if there is one contemporary who matches Turner in his pre-occupation with the sea, it is Charles Dickens. Both artists of London lived by a huge tidal river, and became entranced by the waters. Many of Dickens's novels have settings by the sea's edge, and few of them are not haunted by its presence. There is the sea that Paul Dombey stared into, looking into the ancient fashion of the waves before his impending death; there is gentle Mr Toots wandering by the shore where 'The waves were hoarse with repetition of their mystery; the dust lies piled upon the shore; the sea-birds soar and hover; the winds and clouds go forth upon their trackless flight; the white arms beckon, in the moon-light, to the invisible country far away'. There is the sea upon which Martin Chuzzlewit, and little Emily, and Mr Micawber, variously depart. There is the storm at sea in which Steerforth dies, where 'high watery walls came rolling in, and, at their highest, tumbled into surf . . . a rending and upheaving of all nature'. There is the sea of David Copperfield's memory with 'the sun, away at sea, just breaking through the heavy mist, and showing us the ships, like their own shadows. . . . I have never beheld such sky, such water, such glorified ships sailing away into golden air.' It is the poetry of light and water, equivalent to

what Kenneth Clark called the 'chromatic fantasies' of Turner's sea-
scapes, and in the consonance between the writer and the painter we
may glimpse some stirring of the English genius.

The sea is a constant presence in nineteenth-century poetry, moving
within Byron's *Childe Harold's Pilgrimage*:

> Roll on, thou deep and dark blue Ocean – roll!

and within Tennyson's verse:

> Break, break, break,
> On thy cold gray stones, O Sea!

It also flows within Matthew Arnold's threnody of loss:

> The sea is calm to-night.
> The tide is full, the moon lies fair

There the waves of the tide beat:

> With tremulous cadence slow, and bring
> The eternal note of sadness in

The waters gather in Rossetti's 'sad blueness' and 'the murmur of the
earth's large shell'. The deep peace of the sea is celebrated by Hardy,
'And over a gate was the sun-glazed sea', almost as if it were a rolling
landscape, with its own hills and valleys reproducing the soft curves
of the English countryside; it is a vision of rest, or perhaps of oblivion.
The sea is, perhaps, the true landscape of the English imagination.
In Hippolyte Taine's capacious survey of English literature, there
suddenly emerges a great paean to the sea 'ever intractable and fierce'.
Thus he suggests that 'not in vain is a people insular and oceanic,
especially with this sea and these coasts . . . its waves leap with strange
gambollings, and their sides take an oily and livid tint . . . here and there
on the limitless plain, a patch of sky is shrouded in a sudden shower'.
The mystery and melancholy of England itself are exemplified in
passages such as this.

In the cadences of the most nostalgic and sorrowful music, the sea can
also be heard. 'O past, O happy life' are the plangent words that
accompany the epilogue of Delius's *Sea Drift* in 1908. Two years later,
Ralph Vaughan Williams's *A Sea Symphony* was first heard. Both of
them were based upon the poetry of Walt Whitman but they are filled
with what can only be called 'a recognisably English idiom',[9] matched

by Henry Newbolt's *Songs of the Sea* and John Masefield's *Salt-Water Ballads* of the same period. Two song cycles, Stanford's *Song of the Sea* and Elgar's *Sea Pictures*, suggest the constant awakening presence of surrounding waters. Vaughan Williams composed *Riders to the Sea* while Arnold Bax wrote *The Garden of Fand*, which is the sea, and *Tintagel* 'in which enormous breakers may be imagined crashing against the coast of Cornwall'. In Bax's work the tinctures of myth subtly irradiate the composition, so that the mystery of the sea is deepened and strengthened. The opening bars of his Fourth Symphony 'are said to represent a choppy sea at floodtide on a sunny day',[10] and he died looking out over the Atlantic 'burnished to beaten gold in the rays of the setting sun'.[11] The principle of 'melodic stability' and 'harmonic changeability',[12] so profound a duality in English music, might have been prompted by the sound and movement of the sea.

Vaughan Williams collected folk-songs about the sea, and their melodies inform his own music. Benjamin Britten wrote two celebrated operas concerning the sea, *Peter Grimes* and *Billy Budd*. In *Billy Budd*, based upon a story by Herman Melville, the swell of the sea is musically associated with the murmurs of mutiny on board ship. *Peter Grimes*, inspired by a poem of George Crabbe's, is redolent of the sea in every note but especially in the orchestral interludes which link the separate Acts. The score of *Peter Grimes* has been characterised as 'the grinding of surf against shingle', 'the gulls' cry', 'the jangle of rigging against masts in the storm' and the deep sea-fog.[13] It is impossible not to hear, in this litany of effects, the echoes of the Anglo-Saxon poetry of the sea. There is a continuity.

CHAPTER 34

A brief excursion

The course of an adventurous sea-voyage represents one of the enduring myths of the English imagination. It is charted in the pages of *Utopia*, *Robinson Crusoe* and *Gulliver's Travels*; the fact that all are fiction has not mitigated the effect. Islanders pride themselves on their ability to travel through inhospitable regions of the earth. When Abbot Brendan and his cohort of monks sailed across the cold and lonely ocean, 'and all the while they had nothing to look at but the sea and the sky',[1] they are anticipating the plight of English seafarers everywhere; in particular they are the harbingers of *The Ancient Mariner*.

One of the earliest travel books in the English language was written between 754 and 768, and related the journey of Willibald to Jerusalem. In a sea-locked island such expeditions smack of the marvellous. That is why the Norwegian, Ohthere, and the Dane, Wulfstan, were taken to King Alfred's court, so that they could inform him at first hand of their adventures in the White and Baltic seas. There are beasts called reindeer in the land of the Lapps; in Estonia the dead are 'refrigerated' for six months before the ceremonies of cremation. These may be deemed factual accounts, while Anglo-Saxon productions such as the *Letter of Alexander to Aristotle* and the *Wonders of the East* are filled with centaurs and man-monsters, dragons and satyrs. Other accounts, such as the *Voyage* of St Brendan himself, hover characteristically and ambiguously between 'fact' and 'fiction'. As in many other English narratives, the comparative status of reality and vision is fundamentally in doubt.

This will help to explain the popularity and success of Mandeville's *Travels*; it was written in Anglo-Norman French but by 1400 it had been translated into a number of European languages. The 'insular version' of the text was confined to England, however, from where its author was generally supposed to have come. He claimed to be 'Sir John Mandeville' but this was an assumed or fictitious name. It is sometimes suggested that the *Travels* is the work of a Frenchman, but then why did he adopt the pose of a rusted old English knight who was born and bred in St Albans? In its preface the anonymous compiler insists that he has translated the book out of Latin and French 'into

Englyssch, that every man of my nacioun may understonde it'. There was a great deal to 'understonde'. Its principal focus is Jerusalem and the immediate neighbourhood of that sacred area. In that context travel books could become manuals of devotion, but that was not Mandeville's intent. In true English fashion he borrowed and adapted sections from earlier and more authentic travels, most notably from William de Boldensele and Friar Odoric of Pordenone, before con-flating them within his own homely style. His most daring innovation, however, lay in his suggestion that he himself had participated in the travels and voyages which he disclosed to a no doubt credulous public. He has 'cerched manye full strange places'. He has travelled the land of the Amazons and entered the Imperial Palace at Constantinople; he has been a guest in the household of the Great Khan, and describes the mythological dominions of Prester John. He has seen diamonds that sweat in the presence of poison; he has seen gourds of fruit that, when opened, reveal the bodies of creatures like 'a lytill lomb, withouten wolle'. He was given a thorn from the Crown of Thorns worn by Jesus and with thirteen other travellers had entered the Vale Enchanted, otherwise known as the Vale of Devils or the Vale Perilous, 'but at our going out we were but nine'. This fictional valley later re-emerged as the Valley of the Shadow of Death in Bunyan's *Pilgrim's Progress*.

This joy in the arcane places of the earth is shared by other writers. In a *Cosmography* published in 1652, reference is made to a hill of 'Amara'; it is 'a day's journey high, on the top whereof are thirty-four palaces'. The high and sacred spot then emerges in the fourth book of *Paradise Lost* as

> Mount Amara, though this by som suppos'd
> True Paradise under the *Ethiop* Line

Amhara is the name given by Samuel Johnson to the country of the 'Happy Valley' in his short novel, *Rasselas*, itself a fine addition to the English delight in fictional travel-writing. This valley was 'in the kingdom of Amhara, surrounded on every side by mountains'. There is an element of snugness, or cosiness here, which is the obverse side to the passion for the dangers and hardships of imagined travel. If the same region helped to inspire Coleridge's 'Kubla Khan', where in a vision the poet sees a maid 'singing of Mount Abora', then the fantastic mountain is a truly distinctive feature upon the map of English literature.

Many medieval romances included long passages of description upon the perils and marvels encountered by heroes wandering in far-off lands, but this attraction to enchanted or distant ground may be part of a larger desire for escape. There may be some atavistic longing among islanders to 'get away'. England was from the Anglo-Saxon period an intensely governed country; if it has also been at various times an over-administered one, the desire of many travellers may have consisted in a flight from the conditions of English civilisation itself. The English penchant for the dream and the vision may in turn be part of a general escape from the conventions of practicality and common sense which make up so much of the native psyche. The tradition of empiricism or pragmatism is not in contradiction to the equally large inheritance of ghosts, dreams and visions; they are opposite sides of the same coin of the realm. The evidence may be found in the surviving examples of English cartography; these maps are replete with detailed and accurate information but of course they are flanked by angels, gods, and only semi-human figures.

The traveller depicts all that England is not. Thus Raleigh invokes 'the most beautiful country that ever mine eyes beheld' along the Orinoco, with 'plains of twenty miles in length'. Another traveller, Peter Martyr, confessed that 'Smooth and pleasing words might be spoken of the sweet odors, and perfumes of these countries, which we purposely omit, because they make rather for the effeminating of men's minds'. There are dangers, as well as delights, in these new-found worlds. The women 'be very hot and disposed to lecherdness . . . they live commonly 300 years'. In Sierra Leone resides 'an empress of all these Amazons, a witch and a canniball who daily feeds on the flesh of boys'. The appetite for the marvellous is sufficiently powerful to need no explanation but, in addition, the English affection for such literature springs in part from the need to comprehend and master that which is not English. We may say that English travel-writers define their nationhood by describing other nations; it is an instinctive form of reassurance.

It also reflects, of course, the native passion for seafaring. The title page of Francis Bacon's *Instauratio Magna* contains the engraving of a ship setting forth upon unknown waters beyond the Pillars of Hercules; it is the ship of knowledge, sailing upon strange seas of thought, and is the emblem of an island race which sees water as the natural frontier. Hawkins and Drake, Davis and Frobisher and Raleigh have entered the national consciousness because of their association with the things of the sea; their adventures as pirates, explorers and masters of the burgeoning English empire became the staple material of English fiction and English poetry. These Elizabethan adventurers were joined in later years by Scott and Oates, representative English heroes who faced an uncharted and inhospitable wilderness of ice.

Richard Hakluyt's compilation, *The Principall Navigations, Voiages and Discoveries of the English Nation*, was enormously influential from its first publication in 1589. These sea-works 'created a taste for exotic lands across the sea which in time would become more familiar to English people than the heart of Europe'.[2] J. A. Froude described *The Principall Navigations* as 'the prose epic of the modern English nation', in which England itself becomes the principal actor or character. Hakluyt indeed knew that he was fashioning an epic, and deliberately introduced epic material, but in the words of Richard Helgerson in *Forms of Nationhood* his principal purpose was 'to reinvent both England and the world to make them fit for one another'.[3] He achieves this feat of collation in a very English spirit, in his own words by attempting 'to bring antiquities smothered and buried in dark silence, to light' and by creating 'this homely and rough-hewn shape' of a discourse. Amateurism and antiquarianism are thus aligned in an embarrassed but spirited apology.

His is not a moral or heroic venture, however, but one established upon profit and commerce. His first work was entitled *A Discourse of the Commodity of the Taking of the Strait of Magellanus*, and is an account of putative damage to the English cloth trade; his is a highly pragmatic and practical apologia for sea-travel. Hakluyt's 'later collections are compendia of information . . . organised by geographical region for the easy use of travellers and strategic planners',[4] and he regards 'England as an essentially economic entity, a producer and consumer of goods'.[5] So in this sense tales of travel become shop-windows for putative purchasers; *The Principall Navigations* is a prose epic of commerce. Its two thousand pages, its 216 voyages, its hundreds of supporting documents, are witness to England's 'great trade and traffic in merchandise'. There are no high sentiments or noble rhetorical flourishes; the work is sensible and practical. Where there are two headings on the virtue of spreading Christianity, for example, there are twenty-eight upon the details of trade. Hakluyt himself disparaged the ornate aspirations of the Spanish and Portuguese 'pretending in glorious words that they made their discoveries chiefly to convert infidels to our most holy faith (as they say)' when essentially they were seeking 'goods and riches'. This is the true voice of an English writer who retreats in the face of high sentiment or high language. Instead of quoting books of divinity and scholarship, he employs the archives of the great trading companies. His principal characters are not saints or heroes, or even military adventurers, but London merchants. This is of great significance in any account of the English imagination, where the work of tradesmen is continually being amplified. Even Robinson Crusoe is a kind of merchant. The greatest English enterprise of the age was the East India Company.

The style of Hakluyt's narrative does nothing to dispel this impression; letters of wares and lists of prices are printed in the same 'black-letter folio with decorated capitals'[6] as dedicatory poems. The three volumes contain an 'extraordinary variety of documents ranging from epic fragments of Parmenius and Chapman to commercial lists like Newberg's'.[7] It has been said that the sea-voyages of the sixteenth century were primarily concerned with colonisation and subsequent plunder; the same acts of piracy may be recognised within the English imagination itself, which appropriates the vocabularies of strange lands only to engorge them within its existing structure.

Yet the emphasis in collections of travel literature of the seventeenth century shifted from the marvels of Mandeville to the poetry of fact. William Dampier's *A New Voyage Round the World*, published in 1697, pledges 'the Truth and Sincerity of my Relation'. In 'this plain piece of mine', Dampier has chronicled 'such Observables as I met with'. In his insistence upon 'observable' particulars and circumstantial detail Dampier manifests the English preoccupation with living truth, most profitably to be glimpsed in minute particulars. The pose of the narrator is that 'of the ordinary man of common sense whose personal observations may be trusted by virtue of his lack of specialist skills (especially literary ones)'.[8] In a later volume, *Voyage to New Holland*, Dampier prefaces his narrative with the claim that it is 'a Plain and Just Account of the true Nature and State of the Things described'; the fact that he dedicated this book to the President of the Royal Society suggests his emphasis upon the practicality and usefulness of the information he was concerned to impart. He also had an interesting habit 'of eating most of the strange animals he describes',[9] which might be considered as the height of English pragmatism.

It is also worth noting here that the inventions of English technicians such as the wind gauge, and the discovery of English scientists concerning the properties of magnetism, materially assisted the capacity of sea-voyaging. Volumes such as William Gilbert's *De Magnete* (1600) and Edward Wright's *Certaine Errours in Navigation* (1598) can be said to have 'set the seal on England's supremacy in the theory and practice of navigation'.[10] In that sense travel literature can be understood as an example of native triumphalism. The narratives of eighteenth-century travel, for example, included volumes by explorers and by natural scientists, by clerics and by scholars, by archaeologists and by novelists. The voyages of Cook, Bligh and Vancouver were documented. Fielding described his journey to Lisbon, while Sterne embarked upon 'a sentimental journey' through France and Italy, and William Beckford dallied in Portugal. Tobias Smollett composed his own *Travels through France and Italy*. We might include Samuel Johnson's journey to the Western Islands of Scotland in this company, if only because the great arbiter of English letters had an especial fondness for travel literature. His first published work was a translation of Father Lobo's *A Voyage to Abyssinia*, which helped to fashion his own image of that exotic culture in his subsequent novel *The History of Rasselas, the Prince of Abissinia*. Johnson owned an atlas, for which he compiled his own index at the back, and sustained an enormous appetite for travel literature of every description. Rasselas, despondent in the 'happy valley', finds his amusement in portraying 'to himself that world which he had never seen'; this might be considered as one of the principal delights of travel literature itself, especially for those immured upon an island. The prince's guide, Imlac, had travelled to Agra, the capital of Indostan, as well as Persia and Syria; he had resided in Palestine and Egypt, and sailed upon the Red Sea. Like Robinson Crusoe and Gulliver, however, he was also an explorer of human nature. In one suggestive passage Imlac, on surveying the Red Sea, confessed that his 'heart bounded like that of a prisoner escaped. I felt an unextinguishable curiosity kindle in my mind, and resolved to snatch this opportunity of seeing the manners of other nations.' Here is exemplified the passion of the English mind. The depths of insular melancholy have already been sounded, and in this passage from Johnson we may glimpse another fount and origin of English travel literature.

CHAPTER 35

A miniature

The English affection for miniatures has a long history. It may be that those who live upon a small island take a delight in small things; it may also reflect a preoccupation with the details of practical workmanship.

In the Anglo-Saxon period there was a distinctively English school of miniature painting, which can profitably be aligned with the extraordinary attention to detail in certain Anglo-Saxon poems; even the mythological bird, the phoenix, is depicted in the form of the miniaturist's art. 'His head is green behind, exquisitely variegated and shot with purple. Then the tail is handsomely pied, part burnished, part purple, part intricately set about with glittering spots. The wings are white to the rearward.'[1] In the tenth-century manuscripts executed in the 'Winchester style', the miniatures are characterised by 'the fluttering draperies, and the heavy colours and magnificent gold'[2] where the native passion for ornament is exercised in a small space. In the late Anglo-Saxon miniatures, too, can be found that 'interest in exact detail and love of pattern'[3] which continued over the centuries of English painting. The point may be that miniatures are the appropriate medium for such interests, and that as a result they are more likely to become components of a national art. In the twelfth century there were 'great miniaturists'[4] who travelled round the country, visiting scriptoria and other centres of monastic production, and who in the process created a genuinely national style.

The tradition continued in the illuminations of the thirteenth century, with vigorous human figures 'fitting admirably into the tiny space allotted to them';[5] the notion of general activity within constricted bounds may of course have been a social principle before it became part of an aesthetic. A survey of painting of the thirteenth century has also drawn attention to the prevalence of 'small fantastical initials' of a 'decorative nature' as 'a central and inherent part of the artistic development of the time';[6] many tiny monstrous figures within them derive from 'deep obsessions in their creators' minds', and possess an 'intensity' which reveals them to be 'a central preoccupation of the creative imagination'.[7] This desire to miniaturise obsessions, or to reduce 'grotesques' in size and scale, is interesting if perplexing. Could it possibly be related to the pattern of English detective stories in the twentieth century, when evil and murderous wickedness were seen to operate in small and cosy country villages? In the thirteenth century itself the vogue for the miniature was transposed to other arts and other disciplines; we may note the taste of Edward I for 'miniaturised, encrusted architecture'[8] and in the literature of the period for the 'thumb-nail sketch' and for scenes 'visualised like a miniature'.[9]

In the fourteenth century 'English medieval painting at its best was never monumental in scale' but found its finest expression in manuscript illumination.[10] The embroidery known as *opus anglicanum*, the psalters, the small diptychs in ivory or alabaster, and tomb sculpture 'essentially miniature in its feeling',[11] are all aspects of the same living tradition. One historian of painting has suggested that 'the products of the Gothic Age in England . . . are most impressive on a small scale', and that there was 'no such tradition of monumental scale as steadily developed elsewhere';[12] this may of course represent some diffidence or embarrassment in the native artistic temperament inhibiting the grand or glorious gesture. It does not preclude vitality of form, or liveliness of detail, but exhibits rather 'a sense of what can be done in a small space'.[13] It is an insular art.

Certainly it is the context for an extraordinary flowering in the art of the miniature portrait. The miniaturist Nicholas Hilliard has been designated as 'the central artistic figure of the Elizabethan age' and 'the only painter . . . whose work reflects, in its delicate microcosm, the world of Shakespeare's earlier plays'[14] where wit and fancy strive for mastery. Hilliard confessed that he wished to capture and to evoke 'these lovely graces, these witty smilings and these stolen glances which suddenly, like lightning, pass and another countenance taketh place'. The expressiveness of line, the ornamental pattern of the surface, and the brilliance of colour, all bespeak a native purpose. In this sixteenth-century art, 'the English had no rivals';[15] its loveliness and delicacy materially affected larger compositions, and it has been well said that 'the miniature set the style for oil painting and started a typically English school'[16] where ornate decorative effects and flat linear patterning are once more the characteristic elements. The dominance of portraiture, in this 'English school', need scarcely be emphasised.

It is no surprise, either, that in the seventeenth century 'the art of the miniaturist flourished'.[17] Courtiers, according to Sir Kenelm Digby, 'are ever more earnest to have their Mistresses picture in limning than in a large draught' – a limner, derived from *luminer*, having originally been an illuminator of manuscripts. The achievement of Nicholas Hilliard was followed by that of Isaac Oliver and John Hoskins, and that of Samuel Cooper who for miniatures 'was esteemed the best artist in Europe'.

The obsession with the miniature continued well into the eighteenth century, when 'miniatures were in fact by far the most numerous kind of portraits produced'.[18] It is entirely appropriate that they became a profitable branch of commerce, and this practical benefit may be adduced from the fact that miniatures sprang as much from the skills of goldsmiths as from the art of the manuscript illuminators. It is again characteristic that the miniature, perhaps 'because of its commercial nature . . . rarely shows any form of complex psychological exploration'. Here is a further definition of the English imagination. It has been said that when Delacroix arrived in London, in the spring of 1825, 'English painting he found admirable when on a small scale'.[19] The fidelity to minute detail, so redolent in the paintings of the Pre-Raphaelites, found its counterpart in the poetry of Rossetti and Tennyson with its concentration 'on minute details of the natural world'.[20] And then of course the twentieth-century Australian-born composer Percy Grainger wrote a suite for orchestra entitled 'In a Nutshell'.

One of the most poignant and powerful images within English literature is that of the mustard-seed, or the grain of sand, or the hazel-nut, as an emblem of the spiritual universe. Blake afforded it immortal status in 'Auguries of Innocence':

> To see a World in a Grain of Sand
> And a Heaven in a Wild Flower,
> Hold Infinity in the palm of your hand
> And Eternity in an hour

It might be described as the prophetic *credo* of the English miniaturist. But intimations of that vision were vouchsafed to English mystics of an earlier date. In *The Ladder of Perfection* the fourteenth-century Augustinian canon, Walter Hilton, is intrigued by the 'kernel hidden within the shell of a nut' only to bypass it as an image of divine intercession; Julian of Norwich is shown 'a littil thing' no bigger than a hazel-nut 'in the palm of my hand' and knows it to be an emblem of the universe for 'it is all that is made'. In 'The Prioress's Tale' of Geoffrey Chaucer, the Virgin Mary places 'a greyn' upon the tongue of a murdered infant allowing the child to sing sweetly; this 'greyn' or seed has been variously interpreted as a 'grain of Paradise' or a rosary bead, and later commentators have disputed whether it be 'the smallest, least valuable object' or 'a symbol of immortality'. In truth it is both. In a less sacred context Robert Burton's *Anatomy* prepares a disquisition on the nature of eternity with the sentiment that 'if you did but first know how much a small cube as big as a mustard-seed might hold . . .'. In *David Copperfield* 'the complete idea of snugness . . . lay in a nut-shell'. The same preoccupation can be glimpsed within Marlowe's 'infinite riches in a little room' and the cry of Shakespeare's Hamlet that 'I could be bounded in a nutshell, and count myselfe a King of infinite space'; the soul of Chaucer's Troilus gazes upon 'this litel spot of erthe' as if in the English imagination there is some affection for that which is small and yet also infinite. Blake saw the little fly 'Withinside wondrous & expansive' and in Richard Dadd's visionary painting *The Fairy Feller's Master-Stroke*, the little figures are grouped among hazel-nuts which might have fallen from the hand of Julian of Norwich.

A liking for the miniature has become something of a national speciality. We may note 'the growing pleasure of English writers in creating fantastic miniature worlds which work on their own',[21] and a group portrait of the English poet as miniaturist may be glimpsed in the disparate work of A. E. Housman and Hilaire Belloc, Edward Lear and Walter de la Mare. The Anglo-Saxon riddle and the nineteenth-century limerick are not so far apart. (Is the limerick an English invention? The language, at least, seems designed for it.) A recent study of 'fantasy literature' also proposes the world of Marvell's 'Upon Appleton House', 'where men are tiny, and flowers, grasses and insects are vast',[22] as well as that of the metaphysicals where beautifully shaped tears become worlds or tidal oceans. Consider Donne's 'The Flea'. Pope's *The Rape of the Lock* is a poem in which 'littleness becomes the controlling theme',[23] and the landscape of Lilliput is too well known to require further rehearsal. The pleasure in creating 'fantastic miniature worlds' may have something to do with childishness, or with arrested sexuality. It may also be associated with the creation by the young Brontë sisters of the fantasy realms of Gondal and Angria, where a small and enclosed world serves as a perfect habitat for the English imagination. Of more obvious import, however, is the work of Lewis Carroll whose shrinking Alice seems destined to drown in a pool of her own tears. This delight in littleness is also aligned to 'nonsense' verse. Is it part of some diffidence, some embarrassment at 'sense', or of some reluctance to make any grand statement?

In a celebrated passage Jane Austen adverts to 'the little bit (two Inches wide) of Ivory on which I work with so fine a Brush'. Her remark is complemented by Thomas Hardy's apophthegm that 'it is better for a writer to know a little bit of the world remarkably well than to know a great part of the world remarkably little'. In England it is believed that to know one's locale thoroughly is to understand the forces of the world or, even, of the universe itself.

CHAPTER 36

I saw you, Missis

The tradition of broad comedy has persisted in England for more than a thousand years. The talking ass in an early mystery play, *Balaam, Balak and the Prophets*, is as familiar as Aladdin or Mother Goose:

> Thou wottest well, master, pardy,
> Thou haddest never ass like to me,
> Ne never yet thus served I thee;
> Now I am not to blame

He is the direct if distant ancestor both of the 'Blondin Donkey', with two acrobats concealed inside the skin, and of the pantomime horse; he is the progenitor of all the other talking animals in popular dramas as celebrated as *Old Mother Hubbard and her Dog* and *Puss in Boots*. Noah's Wife and her 'gossips' in *Noah* are siblings of 'the Ugly Sisters' in *Cinderella*. Herod anticipates all the pantomime villains of the twentieth-century stage. Even by the beginning of the sixteenth century he had become the epitome of bombast; he was the buffoon and the braggart, who wore the most extravagant wig and the most extraordinary costume. In one direction he leads to such monstrous tyrants as Tamburlaine and Richard III, in another to such absurd braggarts as Malvolio in *Twelfth Night* and the bombastic Captain Bobadil in Ben Jonson's *Every Man in his Humour*. He is the comic origin of farce and terror.

When Joseph turns to the audience for sympathy, on learning of Mary's unexpected pregnancy, he is the very image of the risible spouse:

> Ya! Ya! All olde men to me take tent
> And weddyth no wyf in no kynnys wyse

He might have been Dan Leno who, four hundred years later, turns in an intimate aside to the audience. 'When she told me the doctor had ordered her to go away for a week, I said "Go away for two years".'

There are local references in the 'York' and 'Chester' cycles, encouraging a sense of community among players and spectators, which are replicated in nineteenth-century comic routines:

Many streets are lighted, and they say that they all shall
But I haven't seen it yet in Walsall

The mechanical serpents of the eighteenth-century theatre 'covered all over with gold and green scales'[1] are descended from a long line of medieval, and indeed Anglo-Saxon, dragons. The fact that men played the women's parts for almost five centuries lends a certain antique respectability to the role of the contemporary 'Dame'. The tradition of the 'good' character making an entrance from the right, and the 'bad' from the left, has similarly ancient roots.

When the braggart in the Tudor interlude, *Thersites*, addresses the audience with 'Aback, geue me roome, in my way do ye not stand' he is anticipating the words of a performer in a modern pantomime, 'Get back, get back, don't crowd the stage.'

Throughout mystery plays, and early comedies, and music-hall, and pantomime, there is the same levelling humour; 'low' comedy, of its nature, does not change significantly over the generations. There is the same passion for sudden violence, particularly when directed at infants or figures of authority, and the same mockery of women; there is the same contempt for foreigners, and the same excremental or sexual humour noticeable in the very earliest English dramas. In the nineteenth century salacious performances were known as 'bringing out the blue bag'. 'Blue' jokes were also the staple of *Carry On* . . . films which represent the apotheosis of broad English humour so different from (and perhaps inferior to) Irish wit and French irony.

This may also account for the English affection for the Fool in stage drama. The Fool emerges out of the medieval Vice, wearing a long coat and tall hat, who engaged in insolent or obscene conversation with the audience. He also retained a tincture of the stage devil, with his crooked or 'bottle' nose. He is the creature who in one of the mystery plays, *The Temptation of Christ*, declares to Jesus that 'I bequeath thee shitte'; he is the same character, under the name of Sedition, who in John Bale's *King John* threatens: 'I wyl beshyte yow all yf ye sett me not downe softe.' So he is already touched by the English love for farce and excremental humour in all of its forms.

His origins in England, however, are mysterious. A thirteenth-century psalter has the picture of a Fool sporting a bladder, but the character may have been part of folk-drama or folk-ritual for many years before that. The post of resident fool, in royal court or rich man's hall, dates from the twelfth century; Henry VIII had a fool, Will

Somers, who was partly copied in the dramatic performances of Will Kempe and Richard Tarlton. Characteristically the Fool was dressed in 'motley', a multi-coloured tunic, with ass-head, bells and fool-stick. In early representations, however, he is depicted as only half-clad and munching upon a white disc like a Host; there are other images which represent him as half-human and half-beast. There may be very powerful forces at work here.

There is an account, from the middle of the sixteenth century, of a Fool whose 'studye is to coine bitter jeastes . . . or to sing bawdie sonnets and ballads'. Another publication, *Robin Good fellow: his Mad pranks and Merry jests*, outlines a similar Fool whose refrain of 'Ho! Ho! Ho!' bears a striking resemblance to that of the giant in nineteenth-century pantomimes and folk-tales. It is interesting that the historian of foolery, Enid Welsford, has determined that Robin himself was a 'very English'[2] figure; thus he turns sentiment into sexual insinuation, feeling into farce, and combativeness into grotesque violence. It is characteristic of the Fool, too, that he employs a wholly native cast of speech, using homely phrases and colloquialisms in order to puncture more sophisticated or ornate diction. 'Your body ys full of Englysch Laten,' one observes, 'I am aferde yt wyll brest.' It is another example of how 'low' comedy was easily translated to the English stage. The demand was, then, that 'I would have the fool in every act'.

Then the Fool became the clown in pantomime, complete with red-hot poker and string of sausages. The first true clown, Joe Grimaldi, was known as the 'Garrick of Clowns' and 'Hogarth in Action', thus testifying to his essential Englishness in a period when 'British clowns enjoyed the highest reputation' throughout Europe.[3] All the tenderness and violence, the mystery and pathos, of daily life were incarnated in their antics and grimaces. In that sense English 'low' comedy has not really changed its nature. As one contemporary theatrical historian has put it, 'Most of the stories that continue to this day to hold the stage as pantomime subjects were first performed between the years 1781 and 1832.'[4] Clowning can be observed, too, in the art of Charles Chaplin. 'I used to watch the clowns in the pantomime breathlessly,' he wrote, 'I used to try it all over when I got home. . . . What has happened is that pantomime, through motion picture developments, has taken the lead in the world's entertainment.'[5] And what could be more English than the exquisite combination of farce and pathos which the 'little tramp' exemplified? The abiding presence of the clown can be glimpsed, too, in the comedy and melancholy of Dan Leno, described by Max

Beerbohm as 'that poor little battered personage, so put upon, with his squeaking voice, and his sweeping gestures, bent but not broken, faint but pursuing, incarnate of the will to live in a world not at all worth living in'. So we return to the Fool himself, who represents 'some quality inherent in the English nature' and thus 'acquired an essentially English character'.[6]

In the middle of the tenth century the monks of Winchester produced a manual of instruction, entitled *Regularis Concordia*. In an embellishment of the Mass at Easter three monks or oblates, dressed as women in order to impersonate the three Maries, arrive at the empty tomb. Another monkish player then questions, '*Quem quaeritis in sepulcro, o Christicolae?*' ('Whom are you seeking in the tomb, dwellers in Christ?') The cross-dressing of the Maries would not have been very extensive, and may only have consisted in changing one ecclesiastical garment for another, but it is suggestive none the less. It is a matter of speculation whether rituals such as the '*Quem quaeritis*' sequence carry the seed from which the mysteries and miracles sprang, but the connection cannot be altogether discounted. From southern England, c.1150, comes an Anglo-Norman drama entitled the *Play of Adam*; it was performed '*devant le puple*' and in '*asez large place*' to hold more than forty actors. The author has added stage directions to the effect that 'Not only Adam but all the actors shall be instructed to control their speech and to make their actions appropriate to the matter they speak of'.[7] After the eating of the apple, for example, Adam and Eve bend their bodies forward as a token of their sorrow. The devils supply the 'low' humour. In the *Play of Adam* they run about '*per populum*' – through the audience – and through the acting area; they dance and gesture throughout the action with a 'freedom to improvise and be intimate with the audience'[8] in a manner instantly recognisable to anyone familiar with the routines of pantomime or music-hall. Satan himself indulges in comic dialogues with Adam in Anglo-Norman vernacular – '*Guste del fruit!*' – while the stock figure of 'the Jew' is used for comic relief in a scene involving the prophecies of Isaiah. Here then are the primal images of English comedy, outlined in an open area by the west end of the church.

The oldest extant secular play in English is an altogether more libidinous affair, concerning an old bawd with her dog, a clerk, and a young girl of easy virtue. The presence of the dog, who performs tricks, testifies to the early use of a characteristically English stage device. The wicked dame herself would of course be performed by a man *en travesti*. *Dame Sirith* seems to have been composed at the end of the thirteenth century, although there must already have been a tradition of comic performance executed by the *mimi* or *histriones* who were being criticised by King Edgar as early as 969. Some of these were nomadic clowns or buffoons; others were mimes or minstrels. But the attacks upon them, both sacred and secular, suggest that they were partly associated with those impersonations of the devil who engaged with the audience. The abundance of 'penis jokes' in Anglo-Saxon riddles complete with *double entendres*, and the preoccupation with farting and excrement in later medieval drama, may suggest the nature of their humour. It has continued ever since.

The broad humour of the medieval theatre lies in direct descent from the Anglo-Saxon originals, therefore, and religious plays were filled with 'low' comedy. Clerics condemned these dramatic interventions as the work of 'fols' who appeared in 'visers' or masks to entertain the populace; they were not honouring God, and their true master was the devil. One *Tretise of Miraclis Pleyinge* condemned those who treated divine matters 'in pley and bourde', with additional 'ribaudry'; it is a clear indication that broad or obscene material was smuggled within the text and context of sacred drama. The verse dramas commonly called 'moralities', only five of which survive, testify to an advanced and relatively sophisticated theatrical culture in which performers and audience react knowingly to one another.

> Make rom, sers, for we haue be longe!
> We wyll cum gyf yow a Crystemas songe

The fact that the song itself is obscene is an indication of the low comic or pantomimic humour involved in this direct address to the audience; the variety and multiplicity of English drama have always encouraged such excursions and extemporisations. It became one of the salient characteristics of the Elizabethan clown, for example, that he engaged in obscene or witty 'back-chat' with the groundlings. In the morality play *Mankind*, there are jovial references to 'pisse' and 'ars'; one performer dresses up in a bear-skin before being baited by his companions.

In the great cycles of the 'mystery plays', played upon pageant wagons or in the open streets, there are farce and obscenity of every kind. From the entrance of Garcio at the beginning of *The Killing of Abel*,

> All hayll, all hayll, both blithe and glad,
> For here com I, a mery lad!

we are in the world of pantomime. He goes on to inform the spectators that anyone still chattering 'must blaw my blak hoill bore', he must blow my black hollow arse. Some of the first words spoken by Cain to Abel are 'Com kis myne ars!' When God speaks to Cain 'from above', Cain's answer is 'Whi, who is that Hob-over-the-wall?. . . God is out of hys wit.' This potent combination of obscenity and blasphemy is not unique to medieval English drama, but it flourished in what might be called the native conditions.

The drama of Noah's Wife, for example, was never so well developed as in England where the comic convention of the shrewish wife has lasted for many generations. In the version of the play prepared by the 'Wakefield Master', Mrs Noah is lewd and combative. On Noah's approach she demands 'Where has thou thus long be?' and engages in battle with him in a series of blows with the war-cry 'Thou shal thre for two', I shall give you three hits for two of yours; they engage in a number of fights, in the manner of Punch and Judy, to great comic effect. In another version of the Noah story, played by the water-drawers of Dee, the wife sits down among the 'good gossopes' for a drinking session even as the waters of the Flood approach.

> NOAH: Welcome, wife, into this boate.
> WIFE: And have thou that for thy mote!

So she punches him. Any admirer of English comedy will recognise these scenes as still fresh and still familiar. Even in the mummings or 'momeries' there appear men 'compleynyng on hir wyves, with the boystous aunswere of hir wyves'. The prevalence and popularity of the subject, however, are not easy to define. Has it to do with some general fear of sexual feeling among the English, incident upon 'the beistlie lust, the furious appetite'? As the Wife of Bath puts it:

> For trusteth wel, it is an impossible
> That any clerk wol speke good of wyves

In the mystery plays Eve is scorned for having first tasted the apple, and of course Noah's Wife is the second mother of mankind. The misogyny latent within the English imagination may derive from buried biblical sources.

Mrs Noah was of course played by a man, as were the other 'good gossopes', and so we must look to the pageant wagons of the medieval period for the first spectacular manifestations of English 'drag'. Combining a fear of the feminine with a latent homo-eroticism, it has been a staple of native humour ever since. The medieval stage convention, particularly of a man dressed as an old or ugly woman, was effortlessly extended into the Elizabethan theatre where Juliet's nurse and Mistress Quickly became comic heroines. The tradition of boy acting is sufficiently well known, although it might be added that French and Italian drama introduced female actresses with more speed and efficiency than the English. Old habits die hard. When French women appeared on the stage of Blackfriars in 1629 their performance was described by the puritan Prynne as 'an impudent, shameful, unwomanish, graceless, if not more than *whorish* attempt'.

Transvestism in England was not confined to the stage. During the Feast of Fools the Lord of Misrule chose 'twenty or sixty of an hundred lustiguts to serve him' who were dressed in female clothes 'borrowed for the moste part of their pretie Mopsies'. The male 'mummers' and 'hobnobs' of succeeding centuries have also characteristically appeared as women, thus emphasising the levelling or anarchic humour present in folk-drama of every kind.

It was present, too, in the manifestations of populist violence in England. There is a pamphlet of 1649 describing 'divers men in women's apparell' who attacked a group of Diggers in Surrey. One historian has commented that cross-dressing was used 'to *enforce* popular morality, or at least to make it known, to *signify* it'.[9] This may be seen as an inheritance from dramatic or festive transvestism. In Wiltshire bands of peasants protested against the enclosure of common land by dressing as women and calling themselves 'Lady Skimmington'; it was a way of breaking class barriers as well as sexual boundaries and testifies, perhaps inadvertently, to the English love of mixing or mingling different forms. Two male weavers in female disguise, calling themselves 'General Ludd's Wives', led a crowd in the destruction of looms and factories in Stockport; the riots against turnpike tolls and other taxes were led by men in 'drag' and became known as the 'Rebecca riots'. Foreign observers noted with some alarm the presence of transvestite clubs or public-houses in London. There were transvestite balls and dances; there were also celebrated transvestites, like the Chevalier d'Eon, who preferred to remain in England rather than risk prosecution overseas. The penalty for transvestism in France was public burning, while the presence of various clubs and pubs in

England indicates a less censorious attitude. This accommodating response must in large part be derived from the continuing dramatic tradition, in which male cross-dressing was associated with fun and badinage. It may be recalled here that in Shakespeare's only 'English' comedy, *The Merry Wives of Windsor* – a play almost entirely devoted to sexual innuendo and double entendre – Falstaff is dressed up as 'the fat woman of Brentford'.

The first Ophelia was played by Nathaniel Field; Lady Macbeth was impersonated by Alexander Cooke; Robert Goffe took the roles of both Cleopatra and Juliet. Even though female actresses were first admitted upon the stage after the Restoration, female impersonators still appeared with them. In 1661 Pepys watched Kynaston in the title role of Ben Jonson's *The Silent Woman* with 'the loveliest legs that ever I saw in my life'. It is part of the English appetite for theatricality and heterogeneity. These female impersonators soon ceased to be credible actors, however; like Tate Wilkinson or James 'Nursery' Nokes, they became comic figures instead. A plump and ill-favoured Charles Bannister played Polly in *The Beggar's Opera*. In a pantomime of 1702 'my counterfeit Male Lady is delivered of her two Puppets, Harlequin and Scaramouche'. Harlequin himself, in later manifestations, was often dressed as a woman in order that he might deceive the Clown. The celebrated Grimaldi played 'Queen Roundabellyana' in *Harlequin and the Red Dwarf*, Dame Cicely Suet in *Harlequin Whittington* and the Baroness in *Harlequin and Cinderella*. He was perhaps the original 'drag' performer.

The 'Dame' part did not properly emerge until the middle of the nineteenth century, however; she arrived on stage with an actress as 'Principal Boy', a feat of double cross-dressing which is unique to the English theatre. The fact that the Dame has stayed and stayed, still bobbing up in the Christmas pantomime season, is evidence enough for the continuing English fascination with this truly native type. Jefferini played one of the Ugly Sisters at Sadler's Wells in 1841; George Robey was the 'Queen of Hearts', Malcolm Scott 'the Woman Who Knows', and the celebrated Dan Leno first appeared as Mother Goose on the stage of the Theatre Royal, Drury Lane, on Boxing Day 1902. Dan Leno played many women – the spinster, the milkmaid, the put-upon servant – and the supposition that 'low comedy' represents the voice of the people is embodied in his small, frail form. One commentator has suggested that Leno's 'insight into the manners and customs of the working class was acute, and his acquaintance with their vocabulary extensive and peculiar';[10] in turn, the audience of the music-hall boxes loved and celebrated Leno as one of themselves. Here we may return to the Dames of the medieval mysteries or the transvestite mummers, in their own way signifying the life of their communities. This may seem a long way from the 'drag' acts in local public-houses, or from those television entertainers who intermittently dress as women for comic emphasis, but the same strong English preoccupation is none the less present. It is one of those manifestations of the English imagination which elicit wonder and incredulity; it is truly inexplicable but there, perhaps, lies its strength and persistence.

English clowns: Richard Tarlton and Will Kemp

An English Bible

Title page to the Bible translated into English, 1539

CHAPTER 37

In the beginning

In the beginning was the word. Aelfric referred to Genesis as *gecyndboc*, the book of beginnings, and we may find in its successive translations and redactions the history of the English word from its origins. The earliest version of Genesis, in the Old English of the late seventh or early eighth century, translated from a mixed Old Latin and Vulgate version, begins

> Her aerest gesceop ece drihten,
> helm eallwihta, heofon and eorthan

'Now first the everlasting lord, protector of all things, made heaven and earth.' The two poems in the Junius manuscript, Genesis A and Genesis B, comprise almost three thousand lines of verse; they are accompanied by ink drawings as illustrations, which emphasise the importance attached to this first book of the Old Testament.

The earliest translation of Genesis in Middle English emerges in a poem of rhyming couplets which opens:

> In firme bigining of noght
> Was hevene and erthe samen wroght

'In the first beginning of nothingness, heaven and earth were made together'. Details and digressions are incorporated within this early biblical narrative; some of them are as familiar and domestic as the marginal scenes in illuminated manuscripts, and some of them are borrowed from the context or content of medieval romance. There is evidence to suggest, too, that the narrative also became the subject of minstrels' song. A later medieval version of Genesis, tentatively dated to the fourteenth century, is composed in the form of a metrical paraphrase:

> how god, that beldes in endlese blyse,
> all only with hys word hath wroght,
> heuyn on heght for hym and hys,
> this erth and all that euer is oght

It is noticeable how the alliterative measure of Old English effortlessly emerges, as if in recounting the story of origins the poet instinctively turned to the original cadences of the language. This is also the pattern of Genesis in the medieval plays:

> At my bydding now made be light!
> Light is goode, I see in sighte

The vocabulary itself is borrowed from Old English to emphasise the ancientness of the theme. Yet that which is most ancient is still of pressing and permanent significance; the actors in the mysteries conceived the drama in contemporary terms, and the words of Old English still lived within the texture of the modern language. The author of *Cursor Mundi*, which paraphrases Genesis in rhyming couplets, remarks that he has translated the narrative into English precisely because of its contemporary presence and significance. 'The Nun's Priest's Tale' and 'The Merchant's Tale' in *The Canterbury Tales* allude by allegory and analogy to the action of Genesis, while Langland uses its themes and images throughout *Piers the Plowman*. He refers to the book as

> Genesis the gyaunt, the engendroure of vs alle

so that the text itself becomes the procreator not only of words but of destinies.

Wycliff's Bible, or the 'Lollard Bible', opens thus: 'In the bigynnyng god made of nought: hevene and erthe / Forsothe the erthe was idel: and voide: & derknessis weren on the face of depthe.' These simple words, translated 'for the profit of English men' in 1395, mark the beginning of what may be called the defiantly English translation of the sacred scriptures. Wycliff was a theologian and philosopher who challenged the jurisdiction of the Pope in England and who questioned the sacramental teaching of the Church itself. He can be seen in one sense as the academic voice of the Lollards, a loosely knit group of religious reformers who called for the removal of episcopal authority and a radical reshaping of the sacramental system. They detested all the trappings of authority, and found the Holy Spirit within the humble worship of ordinary men and women. The words of the 'Lollard Bible', then, may be said to mark the origins of English 'Nonconformity' and to contain the seeds of the Reformation. They represent a genesis indeed. As one biblical historian has written recently, the 'translation of the Bible into English would be a social leveller on an hitherto unknown scale'.[1] If 'simple men', to use Wycliff's phrase, can read and understand the Bible then they may take its lessons to heart; the Bible might then become an agent of social revolution. And if simple men interpret the scripture, without the mediatory agency of the doctors and priests of the Church, the whole fabric of ecclesiastical authority might be shaken. In the prologue to the 'Lollard Bible', written by many hands and not simply by his own, Wycliff cites the example of Bede and Alfred as if the power and significance of the Old English masters could still be employed in the fourteenth century. There is, again, a continuity.

Wycliff's English has been described by Dean Milman as 'rude, coarse, but clear, emphatic, brief, vehement, with short stinging sentences, and perpetual hard antithesis'; Wycliff himself believed that 'a flowery, captivating style of address is of little value compared to right substance'.[2] Here too lies one of the sources of the English imagination, rooted as it is in the speech of the people and conveyed in 'clear' vernacular; this concern for 'substance' is a mark of the native inclination towards the practical and the pragmatic, and is one which emerges in the language of English philosophy and experiment. If indeed we can say that the predilections of Wycliff's faith emerged triumphantly at the time of the Reformation and the Elizabethan settlement, when the vernacular Bible was in the ascendant, then we may agree with one historian of Englishness 'that religion was from the very first mingled with the sense of English identity, and that the history of English religion and the history of England are in many epochs inseparable'.[3] The English became, in one favourite phrase, 'the people of a book'.

The natural successor of Wycliff was William Tyndale who translates the opening lines of Genesis in the following manner:

> In the beginnyng God created heaven and erth.
> The erth was voyde and emptye
> and darcknesse was upon the depe
> & the spirite of God moved upon the water

This represented the first English translation from the Hebrew original, commonly considered to be the language of God Himself, but Tyndale declared that his native idiom was designed to 'sucke out the pithe of the scripture' in knowing or unwitting imitation of Wycliff's desire to elicit the 'substance' of the sacred words. Thus he gives to the serpent a demotic vocabulary not unlike that of the devils in the mystery plays. 'Ah, syr,' the evil one whispers to Eve; and then, in a later passage, he is casually reassuring with 'Tush, ye shall not dye.' The tree itself is 'lustie' to Eve's eyes and, when she and Adam discover their nakedness, 'they sawed fygge leves togedder and made them apurns'; 'apurns' is a sixteenth-century variant of aprons. Tyndale employs such homely terms as 'mesyllynge' for drizzle and 'tyllman' for farmer, emphasising the native and vernacular idiom to which he aspired. In Genesis, Joseph is described as 'a luckie felowe' wearing a 'gaye' coat.

Tyndale translated only the Pentateuch, the first five books, and was never able to expedite an entire translation of the Old Testament. He had left England for Germany in 1525 in order to print and publish his work without fear of harassment or interruption from the authorities. He was already suspected of heresy; it was not clear whether he was a Lollard or a Lutheran but, at a time when the established Catholic Church was being undermined by reformers, it did not much matter. Ten years later, he was entrapped by an English agent in Antwerp, imprisoned and then strangled at the stake before his body was burnt. Yet he had managed to complete an English version of the New Testament which, in its earliest printing, included marginal notes that Thomas More and others believed to be of a Lutheran tendency. He had deemed the work to be in 'proper English', by which he meant a clear and lucid style aptly expressing the meaning of the original. While engaged in that purpose he fashioned a language of devotion that was unparalleled for its beauty and clarity until the publication of the King James Bible, which itself borrows heavily from Tyndale's earlier translations. He came from the Vale of Berkeley in the Cotswolds, an area much loved by Lollards and Lollard preachers in the fourteenth century, and the whole wealth of the native language flooded within his classical and European learning to create an instrument of speech both subtle and supple. 'Axe and it shalbe geven you. Seke and ye shall fynd. Knocke and it shalbe opened unto you.' Tyndale was a master of the short phrase, placed within the movement of a larger cadence, and this in turn is based upon a Gloucestershire dialect touched by wider understanding; it is a paradigm of the English imagination itself. It might be noticed here that Tyndale's English reproduces 'the rhythm of the original Hebrew' as well as that ancient tongue's 'balance, imagery and conciseness of expression';[4] it is another example of the ability of the English to adapt, to borrow and to synthesise. In similar fashion Tyndale created phrases which will live as long as the English language itself, such as 'my brother's keeper' in Genesis as well as 'the powers that be' and 'a law unto themselves'. He invented words, like 'atonement' and 'scapegoat', which have also entered the language as visible tokens of the immense influence which his translation exerted.

The effect of Tyndale's New Testament was, however, immediate and profound. Soon after its publication in Worms, in 1526, copies were smuggled into England from Antwerp, Cologne and Worms; they could be purchased clandestinely in Coleman Street, Honey Lane, or Hosier Lane. Sir Thomas More, then Lord Chancellor, denounced 'nyght scoles' of dissent and sedition, where individuals and families read from Tyndale's translations before worshipping together. A native of Chelmsford, William Maldon, decided to remedy his illiteracy precisely in order to read Tyndale's New Testament; he described the poor men of his town who 'did sit reading in lower end of church, and many would flock about to hear them reading'. When one eminent divine condemned the fact that the teachings of Wycliff were once more abroad – 'trying to infiltrate this country of ours with the old and damnable heresy of Wycliff' – the important connection is made clear. To impart the scriptures in English, apparently plain and simple English at that, was to create an entirely new religious world. As one eminent historian has written of the period after the Reformation, 'Henceforth both those who accepted the Anglican supremacy and those who dissented from it expressed their beliefs in the sanctified idiom of Tyndale. God had found a voice, and the voice was English.'[5]

That is why Thomas More's *The Confutation of Tyndale's Answer* is the most important religious polemic in English culture. With some half a million words of dispute and controversy, it is also certainly the longest. Yet the theme was the single most pressing of the period. As More put it, 'bytwene Tyndale and me no thynge ellys in effecte, but to fynde out whyche chyrche is the very chyrche'. The English translation had in effect subtly shifted both the grounds of belief and the practice of faith; by substituting 'congregation' for 'church', 'elders' for 'priests', 'repentance' for 'penance', 'love' for 'charity' and 'knowledge' for 'confession', Tyndale seriously undermined the Catholic Church's claims of universality and primacy. Their conflict represented a struggle for the soul of England itself and, although this is not the occasion to sift the dust of forgotten theological controversies, it is at least worth observing that More's *Confutation* was entirely composed in English. This is in marked contrast to his most famous and distinguished work, *Utopia*, which was written in Latin for a European audience. Now More was directly addressing his compatriots and fellow citizens. The result was a spirited debate in the vernacular:

TYNDALE:	Marke whyther yt be not true in the hyest degree . . .
MORE:	Tyndale is a great marker. There is nothynge with hym now but marke, marke, marke. It is a pytye that the man were not made a marker of chases in some tenys playe.
TYNDALE:	Iudge whyther yt be possible that any good sholde come oute of theyr domme ceremonyes and sacramentes.
MORE:	Iudge good crysten reader whythyr yt be possyble that he be any better than a beste oute of whose brutyshe bestely mowth, commeth such a fylthye fome.

Tyndale was a grave and learned scholar; More a distinguished humanist on the European model. Yet in this dialogue they resort to the oldest patterns and resources of the language, as if there the real truth might be elicited. Thomas More in particular reverts to the power of alliteration as a way of conveying his anger, and indirectly as a token of the power of inherited speech.

The appetite for English translation, once awakened, became immense; it is as if the whole spiritual history of the world was now available to the plough-boy and the household, and over the next thirty years no fewer than five great translations of the Bible appeared; significantly, all of them were to a large extent based upon Tyndale's original. The first complete English Bible, published in 1535, was the work of Miles Coverdale; he appears to have had little direct engagement with the original texts but, in characteristically English manner, arranged a compilation of all previous translations. His version is characterised by its ease and naturalness, harmonising previous versions and rendering euphonious existing ones; it anticipates the extraordinary achievement of the King James Bible which, despite its role as a translation of translations, is a unique work of art. Coverdale was of pragmatic and conciliatory nature, and he took the middle way; he was concerned to resolve differences between translations, and to smooth out complexities, and it has been said that he possessed a 'real gift in melodious expression' and that his translation 'excels in the music of its phrasing'.[6] This capacity suggests in turn that English music may itself spring out of moderation and conciliation; it is perhaps significant, therefore, that he introduced within the language such phrases as 'loving kindness' and 'tender mercy' which might have sprung from the lips of Richard Rolle or Julian of Norwich.

Two years after the Coverdale Bible was printed and published another English work, known as 'Matthew's Bible', appeared; it was named after the pseudonymous 'translator' rather than the disciple, but it was essentially a conflation of Tyndale and Coverdale to which various marginal notes were appended. The steady pressure of inherited language continued unabated. Coverdale then in turn supervised the revision of 'Matthew's Bible', in order to create what became known as the 'Great Bible'. This reliance upon the translations of translations at least ensured a continuity of language in a period of perpetual change; it testifies also to a profound conservatism among biblical redactors which had a direct effect upon the English language itself. As one biblical scholar has put it, 'the retention of older English ways of speaking in religious contexts' created 'the impression that religious language was somehow *necessarily* archaic'.[7] By the slow and subtle process of the English imagination, the homely directness of Wycliff and the Lollards was replaced by the harmonious simplicity of the now 'authorised' version of the 'Great Bible' which had upon its title page an engraving of Henry VIII handing the volume in question to a grateful Archbishop of Canterbury and assorted clergy. The English Bible had at last become a central token of the national culture. William Strype declared that 'Everybody that could bought the book, or busily read it, or got others to read it to them'. A contemporaneous pamphlet declared that 'Englishmen have now in hand, in every church and place, the Holy Bible in their mother tongue, instead of the old fabulous and fantastical books of the Table Round, Lancelot du Lake, Bevis of Hampton, Guy of Warwick etc and such other, whose impure filth and vain fabulosity the light of God has abolished utterly'.

Another version, 'Taverner's Bible', was disseminated in 1539 but it was overshadowed by the Great Bible which was in turn supplanted by the Geneva Bible or 'Breeches Bible'; Tyndale's 'aprons' had been succeeded, in other words, by 'breeches'. It was the work of several hands but relied once more upon its precursors. Nevertheless it cleared up certain absurdities by direct reference to Hebrew originals and, with the more vigorous expression represented by the use of 'breeches', it revitalised the line of English music as it flowed through the various translations. The first line of its Genesis marks a new beginning in another sense – 'In the beginning God created ye heaven and ye earth' – which has remained ever since the plangent introduction to sacred scripture. Other of its changes have entered the language. The translators altered the wording of the twenty-third psalm so that 'leade me forth besyde the waters of comforte' became '& leadeth me by the stil waters', for example, while 'my cup shalbe full' was changed to 'my cup runneth ouer'. The extraordinary significance of the English Bible, within the English imagination, is testified in phrases such as these which have entered the national consciousness.

Sixty editions of the Geneva Bible appeared during the reign of Elizabeth; by the middle of the seventeenth century 140 had been promulgated. It was produced in compact quarto size, rather than in cumbersome folio. It was the first to be printed in clear roman type, with italics to suggest the meaning of missing words, and was divided into discrete units of verse. More significantly it provided annotations and explanations of difficult passages or 'hard places' for the edification of 'the simple reader'. The Geneva Bible was employed directly by Shakespeare and by Marlowe, thus assuring its place in English cultural history. Here once more is evidence of that curious and powerful tendency within English letters to appropriate and to reformulate foreign texts so that they become thoroughly English in the process; the effect is heightened in the biblical context by the fact that the English of the sixteenth and seventeenth centuries were identified with the Hebrews as the 'chosen race'.

Two other translations appeared at the close of the sixteenth century. A more orthodox 'Bishops' Bible' avoided the taint of Calvinist precepts, while the Catholic Douay Bible preserved a Latinate diction appropriate for the 'old faith'; but these were mere milestones, as it were, to the great achievement of the King James Bible which has aptly been described as the supreme manifestation of the English language. 'In the beginning God created the heaven and the earth. And the earth was without form, and void; and darkness was upon the face of the deep. And the Spirit of God moved upon the face of the waters. And God said, Let there be light: and there was light.' It is impossible to use the language without being influenced by the cadence and vocabulary of this translation; and it says much about the English imagination itself that it should be so moved and modified *by* a translation. It is significant, too, that this extraordinary work should have been produced out of compromise and the wholesale adaptation of different sources. It might act as a mirror of Englishness itself. With the eventual publication of the King James Bible, it could even be asserted that 'God is an Englishman'.

James I had been so disturbed by the popularity of the Geneva Bible, which seemed in its annotations to deny the divine right of kings as well as to perpetrate other puritanical abuses of scripture, that he assembled a conference at Hampton Court 'for the reformation of some things amiss in ecclesiastical matters'. In the course of this conference it was proposed that a company of translators be established in order to begin work upon a wholly new translation which would avoid the excesses of Puritanism, Presbyterianism and Roman Catholicism. Their standard text was to be the Bishops' Bible but other versions were to be employed when they were closer to the sacred originals, in the sequence of 'Tindoll's, Matthew's, Coverdale's, Whitchurch's, Geneva'. Here is one 'line' of English music whereby each version harmonises with, and amplifies, its predecessor. There were fifty scholars whose 'endeavour' or 'mark' was 'to make a good one better, or out of many good ones, one principal good one'. Their purpose was to redeploy the resources of an older English – Tyndale's translation, which comprises some nine-tenths of the King James version, had been published almost a century before – so that it might reverberate in another era and, indeed, in subsequent centuries. It is a memorable fact of English continuity or conservatism that all the changes wrought in the language during the period of Shakespeare and Marlowe were set aside for the simplicity and directness of Tyndale's vernacular.

The preface to the King James Bible is itself an epitome of the English genius for assimilation and adaptation, since translation 'it is that openeth the window, to let in the light; that breaketh the shell, that we may eat the kernel . . . that removeth the cover of the well, that we may come by the water'. Yet by that curious transformation, already observed in a variety of contexts, this translated work 'played no small part in shaping English literary nationalism, by asserting the supremacy of the English language as means of conveying religious truths'.[8] Indeed it became the touchstone of English literary culture itself. In his lectures, 'On Translating Homer', Matthew Arnold declared that there is 'an English book and one only, where, as in the *Iliad* itself, perfect plainness of speech is allied with perfect nobleness; and that book is the Bible'. Thus it had become known as an 'English book'. Many phrases from Hebrew, Greek and Latin were internalised and domesticated so that they seem as much part of the language as any phrase out of Old English. Alister McGrath, in his erudite study of the King James Bible entitled *In the Beginning*, records many of these now idiomatic phrases taken out of the Hebrew; among them 'sour grapes', 'rise and shine', 'a fly in the ointment', 'a drop in the bucket', 'to lick the dust', 'the land of the living', 'the skin of my teeth' and to 'go from strength to strength'. From the Greek originals spring 'the salt of the earth' and 'a thorn in the flesh'. No one would now know that these were originally foreign phrases imported in the early seventeenth century; it is testimony to the plastic power of the English language, and of course the English imagination, that they have been so thoroughly absorbed that they are now an instinctive and intimate part of speech. As McGrath put it, the King James Bible demonstrated the fact that English is 'perhaps the global language which has been most welcoming to words whose origins lie elsewhere'.[9] Perhaps this extraordinary adaptive ability is the very reason why the language has attained its contemporary global status, far surpassing the Latin tongues of the classical and medieval centuries.

The King James Bible was not simply a translated work but, as has been intimated, already an antiquated one. This in turn suggests the almost intuitive antiquarianism of the English imagination, since within this new version were perpetuated 'thou' rather than 'you' and 'sayest' rather than 'says'. Then, on a more general scale, the cadences and syntactical variations of an earlier language were also maintained. By remaining faithful to earlier English translations, the King James Bible did in fact preserve old forms of speech. Here lies another aspect of the fidelity to an older English tradition; the scholars read out their translations to one another, so that in a sense the native breath or breadth might enter their words. The spoken word is always a more conservative form than the written language; one of the secrets of the King James Bible's success, and of its continuity, lies in its employment of this natural power.

It is perhaps appropriate that the King James Bible should have been published in 1611, the presumed date of Shakespeare's retirement from the public theatre; in one sense it continued the dramatist's tradition and, by inheriting the language from Chaucer as well as Genesis, from Spenser as well as from the Psalms, it continued the line of English music itself. The Coverdale Bible translated the phrase from I Kings 19 as 'a styll softe hyssinge' but the Matthew Bible changed this to 'a small styll voyce' until the King James Bible rewrote it memorably as 'a still small voice'. Thus the line of biblical translations into English has been described as 'both cumulative and progressive, like the course of a river' while the King James Bible itself has been characterised 'by its smoothness, its even-flowing tempo, its ease and naturalness and harmony'.[10] As one biblical scholar has put it, 'all previous versions . . . resonate somewhere in their text'. In translation, too, there is also a measure of self-effacement. As the Preface to the King James Bible stated of its contributors, 'There were many chosen, that were greater in other men's eyes than in their own, and that sought the truth rather than their own praise.'

We may look for its influence in the language itself or, as John Livingston Lowes puts it, 'its phraseology has become part and parcel of our common language – bone of its bone and flesh of its flesh'. We can trace it in the work of Milton and Bunyan, Tennyson and Byron, Johnson and Gibbon, Walton and Thackeray, none of whom according to Sir Arthur Quiller-Couch could resist 'the rhythms of our Bible . . . it is everything we see, hear, feel because it is in us, in our blood'. More significantly for this study, perhaps, we may trace its effect in the immediate outpouring of religious literature in the vernacular. The King James Bible invigorated the consciousness of the nation, and prompted some of its most eloquent manifestations. The religious controversies of the seventeenth century were now conducted within an entirely national context, and the publication of the Bible heralded a vast outpouring of religious poetry, books of devotion, tracts and pamphlets of every kind; religious poetry had a political dimension, and political poetry wore a spiritual aspect. It has been estimated that, in the first forty years of the century, one half of the books printed were concerned wholly or partly with religious topics. The enthusiasm attendant upon the assorted creeds of Anabaptists, Laudians, Levellers, Presbyterians, Calvinists, Puritans and Anglicans, was itself directly related to the translation of the Bible; but even after the civil war and the Protectorate religious texts were at a premium. Volumes such as Jeremy Taylor's *Holy Living* and *Holy Dying* and John Rawlet's *The Christian Monitor* passed through innumerable editions; one optimistic publisher believed that Benjamin Keach's *War with the Devil* and *Travels of True Godliness* would sell 'till the end of time'. Volumes of sermons were also in great demand, while religious poetry flourished in the form of songs and emblems, odes and cantatas.

In this context both the new prominence of the hymn, in a church service set in the vernacular, and the popularity of the psalms, newly translated into English, are instructive. They could now be sung by congregations, to readily recognisable tunes. The central principles of devotional writing had become those of simplicity and intelligibility; the central role afforded to the English Bible led naturally and ineluctably to a more profound attention to the word, written or spoken, rather than to the drama and gesture of the Mass. Multiple interpretations of the Bible, the scholastic equivalent of polyphony, were displaced by a plainer and more literal elucidation of the sacred texts. Thus the *Westminster Directory* of 1644 suggests that 'in singing of Psalms the voice is to be tunably and gravely ordered, but the chief care must be to sing with understanding, and with grace in the heart, making melody unto the Lord'. In a sermon preached at Oxford in 1668 Robert South, the Public Orator to that university, disparaged pulpit eloquence which consisted in 'difficult Nothings, Rabbinical Whimsies, and remote Allusions'. The sentiments are part of a general English aversion to florid discourse or openly expressed sentiment, but the tone and rigour of this return to 'plain' and traditional English are a direct consequence of the publication of the King James Bible.

No more striking evidence of its influence can be found than in the pages of John Bunyan's *The Pilgrim's Progress*, where the plain-speaking narrator weaves the words of the King James version within the texture of his prose. In this passage, 'Safe for those for whom it is to be safe, *but transgressors shall fall therein* . . . for saith he, *Concerning the works of men, by the word of thy lips, I have kept them from the paths of the destroyer*. Thus they lay bewailing themselves in the Net', the italicised words are taken from that version. It has been said of Bunyan himself that 'some phrase or sentence from the English Bible suddenly speaks to him in an hour of crisis . . . the thought as it is incarnated in the familiar words of the Authorized Version'.[12] Bunyan emphasised the traditional plainness of King James when he declared that 'I have not writ at a venture, nor borrowed my Doctrine from Libraries. I depend upon the sayings of no man: I found it in the Scriptures of Truth, among the true sayings of God.' The plain speaking of this plain man, inherited in one sense from William Langland and *Piers the Plowman*, is here given doctrinal authority from the example of the vernacular Bible. Thus at any point in the text passages may be selected which derive from the same source. 'Ah thou sinful sleep! How for thy sake am I like to be benighted in my Journey! I must walk without the Sun, darkness must cover the path of my feet, and I must hear the noise of doleful Creatures, because of my sinful sleep!' None of this could have been written without the influence and example of the English Bible; its vocabulary and cadence are every-where apparent and, if we concur that *The Pilgrim's Progress* is 'the first modern English novel',[13] then the King James Bible has been influential indeed. In the nineteenth century, however, Southey made the essential point that Bunyan's 'homespun style' represented 'a clear stream of current English'. So it may be inferred that the King James Bible helped to confirm and to emphasise an existing tradition within the language. That is why it has been suggested that *The Pilgrim's Progress* represents 'a bridge between two worlds, the medieval and the modern'[14] in precisely the manner that the Authorised Version may be said to 'bridge' that gap or transition between Wycliff and the seventeenth century.

The connection between English spirituality and the English imagination is in fact a continuous and permanent one. It is only necessary to note, in the eighteenth century, the unique popularity of the biblical oratorio. The success of Handel's productions, in particular, rested partly on the identification of the English with the Israelites of the Old Testament and their especial rank as God's 'chosen people'. The oratorios, in the words of one musical historian, 'made the history of the Hebrews into a kind of "national epic" in which Englishmen could see themselves'.[15] It is an ancient and well-worn theme; a century before, John Milton remarked that 'God reveals himself to his servants and, as his manner is, first to his Englishmen'. It is the secret of Handel's *Messiah* which, according to one commentator, 'sums up to perfection and with the greatest eloquence the religious faith, ethical, congregational, and utterly unmystical, of the average Englishman'.[16] Handel himself became a naturalised Englishman in 1727, after his art had been thoroughly assimilated. The power of place is once again manifested. We may call it placism, as an antidote to racism. The English oratorio was in fact a distinct and readily identifiable form; it was adapted from continental models and from its inception incorporated English, French, Italian and German elements to create a familiar mixed and 'mungrell' style. It was part drama, part anthem, and part epic; it moved from the sublime to the tender, and thus amply fulfilled the English appetite for variety and theatricality. Just as the Elizabethan settlement of the sixteenth century afforded a practical 'middle ground' for those of different political persuasions, so the eighteenth-century oratorio 'established a common ground for expressing certain basic religious beliefs that reunited the English as no other area of the nation's culture had done'.[17] A pragmatic instinct is at work, whereby the beliefs and practices of the Church are subtly united with the rituals of English social life.

The popularity of the hymn, in the eighteenth century, manifests a similar spirit of commonality drawn in large part from the fellowship of the vernacular in biblical translations. The fact that Isaac Watts, Charles Wesley and Joseph Addison all wrote popular hymns is a clear indication, also, that they could encompass various forms of popular devotion. The hymn itself has been described by Helen Gardner as 'the great eighteenth-century lyric form', so that 'the glory of the eighteenth century in religious poetry lies in its hymns'.[18] When they are praised for their clarity and plainness, as well as for their 'impersonal majesty', the affiliations with the English translations of the Bible are again manifest. When Isaac Watts wrote:

> My best-Beloved keeps his Throne
> On Hills of Light, in Worlds unknown;
> But he descends, and shows his Face
> In the young Gardens of his Grace

he could not have composed the lines without the direct impress of the King James Bible and of the religious poetry which sprang from it. 'O God Our Help in Ages Past', perhaps the most famous of all English hymns, is directly based upon a psalm translation. When it is stated that 'the purpose of a hymn is to create the sense of belonging to a continuing fellowship . . . a sense of unity with fathers and forefathers',[19] that unity is the English imagination itself.

Cockney visionaries

'A Harlot's Progress', plate two, 1732. By William Hogarth

CHAPTER 38

London calling

The Cockney visionary tradition began early. William Langland, who lived in a hovel along Cornhill, has often been compared with William Blake and John Bunyan. But he has also been associated with William Hogarth. The first scholarly edition of the text of *Piers the Plowman*, edited by W. W. Skeat in 1869, remarks that 'to remember the London origin of a large portion of the poem is the true key to the right understanding of it'. The conflation of Blake and Bunyan, Langland and Hogarth, however, is itself a 'true key' to the London imagination. To hear the music of the stones, to glimpse the spiritual in the local and the actual, to render tangible things the material of intangible allegory, all these are at the centre of the London vision. There is a film made in 1946, *Hue and Cry*, in which one of the protagonists is asked, 'So you're the boy who sees visions in the middle of London?' It is a most pertinent question for Langland, too, who in the middle of a London tavern sees the everlasting figures of Gluttony and Sloth. They are his living companions, but they are also types of eternity.

In a city where the extremes of the human condition meet, wealth beside wretchedness and famine beside avarice, there must be room for imaginative extremity. The presence of hyperbole in Chaucer's writing, for example, has often been noted in phrases such as 'Ther nas no man nowher so vertuous. . . . So greet a purchasour was nowher noon. . . . In al this world ne was ther noon hym lik. . . . A bettre preest I trowe that nowher noon ys.' But it has escaped the attention of those who characterise Chaucer's poetry that exaggeration was in fact a familiar aspect of London speech. We may turn to the sixteenth-century diaries of Henry Machyn to register a bravura or bravado which has never since been lost: 'the goodlyest scollers as ever you saw . . . the greth pykkapus as ever was . . . ther was syche a cry and showtt as has not byne'.

If we are to denote a London style, then this is one of its most significant tokens. It suggests aggression, and a measure of latent cynicism, which have never been absent from the city; it reveals also the need to impress, in a milieu where everyone and everything competes to demand attention, as well as an appetite for extravagance and theatricality. These are all qualities which may be traced in the line of Cockney visionaries, no less in Milton and More, Blake and Turner and Dickens, than in Chaucer.

Dickens was known for his superlatives and over-statements: never had he seen such excitement, never had he sold so many copies, never had he entertained so large a number. It is, in turn, one plausible context for that mingling of the comic and the pathetic, the farcical and the tragical, which plays so large a part in Chaucer's narrative; the variety itself represents that striving after effect which characterises the novels of Dickens just as much as *The Canterbury Tales*.

There is a further, if less familiar, conclusion to be drawn. It has been suggested that, in Chaucer's narratives, 'causation and analysis have little place'.[1] This is demonstrably true of his fabliaux and saints' stories, where psychological complexity is altogether unnecessary, but it has been traced in other tales. In *Troilus and Criseyde*, for example, idiosyncratic characterisation is of more significance than any profound growth or naturalistic development. In a curious parallel the same habit of mind has been found in the King James Bible, which manifests an 'additive, non-analytical style'.[2] Is it possible, then, that this aversion to causation and complexity is part of the English imagination? It might account for that delight in caricature, that preference for varied spectacle over profound feeling, which is so much part of a specifically London genius.

It might also be glimpsed in the early urban appetite for allegorical pageants on a glittering, if occasionally grotesque, scale; in the fourteenth and fifteenth centuries giants and saints, classical gods and Christian emblems, contemporary and legendary figures, were all jumbled together in a common aspiration towards the scenic and the magnificent. Painted castles, naked children, fountains gushing with wine, white and red, were part of the stage business; the action itself consisted of dramatic monologues, allegorical dialogues and scenic tableaux. It was a rich mixture indeed, and materially affected the staging of Tudor and Elizabethan drama where the same penchant for spectacle and melodramatic excess is evident.

That passion for the marvellous in fact animates a more general London vision, whether it be in an eighteenth-century masquerade where 'Tom Jones meets the Queen of the Fairies' or in the spontaneous combustion of Krook in Dickens's *Bleak House*. It is present in those riverine scenes of Turner where Dido and Aeneas are glimpsed in the landscape of the River Tamar, provoking the comment of Sir George

Beaumont that the Cockney artist was 'perpetually aiming to be extraordinary'.

Handel caught an air from a whistling tradesman, Turner borrowed scenic effects from a pantomime starring Polyphemus, and Blake adopted images from the Gothic dramas of the London patent theatres. Much has been written about 'high' art influencing 'low', but the traffic often goes in the other direction.

When in the mid-sixteenth century the Princess Elizabeth asked her governess, 'What news?', she heard that she was about to marry Lord Admiral Seymour. She replied that 'it was but a London news' concocted for the sensation and rumour of the moment. In a similar spirit the playhouses of the 1590s incorporated scandal and gossip, where one contemporary moralist depicted Londoners as 'learning at the play what is happening abroad'. There was much enthusiasm among 'London audiences for this kind of journalistic news and topical comment'.[3] The demands of novelty were clamant and persistent, with the result that 'sonnet sequences, plays, epigrams, satires and prose pamphlets had each year to differ from last year's model'.[4] Generic mutations and imitative flourishes abounded, but again we may see this as the condition of all successful London compositions where immediate effect and local sensation become indispensable. That is why in the sixteenth century new words were being constantly introduced within the ordinary vocabulary, with an affection for extravagant jargon. With the jargon came absurd mistakes in the use of overly expressive words, so intimately parodied by William Shakespeare in the argot of Mistress Quickly and others.

One of the great masters of jargon and topicality was Thomas More, the saint who all his life walked through the streets of London. He was indeed a Cockney visionary who created his Utopia out of an inverted and idealised image of his city; he lectured upon St Augustine's *City of God* in the church of St Lawrence Jewry, and in his devotions at the Charterhouse tried to realise the divine city within the lineaments of the mundane one.

Paradoxically amongst the noise and mire of London it is possible to glimpse the spiritual destinies of humankind. That is what another Cockney visionary, William Blake, understood about his great city predecessor, Geoffrey Chaucer, when he remarked that 'The characters of Chaucer's Pilgrims are the characters which compose all ages and nations: as one age falls, another rises, different to mortal sight, but to immortals only the same . . . Accident ever varies, Substance can never suffer change nor decay.' Only in the busy concourse of struggling existence, and among the transient movement of vast crowds, can such truths be vouchsafed.

Yet the spectacle of the city, with all the woes of the world, can produce hardness; the experience of its crowds might elicit only indifference to the undifferentiated mass. Thomas More's writing against the 'reformers', Tyndale and Luther, is notorious for its spite and intemperance. In his Latin polemics More condemned Luther as *'Furfuris! Pestillentissimum surram!'* Luther was an ape, an arse, a drunkard, a lousy little friar, a piece of scurf, a pestilential buffoon. It is an example of Cockney invective which was used also by John Milton and William Blake in their attacks upon their adversaries. It is the language of the street. Thus More declares that Luther *'volutatur incestu'* and *'clunem agitat'*; he writhes in incest and wriggles his bum. There is a scatological tinge to More's polemics, also, which is wholly characteristic of the Cockney vision; Blake was preoccupied with 'shite', and More accused Luther of celebrating Mass *'super fornicam'* or upon the toilet. Luther is a shit devil; he is filled with *'merda'* and dung and filth. It is right to shit (*'incacere'*) and to piss (*'meiere'*) into his mouth and, look, my own fingers are covered with shit when I try to clean his filthy mouth. It is not the language of a saint, perhaps, but it is the language of a Londoner. It may be aptly compared with Pope's excremental vision of London in *The Dunciad.* More's writings in English also accommodate a wealth of colloquial speech that springs directly out of the people – 'lyke a flounder out of a fryenge panne in to the fyre. . . . The lytle apple of myne eye . . . that can perceyue chalke fro chese well ynough . . . one swalow maketh not somer.' No account of the English imagination can ignore the persistence and power of such phrases; they have endured for perhaps a thousand years (certainly they were already proverbial in the late fifteenth century) and have become part of the folk-memory of the country.

It is appropriate to set Milton in the context of More's polemic because he was also a master of Cockney invective. Milton was born in Bread Street, a few yards south of More's childhood home in Milk Street, but they share more than local topography; they share the inheritance of that small London area where merchants and thieves and prostitutes thrived. 'Noise it till ye be hoarse', Milton exclaims in *The Reason of Church Government*, '. . . that ye be fat and fleshy, swoln with high thoughts and big with mischeivous designs. . . . O rather the sottish absurdity of this excuse!' He attacks the prelates who 'have glutted their ingratefull bodies' with 'corrupt and servile doctrines'; they were fed with 'scraggy and thorny lectures . . . a hackney cours of literature', and filled with 'strumpet flatteries . . . corrupt and putrid oyntment'; they are scum, and harlots and open sepulchres. In an attack upon a rival scholar, *An Apology Against a Pamphlet*, he declares that the scholar's papers 'are predestin'd to no better end than to make winding sheetes in Lent for Pilchers'. 'Delicious!' he announces while transcribing an argument, and declares: 'How hard it is when a man meets with a Foole to keep his tongue from Folly.' His voice echoes that of another Londoner, John Donne:

> Who wasts in meat, in clothes, in horse, he notes;
> Who loves whores, who boyes, and who goats

And then that of Pope:

> Shut, shut the door, good *John*! fatigu'd I said,
> Tye up the knocker, say I'm sick, I'm dead

It is the direct and colloquial speech, albeit turned into fluent cadence, which arrests the attention; the language of the streets has become golden.

Milton wrote polemical dialogues, like More, in which the demotic of the streets also enters. 'Wee know where the shoo wrings you, you fret. . . . Y'are a merry man, Sir, and dare say much. . . . A quick come off!' He compares the prelatical liturgy to 'an English galloping Nun, proferring her selfe' for intercourse, and to a 'Queene . . . that sanke at Charing-Crosse, and rose up at Queene-hithe'. He savours 'a more perfect and distinguishable odour of your socks'. He works himself into a fine fury of discrimination and denunciation, trading insults as if they were blows and ending in withering asides such as 'Wipe your fat corpulencies'. The same tone and manner emerge in the polemic of William Blake. The scatological emphasis –

> The Hebrew Nation did not write it
> Avarice & Chastity did shite it

– can be set beside another couplet:

> If Blake could do this when he rose up from shite
> What might he not do if he sat down to write

It is a characteristic London voice.

There are images in Thomas More's writing which are also of urban provenance, particularly those of the prison and of the theatre. What better metaphors could, in any case, be chosen to represent the condition of the city? Allusions to the world as a prison run deep through London writing, and it may be significant that the earliest extant text discovered in the city was a prisoner's prayer. More continued that theme with a threnody on the world as representing a city gaol, with 'some bound to a poste, some wandring abrode, some in the dungeon, some in the upper ward, some bylding them palaces in the prison, some weping, some laughing, some laboring, some playing, some singing, some chiding, some fighting'. We may put this beside Dickens's strictly comparable vision in *Bleak House* and *Little Dorrit*, where the whole world is described as a type of prison with all of its inhabitants as prisoners. In the final double number of *Little Dorrit*, in which the images of the gaol invoke all the weariness and melancholy of that London novel, there is a glimpse of sunset. 'Far aslant across the city, over its jumbled roofs, and through the open tracery of its church towers, struck the long bright rays, bars of the prison of this lower world.'

The prison is everywhere in London writing. Thus John Donne, in a sermon preached to the Lords at Easter, surmised that 'Wee are all conceived in close Prison . . . when we are borne, we are borne but to the liberty of the house; Prisoners still, though within larger walls'. He continued with this striking simile: 'Now was there ever any man seen to sleep in the Cart, between New-gate, and Tyborne? between the Prison and the place of Execution, does any man sleep? And we sleep all the way . . .'. It is true that metaphors of prison arise naturally from our human state, and are to be found within many cultures, but the conditions of London in earlier centuries rendered it a particularly pressing and persistent motif. The dominant image of London in *Tom Jones* is that of a prison in which the hero wanders looking for relief; he may congregate in the prison yard of the city with 'the mob' who have 'one of their established maxims, to plunder and pillage their rich neighbours without any reluctance' or remain in solitary confinement, where 'a man may be as easily starved in Leadenhall Market as in the deserts of Arabia'. In *Amelia*, another of Fielding's novels, Booth and the eponymous heroine 'are close prisoners in a metropolis of evil'.[5] Wordsworth condemned London as 'A prison where he hath been long immured', and where its citizens are 'Dreaming of nought beyond the prison wall'. William Morris maintained the imagery of incarceration with his apostrophe to the city as 'this prison built stark / With all the greed of ages'. Matthew Arnold considered it to be a 'brazen prison' and, in the twentieth century, V. S. Pritchett described it as 'this prison-like place of stone'. The imagery employed by More, let loose as it were into the language, has a long history.

But if London is a prison it is also a theatre in which each man and woman must play a part. Thomas More understood very well the vagaries of the city as a stage, since he walked in costume all his life, and he offers one of its very first metaphors in his history of Richard III. 'They said that these matters bee Kynges games, as it were stage playes, and for the more part plaied vpon scafoldes. In which pore men be but ye lokers on. And thei yt wise be, wil medle no farther. For they that sometyme step vp and play with them, when they cannot play their partes, they disorder the play & do themself no good.' He is describing political activity within a city which, in more than one sense, was devoted to drama.

There was extravagance, and hyperbole, and variety, in every form. The citizens attended the theatre in order to see themselves in 'city comedies', such as *The Shoemaker's Holiday*, *The Knight of the Burning Pestle* and *Bartholomew Fair* which were set among their familiar shops and houses. It may also be that the manner and behaviour of the citizens were subtly changed by these dramatic representations. Just as it has been observed that Londoners became more extravagant in the presence of Charles Dickens, so that they might appear more Dickensian, so the Londoners of the sixteenth and seventeenth centuries reverted or aspired to type. It is a fundamental feature of city life, and thus an aspect of the city imagination. That is why sentimental characterisation, rather than psychological complexity, became the standard; there is no depth or consistency to melodramatic portraiture, and realism necessarily is displaced by spectacle and energetic movement. The whole range of urban entertainment is thereby characterised in these terms. The heroic operas of seventeenth-century London 'were not concerned with growth within the mind . . . not concerned with the interaction of character';[6] musical theatre used songs 'to break up the dramatic action, which was reduced in complexity';[7] prose fiction of the seventeenth century contains 'little psychological insight';[8] Fielding's novels display 'limited psychological range . . . seem to embody a certain moral, social, or psychological *idée fixe* and display little of that symbolic variability and emotional ambivalence'.[9] There was even a 'London School' of painting which utilised all the special effects of stage scenes to create history paintings, classical tableaux and dramatic episodes in the alcoves of Vauxhall or the walks of Ranelagh Gardens.

When William Wordsworth composed that part of *The Prelude* entitled 'Residence in London', he chose to remark upon its 'shifting pantomimic scenes' and 'dramas of Living Men'; this 'great Stage' encouraged 'Extravagance in gesture, mien, and dress' so that even the roadside beggar wore 'a written paper' announcing his story. This last detail may be the fruit of accurate observation; as early as the sixteenth century the beggars of London were renowned for their theatrical tendencies. A seventeenth-century beggar, Nan Mills, depicted by Marcellus Laroon in *The Cryes of the City of London Drawne After Life*, was known as an excellent actress and mimic who 'could adapt her countenance to every circumstance of distress'.

In one of his essays in the *Spectator*, composed primarily for a London audience, Addison alludes to the notion of the world as a theatre in which 'the great duty . . . upon a man is to act his part to perfection' and 'to excel in the part which is given us'. According to one literary historian Addison was here alluding to the 'arbitrariness' and 'inscrutability' of the theatre itself.[10] But these are of course precisely the characteristics of the city and, by an ineluctable process, of the theatrical art associated with it. In Henry Fielding's 'Essay on the Knowledge of the Characters of Men', he declares that 'the whole world becomes a vast Masquerade, where the greatest Part appear disguised under false Vizors and Habits'. It was this vision which prompted Daniel Defoe's vast assemblage of journalistic and fictional reportage, generally concerning the sensation of the moment; he was one of the true originators of the English novel.

The monkey, the mask and the mirror in the second stage of William Hogarth's *The Harlot's Progress* are all tokens of theatricality and imitation; the pictorial series itself presents a number of highly dramatic scenarios in which Hogarth introduces his characters as if they were already on stage. One chapter of *Tom Jones* is entitled 'A Comparison Between the World and the Stage', in which Fielding suggests that 'life more exactly represents the stage, since it is often the same person who represents the villain and the hero; and he who engages your admiration to-day, will probably attract your contempt to-morrow'. Hogarth confessed that 'my Picture was my Stage and men and women my actors'. The conjunction of Hogarth's name with those of Defoe and Fielding does indeed suggest a new and uniquely urban sensibility within the English imagination.

A wealth of characters

Henry Fielding. Engraving after William Hogarth. Circa 1762

CHAPTER 39

An essay on the essay

The art of fictional dialogue imitates the practice of conversation. In the middle of the eighteenth century, when the novel emerged fully armed upon the stage of the world, there were in London 'conversation assemblies' and *conversaziones*. In high art 'conversation pieces' were considered to be distinctly modern, because conversation itself had become the single most important medium for understanding. The idea of conversation, as the proper form for public and socialised truth, was pre-eminent in a culture of coffee-houses, clubs and weekly periodicals.

London had of course always been the centre of political and economic debate. But the notion of polite conversation, making judgements and recording opinions, spread as rapidly and as widely as the newly emerging 'middling classes' of London merchants and professional men. The discussion of essays played a large role in these informal debates where, by general report, the latest *Spectator* or *Idler* would be commended or disparaged. The *Spectator* was primarily designed for readers 'in Clubs and Assemblies, at Tea-Tables and in Coffee-Houses', with the assumption expressed by the Earl of Shaftesbury that 'All Politeness is owing to Liberty. We polish one another, and rub off our corners and rough sides by a sort of amical collision.' The civic virtues of the seventeenth century had been those of hardy frugality and moral independence, but these in turn gave way to condescension and civility. The unamiable rigours of Hobbes's *Leviathan*, for example, were replaced by a blander benevolence. The martial spirit was outmoded and unfashionable; the new key-word was sensibility not untouched by sentimentalism.

The success of the essay depended upon a shared set of values and assumptions, therefore, in turn allowing an intimacy or familiarity of tone; a certain *rapprochement* between author and reader was to be desired. Johnson, in one of his own essays in *The Rambler*, associated himself with Francis Bacon. 'Bacon, among all his pretensions to the regard of posterity, seems to have pleased himself mainly with his essays, "which come home to mens business and bosoms" and of which, therefore, he declares his expectation that they "will live as long as books last".' It is this desire to reach 'bosoms' as well as 'business' which suggests a connection between the essay and the novel, but with its unique form and its formidable strength the essay itself takes its place as a true feature of the English imagination.

The first collections were published in the 1780s, the great contributors being Johnson and Goldsmith, who had succeeded Addison and Steele; after them came Hazlitt, Lamb, and the series of *English Essayists* published between 1802 and 1810. Samuel Johnson was a natural and prolific essayist, so there is more than a touch of humorous self-abasement in his remark that a writer 'needs only entitle his performance an essay, to acquire the right of heaping together the collections of half his life, without order, coherence, or propriety'. Here again is the English aptitude for variety, even if it is ironically expressed. Essays were not only conversational and various, however; they were also practical and useful. They were modes of instruction and exhortation; where once the circulation of learning was maintained by the pilgrimage to European libraries or by the work of scholarly exegetes, the demands of knowledge were now amplified and communicated in the various journals and periodicals of London coffee-house society. Matters of theology and of physics, of medicine and of economics, were now the subject of the 'easy' and 'familiar' style of the English essayists. The contribution of the essay to moral and homiletic literature was therefore immense. As Addison remarked in the tenth number of the *Spectator*, 'I shall be ambitious to have it said of me that I have brought Philosophy out of closets and libraries, schools and colleges, to dwell in clubs and assemblies, at tea-tables and in coffee-houses'. The other merit of the essay lay in its brevity; as one writer of the early eighteenth century put it, it was more appropriate to 'the Brisk and Impetuous Humour of the English, who have naturally no Taste for long-winded performances, for they have no sooner begun a Book but they desire to see the End of it'. That is perhaps why the essays of Montaigne, translated by Florio in the early seventeenth century, acquired such an enormous popularity at an earlier date. So the form, first popularised in English by Francis Bacon, sets its seal upon eighteenth-century civilisation. It has been concluded that the essay was 'the only literary form used by every major author of the century';[1] its influence can be traced in the more fluent and informal tone of dialogues and sermons, treatises and poems. And, of course, shortness was all.

CHAPTER 40

The Hogarthian moment

Samuel Johnson wrote poetry and essays while also attempting drama and fiction; Fielding and Smollett began as dramatists before they ever considered writing novels; Defoe mastered every single form of the eighteenth century, and invented several new ones. This variousness can of course be studied as part of the English appetite for heterogeneity in all its forms, but variety is also an old London dish. Dryden's dramatised version of *Paradise Lost*, *The State of Innocence*, has been described as that of 'a London citizen and his wife mixing on familiar terms with angels and archangels',[1] a dialogue which has less to do with seventeenth-century London than with the inheritance of the medieval mystery plays on the streets of Clerkenwell and Cheapside. It is the same appetite which Dryden himself apostrophised in his dedication of *Love Triumphant*; he declared that the mixture of tragedy and comedy was 'agreeable to the English Genius. We love variety more than any other Nation; and so long as the Audience will not be pleas'd without it, the Poet is oblig'd to humour them.' The condition of London itself encourages a life, or sense of life, in which contraries meet. Without contraries, one Cockney visionary once wrote, there is no progression.

Yet when everything is contiguous, there is danger of so close a contact that distinction ends. This was conveyed by metaphors of the plague, when in one essay Fielding suggested that public assemblies in the city were 'as infectious by Example, as the Plague itself by Contact'. The same vision was promulgated by Charles Dickens when he surmised that it is certain 'that the air from Gin Lane will be carried, when the wind is Easterly, into May Fair, and that if you once have a vigorous pestilence raging furiously in Saint Giles, no mortal list of Lady Patronesses can keep it out of Almacks'. It was often observed that in London the living must keep close company with the dead. Hogarth depicted this in *Gin Lane*. The same sense of mortal contagion infects the dramatic and novelistic representations of urban life, where 'fever' and 'fevered dreams' are constantly invoked.

In a world where all marks of rank and distinction can also be blurred, as if in masquerade, there is the danger of social slippage. That is precisely why the novels and plays and paintings of the period are concerned with the ambiguities of gentility and criminality, as well as by the urgent aspirations of one or another character to move forward in the social hierarchy.

The role of chance meetings and unexpected events, generally against the background of the 'mob' or crowd, is as integral to the fiction of Fielding or Smollett as to that of Dickens. Thus in Fielding's *Amelia* (1752) a 'trifling adventure', a perambulation in 'the green fields in London' by the heroine and her husband, is capable 'of producing the most unexpected and dreadful events'. Such is the quality of chance or fortune in London, where a population of socially fluid characters are engaged in incidents over which they have no control; the 'events' are 'unexpected' because they conform to no observable plan or pattern. This mutability is mimicked by the novels themselves, which shift unexpectedly from allegory to history, from heroism and high sentiment to pantomime and melodrama. Pierce Egan's *Life in London* is a narrative adventure diverted and diffused by verse, philosophical speculation, topographical enquiry, romance and passages of song. Egan even manages to include an operatic score. This vision of the world is comprehensive and capacious without necessarily being complex or profound. It accommodates arbitrariness, inscrutability and endless change.

Yet Charles Dickens, of all novelists, knew that the city was not necessarily random or inscrutable; rather, that the mystery of London lay in its interconnectedness. His own novels represent by means of image and symbol such an interpenetration of lives and destinies that London itself is packed to blackness with accumulations of suffered or shared experience. 'Draw but a little circle', he wrote in *Master Humphrey's Clock*, 'above the clustering housetops, and you shall have within its space everything, with its opposite extreme and contradiction close by.' Here 'life and death went hand in hand; wealth and poverty stood side by side; repletion and starvation laid themselves down together' and here also were 'wealth and beggary, vice and virtue, guilt and innocence . . . all treading on each other and crowding together'. He described 'the restlessness of a great city, and the way in which it tumbles and tosses before it can get to sleep', as if it had somehow to encompass its multitude before it rests; if it ever can rest, that is, with the 'streams of people apparently without end . . . jostling each other in the crowd and hurrying forward'. Spectacle and melodrama are intrinsic aspects of the London vision and thus, by extension, of the English imagination itself. Yet it is not a false or ignoble sensibility. It allows pathos and sublimity no less in the canvases of Turner than in the pages of Dickens where 'every voice is merged, this moonlight night, into a distant ringing hum, as if the city were a vast glass, vibrating'.

Hogarth's *Night*, executed in 1738, is very much a stage-set or a nocturnal tableau in which the tall buildings of brick are its 'wings'; crowded upon the stage of stone and cobbles are vagrant children, drunks and an overturned coach. Gin is being poured into a keg, while urine is discharged from a chamber-pot out of a first-floor window. Fire is spreading in the foreground, and in the background are signs of a larger conflagration. 'We will therefore compare subjects for painting,' Hogarth wrote, 'with those of the stage.' In his graphic works action and contrast thrive in dramatic chiaroscuro; exits and entrances are manifold. Healthy 'Beer Street' and noxious 'Gin Lane' exist side by side; the purse-proud milliner passes a wretched whore, and the plump child of esteemed parents struts beside a vagrant girl eating broken crusts out of a gutter. Here dwell incongruity and difference but, curiously, in the light and atmosphere of London they are for a moment united. It may be wrong, then, to conclude that London artists are not capable of profundity.

In every respect Hogarth conceived of himself as a distinctly and defiantly English artist. He was born at Smithfield in 1698, and his art became identified with the raucous streets of the city. He began in a hard trade, that of a goldsmith's engraver, but quickly realised the commercial possibilities of political satire. He was a wonderful artist, who excelled in the realm of portraiture, but he managed to combine genius with business in an exemplary manner. He secured the passage of legislation, known as 'Hogarth's Act', to protect the copyright of engravers. Like Blake and Turner, he was short, stocky and pugnacious. In a letter to the *St James's Post* in June 1737, he condemned those dealers in art who 'depreciate every English work, as hurtful to their trade, of continually importing shiploads of dead Christs, holy families, Madonnas . . . and fix on us poor Englishmen the character of *universal dupes*'. He declared that he would rather depict an 'English cook-maid' than a Venus, and in one print displayed crowds attending an Italian opera while the works of Dryden, Congreve and Shakespeare are cried out as 'waste paper for shops'. So Hogarth aligned himself with an English dramatic tradition at the same time as he promulgated a wholly native art. That is perhaps the reason for the marked resemblance between some of his caricatures or grotesques and the 'babooneries' in the margins of medieval psalters; the same spirit of gross and popular art is abroad. It is of course in the nature of English genius that it steals from foreign compositions even as it disparages them, and Hogarth borrows from European artists as disparate as Raphael and Watteau; there is always this sense, in even the most defiantly 'nationalist' art, that the English imagination has been quickened and revivified by contact with European sources. Yet ultimately the scene is that of contemporary London, and the tradition Hogarth invokes is that of Shakespeare and Pope, Swift and Defoe.

His first paintings were of scenes from Gay's *The Beggar's Opera*, in which 'high' and 'low' are confounded, but his gift for moral portraiture can be seen most clearly in relation to Langland or Chaucer. Only in the city can true drama and allegory be discovered. 'In these compositions,' he wrote, 'those subjects which will both entertain and improve the mind, bid fair to be of the greatest utility, and must therefore be entitled to rank in the highest class.' That emphasis upon 'utility' might of itself be enough to characterise his English genius, but his demotic and egalitarian temper is also pertinent. He dwelled keenly upon the details of 'low life', and crowded his engravings with the weak and helpless. In part it represents a Hogarthian defiance of 'high' art, and a kind of embarrassment at the striking of heroic or historical attitudes; in practice, too, it relies upon the representation of homely or familiar details rather than the grandly or generally expressive painterly gesture. The deflation of magnificence has always been part of the English imagination.

Hogarth also depicts pantomimes and masquerades on the streets of London, as if in implicit homage to the theatrical reality by which they are surrounded. In an engraving completed in the early months of 1724, *Masquerades and Operas*, the London crowd is seen to patronise a pantomime entitled *The Necromancer*; in the same street, Haymarket, is displayed the notice for a midnight masquerade. Hogarth also drew Punch, whom in *The Analysis of Beauty* he called 'droll by being the reverse of all elegance, both as to movement and figure'. The same may be concluded of the Londoners in his engravings, who are often rendered as caricatures or as types.

Hogarth is of London, too, in his disregard for the conventional pieties of Christianity. Turner died murmuring that the sun was god, and this pagan spirit is very much part of the city's instinctive and energetic life. In the fifth plate of *Marriage-à-la-Mode*, Hogarth parodies the Descent from the Cross in the dying posture of a nobleman; he also parodied the effects of sermonising in *The Sleeping Congregation* and burlesqued William Kent's altar-piece at St Clement Danes Church. One curious detail may be mentioned in this context. In *The Sleeping Congregation* Hogarth has included an hour-glass, but this is only one of the many time-pieces which he incorporates within the scenes of London. In the work entitled *Morning* the clock of St Paul's Church is clearly visible, with an image of Father Time above it and the legend '*Sic Transit Gloria Mundi*' below. Smoke rises from a chimney pot towards these emblems of time, as if to represent the elements of transitoriness and forgetfulness in the passages of London life. In such paintings as *The Graham Children* and *The Lady's Last Stake*, clocks appear as emblematic features of a rushing or decaying world. In his last completed work, *Tailpiece*, or *The Bathos*, he again depicts Father Time with his scythe at a ruinous tavern in Chelsea known as 'The World's End'; here on the edge of London is the broken portal of eternity. So Hogarth was vouchsafed an intuition of London existence in the context of time and evanescence. It has been remarked that, the more local and specific a sensibility, the more it may aspire to universality. It is appropriate, therefore, that, in the words of one historian of art, Hogarth 'was the first British artist ever to achieve international fame'.[2] We may go further, and suggest that he was one of those Cockney artists who saw real visions in the streets of London.

His influence was profound, but also particular. Rowlandson, Gillray and Cruikshank were the three principal English caricaturists who considered themselves to be in the Hogarthian tradition of London portraiture, combining a fluency of line with a gift for grotesque or comic observation. The cartoons of Gillray and Rowlandson are vigorous and energetic, filled with the life and variety of the city, savagely denunciatory or gargantuan and tumultuous. They were true London artists because they were entranced by the scenic and the spectacular; in a city built upon greed and upon commerce, Gillray in particular was preoccupied with the shadows of money and power. His great works are striated with light and darkness, as if he were an heroic artist of the streets. He was neither sentimental nor introspective; his power came out of caricature and theatrical display, even though a note of rancid poetry emerges in some of his more demonstrative compositions. Each one strikes a different attitude, some grave, some gay, with a readiness of wit and rapidity of association which are also associated with urban life. As one historian of the national character has observed, the dweller in a great town 'is always receiving fresh impressions; and he may readily fall into a longing for a constant renewal of his sensations'.[3]

The book illustrations of Cruikshank were perfectly equivalent to the early urban vision of Charles Dickens, too, with their fierce air of constriction and incarceration. There is a famous illustration of Fagin in the condemned cell at Newgate, of which Chesterton wrote that 'it does not merely look like a picture of Fagin; it looks like a picture by Fagin'. There is something feverish about Cruikshank's genius, peculiarly apt in a city itself often described as fevered. In later life Cruikshank often declared that he had been the principal begetter of Oliver Twist and his sad history, and it is possible that he did in fact conceive of an Hogarthian 'progress' of the orphan from poverty and misery to wealth and happiness.

One critic wrote, in 1844, that anyone who wished to 'estimate the genius of Mr Dickens' should 'read the essays by Charles Lamb and by Hazlitt, on the genius of Hogarth'. There is indeed a true and powerful affinity. Dickens was often described as 'Hogarthian'; the novelist and the artist were believed to possess the same strident urban sensibility. The resemblance is not fortuitous. Dickens was a keen admirer of Hogarth's work, and his imagination was partly trained by his absorption of Hogarth's engravings. Hogarth's depiction of *Gin Lane* helped to create Rowlandson's *The Dram Shop* and Cruikshank's *Gin Shop*, for example, but it was also the inspiration for an early essay by Dickens entitled 'Gin-Shops'; the young novelist describes in vivid terms precisely the same spot which Hogarth had depicted eighty-seven years before. Just as Hogarth dwelled in loving detail upon the critical mass of crowds in *March to Finchley* and *Southwark Fair*, so Dickens exclaimed that 'we revel in a crowd of any kind – a street "row" is our delight'. Hogarth and Dickens were both preoccupied with gaols and asylums, as if they represented a true image of London; the third plate of *A Rake's Progress* is best and most fully interpreted in the account of Mr Pickwick's incarceration in the Fleet Prison. But they were both entranced by fairs and street carnivals so that Hogarth's *Southwark Fair* is amplified by Dickens's essay on 'Greenwich Fair'. In their works the city becomes both prison and theatre, fairground and madhouse. *Oliver Twist* has as its subtitle 'A Parish Boy's Progress' in direct homage to Hogarth, while the more pathetic scenes of *Nicholas Nickleby* were described by Forster as 'like a piece by Hogarth, both ludicrous and terrible'. They both dwelled upon minute particulars. In Hogarth's third plate of *Marriage-à-la-mode*, for example, a quack's surgery is seen to contain a fish's skeleton, a tripod, an odd shoe, a sword, a model of a human head, a top hat, pill boxes, and so on. Dickens describes the interior of the old curiosity shop as containing 'suits of mail standing like ghosts in armour . . . fantastic carvings brought from monkish cloisters, rusty weapons of various kinds; distorted figures in china, and wood, and iron, and ivory; tapestry and strange furniture'. Both artists packed their work with strong detail, as if attempting to convey all the fragmentation and adventitious chaos of the urban world. It could even be argued that some of Dickens's success and popularity sprang directly from the fact that he rendered Hogarth's engravings legible and readable; he gave the artist's vision a literary life.

The example of Charles Dickens will in any case confirm that the influence of Hogarth's vision was not confined to artists. Just as Hogarth borrowed some of his satire from Pope – particularly from that visionary poem of London, *The Dunciad* – so in turn Hogarth influenced Samuel Johnson. One of Johnson's essays for *The Idler* is a direct commentary upon Hogarth's print of *Evening* in the city. Yet the artist's most formidable bequest was to those eighteenth-century novelists who shared his sense of the urban world. Hogarth and Samuel Richardson were on terms of familiar acquaintance, for example, and Richardson's *Pamela* borrows directly from *A Harlot's Progress* and *A Rake's Progress*. Richardson's *Apprentice's Vade Mecum* wishes that 'the ingenious Mr Hogarth would finish the portrait'. Henry Fielding called Hogarth one of the most 'useful Satyrists that any Age hath produced' and, in his preface to *Joseph Andrews*, praised 'the ingenious Hogarth' for his ability 'to express the affections of men on canvas . . . it is a much greater and nobler applause, that they appear to think'. In *Tom Jones*, also, Fielding interrupts his narration to exclaim 'O Hogarth! had I thy pencil!' Hogarth himself was not averse to borrowing from Fielding; his *Industry and Idleness*, which recorded the careers of industrious and idle apprentices, was clearly indebted to the novelist's account of criminality in *Jonathan Wild* published four years earlier. There is here a consonance of attitude and taste which surely belongs to the broader history of the English imagination.

It has been observed that Laurence Sterne is heavily indebted to Hogarth's *The Analysis of Beauty* – Corporal Trim's flourish with his stick copies the artist's 'serpentine line of beauty' – and Sterne's sermon upon 'Felix's Behaviour Towards Paul' serves as a commentary upon

Hogarth's *Paul Before Felix*. Tobias Smollett invokes Hogarth in his principal novels. 'It would take the pencil of Hogarth', he wrote in *Roderick Random,* 'to express the astonishment and concern of Strap'; an expression in *Humphry Clinker* 'would be no bad subject for a pencil like that of the incomparable Hogarth, if any such ever appear again, in these times of dullness and degeneracy'. In the context of this admiration, then, it may be appropriate to consider the novel as a specifically London form.

CHAPTER 41

Some eminent novelists

Prose fiction, which is believed to be of Graeco-Roman origin in the centuries before Christ, is ancient and ubiquitous. The Anglo-Saxons translated *Apollonius of Tyre* into Old English prose, which can properly claim to be the first novel in the vernacular. But if it can be argued that a broad tradition of popular fiction began with the work of Defoe and Richardson, Smollett and Fielding, then the springs or sources of its inspiration are most likely to be found in the circumstances of eighteenth-century London. The city was the centre of novelty and of change, of social mobility and of sociable excitement; most eighteenth-century novels are set in London or send their characters spinning in that direction, as if they were being drawn ineluctably by a 'vortex' or a 'lodestone'. The conditions of the novels of Smollett or of Fielding are populous and multifarious, with characters led by chance or exigency into one another's company. The symbolic power of the capital was, therefore, immense. It was itself one giant novel.

Eighteenth-century fiction is hybrid and various, part realistic and part allegorical, combining heroism and farce in equal measure; it conflates epic with romance, and even includes critical theory. The tone is never constant, and the instability of the narrative mimics the fluidity of the action. At the time of the city's greatest expansion, the novel is endlessly prolific. It has no boundaries of form or genre, mingling fact and fiction indiscriminately; in that sense, too, it reflects the nature of the city. Masquerades are to be found in Richardson's *Pamela*, in Fielding's *Amelia* and *Tom Jones*, in Fanny Burney's *Cecilia*, in Smollett's *Peregrine Pickle*, in Defoe's *Roxana*, and in a score of other fictions.[1] Upon these occasions a 'strange medley' of persons in disguise disport themselves; this is the condition of the city, and also the nature of the novel. Masquerades represent the shifting crowd, an unnatural assembly in every sense which in *Cecilia* includes men dressed as 'Spaniards, chimney sweepers, Turks, watchmen, conjurors and old women'; these are of course the inhabitants of the city itself who are here portrayed in caricature as if in homage to the *genius loci*. The fear of enforced touch, and of contagion, is also evident in the descriptions

327

of untidy or unnatural couplings: 'a Devil and a Quaker, a Turk and female Rope-dancer, Judge and *Indian* Queen, and Friars of several Orders with *Fanatick Preachers*, all pair'd'. There is a suggestion here of sexual licence underlying the incoherence and arbitrariness of the proceedings; the city itself is portrayed in eighteenth-century fiction as the haven for lusts natural or unnatural. As Addison remarked, 'the secret history of a carnival would make a collection of very diverting novels'.

Many fictions present a journey towards the city as a colourful pilgrimage – the most celebrated example being that of Tom Jones – and in a similar spirit novelists such as Fielding and Defoe relish disorder and mutability. Just as the 'low' can be disguised as their betters at a masquerade, so in eighteenth-century fiction servants and masters often find their roles reversed; Pamela is transformed from a chambermaid into a lady, even if her gentility is somewhat theatrical. But then this is also the condition of the city, where servants were chastised in pamphlets and tracts for dressing up as their employers and imitating their manners. The novel was often criticised, in oblique terms, for the size and nature of its audience. There is no doubt that the vogue for fiction helped to create a 'reading public' but the moralists observed that fiction had become the especial delight of women, tradespeople and servants. The appeal to women is perhaps exemplified by the plethora of titles devoted to heroines – Pamela, Amelia, Cecilia – where the Anglo-Saxon and medieval tradition of female saints' lives is continued in another guise.

Despite the complaints of moralists, however, fiction was far from being simply an entertainment or diversion for servants and trades-people; it acted, on the contrary, as an instruction manual or 'pattern book'. The fictions of the eighteenth century were on one level designed to 'describe manners, paint characters, and try to correct the public'. It was advertised that *Pamela* was 'published in order to cultivate the principles of virtue and religion in the minds of the youth of both sexes; a narrative which has its foundation in truth'. Novels, however, were concerned with practice as well as principle. They were manuals of etiquette and guides to polite society. It is no simple coincidence, therefore, that 'they depict more often than not attempts to acquire status (or wealth and power) through isolated and individual virtue and action rather than by inheritance or through corporate involvement'.[2] So the elements of pantomime and masquerade also hold the slivers and glimmerings of individualism; just as the city is the true arena for the human striving after profit or power, so the novel celebrates individual and practical exertion.

It is striking and significant that Daniel Defoe, for example, should select as the subject of his fictions solitary and generally fearful individuals. Robinson Crusoe, who has variously been described as the representative of 'economic man' and the Protestant conscience, has become a key figure of the English imagination; in that context, his earnest practicality and hesitant spirituality, as well as his position in 'the middle state, or what might be called the upper station of low life', are at least as important as the variety of his 'strange surprizing adventures'. He was as isolated upon his desert island as in any London garret.

Daniel Defoe was born in Cripplegate, in 1660, the son of a tallow chandler; he shared that shopkeeper parentage with William Blake, whose father was a hosier, and Defoe can best be seen in the light of a broad tradition of London dissent. It is an honourable and old tradition, which has continued into the present century. He attended a Dissenting academy in Newington Green before taking up the trade of hosiery. He was never a successful businessman, however, and soon adopted the role of journalist and pamphleteer in the cause of William of Orange and the Whigs; the new king had invaded England in 1688, turning out the Catholic James II in the process, and reinstated a Protestant dispensation. Yet Defoe was not successful as a creature of party politics; he was constantly imperilled by bankruptcy and the threat of prison. As one of his most recent biographers has suggested, he had turned 'from a conventional city merchant into a lonely, hunted and secretive outsider'.[3] He had experienced all the splendours and disasters of the city, in other words, and out of that confusion created the rapid and avaricious careers of Roxana and Moll Flanders. Yet he did not turn to fiction until he had exhausted his influence as a journalist; he did not believe his novels to be a substitute for, but rather an extension of, his reportorial and polemical work. He wrote discourses on family life and on trade; he wrote stories about pirates and thieves and murderers; he composed political as well as economic treatises; he wrote biographies of Peter the Great and Charles XII of Sweden; he finished a history of the Church of Scotland and a history of the devil; he issued a great many pamphlets and wrote down many accounts of London 'marvels' such as hauntings and healings. Like many London writers, he tried his hand at anything.

It is important, also, to note that the novels sprang out of this prodigal inheritance and that they were conceived from Defoe's confusion of fact and fiction. *Robinson Crusoe* was advertised as a true history 'Written by Himself', with Defoe's name absent from the frontispiece. *A Journal of the Plague Year* is nothing of the kind, but a rich concoction of true report and fictive imagining, while *A Tour of the Whole Island of Great Britain* was written from Newington Green. If fact proves to be fiction, then Defoe's fiction has often been granted a factual status. The adventures of Robinson Crusoe were taken to be literal truth, while in more recent years Moll Flanders has been identified as Moll King or Mary Godstone. Yet all of these characterisations and attributions are beside the point. In the eighteenth-century city Daniel Defoe discovered the poetry of fact, and in that combination of the marvellous and the real he found his true subject. It is a token once more of that hybrid art which London seems to nurture; in an unstable and fluid society, where all may walk in disguise, there is no value to be found in generic identity and stability. It could be said that Defoe's fiction is a simulacrum of his journalism, but in truth there need be no distinction. This may be profoundly unsettling for the more solemn critics, who wish to find in 'the English novel' some intrinsic virtue or some reliable touchstone of excellence, but it is true to the mixed and various nature of the English imagination.

Defoe loved sensation and adventure, excessive delight and character in violent action. The energy and motion of London fill his sentences with their rapid and impersonal beat, their digressions and divagations; all the fever and fearfulness of Roxana's life, for example, can be sensed in the restless and repetitious cadences of her autobiographical narrative. The speed and acceleration of the London streets are visible in Moll Flanders's quick way of explaining herself – 'for the next time I try'd it at *White-Chappel* just by the corner of *Petty-Coat-Lane*, where the Coaches stand that go out to *Stratford* and *Bow* and that Side of the Country; and another time at the *Flying Horse*, without *Bishops-gate*, where the *Chester* coaches then lay'. The language of the streets emerges, too, in Moll's strong phrases. 'So there was her mouth stopped. . . . That's by the way.' There is a wonderful scene in Newgate between Moll and a condemned woman. 'Well *says I*, and are you thus easy? ay, *says she*, I can't help myself, what signifies being sad? If I am hang'd there's an End of me, and away she turn'd Dancing . . .' Here is further confirmation of the foreign belief that the English disdained death as a cheat or a thing of no moment, but it is also a tribute to Defoe's remarkable fluency. In recent years his tone has become a

England is the only European country to have a national portrait gallery:
(*Above left*) John Milton. (*Above right*) Edward Gibbon. (*Below left*) Mrs Gaskell.
(*Below right*) Ralph Vaughan Williams.

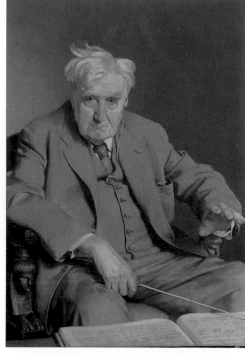

(*Above*) 'Self-Portrait' by William
Hogarth, whose individual portraits are
suffused with homeliness and intimacy
of response. (*Left*) His 'Shrimp Girl'
has, perhaps, a typically English face.

One of the portraits by Sir Joshua Reynolds
of Samuel Johnson, 'the scholar with intense
and serious gaze, deeply preoccupied or
deeply troubled by some inner vision'.

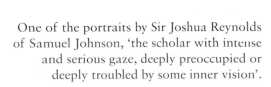

Kemble as Hamlet, painted by
Sir Thomas Lawrence. The image
of the introverted romantic hero,
'dark cloaked against murky skies'.

'No reasonable offer refused.'
Widow Twankey, like Juliet's Nurse
and Cinderella's Ugly Sisters, was a
descendent of the nagging Mrs Noah,
played for broad comedy by a man in
skirts. Equally, Dan Leno's comic asides
to the audience found their roots in the
medieval mystery plays.

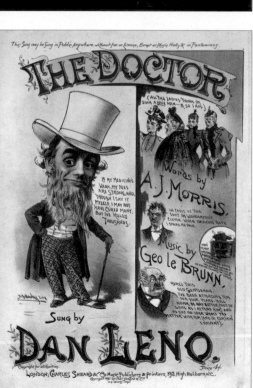

Theatre in painting:
'Mr B finds Pamela
writing.' From Joseph
Highmore's illustrations
for Richardson's
novel *Pamela*.

Hesitancy and awkward formality: 'Mr and Mrs Andrews' by Thomas Gainsborough. Are they embarrassed to be the owners of such a landscape?

Pegwell Bay, Kent, 'A Recollection of October 5th 1858' by William Dyce: the landscape of the English shore-line 'touched by mystery and enchantment'.

'Margate from the sea' by J.M.W. Turner, 'the Cockney boy who felt the romance of the ocean, becoming once more the seafarer of the Anglo-Saxon lament'.

The romantic imagination: 'The artist is then one surrounded by invisible powers.' 'The Great Day of His Wrath', from John Martin's Judgement series.

The celebrated painting by Henry Wallis of the doomed young poet, Chatterton, the most successful faker of the 18th century.

'Stroud: An Upland Landscape' by Philip Wilson Steer.
It was in the Malvern Hills that Langland dreamed his marvellous dream and Elgar was inspired to express yearning and nostalgia in *The Dream of Gerontius*.

'Reliance upon practical detail and purposeful experiment seems to breathe an English spirit.' 'An experiment on a Bird in the Air Pump' by Joseph Wright of Derby.

The open elaboration of the Lloyds Building reflects an English love of surface decoration.

matter of debate. Is he being ironic at his characters' expense, or does he expect the reader fully to sympathise with their respective fates? A similar question has been raised about his style, which has been praised as a triumph of literary artifice and condemned as artless and prolix. Yet these considerations need not apply, especially within the new form of prose fiction which confounds distinctions of every kind. Defoe was an instinctive and prolific writer who effortlessly combined all the materials that were closest to hand without any attempt to discriminate between them. In this context it is perhaps worth noting that 'Defoe's prose contains a higher percentage of words of Anglo-Saxon origin than that of any other well-known English writer except Bunyan'.[4] The old language emerged naturally, almost instinctively.

The metaphor of London as a stage also came spontaneously to Defoe, so that Moll Flanders may declare that 'generally I took up new Figures, and contriv'd to appear in new Shapes every time I went abroad'; in particular, 'I dress'd myself like a Beggar Woman, in the coarsest and most despicable Rags I could get'. Defoe himself dressed in strange shapes, and was for a long period a paid political spy in the service of Robert Harley; like Moll herself, he was consigned to Newgate Prison which was 'an Emblem of Hell itself, and a kind of an Entrance into it'. So he was always drawn to the condition of the confined and the desperate, and the birth of individual character in English fiction can confidently be ascribed to the condition of London itself. As Moll Flanders observes while living in the Mint, a poor area of Southwark, 'I saw nothing but Misery and Starving was before me'. These are the afflictions which haunt Robinson Crusoe and Roxana, albeit in different guises. The general plot of Defoe's fictions, which include the 'true' histories of the criminals Jack Sheppard and Jonathan Wild, is of a provincial's journey to London; it is also a pilgrimage towards sexuality and crime, with the imminent threat of the gaol and the gallows.

Defoe's *Journal of the Plague Year*, published in 1722, is itself a tabulation of fears. London 'might well be said to be all in tears', and Defoe's frequent image of the city as a human body takes on a piteous aspect. It exudes 'steams and fumes' so that its streets reproduce 'the Breath . . . the Sweat . . . the Stench of the Sores of the sick persons'. In this world of steam and suffering the inhabitants of the city run mad, 'raving and distracted', with others 'frighted into idiotism, and foolish distractions, some into despair and Lunacy, others into melancholy madness'. The *Journal* is in fact itself a narrative of melancholy madness, that condition to which the English were most prone. If London resembled an asylum, however, it was also compared to a prison with every house its own gaol since 'here were just so many prisons in the town as there were Houses shut up'. Many people, naked and delirious, ran through the streets screaming or plunged into the Thames while others grew 'stupid with the insupportable sorrow'.

In Defoe's account we see as much evidence of the English imagination as of the London plague. It purports to be the work of 'a Citizen who continued all the while in London' but in fact Defoe was a small child at the time of the distemper, and this highly wrought account is essentially a fiction with details taken from contemporary annals and memoirs. It is literally a work of sensation in the most strident urban style, relying upon anecdote and adventure, filled with short character studies of the afflicted and suffused with practical detail. Defoe is always seeking for extremes, so that the sensationalism is effectively a literary device. Here we may make the connection with Hogarth or with Gillray, whose vivid and animated visions dwell in the region of sublime distortion. The artists employed a 'strongly engraved, expressive line',[5] just as Defoe coined a powerful and fluent style heavily influenced by short Anglo-Saxon derivations; all of them came out of a popular tradition of print or journalism, and all appealed to a varied and urban market. But if it was a London vision, it also rested upon a native spirit and tradition.

The theatricality and excess of Henry Fielding's novels are not in doubt; he was a highly successful dramatist before he became a novelist. During his early career in London he wrote comedies and farces for the popular stage, composing some thirteen plays in less than three years, with titles such as *The Author's Farce*, *Rape Upon Rape* and *Tom Thumb*. In the tradition of Defoe, he also found employment as a journalist before he turned to fiction; he became assistant editor of *The Champion: or, The British Mercury* and wrote most of its leading articles. He created a character upon the model of Addison's 'Mr Spectator', Hercules Vinegar, who with the members of his immediate family commented upon the affairs of the day. In fact he continued writing journalism for the rest of his life. He edited two political news-sheets, *The True Patriot* and *The Jacobite's Journal*; even after the success of *Joseph Andrews* and *Tom Jones*, he took on the editorship of a twice-weekly periodical called *The Covent-Garden Journal*. In that sense he shares a curious affinity with Charles Dickens, who edited

Household Words and *All the Year Round* while engaged upon his great works of fiction.

There is in fact a skein of associations and resemblances between these three London novelists. Dickens wrote for the stage, also, and enjoyed great success as an amateur actor for much of his life. And all three men were touched by the shadow of the prison-house. Defoe was incarcerated at various times in Newgate, the Marshalsea and the King's Bench, while Dickens's youthful experience of London included the imprisonment of his father for debt in the Marshalsea. In turn Fielding was arrested and imprisoned for debt; he may have escaped Newgate, but he could not have avoided the 'spunging house' or half-way house to gaol. Defoe's fiction is filled with images and scenes of imprisonment; the novels of Dickens are preoccupied with prison and prisoners; the opening chapters of Fielding's *Amelia* are set in a London gaol, and Tom Jones may be said to have been incarcerated with Moll Flanders in Newgate. It might also be mentioned here that for five years William Hogarth's father was imprisoned for debt in the Fleet.

Fielding, like Defoe and Dickens, also wrote essays on social and political matters – among them 'An Attempt Towards a Natural History of the Hanover Rat' and 'A Dialogue Between the Devil, the Pope and the Pretender'. Like Defoe, he composed poetical satires and dubious 'factual' accounts of famous criminals. His *Life of Mr Jonathan Wild the Great* is a classic of its kind, supplanting even Defoe's *True and Genuine Account of the Life and Actions of the Late Jonathan Wild*. These London authors were prodigal of genres as well as words so that urban writing becomes the stuff or material out of which are shaped novels, newspapers and pamphlets. Fielding himself called the novel 'a newspaper, which consists of just the same number of words, whether there be any news in it or not'; but he also described *Tom Jones* as 'this heroic, historical, prosaic poem'. Just as the eighteenth-century term 'cartoon' could be applied equally to a caricature and to an historical painting, so the word 'history' applied to *Joseph Andrews* as well as to more sober narratives. Out of many forms came that formless jumble, the English novel.

The truest metaphor for Fielding, however, remains that of the theatre. The master of burlesque and farce, once called 'the English Molière', he translated his talent for stage comedy into another sphere. In defending his heterogeneous entertainments, filled with the spirit of 'contrast', he invokes 'the inventor of that most exquisite entertainment, called the English pantomime' who mixes 'the serious and the comic'. In Hogarth's frontispiece to Fielding's collected works, the image of the novelist is placed above the masks of comedy and tragedy in true interpretation of his genius. In *Jonathan Wild* he compares the political life of the nation to a street theatre – 'these Puppet-shows', as he puts it, 'which are so frequently acted on the GREAT stage'. That is why his own work was often considered to be 'low'. His reputation as a writer of farce and burlesque was held against him, and he was accused of importing these qualities into his fiction. His characterisation was implausible, his plots impossible, and his characters disgusting. 'Common charity, a f——t' exclaims Mrs Tow-Wouse. In *Tom Jones* Squire Western declares that he regards his sister's politics 'as much as I do a f——t'. Which word 'he accompanied and graced with the very Action, which, of all others, was the most proper to it'. Whereupon the periodical *Old England* described *Tom Jones* as 'a Book so truly profligate, of such evil Tendency, and offensive to every chaste Reader, so discouraging to Virtue and detrimental to Religion'.

Dickens avoided any taint of obscenity and impropriety – there could be no Hogarth or Fielding in the nineteenth century – but his own fiction was also derided for inconsistency and implausibility. The plots of his later novels were considered to be unrealistic 'twaddle'. It is the response of earnest intelligence to an urban sensibility which embraces the pantomimic and the scenic, which revels in energy and adventure, and which betrays little interest in psychological or moral complexity. It is no accident that both Fielding and Dickens, for example, defended their use of coincidence in plot-making as a natural device; their experience of the city convinced them that coincidence is a strong force in human life and that it reflects a greater underlying network of relations. Theirs is a London vision.

If we reflect upon the different virtues of Tobias Smollett and Samuel Richardson, however, we may understand the actual capaciousness of that vision. Smollett was born and educated in Scotland, but moved to London in order to pursue his career as a surgeon. Very quickly he assumed the role of a London writer, however, by becoming in quick succession a journalist, dramatist and pamphleteer as well as a novelist. He helped to edit the *Critical Review*, he compiled a selection of *Authentic and Entertaining Voyages* and wrote a history of England; he even tried his hand at farce and tragedy. A recognisable pattern of prodigal achievement once more emerges.

Charles Dickens had Smollett's novels by heart, having first encountered them in childhood when living in lodgings beside the Marshalsea Prison. Smollett was himself imprisoned in the King's Bench, just south of the Marshalsea, affirming in his own life the connection between urban fiction and the London gaols. As a result, perhaps, his art is one of extremity and intensity. When Roderick Random, the eponymous hero of *The Adventures of Roderick Random*, meets his benevolent uncle who releases him from debt and confinement, 'I was utterly confounded at this sudden transition . . . and a crowd of incoherent ideas rushed so impetuously upon my imagination, that my reason could neither separate nor connect them'. This is a fair measure of the sudden and rapidly changing sentiments which invade Smollett's characters, and which prompted Sir Walter Scott to suggest that he 'loved to paint characters under the strong agitation of fierce and stormy passions'. His metaphor of the 'crowd' here suggests, in fact, how his sensationalism and excitation are related to the feverish life of the city. It is the life which he portrays in *Humphry Clinker*, where Matt Bramble remarks of Londoners that 'All is tumult and hurry; one would imagine that they were impelled by some disorder of the brain, that will not suffer them to be at rest . . . how can I help supposing they are actually possessed by a spirit, more absurd and pernicious than any thing we meet within the precincts of Bedlam?'

Smollett was aware of the violence and despair which are the condition of the city, London 'being an immense wilderness'. Roderick Random is beaten, robbed, press-ganged, swindled until he eventually languishes in the Marshalsea Prison with an 'imagination haunted with such dismal apparitions, that I was ready to despair'. One critic has written of this novel that there 'can be no movement but from one extreme to another, from shock to shock, from terror to hysterical laughter'.[6] The life of the novel then replicates the life of the streets, filled with rapidly changing scenes and imbued with a certain spontaneity or incoherence of tone. All is action and confusion. When it is further concluded that, in the novels of Smollett, 'each statement is in competition with all the other statements; there is no remission from the struggle for attention'[7] we are truly in the little world of London. Here are strident 'types' who may clamour for notice – 'There were also my Lord Straddle, Sir John Shrug, and Master Billy Chatter, who is actually a very facetious young gentleman' – but they must also struggle to be seen and heard among 'the modish diversions of the town, such as plays, operas, masquerades, drums, assemblies, and puppet-shows . . . surprisals and terrifications'.

Prison and pantomime, death and excremental farce, are all in consort together. The city then becomes a kind of dream or hallucination in which irreconcilable states are jumbled together. 'I could not believe the evidence of my senses,' declares Roderick Random, 'and looked upon all that had happened as the fictions of a dream!' Life, for Henry Fielding, is no more than 'an idle, trifling feverish dream'. 'It was all a troubled dream?' asks Richard Carstone at the end of his unhappy life in *Bleak House*. It is the great dream of London.

If there is one aspect of Smollett's art which is of particular significance, however, it lies in his creation and embellishment of eccentric character. A general delight in eccentricity, in all its forms, in fact animates the English genius. It is related to the habits of individualism and defensive privacy which the English have adopted; eccentricity then becomes the natural, if unacknowledged, issue of a native virtue. So Smollett introduces certain stock characters, such as the formidable Mrs Trunnion who 'by the force of pride, religion and Coniac, had erected a most terrible tyranny in the house'. But her unfortunate spouse, Commodore Trunnion, is of quite another order of creation. He is perhaps the first eccentric in English prose fiction. With his companions, Pipe and Hatchway, he lives in a nautical dream. 'I have been a hard-working man, and served all offices on board from cook's shifter to the command of a vessel. Here, you Tunley, there's the hand of a seaman, you dog.' He is the immediate ancestor of innumerable Dickensian characters, from Captain Cuttle to Major Bagstock, and the preposterous if amiable ex-seaman has entered the list of English immortals. He calls his house a 'garrison', has a drawbridge over a ditch, and sleeps in a hammock; he 'swears woundily' but 'means no more harm than a suckling babe'. He is located in an English county 'bounded on one side by the sea', and he can be seen as a burlesque upon the private and enclosed English character. That is why he has achieved such exemplary status. His constant memories of the sea, and of nautical battles, render him an Anglo-Saxon *revenant*; his fear of women and his whimsical sentimentality can also be seen as marked characteristics of the English temper. He is a reluctant and hen-pecked husband who finds comfort with his male companions, generally in the tavern, but he makes a very good death. On his death-bed he declares, of his gravestone, that 'it may not be ingraved in the Greek or Latin lingos, and much less in the French, which I abominate, but in plain English, that when the angel comes to pipe *all hands* at the great day, he may know that I am a

British man, and speak to me in my mother tongue. And now I have no more to say, but God in heaven have mercy upon my soul, and send you all fair weather, wheresoever you are bound.' It has been said that Smollett based the death scene upon that of Shakespeare's Falstaff; in the calm dignity and cool despatch there are resemblances, but it might also be fair to claim that in its reticence and disinclination to lament it is a very English death. The sensibility endures to the very moment of its surcease.

The emphasis upon eccentricity of behaviour or demeanour is also part of a larger English preoccupation, best exemplified by what became known as 'the novel of character'. Its first and best practitioner was another urban writer, a tradesman and pamphleteer who like his contemporaries in eighteenth-century London seemed to adopt the novel form almost by accident. Samuel Richardson once confessed that 'I almost slid into the writing of *Pamela*'. Thus was born the novel whose intense interest centred on the development of character under the pressure of circumstance and extremity, with a highly coloured presentation of the individual formed upon the anvil of adversity. Richardson's novels betray their London origins.

Richardson himself, in characteristic London fashion, was a businessman and pamphleteer before turning to the business of writing novels. He was a printer by trade, with a shop at the top end of Fleet Street, who had already fashioned a successful career out of publishing political literature and periodicals such as the Duke of Wharton's *True Briton*; he had a licence to print parliamentary debates and launched himself into the public domain with a scholarly account of seventeenth-century English diplomacy. His fictional skills emerged out of that practical or pragmatic interest which has served the English imagination so well; he had been asked to compose a manual on the art of letter-writing 'in a common Style' for the use of 'Country Readers', and on the basis of these models he hit upon the plot of *Pamela* which is itself an epistolary novel. The story of the kidnapping and imprisonment of the unfortunate heroine took him two months to complete; in fact it can be said, of all the eighteenth-century London novelists, that they wrote fast and furiously, as if in consort with the life all around them. In a period when a pamphlet could be written in the morning and printed (by Richardson among others) in the afternoon, when a play and its prologue could be ready in published form the day after their first performance, there was a premium upon speed of execution.

Written at this rapid pace, *Pamela* instinctively and effortlessly incorporates such familiar characteristics as melodrama and theatrical caricature. The portrait of Pamela's unofficial gaoler, Mrs Jewkes, has been variously described as resembling Hogarth and Dickens but the family likeness is clear. 'Her face is flat and broad; and as to Colour, looks as it had been pickled a month in Saltpetre: I dare say she drinks. She has a hoarse man-like Voice, and is as thick as she's long . . .' She might be the procuress in *A Harlot's Progress* or Mrs Gamp in *Martin Chuzzlewit*. She is, in other words, a London type. She has an 'ugly horse-lip', calls Pamela 'lambkin' and tells dubious jokes. 'Hey-day! why so nimble, and whither so fast?' she calls out. 'What! are you upon a wager?' Yet the principal emphasis is upon the intense and heightened sensations of Pamela herself, all the time fearing that she is about to be raped by her 'master', and the novel is filled with apprehension and passionate reproach. It is written in the form of apparently artless and spontaneous letters, so that everything happens in the foreshortened space of a day or a passing hour; the intensity of the action is proportionately increased. It is not difficult to enter the movement of feeling, therefore; the reader keeps pace, as it were, with the consciousness of the principal characters.

In that sense, if in no other, Samuel Richardson changed the course of the English novel. He had a direct influence upon the work of Jane Austen who, in her *Sanditon*, reveals a character very like herself whose 'fancy had been early caught by all the impassioned & most exceptionable parts of Richardson; & such Authors as have since appeared to tread in Richardson's steps, so far as Man's determined pursuit of Woman in defiance of every opposition of feeling and convenience is concerned'. It has also been said that the novels of Richardson, with their steady attention to a sequence of fleeting impressions, materially influenced Virginia Woolf and James Joyce; in addition, he affected European writers as diverse as Rousseau and Goethe. Diderot composed a poem in his honour, 'O Richardson, Richardson, first of men in my eyes, you shall be my reading at all times!' So did this successful and somewhat prim London tradesman enter the history of European romanticism.

It could be said that Richardson provided a peculiarly English contribution to that history since, according to Paul Langford in *Englishness Identified*, the 'English novel, the single most potent agent of English culture on the Continent, was *par excellence* about character and manners'. By the latter half of the eighteenth century, 'it was the sensibility of the English novel rather than the brutality of English history that informed Continental assumptions'.[8] A French critic said, of innkeepers, that 'the English novel writers who are so fond of painting these characters copy from a given model which, though it admits of but little scope for variety, is nevertheless true to nature'. Fanny Burney's novels were celebrated for forming 'a history of National Manners in themselves'[9] while an Italian critic believed that the novels of Fielding and Smollett comprised a vast encyclopaedia of 'English manners and peculiarities'. As Mr Langford remarks in another place, 'Continental observers were fascinated by the English preoccupation with originality of character';[10] it is manifest no less in portrait-painting than in satirical caricature, English drama and English fiction.

CHAPTER 42

A character study

There is perhaps no greater English character than Dr Johnson. The shambling, obsessive, melancholy figure has become representative no less of London than of literature; he walks through both accompanied by a fluent and sharp-witted Scotsman. In his bad temper and solicitude for others, in his prodigious learning and no less prodigal speech, in his hack work and in his high endeavours, in his gregariousness and in his melancholy, he is characteristic and unmistakable. He attempted every form of writing and excelled in each one of them. In his essays for *The Rambler* and *The Idler*, in his commentaries upon Shakespeare, he evinces a kind of sublime common sense – literally *communis sensus*, the feelings common to mankind – so that his poetry and prose are marvellously freighted with general reserves of taste and judgement. His gravitas lies also within the weight of his language, which contained all of its classical affiliations. When introduced to French scholars and divines he spoke in Latin; like More and Milton before him, he trusted the efficacy of European humanism and what has been called 'the Anglo-Latin tradition'. His two greatest poems, 'London: A Poem' and 'The Vanity of Human Wishes', are imitations of Juvenalian satire; he translated Horace, and wrote poetry in Latin. In his own tone of dignified melancholy he adverted to his position as 'scholar' rather than 'author':

> There mark what Ills the Scholar's Life assail,
> Toil, Envy, Want, the Patron, and the Jail

He was possessed by the idea of translation as a major force within English letters, therefore, and in the second volume of *Lives of the Poets* he wrote that 'the affluence and comprehension of our language is very illustriously displayed in our poetical translations of the Ancient Writers; a work which the French seem to relinquish in despair'. This concluding note suggests a certain nationalism of response, even in so learned a context, and once again the English genius seems to spring out of a confluence of European or classical influences. It is what Johnson remarked of Pope, when he declared that the earlier poet's translation of the *Iliad* was 'certainly the noblest version of poetry

340

which the world has ever seen; and its publication must therefore be considered as one of the great events in the annals of Learning'; it was 'a performance which no age or nation can pretend to equal'. This is high praise, but praise for an English poem rather than a Greek epic.

That Johnson understood the dimensions of his national culture is not in doubt. Of the proposal to establish a society for the reformation and standardisation of language upon the French model, Johnson wrote that 'such a society might, perhaps, without much difficulty, be collected; but that it would produce what is expected of it may be doubted'. In England its proposals 'would probably be read by many, only that they might be sure to disobey them'. He understood the native sensibility too well to imagine its renovation in a Gallic or neo-classical spirit. Of course his own *Dictionary* might be seen as an exercise in authoritarian linguistics but, like his work upon Shakespeare and his *Lives of the Poets*, it is more profitably to be regarded as an attempt to restore a native tradition. In his preface to that great enterprise Johnson insisted that he wished to recall English to its 'original Teutonick character' and that he felt obliged to take 'examples and authority from the writers before the restoration [1660] whose works I regard as the wells of English undefiled, as the pure sources of genuine diction'. In that sense the *Dictionary* might be considered to be a project filled with the spirit of English antiquarianism – what Johnson himself termed 'my zeal for antiquity' – and the learned lexicographer did indeed insist upon 'making our ancient volumes the ground work of stile'. This reverence for 'the genius of our tongue' is then entirely consonant with his deep regard for history and the historical process, or what one biographer has called 'Johnson's lifelong concern for historicity'.[1] The *Dictionary* itself is devoted 'to the honour of my country' whose 'chief glory . . . arises from its authors'.

His declaration that 'No man but a blockhead ever wrote, except for money' has been widely regarded as a 'typically' English statement of disregard for theoretical or ideal aspirations. It is an aspect of his pragmatism or, at least, of his practicality. The tone is continued in his reply to James Boswell's enquiry about the meaning of human activity – 'Sir (said he in an animated tone) it is driving on the system of life' – upon which he further elaborated in an essay for *The Rambler*. 'We proceed, because we have begun; we complete our design, that the labour may not be in vain.' It is possible to glimpse here, also, that peculiarly native combination of fatalism and melancholy inherited from the Anglo-Saxon poets and continued ever since.

Perhaps Johnson's most famous gesture was his kicking of the stone in contempt of Bishop Berkeley's theory concerning the non-existence of matter. 'I refute it thus' is a sufficiently English rejoinder to have entered what might be called the canon of native sensibility. It also touches upon the most perplexing aspect of his Englishness or, rather, his English reputation. Samuel Johnson is better known for his character than for his writing. It is part of a native tradition.

The English were preoccupied with character as the determining force in human relations and the agent of social change. It was conjectured, for example, 'that English educators were obsessed with the development of character rather than the inculcation of knowledge'.[2] We may find its traces within the texture of English common law and religious thought, both of which emphasise individual rights and responsibilities, while one historian finds its origins in the English language and its 'individualism of style, which corroborates a passion for individuality'.[3] These are profound matters indeed, suggesting the transmission 'of some common substance of thought from a dim and forgotten past'.[4] The English language will not yield to the blandishments of academic discipline, and English literature is marked by 'an absorption in character and its development'.[5] These concerns are to be found in Elizabethan drama no less than in the comedy of 'humours', in the historical characters who populated Clarendon's *History of the Rebellion* or Burnet's *History of My Own Times*, and in the philosophy of Locke which sustained the natural rights of the individual. They are, in short, to be found everywhere.

It is the merest truism to note, in this context, that the art of portrait painting became for all intents and purposes a national pursuit. Hogarth once surmised that 'portrait painting ever has, and ever will, succeed better in this country than any other' and an historian of art has confirmed this observation with the remark that 'portraiture set the agenda for other forms of painting'.[6] It is a practical art; it is a useful art; it is a commercial art. These may be considered English virtues. The obsession with character may be traced in medieval babooneries and misericords, in Rowlandson's cartoons and in Frith's crowded paintings. No other European nation has a National Portrait Gallery.

It has been said of Holbein's portraiture that 'his sense of character in itself gives an English appearance to his work',[7] which suggests that there is something in the soil or air or atmosphere of England which impregnates even a foreign genius. Roy Strong has also written of

Holbein that 'the longer he stayed, the more his work moved away from being three-dimensional towards being flattened into a two-dimensional pattern'[8] which is also part of a native aesthetic. There is a continuity, therefore, manifested in thirteenth-century manuscripts which display a 'purely English skill in portraiture'[9] and in the carved heads of Early English architecture; it has been observed, of these artefacts, that 'in no other country are such heads found in such quantities, a fact that indicates the English interest in physiognomy, an interest which in the future was to lead to the prominence of portrait painting'.[10]

The English Renaissance has been called 'an age of portrait-painting'[11] so that in the sixteenth century there was a 'near monopoly by portraiture'.[12] The twin ideals of the Renaissance and the Reformation, if such intellectual shorthand be permitted, encouraged the presumption that religion was the domain of the individual and that history was the arena of the hero. It is of some significance, too, that 'in all its varied aspects only the formalised linear portrait is to be found in England'[13] so that the preoccupation with the hard or simple outline is of a piece with the interest in character. English miniatures of the period are also entranced by the individual sitter, with 'the insistence on the facial likeness, on the vocation or status of the sitter, on the memorial nature of the works';[14] the practicality of the exercise is not in doubt. In these miniature portraits an exquisite individuality is to be found, complementing the rich colour and decoration so that there is an exact equivalence between face and surface.

In the seventeenth century 'family portraits and portraits of friends and political associates predominated',[15] while the most interesting sculpture is to be found in funereal effigies and portrait busts; the head of Sir Christopher Wren by Edward Pierce is justly celebrated. One of the attributes of English painting in this period is that of 'a fresh approach to character', and the sojourn of artists such as Anthony Van Dyck and Daniel Mytens in England is often invoked to explain their deepening sense of individual or at least courtly personality. The work of a native painter like William Dobson, on the other hand, has been exemplified in the remark that his 'feeling for character is entirely English'.[16] In the single heads of the early seventeenth century, as opposed to the full-length portraits, 'the beginnings of what may perhaps be called a native British tradition can first be found'.[17] Cornelius Johnson, for example, was 'the first to seize (as only an Englishman could) upon that shy and retiring streak in the English temper, whose presence in a portrait is a sure sign of native English art'.[18] This is an interesting perception, and does much to explain the feeling of hesitancy and awkward formality in subsequent portrait-painting. In many of Gainsborough's portraits, it might seem that the sitter did not wish to be painted at all. It is a form of English embarrassment, manifest in Gainsborough's delicate and ambiguous line.

The exception may be made here for seventeenth-century 'family pieces', or 'conversation pieces', in which tribal or social imperatives triumph over the individual sensibility. That is why Steele could write in the *Spectator* that 'no nation in the world delights so much in having their own, or Friends or Relations pictures. . . . We have the greatest number of the Works of the best masters in that kind [portraiture], of any people', which compliment he followed with 'Face Painting is nowhere so well performed as in England'.

His own likeness by Godfrey Kneller emphasises the sociability of the English portrait: he was painted as one of the forty-eight members of the 'Kit-Cat Club', a club of Whig notables which met in Shire Lane. These portraits are not representations of the isolated or self-communing individual but of something close to a collective identity. When Jonathan Richardson elaborated upon the theory of portrait-painting in the early eighteenth century he chose to emphasise the importance of 'beauty, good sense, breeding and other good qualities of the person', as if he were constructing a racial or national model to which the representation of the sitter must aspire; they are social rather than personal qualities.

One collector of contemporaneous English art was asked by his son why he had not purchased one of Benjamin West's classical compositions, to which came the reply, 'You surely would not have me hang up a modern English picture in my house unless it were a portrait?' He might have included in this category the somewhat more formal portraits of actors in role, or actors in costume, which form a significant part of the English canon. They reflect the national appetite for theatrical illusion, and in the work of such artists as Zoffany and Wright the tinctures of stage lighting reveal action as if it were on a proscenium. Hogarth's renditions of *The Beggar's Opera*, and Highmore's representations of the more dramatic moments in *Pamela*, are also part of this tradition.

Yet Hogarth was equally capable of composing individual portraits which are suffused with a certain homeliness or intimacy of response; the portrait heads of his servants are sufficiently well known but, in his representations of *Captain Thomas Coram* or *The Graham Children*, the expressions and gestures of the subject manifest Hogarth's extraordinary alertness to the springs of human character. It has always been said of him that he specialised in the English face, with *The Shrimp Girl* as one of the more notable examples, but this abiding interest is connected with what has been called Hogarth's 'rugged individualism' of style and manner[19] as well as the 'homely simplicity'[20] upon which the English prided themselves. He is preoccupied with the trajectory of the living character, and with the practical expression of life itself beyond the range of authority and theory. England is a biographical nation.

Bust of Sir Christopher Wren by Edward Pierce. Circa 1673

CHAPTER 43

The fine art of biography

The extant portraits of Samuel Johnson, no less than five of which were executed by Sir Joshua Reynolds, have created a familiar compound image of the scholar with intense and serious gaze, deeply preoccupied or deeply troubled by some inner vision. More circumstantial detail is supplied by contemporaries who have remarked that 'his immense structure of bones was hideously striking to the eye, and the scars of the scrofula were deeply visible'. At a later date 'down from his bed-chamber, about noon, came, as newly risen, a huge uncouth figure, with a little dark wig which scarcely covered his head, and his clothes hanging loosely about him'. His clothing was often dirty, his shirt collar and sleeves unbuttoned, his stockings around his ankles. James Boswell noted that 'he is very slovenly in his dress, and speaks with a most uncouth voice'. Fanny Burney has left the most interesting account, however, with her observations that 'He is tall and stout; but stoops terribly; he is almost bent double. His mouth is almost constantly opening and shutting as if he was chewing. He has a strange method of frequently twirling his fingers, and twisting his hands. His body is in continual agitation, see-sawing up and down; his feet are never a moment quiet; and, in short, his whole person is in perpetual motion.' His curious gait meant that he was a constant object of amuse-ment to children or to the 'mob'. He would 'zigzag' across the London streets, often colliding with people without realising that he had done so, and he had an obsessive habit of knocking every post with a stick; if he missed one, he would retrace his steps and give it a tap. He would suddenly come to a halt in the middle of these thoroughfares, and raise his arms above his head in a spasmodic movement; before crossing any threshold he would whirl about, twisting his body before making a sudden stride or leap. He enjoyed rolling down hills and climbing trees.

This is not a diversion but, rather, an example of biographical description in the English manner. Here is Samuel Johnson, for example, upon the life of Jonathan Swift:

> He thought exercise of great necessity, and used to run half a mile up and down a hill every two hours. . . . He was always careful of his money, and was therefore no liberal entertainer, but was less frugal of his wine than

of his meat. When his friends of either sex came to him in expectation of a dinner, his custom was to give everyone a shilling that they might please themselves with their provision. At last his avarice grew too powerful for his kindness; he would refuse a bottle of wine, and in Ireland no man visits where he cannot drink.

Johnson himself believed that biography, the history of character in the world, was a noble and salutary pursuit. 'I have often thought', he once wrote, 'that there has rarely passed a life of which a judicious and faithful narrative would not be useful.' Whether he would have praised Boswell's *Life* of him in these terms is an open question; but his own *Lives of the English Poets* amply fulfils his principles. 'Biography', he wrote, 'is of the various kinds of narrative writing, that which is most eagerly read, and most easily applied to the purposes of life.' He told a gathering of friends in the Mitre public-house 'that he loved the biographical part of literature most',[1] and once explained to Boswell that 'I esteem biography, as giving us what comes near to ourselves, what we can turn to use'. This emphasis upon usefulness partakes of the English spirit, but Johnson's preoccupation with individual life and character is also of English provenance.

In an essay for *The Rambler* he proposed that biography was an extension of imaginative literature since 'all joy or sorrow for the happiness or calamities of others is produced by an act of imagination, that realises the event, however fictitious, or approximates it, however remote, by placing us, for a time, in the condition of him whose fortune we contemplate'. The biographer will 'conceive the pains and pleasures of other minds' but must also 'excite' them in the act of imaginative re-creation. This dictum has profoundly affected the course of the English imagination, even as it arises naturally out of it. The novel and the biography are aspects of the same creative process. In fact it might be suggested that the greatest writers are those, like Johnson, who effortlessly transcend the limitations of genre; their writing, whatever temporary form it takes, is of a piece. If his poetry becomes a 'just representation of general nature', then so must his life of Milton or of Dryden.

But there is a further refinement to Johnson's art, in those passages where he fashions his prose in the image of his subjects. When in his life of Milton he exclaims upon 'these bursts of light and involutions of darkness; these transient and involuntary excursions and retrocessions of invention', he is translating within his own style the idiom and cadence of Milton's verse. In a less elevated mode he notes that 'the death of Pope was imputed by some of his friends to a silver sauce-pan, in which it was his delight to eat potted lampreys'; he employs here the delicate and familiar imagery of Pope's satires to make his own point. The collusion of style is also evidence of further intimacy, since Johnson is drawn into autobiography by the pressure of biography. He re-creates himself in passages ostensibly dedicated to others. He identifies himself with Richard Savage, the destitute young dramatist and poet with whom he walked the streets of London at night in endless conversation. When he writes of the wild and penniless Savage that 'His mind was in an uncommon degree vigorous and active. His judgement was accurate, his apprehension quick and his memory so tenacious that he was frequently observed to know what he had learned from others in a short time, better than those by whom he was informed' he is also limning a self-portrait. When he wrote of the scientist, Boerhaave, he was also engaged in an act of self-definition. 'There was, in his air and motion, something rough and artless, but so majestic and great at the same time, that no man ever looked upon him without veneration.' There were less happy resemblances, however, and in his account of William Collins's mental decline there is a suggestion of his own incipient madness. Collins 'languished some years under that depression of mind which enchains the faculties without destroying them, and leaves reason the knowledge of right without the power of pursuing it'; this is the composition of one who desired to be tied and whipped, and whose own depression of spirits was heavier than many other men could bear.

All the pity and sympathy of his nature, therefore, went out to the bereft Savage. Indeed his entire description of the young outcast, this uncommon writer thrown away destitute into the alleys and doorways of London, is an image of Johnson as he might have been or might one day become. He wrote his friend's life when he was himself an impoverished hack in the employment of the *Gentleman's Magazine*, often forced to wander the streets at night for want of settled lodgings. And so when Johnson writes of Savage that 'when he left his company, he was frequently to spend the remaining part of the night in the street, or at least was abandoned to gloomy reflections', he writes about himself as eloquently as he writes about Savage. The associations and affiliations are formed. When in the same life-story he declares that Savage was 'disowned by his mother, doomed to poverty and obscurity, and launched upon the ocean of life only that he might be swallowed by its quick-sands or dashed upon its rocks', he is outlining the entire plot of Smollett's *Peregrine Pickle* with more than a little seasoning of *Tom Jones*. A common language creates a common vision of the world; this is the English imagination at its primary and pre-eminent work.

In his absorbing study of Johnson and Savage, *Dr Johnson and Mr Savage*, Richard Holmes noted that literary biography is a hybrid art and amplified the argument by suggesting that this mixed and mingled form – this essentially English form – helped to create the romantic sensibility. He surmised that Johnson's naïve romanticism[2] seized upon Savage as an outcast poet, and that he had 'glimpsed in the back streets the first stirrings of the new Romantic age'.[3] It is only another step then to claim, as Mr Holmes does, that biography itself 'is essentially a Romantic form'[4] which, in the eighteenth century, 'became a rival to the novel'. It is perhaps more appropriate to suggest that it incorporated the novel, just as it manifested certain tendencies which come under the rubric of 'romanticism'. Like the language, and the culture, it assimilates anything.

In truth English biography was, from the beginning, a collection of fictional or dramatic episodes united by a commentary of a didactic or homiletic nature. The twin deities of 'Fortune' or 'Fate' were invoked in medieval narratives, while North's preface to his translation of Plutarch's 'Lives' – one of the key influences upon the development of the native tradition – reveals the moral aspect of biography in the typically English injunction that 'it is better to see learning in noble mens lives than to read it in Philosophers writings'. The perception was extended by Fielding in his novel, *Joseph Andrews*, in which he remarked that 'examples work more forcibly on the mind than precepts'. The pragmatic dimension of biographical study is here made explicit, and that practicality helps to explain the love of biography among English rather than French or Italian readers. With its approximation to fact it is considered to be an instructive and useful art, implicitly opposed to the fanciful and useless – if entertaining – allurements of fiction.

There has never been any distinction between 'fiction' and 'fact', however. Just as early biographies followed the tragic pattern of the drama's 'wheel of fortune', so the early novelists insisted upon the basis of their fictions in true sources and authentic reports. It is appropriate that a dramatist, Thomas Heywood, proposed to write 'the Lives of all the Poets, foreign and modern' while Thomas Fuller's *Worthies of England* (1662) promised a narrative 'interlaced with many delightful stories'. Izaak Walton's *Lives* maintain the hagiographical tradition of medieval biography; his accounts of Donne and Herbert, Hooker and Wotton, resemble threnodies or laments, and he did not scruple to invent lengthy conversations in order to transmit the nobility or sanctity of his subjects. More's *Richard III* reverses the equation by constructing an almost wholly inaccurate report of that monarch as false and malevolent. More's son-in-law, William Roper, in turn fashions a biography of More which proposes him as a secular saint and martyr. Cavendish's biography, *The Life and Death of Cardinal Wolsey*, is filled with imprecations to Fortune – 'O madness! O foolish desire! O fond hope!' – while Foxe's *Book of Martyrs* thoroughly exemplifies the English tradition in its combination of improbable anecdote and broad theatricality.

If the eighteenth century witnessed the first flowering of the novel, it was wholly appropriate that it should also have nurtured the more extensive development of prose biography. They grew up together in an act of symbiosis. There were volumes entitled *The History of the lives of the most noted highway-men, footpads, house-breakers, shop-lifts and cheats* as well as *The lives of the most eminent persons who died in the year 17——*; the *Biographica Britannica* was begun, and the seventeen volumes of John Nichols's *Literary Anecdotes of the Seventeenth Century* were completed. It is also highly appropriate – indeed it is fitting and significant – that Samuel Johnson himself has been made more generally known to posterity through Boswell's biography rather than through any of his own books or essays.

Yet we must pause before we cross the threshold of this great work, and examine Boswell's practice of mingling representative fact and selective fiction. In his advertisement to the second edition of the *Life of Johnson* Boswell compares his narrative with that of Homer's *Odyssey*: 'Amidst a thousand entertaining and instructive episodes the HERO is never long out of sight; for they are all in some degree connected with him; and HE, in the whole course of the History, is exhibited by the Author for the best advantage of his readers.' Boswell less resembles the writer of the verse epic, however, than the novelist. He is concerned with his subject's important actions but also with 'what he privately wrote, and said, and thought'; he wishes to display 'the progress of his mind and fortunes', like any fictional hero, principally by dwelling upon 'innumerable detached particulars'. Boswell admired Rembrandt and Vermeer in this respect, noting 'with what a small speck does the painter give life to an eye!' He quotes Johnson himself to the effect that the biographer must examine 'domestick privacies and display the minute details of daily life'. The biographer thereby congratulates himself that Samuel Johnson 'will be seen in this work more completely than any man who has ever yet lived'. But when he states that 'I have spared no pains to ascertain with a scrupulous authenticity' the facts of the matter, and that 'I have sometimes been obliged to run half over London, in order to fix a date correctly', we may recall Daniel Defoe's similar protestations in the prefaces to his fictional accounts. There are indeed scholars who have dismissed Boswell's *Life* as a work of the imagination, but of course it is only in the imagination that writing lives. The imagination is the secret of Boswell's art.

He informed one acquaintance that he wished to cast Johnson's biography 'in scenes', as if he were somehow impelled by the theatrical nature of London life to proceed upon a dramatic model; then Johnson might become the chief actor surrounded by secondary players. If it is the business of the biographer to create drama, however, he must introduce pace or tempo into various confrontations. He must rehearse moments of significant action, such as that of Johnson kicking a stone in refutation of Bishop Berkeley's theories. Most importantly he must create, or shall we say fabricate, memorable dialogue. Since Boswell himself was engaged in many of these conversations, he was also obliged to enter his own narrative with all the attendant problems of repression and revision.

There is a very interesting account of Boswell's procedures in Adam Sisman's *Boswell's Presumptuous Task*, in which he suggests that Boswell subjected his narrative 'to every type of revision: summary, paraphrase, expansion, contraction, conflation, interpolation, and so forth'.[5] Stories were abbreviated, and anecdotes transposed; short notes were amplified and, significantly, 'details that did not fit were altered or discarded'.[6] That this is also the practice of most other biographers underlines its suggestiveness. The radical reshaping of a life is primarily the imperative of the artist who must fashion the narrative to accord with his or her own personal vision; it is also necessary to alter or discard facts and details in order to create a coherent character out of the raw materials lying all around. When Mr Sisman goes on to suggest that Boswell was to some extent 'forced to rely on his imagination to elaborate stories of Johnson's early years',[7] all the formal boundaries of discourse are dissolved. The overriding concern is with the creation of character.

Certainly Boswell did not scruple to invent facts, or omit inconvenient ones. He made only a few notes at dinner in May 1776 when Johnson and Wilkes, the radical London politician, were introduced; but out of these random jottings a fully prepared and described scene, of some four thousand words, was produced twelve years later. Boswell also engaged in what he described as 'nice correction', by which characters and scenes were omitted or refined for the sake of the narrative argument.

One of his more obvious procedures was to render originally short Anglo-Saxon words into their Anglo-Latin equivalents, thus adding sonority to Johnson's stated opinions. Yet this was also a device which Johnson himself employed. On hearing himself say, of a drama, 'It has not wit enough to keep it sweet,' he corrected himself and continued, 'it has not vitality enough to preserve it from putrefaction.' There may have been an element of irony or self-parody here, but it may also have been a genuine attempt by Samuel Johnson to preserve a respectable mien for the benefit of his biographer; both men were involved in a process of artistic collusion.

Boswell also believed it to be necessary to bowdlerise or boswellise Johnson's correspondence, so that no trace of grossness or vulgarity remained. But Boswell's desire to maintain a stable identity for Johnson was designed to reassure himself as well as his readers. As one critic has suggested, 'the impulse to create or construct a Johnson answering his private needs is overwhelmingly visible'.[8] There is often some consonance between the biographer and the subject of the biography, as if the biographer were ineluctably drawn towards certain destinies. In the act of inspection or observation, there is also an element of self-examination. It might account for Mrs Gaskell's biographical interest in Charlotte Brontë, for example, or for that of Carlyle in Frederick the Great.

There is another way of conveying biographical identity in a covert or factitious manner. Boswell admitted that, while composing his narrative out of notes or stray anecdotes, 'he had rewritten some of these sayings of Johnson's into what he considered the authentic Johnsonian style.'[9] It is once more a question of artistry, and has nothing to do with factual or historical concerns. That is why the 'Johnsonian' style, as invented or embellished by Boswell, was powerfully influential. The biographer relates how, after publication of the Life, an acquaintance spoke of its success 'in the circles of fashion and elegance'. He informed Boswell that 'you have made them all talk Johnson', to which remark Boswell appends: 'I have Johnsonised the land.' The conversations invented by Boswell were anthologised as 'Johnsoniana', and in subsequent years his biography became the only official or extant source of Johnson's life. This was his success as an artist – to have created a character who over the intervening years has become as recognisable and as familiar as Mr Pickwick or Mr Micawber. In 1835 Francis Jeffrey concluded in the *Edinburgh Review* that Boswell 'has raised the standard of his [Johnson's] intellectual character, and actually made discovery of large provinces in his understanding of which scarcely an indication was to be found in his writings'. He did not pause to consider whether those provinces were the rightful territory of Johnson or of Boswell himself. Yet this invented biography created the first 'romantic' hero. Out of artificial material a great truth was born; romance, epic, fiction and drama come together to form biography.

Mrs Gaskell's *The Life of Charlotte Brontë* was one of the most popular and most controversial lives of the nineteenth century. A modern editor of this interesting volume has remarked that 'she seems to have forgotten that it was not a novel that she was writing'.[10] There are indeed some startling resemblances between Mrs Gaskell's biography and her fiction, to the extent that Charlotte Brontë becomes the heroine of a novel rather than of her own life.

When Elizabeth Gaskell first met Charlotte Brontë, she wrote that 'the wonder to me is how she can keep heart and power alive in her life of desolation', a sentiment similar to the themes of female anguish and self-sufficiency in her novels *Ruth* and *Mary Barton*. The opening of her *Life* follows the same trajectory as that of *Ruth* and *Sylvia's Lovers*, as the narrator walks through the landscape and setting of her story. The parsonage at Haworth 'is of grey stone, two storeys high, heavily roofed with flags, in order to resist the winds that might strip off a lighter covering'. In *Sylvia's Lovers* Hope Farm is 'long and low, in order to avoid the rough violence of the winds that swept over that bleak spot'. In *Ruth* are to be found 'grey, silvery rocks, which sloped away into brown moorland', while in *Sylvia's Lovers* stretch 'the moorland hollows' and purple heather; in *The Life of Charlotte Brontë* are to be found 'the dense hollows of the moors'. The first chapter of *Ruth* opens with a description of a town 'in one of the eastern counties' where the streets 'were dark and ill-paved with large, round, jolting pebbles, and with no side-path protected by kerbstones'. The first chapter of the *Life* opens with a description of Keighley where 'the flagstones . . . seem to be in constant danger of slipping backwards'. There is a remarkable consonance of tone and theme. In each case the landscape creates a steadfast heroine, and what Mrs Gaskell called Charlotte Brontë's 'wild, sad, life'. As Virginia Woolf suggested, 'the *Life* gives you the impression that Haworth and the Brontës are somehow inextricably mixed. Haworth expresses the Brontës; the Brontës express Haworth; they fit like a snail to his shell.' This formula is itself so perfectly adapted to the English imagination that it might serve as its introduction; the mingling of character and landscape expresses a great truth, and out of this essentially fictional intuition by Elizabeth Gaskell have sprung a myriad books and literary pilgrimages.

It is appropriate, therefore, that Haworth Parsonage itself is perhaps the principal object of popular affection. Mrs Gaskell did not start the identification of writer and place – the Shakespeare Jubilee of 1769 in Stratford has some claim to that honour – but Mrs Gaskell's setting of the Brontë sisters on the edge of the moors has greatly influenced the English literary inheritance. It combines a peculiar reverence for place, and a preoccupation with the formation of character. Just as artists have found inspiration on Salisbury Plain or among the Malvern Hills, so others have found consolation in areas which have become sacred or enchanted through their association with writers. From the 1870s forward there emerged a fashion for topographies or itineraries based upon the life of famous writers – *The Homes of Tennyson*, *In the Steps of Charles Dickens*, *Bozland*, *Dickens' Places and People*, *The Home and Early Haunts of Robert Louis Stevenson* are among the scores of volumes which appeared upon the subject. It became a national pursuit, and Tennyson was forced to move house in order to avoid the attentions and depredations of these literary tourists. There are many volumes upon the neighbourhood of the Lake District and Thomas Hardy's semi-fictional 'Wessex', and there are books entitled *A Writer's Britain* and *The Oxford Literary Guide to the British Isles*. The *genius loci* has many hearths in England.

So Elizabeth Gaskell, inspired by the imaginative vision of her novels, re-created Charlotte Brontë. As a novelist she was preoccupied with details, and in similar fashion requested information on 'the peculiar customs & character of the population towards Keighley'. As one of Mrs Gaskell's biographers has put it, 'Charlotte Brontë's life already fell easily into the patterns of Gaskell's fiction, with its suffering daughters, profligate son and stern father, and its emphasis on upbringing and environment, female endurance and courage'.[11] Mrs Gaskell lends strong imaginative shape to her biography, also, with letters and anecdotes reinforcing the pace and emphasis of the narrative. She was commenting upon Charlotte Brontë's husband as an 'exacting, rigid law-giving man' at the same time as she was creating just such a character, John Thornton, in *North and South*. In the *Life*, too, Elizabeth Gaskell comments that standards of behaviour and morality 'in such a manufacturing place as Keighley in the north' are very different from those of any 'stately, sleepy, picturesque cathedral town in the south'; this of course is a principal theme of her novel *North and South*. But the resemblances do not end there. After the publication of the *Life* Charlotte Brontë's father, Patrick Brontë, wrote to its author and informed her that 'the truth of the matter is that I am, in some respects, a kindred likeness to the father of Margaret Hale in "North and South" – peaceable, feeling, sometimes thoughtful'. The circle of 'fact' and 'fiction' becomes complete.

It has also become evident that Mrs Gaskell, like Boswell before her, omitted, edited and distorted details so that they might more accurately reflect her imaginative concerns. It was necessary for her purposes to emphasise the private and domestic life of Charlotte Brontë, for example, rather than to examine her professional career in proper detail. When Charles Kingsley wrote to congratulate her upon fashioning 'the picture of a valiant woman made perfect by suffering' he touched upon an important truth; hers is a 'picture' rather than a defined or definite reality. Gaskell omitted unfortunate facts, such as her heroine's obsession with a Belgian schoolmaster, and frequently cut out significant details from Charlotte Brontë's correspondence; she also chose to emphasise the endurance and courage of the three sisters, at the expense of downgrading their unhappy brother Branwell. Gaskell, in other words, created the myth of the Brontës which may still linger among the readers of *Jane Eyre* and *Wuthering Heights*.

The ambiguity of Mrs Gaskell's achievement was recognised at the time. George Eliot praised her for creating 'an interior so strange, so original in its individual elements and so picturesque in its externals . . . that fiction has nothing more wild, touching and heart strengthening to place above it'. The anonymous writer in the *Edinburgh Review* declared that 'Mrs Gaskell appears to have learnt the art of the novel-writer so well that she cannot discharge from her palette the colours she has used in the pages of "Mary Barton" and "Ruth". This biography opens precisely like a novel.' But of course it is precisely because it is 'like a novel' that it has created an enduring impression upon successive generations of readers. It represents a very English art.

Women and anger

Jane Austen

CHAPTER 44

Femality and fiction

There is a report this day, 6 June 2001, on the 'Orange' prize for women's fiction in which a male and female jury chose a notional winner; it is reliably stated that the jury of women were impressed by the 'feeling' of the book, Kate Grenville's *The Idea of Perfection*, while the men were enthusiastic about its 'artistry'. The commonplaces of the English imagination, as they are applied to women writers, still survive.

It has generally been agreed, for example, that femality and fiction are related more naturally than femality and poetry; the novel, after all, is supposed to reside in the domain of lived experience, and to be guided by the promptings of observation or sentiment rather than the precepts of reason or theory. It has even been suggested that 'the English novel seems to have been in some sense a female invention'[1] with such paradigms as Fanny Burney and Jane Austen, Maria Edgeworth and Ann Radcliffe. Fiction has been deemed a feminine occupation, too, 'because it is commercial rather than aesthetic, practical rather than priestly'.[2] In the eighteenth century there was indeed 'a common notion, or fear, that the novel had become a feminine genre',[3] not in the male tradition of theatrically conceived picaresque but in the sphere of moral or sentimental fiction. The epistolary novel was also considered to be a female form, despite or perhaps because of the example of Samuel Richardson (who was clandestinely described as 'old-maidish' precisely because of the nature of his fiction). Letters and diaries had always been modes of writing considered to be appropriate for women, because they were not of their nature available in a public forum; now all that had changed. By the last decades of the eighteenth century the novel itself 'was virtually taken over by women' to the extent that it came 'to be identified as a woman's form' with over half the inordinate production of fiction in that century emerging from female writers.[4] In the nineteenth century, too, the female prerogative was clear. Marian Evans, in her days before the baptism of George Eliot, wrote in the *Westminster Review* that 'fiction is a department of literature in which women can, after their kind, fully equal men . . .women can produce novels not only fine, but among the very finest – novels, too, that have a precious specialty'.

Equally significant, too, were the number of female readers. In *Arcadia*, written in the 1580s and regarded as one of the first English novels, Philip Sidney addressed the 'fair ladies' who would read his romance; it might even be suggested that ever since the time of the courtly *lais* the association between fiction and a female audience was established. It has been surmised that three-quarters of the reading public, in the eighteenth century, were female; it was considered to the discredit of the novel, in particular, that it was read by scullery maids as well as by high-born ladies. The prolixity and heterogeneity of the form thus seemed to create an audience similarly disposed. In that century, too, 'fiction was often thought to be the most powerful (although also the most condemned) element in girls' education.'[5] But the question, why Marian Evans and the Brontë sisters originally wrote under assumed male names, is not difficult to determine. They knew their strength, and wished to be judged on equal terms with male writers. They did not wish to be patronised or dismissed.

Yet the question of 'precious specialty', in Marian Evans's phrase, remains perplexing. Did the female novel exhibit the inflections of a special kind of experience or an inimitable form of expression? Was it a matter of a new and ingenious subjectivity, for example, or a peculiar access of spontaneity? There have been many attempts to decipher 'female patterns' within fiction, especially in recent years; the authors of *The Madwoman in the Attic*, a study of female literature, have suggested 'a distinctively female literary tradition' which accommodates 'images of enclosure and escape' as well as 'obsessive descriptions of diseases'.[6] They discuss George Eliot's 'self-conscious relatedness to other women writers, her critique of male literary conventions', and cite her 'interest in clairvoyance and telepathy, her imagery of confinement, her schizophrenic sense of fragmentation'.[7] In that sense, of course, she is close to the female authors of Gothic fiction whom in no other area does she resemble; her preoccupation with 'clairvoyance and telepathy' not only links her with Charlotte and Emily Brontë but also with that broad school of women writers who eschew 'realism' as part of a male-ordered or mail-ordered universe.

For some female writers, however, there was no such alternative. In the seventeenth century Aphra Behn demanded 'the Privilidge for my Masculine Part the Poet in me . . . to tread in those successful Paths my Predecessors have so long thriv'd in', but complains that in practice 'such Masculine Strokes in me, must not be allow'd'. The 'masculine' powers which she invokes here are those of imagination and invention which, in the latter decades of the seventeenth century, were not deemed suitable for a woman. Behn remains important as the first professional female writer in England, however, 'forced to write for Bread and not ashamed to owne it', and as such she became synonymous in the English imagination with cupidity and immorality. She wrote everything – plays, poems, novels – and displayed a vivacious energy. 'Whilst that which Admiration does Inspire / In other Souls', she wrote in one verse, 'kindles in Mine a Fire' where 'Fire' is the single most important and significant quality of her art. Thus was she branded a shame to all her sex, since her emphasis upon sexual gender in the act of self-assertion was also implicitly a reference to sexuality itself. This is the sub-text in all her compositions. Her witty juxtaposition of 'masculine' and 'feminine' parts in defence of her art led Virginia Woolf to define her 'androgynous' mind as subtly subversive. In the public sphere she sympathised with the oppressed and exiled Stuarts, perhaps in native sympathy for all kinds of oppression, but her 'Fire' is derived from passionate experience.

There were of course women writers in the seventeenth century other than Aphra Behn – Mary Wroth and Rachel Speght among them – and it has been claimed that by the end of that century 'women were participating in the major historical and literary shift that was to place prose at the heart of modern written culture'.[8] Women were no longer intruders, but inhabitants, in the house of English literature. That is why, in the eighteenth century, there were at least traces of a recognisable tradition; women writers began to cite one another as authorities rather than as object lessons in extravagance or licentiousness. There was a great outpouring of literature which reached its apogee in Austen, Eliot and the Brontës. It has been surmised that in the 1790s there emerged 'the first concerted expression of feminist thought in modern European culture'[9] as well as a number of books written specifically by women in the sphere of conduct, children and education. Printers and booksellers also responded to changes in female taste.

The example of Fanny Burney, one of the most popular novelists of the eighteenth century, is of some significance. She was considered by Samuel Johnson to be 'a writer of romances', but from the beginning she was aware of the necessity for escape – escape, in particular, from 'that inertness which casts the females upon themselves'. We may remark here upon a note of frustration, or anger, which seems to impel female creativity. As a child she had been denied the possibilities of education, while her brother was despatched to Charterhouse, and she describes herself in a biography of her father as 'merely and literally self-educated'. She continues in an ironic fashion; 'her sole emulation for improvement, and sole spur for exertion' was her father 'who, nevertheless, had not, at the time, a moment to spare for giving her any personal lessons; or even for directing her pursuits'. She found herself to be a charmed progenitor of language, however, and reported in her journal: 'Making Words, now & then, in familiar writing, is unavoidable, & saves the trouble of *thinking*, which, as Mr Addison observes, we Females are not much addicted to.' The vexation is once again evident. Her biographer has commented upon the fact that her 'freedom with language reflects her self-image as an "outsider" in literature and her defiance of conventional limitations in a manner that could be seen as rebellious, even revolutionary'.[10] Fanny Burney was known to Virginia Woolf as 'the Mother of English fiction', and Macaulay suggested that her novels 'vindicated the right of her sex to an equal share in a fair and noble province of letters'. But she remained unassuming, even though her spirit and her career were devoted to the acknowledgement that 'experience has a complex texture and that truth about it is elusive'.[11] In a sense she left the theory, or at least its explication, to her successors.

One philologist has described her 'relaxed enjoyment of language for its own sake, and an unabashed pleasure in its flexibility',[12] which in turn lends a further significance to the remark of a literary historian that 'for women the creation remained part of the creator'[13] rather than a detached product to be viewed ironically or dispassionately. This is as much to say that the 'natural' language of female writers is much closer both to the expression of the physical body and to the inflections of subjectivity. So when, for example, 'the Victorians thought of the woman writer they immediately thought of the female body'.[14] The experience of the body, and the experience of anger, are curiously entwined. One female critical theorist has described the process by which 'feminine texts are very close to the voice, very close to the flesh of language . . . straight away at the threshold of feeling . . . I see it as an outpouring'.[15] In her essay upon women's literature in English, 'A Room of One's Own', Virginia Woolf suggested that 'the book has somehow to be adapted to the body' and that 'it is much more important to be oneself than anything else. . . . Think of things in themselves.' If this is the peaceful 'stream of consciousness', as adumbrated by Woolf, then it must be related to Julian of Norwich's perception that her book of visions was 'still in process'.[16] The process is that of the interior life which cannot be ordered by rational perception, and of a female subjectivity which cannot become subject to male disciplines. It is what Fanny Burney meant, in self-deprecating fashion, by her 'scribbleration'.

In her second novel, *Mary: and The Wrongs of Woman*, Mary Wollstonecraft depicted 'feeling as the necessary instrument of female liberation', with the addendum that if 'feminine sensibility was an oppressive social construct, true feeling was a positive womanly quality and the hope for the future';[17] the male expectation of what is feminine and unfeminine must be wholly overturned. While the heroine Maria is languishing in prison it becomes plain that sorrow 'must blunt or sharpen the faculties to the two opposite extremes; producing stupidity, the moping melancholy of indolence; or the restless activity of a disturbed imagination'. It is the imagination of Aphra Behn and Emily Brontë kicking, as it were, against the pricks.

By the middle of the eighteenth century the female component of the English imagination was understood and celebrated. In 1748 *The Female Right to Literature* and, four years later, *Memoirs of Several Ladies of Great Britain who have been celebrated for their Writings* appeared; in 1755 an anthology of poems written by women was issued under the title of *Poems by Eminent Ladies*. The fact that all of these volumes were composed and compiled by men does not alter the historical significance of the change in literary perception. Eliza Haywood launched the *Female Spectator* as a direct challenge to the male periodical, while the cult of the 'Blue-Stocking' opened up hitherto inaccessible areas of male learning. 'In former times, the pen, like the sword, was considered as consigned by nature to the hands of men', Samuel Johnson wrote in 1753, but 'the revolution of years has now produced a generation of Amazons of the pen, who with the spirit of their predecessors have set masculine tyranny at defiance.'

Jane Austen herself was indebted to her eighteenth-century predecessor, Fanny Burney. The last chapter of Burney's *Cecilia* intimates that 'if to PRIDE and PREJUDICE you owe your miseries . . . to PRIDE and PREJUDICE you will also owe their termination'. Austen also celebrated the nature and role of the novel in opposition to Burney's own somewhat self-deprecating attitude towards the form she had helped to fashion. 'I will not adopt that ungenerous and impolitic custom so common with novel writers', she stated in the fifth chapter of *Northanger Abbey*, 'of degrading by their contemptuous censure the

very performances to the number of which they are themselves adding
. . . Although our productions have afforded more extensive and
unaffected pleasure than those of any other literary corporation in the
world, no species of composition has been so much decried.' She
imagines the response of a female reader, 'Oh! It is only a novel!', to
which she adds her own acerbic commentary, 'only some work in
which the greatest powers of the mind are displayed, in which the most
thorough knowledge of human nature, the happiest delineation of its
varieties, the liveliest effusions of wit and humour, are conveyed to the
world in the best chosen language'. Since in this context Austen cites
Maria Edgeworth's *Belinda* as well as Fanny Burney's *Cecilia* and
Camilla – in opposition to the work of Milton, Pope, Prior, Sterne and
Addison – we are entitled to suggest that she was celebrating the merits
of the female novel rather than those of male discourse.

The theme of female anger in the writing of Jane Austen has often
been surveyed, partly in response to her remark that 'Pictures of
perfection as you know make me sick & wicked'. A psychologist,
reading the novels, once remarked, 'You know – she *hated* people.'[18] It
is another way of putting what W. H. Auden meant:

> You could not shock her more than she shocks me;
> Beside her Joyce seems innocent as grass

In her anatomies of provincial society, and in her close attention to the
relationship between economics and sexual politics, her frustration and
dissatisfaction are clarified by her high comedy. One of her abiding
themes is the pressure of loneliness among a group of people who are
forced to inhabit a system of social relations over which they have no
control; the heroines of *Mansfield Park* and *Persuasion* must learn to
subdue their feelings or manage a nice reticence in the face of snobbery
and greed. The individual woman cannot speak out. Anne Elliot
remarks to Captain Harville in *Persuasion*, on the role of women, that
'we certainly do not forget you, so soon as you forget us. . . . We cannot
help ourselves. We live at home, quiet, confined, and our feelings prey
upon us.' He then raises the question of 'women's inconstancy' and
argues that 'all histories are against you, all stories, prose and verse'.
But she answers in spirited terms which somehow transcend the
context in which they are placed. 'Yes, yes, if you please, no reference
to examples in books. Men have had every advantage of us in telling
their own story. Education has been theirs in so much higher a degree;
the pen has been in their hands. I will not allow books to prove

anything.' With whatever velleities of regret and nuance, there is genuine indignation in these sentiments. It is aligned with the harshness and evident contempt with which Austen treats those of whom she disapproves, 'which taste cannot tolerate – which ridicule will seize'.

It should be recalled that in her first novel, the epistolary *Lady Susan*, she creates a commanding and brilliant woman whose articulacy and powers of persuasion are far greater than any of the stupid or faintly sanctimonious men who surround her. Jane Austen's first extant letter, written in 1796 when she was twenty-one years old, shows that in the words of one recent biographer, Claire Tomalin, she 'is clearly writing as the heroine of her own youthful story, living for herself the short period of power'.[19] All this excitement, and sense of power, would eventually be subdued. In her correspondence, particularly with her sister Cassandra, she evinces her resentment and frustration at those around her. 'Caroline is not grown at all coarser than she was, nor Harriet at all more more delicate. . . . Ly Elizth for a woman of her age & situation has astonishingly little to say for herself, & . . . Miss Hatton has not much more.' A certain harshness, or hardness, of temperament is also manifest in remarks upon a Mrs Hall giving birth to a dead child, 'some weeks before she expected, oweing to a fright – I suppose she happened unawares to look at her husband'.

After her unwilling removal to Bath, from her childhood home in Steventon, her anger seems to increase. 'Another stupid party last night,' she wrote, '. . . I cannot anyhow continue to find people agreeable.' It has been suggested in this context that Austen 'was schooled to keep up appearances, even if she was screaming inside her head' and that 'she had deep and often painful feelings'.[20] But she was trained in female reticence, which was designed to cover the springs and manifestations of anger. There is a passage in Claire Tomalin's biography where she speculates upon the nature of Jane Austen's silence. That silence encompassed the world of politics and of public events, the matter of women's rights, and the nature of religion. Her silence upon the rights of women, however, is modified by her insistence 'on the moral and intellectual parity of the sexes'[21] which no even half-attentive reader of her novels can fail to notice. There was her own silence as a writer, too, which endured for ten years. Other biographers have described her irritability, her coldness and frustration. She once referred to herself as a 'wild Beast'.

It is important to insist upon her anger, in all of these examples, because it is one of the great resources of the English woman writer; the

365

commonplaces about the female interest in sensibility, or in feeling, derive from this abiding experience of wrath. It is the single most significant source of inspiration and ambition. Of Charlotte Brontë and her creation Jane Eyre, for example, it has been suggested that 'what horrified the Victorians was Jane's anger' and her desire 'to escape entirely from drawing rooms and patriarchal mansions'.[22] 'Why was I always suffering,' Jane speculates of her childhood, 'always brow-beaten, always accused, forever condemned?' When she had read Goldsmith's *History of Rome*, with its history of male tyrants, the young Jane Eyre 'had drawn parallels in silence'. The female silence here, as in other examples, is filled with exasperation and despair. When Mrs Gaskell asked Charlotte Brontë about women in the nineteenth century, she replied that there were 'evils – deep rooted in the foundation of the social system, which no efforts of ours can touch: of which we cannot complain; of which it is advisable not too often to think'. Here is the true recognition of oppression almost too deep for words. When Harriet Beecher Stowe's *Uncle Tom's Cabin* was published, Brontë remarked that 'I doubt not Mrs Stowe had felt the iron of slavery enter into her heart, from childhood upwards'. The iron had entered Charlotte Brontë's soul, also, and the apparently shy and self-deprecating author had been moulded in the fire. Matthew Arnold, on reading *Villette*, surmised that the mind of its author was one 'containing nothing but hunger, rebellion and rage' to which the answer can only be – and why not? She had every reason. At the beginning of *Jane Eyre* the narrator recalls how 'my habitual mood of humiliation, self-doubt, forlorn depression, fell damp on the embers of my decaying ire'. Yet the fury still burned within her, occasionally striking fire in impulsive and vehement speech: 'Forgive me! I cannot endure it –'

The romantic genius flourished essentially in Charlotte Brontë; her anger propelled her into a sphere of consciousness where exultation and fury meet. 'My soul began to expand, to exult, with the strangest sense of freedom, of triumph, I ever felt. It seemed as if an invisible bond had burst, and that I had struggled out into unhoped-for liberty.' The call is always for liberty in Charlotte Brontë's fiction – to take the iron out of the soul and fashion it into a sword. 'I desired liberty;' Jane Eyre confides, 'for liberty I gasped; for liberty I uttered a prayer.' Then she might enter the world with courage 'to go forth into its expanse, to seek real knowledge of life amidst its perils'. That is why the theme of confinement runs so deeply within female writing, whether it be in the measured narratives of Jane Austen or in the insalubrious caverns of Gothic fiction. Jane Austen had adverted to the false example of books written by men, and in turn Jane Eyre remarks that 'I have observed in books written by men' that marital ardour lasts only a short space. Here, again, are the pride and assertion. It is a matter of gender, since as Jane Eyre declared 'women feel just as men feel . . . they suffer from too rigid a constraint, too absolute a stagnation, precisely as men would suffer. . . . It is thoughtless to condemn them, or laugh at them, if they seek to do more or learn more than custom has pronounced necessary for their sex.' So Emily Brontë's Catherine, in *Wuthering Heights*, in her weary sickness, exclaims, 'Oh, I'm burning! I wish I were out of doors . . . I'm sure I should be myself were I once among the heather on those hills. . . . Open the window again wide, fasten it open!'

We may look, then, to female anger as one means of access to a new sensibility; it represents the unremitting flow of feeling or what Virginia Woolf called 'the psychological sentence of the feminine gender', marked by its musicality and its fluency of association. This female music is the reason that, three hundred years before, Aemilia Lanyer had identified the origins of her poetry in Nature rather than that of 'scholars who by Art do write'. It is the technique of the Duchess of Newcastle who wrote 'so fast as I stay not so long to write my letters plain' which suggests a natural susurrus hastening her along. Thus the early twentieth-century novelist May Sinclair 'wishes to remind us how ideas exist in a whole context of feeling and mundane activity by which they are shaped',[23] so that the novel itself is the form perfectly complemented by the female consciousness of experience. It is what Austen meant by 'the happiest delineation' of human nature in all its variability and variety. The 'stream of consciousness' itself may be compared to a sentence from Doris Lessing's *The Golden Notebook*: 'That's how women see things. Everything in a sort of continuous creative stream.' When Virginia Woolf considered the nature of the female sentence, she described it as one 'of a more elastic fibre than the old, capable of stretching to the extreme, of suspending the frailest particles, of enveloping the vaguest shapes'. Is this not also a definition of the pregnant female form? All paths seem, indirectly, to lead to the same beginning.

Melodrama

The Spanish Tragedy by Thomas Kyd. Woodcut dating from 1615

CHAPTER 45

Blood and gore

One of the delights of the English theatre has always been its morbid sensationalism, not unconnected with a fascination for the 'Gothic' and the grotesque. It has a long history. We may recall Grendel's indiscriminate slaughter in *Beowulf* where the *scop* did not spare the bloody detail, and the episode of *Sir Gawain and the Green Knight* in which Sir Gawain slices off the head of the knight; the head, in characteristic fashion, then speaks. In both cases the emphasis is upon the physical detail of the butchery, which in the narrative of *Gawain* is treated with a vigour that marries comedy and grotesquerie. To laugh in the midst of horrors – it is another example of that heterogeneity, that medley of moods, which makes up the English imagination. There are moments of sensational horror in the mystery plays, and Malory never refrains from narratives of carnage.

There are on-stage hangings in *Horestes* and *Sir Thomas More*, decapitations in *Apius and Virginia* and *The Atheist's Tragedy*, scenes of terrible torture in *Cambyses* and *Bussy D'Ambois*. *The Spanish Tragedy* of Thomas Kyd has been considered by some to be the first modern English tragedy, and it is entirely appropriate that it should open with the entrance of a ghost seeking bloody revenge; in the penultimate scene Hieronimo bites out his tongue, which in a twentieth-century production was accompanied by 'trickles, spurts, and finally showers of stage blood . . . in which black comedy and horror were inextricable'.[1] The predilections of actors and audiences have not changed through a period of four hundred years, particularly in that area of sensationalism where 'black comedy' and 'horror' meet. Is it not the first principle of English philosophy, at least according to Locke, that all knowledge derives from sensation?

Of early English tragedy and tragi-comedy, then, the secret lies in a combined 'taste for horror, a taste for rhetoric, a taste for ethical commonplace';[2] they have in turn been related to the appetite for public executions, and even to the bloody detail of the suffering Christ in the medieval mysteries. Shakespeare was not immune to the attraction of melodramatic death and violence, using various sanguinary effects in *Titus Andronicus*, *Macbeth* and *King Lear*. The authors of the revenge tragedies were inclined to murder and torture on a large scale, until in the end the English stage was filled with examples of gratuitous sensationalism.

Rupert Brooke once described a play by John Webster as 'full of the feverish and ghastly turmoil of a nest of maggots'. In Webster there is the striking concordance of wonderfully heightened speech and grandiloquent or melodramatic action; ghosts consort with metaphors, and there are such stage directions as 'They shoot and run to him and tread upon him'. Most famously, in *The Duchess of Malfi*, the imprisoned duchess is surrounded by a 'wild consort / Of madmen' who plague her out of her wits. In this scene she asks 'Who am I?', to be granted the reply which seems to epitomise the English tendency towards sensational disquiet. 'Thou art a box of worm seed, at best, but a salvatory of green mummy: what's this flesh? a little crudded milk, fantastical puff-paste: our bodies are weaker than those paper prisons boys use to keep flies in: more contemptible; since ours is to preserve earth-worms . . .' She is then strangled. Her twin brother suffers from lycanthropy and imagines himself a wolf in duke's clothing. It is a very English production. It is curious to note, however, that many such revenge tragedies are set in Italy, which is also the land of the Gothic novel; it is as if the conflation of papistry and Catholic superstition preyed upon the Protestant conscience. It returns like a guilty thing to its mother, who has grown monstrous out of her abandonment. We will also find that English ghost stories bear traces of a buried but unquiet Catholic past.

That sensational violence was a native taste is illustrated by the delight of audiences in the crudities of English pantomime, when babies were regularly boiled in kettles or fried in pots. In a more serene context we might observe, in English prose, an equivalent fascination for death and decay. In John Donne the macabre and the rhetorical join together in a manner which is heavily reminiscent of Webster's dramatic rhetoric. One of Donne's editors remarks that his fondness for metaphor can become 'grotesque', and that he reserved 'his more macabre performances for weddings'.[3] It suggests a curious aspect of the English grotesque, as if it were related to sexuality; the appetite for morbid description is related to the physicality of the body, and may be connected to sexual embarrassment or repression. It brings to mind Sir Thomas Browne's divagations on eating, since 'all this masse of fleshe that wee behold, came in at our mouths'.

The connection of the 'Gothic' with thwarted or perverse sexuality is well attested, and that is perhaps the reason why the 'Gothic novel' of terror and of the supernatural became an English speciality if not exactly an English possession. Smollett's *The Adventures of Ferdinand Count Fathom* (1753) and Walpole's *The Castle of Otranto* (1764) were two of the earliest examples of that national 'craze' which was eventually satirised in Jane Austen's *Northanger Abbey*. We may include in this list Ann Radcliffe's *The Mysteries of Udolpho*, M. G. Lewis's *The Monk* and Mary Shelley's *Frankenstein, or The Modern Prometheus*, which in turn prepared the way for the peculiarly English institution of the 'horror' film or 'Hammer horror'. An authority upon the subject has concluded that, in distinction to the English version, German Gothic was 'politically committed' and 'critical social comment . . . was implicit and explicit in the stories'.[4] German Gothic had a higher purpose, therefore, whereas the English revelled in the macabre or sensational for its own sake. The effect is similar to that of English translations of French romances; the 'romance' is trimmed, and only the story or adventure remains.

Aspects of the Gothic are to be found in all areas of the English imagination. Leigh Hunt remarked that 'a man who does not contribute his quota of grim stories nowadays, seems hardly to be free of the republic of letters. He is bound to wear a death's head as part of his insignia. If he does not frighten everybody, he is nobody.' Hunt's contemporary, Charles Lamb, remarked of English pantomime that it resembled 'the grotesque Gothic heads that gape, and grin, in stone around the inside of the Round Church of the Templars'.

Gothic effects lie somewhat uneasily on the border between comedy and tragedy. This heterogeneity of effect is entirely congenial to the English imagination which does not care to dwell upon a single emotion for very long. Gothic drama itself was advertised as 'a drama of mingled nature, operatic, comical and tragical'. Havergal Brian named his masterwork *The Gothic Symphony* precisely because of its mixed musical nature.

There are other suggestive associations. The Gothic fiction of the eighteenth century was largely set in an imaginary medieval civilisation, or at least one overtly Catholic in its paraphernalia. It represents once more the fear of an ancient but not forgotten past. It has a flavour of antiquarianism, therefore, in particular of the English reverence for 'the imagined vitality of past ages';[5] but it also represents 'a fear of historical reversion . . . of the nagging possibility that the despotisms buried by the modern age may prove to be yet undead'.[6] This may account for the popularity of Gothic fiction 'within the British and Anglo-Irish middle class'.[7] It is curious, too, that Anglo-Irish writers were responsible for the development of the ghost story; Sheridan Le Fanu was an Irish Protestant.

The Gothic story is characteristically set within an ancient dwelling – a castle, a monastery, a ruined house. The English family house itself embodies the desire for privacy and individuality, for protection and defence, but it can grow sour and induce claustrophobia or fear. It can become a labyrinth, or a wilderness of corridors. Its very Englishness decides its fate, and the Gothic novel is concerned with ancient foundations and decaying structures. A leprous or clammy moisture infects its walls, manifesting a native fear or dislike of the physical body. The physiological or psychological dwelling is invaded by strange and perverse desires. Many of the greatest writers of Gothic fiction were women – among them Ann Radcliffe and the Brontë sisters – so the old house can exemplify the horrors of the patriarchal condition. In Gothic fiction, too, there are references to parchments and manuscripts which often unravel the mysteries of torture and pursuit; these fragments resemble the incomplete 'Rowley' poems of Thomas Chatterton.

Gothic literature itself is a rancid form of English antiquarianism. The picturesque ruins assembled by eighteenth-century dilletanti might be said to mimic the haunted residences of the Gothic imagination; in their proliferation across the countryside, England spawned a living or tangible Gothic. It has been noted of the Gothic melodrama upon the nineteenth-century stage that it was 'deliberately archaic'.[8] The resonances may go far back, indeed, in the sense that Gothic fiction also 'appropriates the marvellous and supernatural from folk tales'.[9] It is a constant feature of the English imagination, caught in some helpless reversion to the past.

CHAPTER 46

Ghosts

In 'Oh, Whistle, and I'll Come to You, My Lad' a scholar finds a bronze whistle among the buried fragments of a Templar church; it bears a legend in Latin, '*Quis est iste qui venit?*', 'Who is this who is coming?' What comes is an indistinct figure, a dim presentiment of human form, with a 'face *of crumpled linen*'. One character in these macabre proceedings remarks, at the end of the short story, that they 'served to confirm his opinion of the Church of Rome'. The scholar himself 'cannot even now see a surplice hanging on a door quite unmoved'. The author of this story, M. R. James, is acknowledged to be the pre-eminent master of English ghost fiction; in this particular tale, many of his characteristic themes and devices are to be found.

His 'heroes', or rather those to whom the ghostly visitants are drawn, tend to be of scholarly or antiquarian temper. His first volume was entitled *Ghost Stories of an Antiquary*. M. R. James was himself a noted scholar and palaeographer, who made a particular study of the apocrypha of the New Testament. He had a thoroughly English mind, steeped in bibliography and iconography. Yet the apparatus of his remarkable historical knowledge is presented in his stories as a 'faintly ironical, at times almost self-mocking image of himself as a scholar and an antiquary'.[1] This ironic diffidence, so much part of the native imagination, permeates his fictions.

There are other characteristic touches. In that parody of learning which seems endemic among the English learned, James manufactures references to British Museum manuscripts and alludes in one par-ticularly nasty haunting to 'the publications of the Swedish Historical Manuscripts Commission'. Many of the stories are concerned with libraries and with the ancient volumes buried therein. The antiquarian and the hunter after ghosts is, therefore, a twin being intent upon gathering the living presence of the past. The English tradition may itself then be glimpsed as a *revenant*, reaching out to the living with uplifted arms. That is why the ghost story is recognised to be a quintessentially English form. It has been calculated that 'the vast majority of ghost stories (around 98 per cent) are in English and roughly 70 per cent are written by English men and women'.[2]

The genre or medium of the ghost story emerged in the 1820s, but of course the island has always been filled with ghosts. The legionaries of the Roman Empire reported that this remote place was inhabited by spirits; England was once characterised as a land of dreams and visions. There are ghosts in Dickens and in Chaucer, in Shakespeare and in Emily Brontë, in Webster and in Wells. They may be said to haunt the English sensibility. English translations of continental romances typically added elements of magic and of supernature; the appetite for violence was equalled only by that for the mysterious and the grotesque. The English tone has been described as one of 'romantic strangeness'.[3]

M. R. James wrote that certain places had been 'prolific in suggestion'; he was particularly enamoured of the ancient landscapes of East Anglia. In 'A Neighbour's Landmark' the landscape itself seems haunted with 'stretches of green and yellow country . . . and blue hills far off, veiled with rain. Up above was a very restless and hopeless movement of low clouds travelling north-west.' Like Sherlock Holmes in *The Valley of Fear* James was 'a believer in the *genius loci*'. It is the sudden silence in a wood, or the sound of footsteps in an empty street; it is the English sense of being haunted by place and by a specific history associated with it. A country so preoccupied with its past, and with the traditions of that past, cannot help but be haunted by time itself. As Rudyard Kipling said of the countryside around his house 'Batemans', in Burwash, it harboured a 'long overgrown slag-heap of a most ancient forge, supposed to have been worked by the Phoenicians and Romans and, since then, uninterruptedly till the middle of the eighteenth century. . . . Every foot of that little corner was alive with ghosts and shadows.' Kipling was an expert writer of ghost stories and, in *Puck of Pook's Hill*, he re-creates 'an earth spirit, and, for Kipling, specifically that of the English earth'.[4]

There are sites in the natural world which also become sites of the imagination. In English ghost stories these include ancient churches, abandoned churchyards and ruined monasteries. In 'Oh, Whistle, and I'll Come to You, My Lad' the ghost or shape is specifically associated with a Catholic past. This is in fact a central motif in the work of M. R. James. In 'Canon Alberic's Scrap Book' an Englishman or 'North Briton' of Presbyterian faith inadvertently raises the spectre of a Catholic canon. In 'Number 13' a spectral chamber and its occupant are intimately related 'to the last days of Roman Catholicism' in Jutland. In 'Casting the Runes' an evil protagonist is described, in a cancelled passage, as 'formerly a Roman [Catholic]'. In 'Count Magnus' another spectre is reported to be 'a Roman priest in a cassock'. The presence of the great medieval cathedrals is acutely felt in the ghost stories, as if the stripping of the Catholic altars and the weight of all that rejected knowledge had somehow created a flaw in time through which spectral visitors could still move. As a child M. R. James had studied Church history, and in particular 'the martyrdom of the saints',[5] so he was not untouched by intimations of the Catholic past. In many of his stories a Latin inscription is revealed, in words which amount to a curse.

M. R. James was a skilful pasticheur, able effortlessly to reproduce the language and cadence of the sixteenth and seventeenth centuries; like Chatterton's, it was a gift which he first employed as a schoolboy, and represents once more an instinctive turning towards the past. In his life and in his art he practised restraint and detachment. Horror and malevolence were necessary in ghost stories, he wrote, but 'not less necessary . . . is reticence'. One critic has remarked of his stories that they are 'strongly impersonal, as if the teller in no way wishes to commit himself to his tale'.[6] In particular he was dismayed by any allusion to sexuality – 'sex is tiresome enough in the novels; in a ghost story, or as the backbone of a ghost story, I have no patience with it.' Here is the general English embarrassment at sex and, indeed, at physicality itself. Most of James's spectres are touched before they are seen, and there is such an emphasis upon noisome tactility that his editor has suggested 'this repulsive moment of intimacy perhaps exteriorises a fear of sexual contact in James himself'.[7] 'I was conscious', one protagonist remarks, 'of a most horrible smell of mould and of a cold kind of face pressed against my own and moving slowly over it.' And another of James's characters observes of a ghost or apparition 'how the mouth was open and a single tooth appeared below the upper lip'. These are the limits of frightfulness, fuelled by many different fears. 'What he touched was, according to his account, a mouth. With teeth and with hair about it, and, he declared, not the mouth of a human being.' James is a miniaturist in horror; he is alert to the small detail and to the significant fact. He is interested, too, in physical circumstance. On another occasion 'wet lips were whispering into my ear with great rapidity and emphasis for some time together'.

Here, once more, we may trace elements of that morbid sensationalism everywhere encountered. The English sense of mystery, beyond the sphere of the practical and the pragmatic, is, however, perhaps best summarised in the following exchange. 'Do you believe in ghosts?' 'No. But I am afraid of them.'

M. R. James himself remarked that 'the recrudescence of ghost stories in recent years', by which he meant the 1920s and 1930s, 'corresponds, of course, with the vogue of the detective tale'. The assumption of some natural connection is perhaps explicable; the detective story, like the ghost story, was considered to be a characteristic English genre suffused by a native conservatism of form and address. Both share a delight in death, albeit from different perspectives, which has been seen to be an aspect of the English imagination. Both characteristically deal with small communities or groups of people – the inhabitants of a village, or a house – upon which strange forces or unsettling passions descend. But there are perhaps more interesting parallels. The great English fictional detectives – Sherlock Holmes, Miss Marple, Father Brown – are curiously sexless figures, while sex itself is the instigator of crime and iniquity. It is a very native displacement of passion.

If we take one of the classics of the genre, *The Body in the Library* by Agatha Christie, we may note with surprise that it opens with a dream sequence in which the vicar's wife wanders 'dress'd in a bathing suit'. It is already being suggested that the furtive lusts of the unconscious mind may be dangerous. The dreamer, Mrs Bantry, had been reading a detective story entitled *The Clue of the Broken Match*; like some Chaucerian protagonist, in an earlier English setting, the book had provoked the dream. The amateur detective is soon introduced as Miss Marple, a 'prim spinster'; her neighbours in St Mary Mead include an 'acidulated spinster', 'a rich and dictatorial widow' and of course a vicar. It is almost as if the pent-up rage of repression in a small space had created the crime, the murder of a blonde woman whose body had been left in a library which itself 'spoke of long occupation and familiar use and of links with tradition'. It is, in other words, a very English murder.

The mind of Miss Marple is described as one 'that has plumbed the depths of human iniquity' and is depicted by the lady herself in no very complimentary terms. 'I have a mind like a sink . . . most Victorians have.' The remark is made in the context of a particularly unpleasant child-murder, and we enter that morbid and faintly musty world of perverse passion entirely congenial to the Victorians themselves. 'One does see so much evil in a village', as Miss Marple maintains.

Despite the morbid and manifest 'evil' within Agatha Christie's novel, however, there is little interest in the discovery of emotion or the exploration of character. This is as entirely characteristic as the emphasis upon plot and action. The serpentine line of the story is of the utmost importance, and the principal character is concerned with observation and deduction. The fiction is the purest expression of the practical English imagination, therefore, concerned with the pragmatic solution best achieved by the exercise of uncommon common sense.

Ronald Knox established a Detection Club in 1929 for the sole purpose of excluding 'Divine Revelation, Feminine Intuition, Mumbo-Jumbo, Jiggery-Pokery', an antipathy which represents an index of the English sensibility itself. As a consequence the detective story 'stays in line with the basic storytelling requirements of straightforward progression and a proper finale'.[8] It is indeed a curiously linear way of dealing with human desire, as if the 'evil' could best be arranged in those two-dimensional patterns employed by English painters and miniaturists. And yet a reading of these stories might suggest that the English imagination sometimes resembles the 'mould' upon M. R. James's spectre, harbouring the living remnants of death itself.

Philosophy, mockery
and learning

Thomas Hobbes. Engraving by Wenceslaus Hollar, after J.B. Caspar

CHAPTER 47

Practice makes perfect

The prose style of Alfred, father of the English nation, was 'verbal and concrete', filled with 'concrete examples'[1] of law and governance. A greater number of texts, denominated as 'practical', 'survives from Anglo-Saxon England than from any other Western European country'.[2] Anglo-Saxon scientific writings, for example, 'constitute a large corpus of writings – far beyond anything produced contemporaneously on the continent'.[3] That curiously English heretic, Pelagius, asserted that Christian worship lay in the sphere of practical and moral action rather than in the cultivation of a more exalted spirituality. We read of the Anglo-Saxon theologian, Eadmer, who manifested a 'practical working simplicity in religious matters [which] was characteristically Anglo-Saxon' together with 'a turn of mind which to some extent has remained a feature of the English way of thought'.[4]

That there is a spiritual continuity cannot seriously be in doubt. One contributor to the *Cambridge History of Medieval English Literature* has noted that French scholars believed 'English spirituality before 1300 . . . to have been pragmatic and particularist' and one which 'generated little by way of complex abstract reflection'.[5] When Julian of Norwich is described as evincing a 'very practical and common-sense outlook',[6] and in another context Wycliff is claimed as 'a realist philosopher',[7] the associations and affiliations become clear.

When Roger Ascham composed *The Schoolmaster* he was intent upon a highly practical course of learning to create a 'Civil Gentleman' in whom learning would be utilised to instigate a right course of action. At a slightly later date Gabriel Harvey 'was urging young wits in 1593 to leave poetry for studies of more "effectual use" '.[8] The burgeoning publishing industry of the sixteenth century satisfied the taste for efficacy, too, with books upon medicine and husbandry, navigation and arithmetic. John Dee may now be remembered only as a magician or mystic, but he also wrote treatises upon navigation and mechanics. John Aubrey lists him as a mathematician. In the English imagination, scholarship is applied and learning utilised. Even the finer arts came within the same orbit of practical taste. Sir Philip Sidney suggested that

383

the poet, eschewing the 'wordish description' of philosophy, was in truth 'a right popular philosopher'. Of sixteenth-century English composers it has been written that 'their approach was pragmatic; what was congenial, they used, adapting it to native traditions',[9] where pragmatism can be seen to have a double perspective; it creates a tradition, but is also applied to it.

The history of English philosophy is also the history of empiricism, from the writings of Duns Scotus in the thirteenth century to the logical positivism of the twentieth century. W. R. Sorley's *A History of British Philosophy* might in fact be described as a text-book of pragmatism. As the German philosopher Hegel summarised the matter, 'abstract and general principles have no attraction for Englishmen'. In *The German Ideology* Marx and Engels distinguished between French 'philosophical system' and English 'registration of fact'. Duns Scotus was himself 'critical of all intellectual arguments in the domain of theology'[10] and thus may be described as the harbinger of that anti-intellectualism which has always been so prominent an aspect of the English sensibility. His successor and follower in more than one sense, William of Ockham, propounded the theory that 'all knowledge is derived from experience',[11] a native sentiment which now needs no introduction or interpretation.

In the sixteenth century William Temple's logic 'had the advantage of clearness and practicality',[12] and Francis Bacon can be claimed as the first significant proponent of experimental science. 'The matter in hand is no mere felicity of speculation', he wrote in *Novum Organum*, 'but the real business and fortunes of the human race, and all power of operation.' The swipe against mere 'speculation' may have been instinctive, a manifestation of native taste, since Bacon's method 'had affinities with the practical and positive achievements of the English mind'.[13]

The first English philosopher of empiricism was Roger Bacon, an English Franciscan of the thirteenth century whose speculations upon science were maintained by the 'high value' he placed 'on experiment, with numerous but odd concrete illustrations'.[14] Yet there is no doubt that his namesake, Francis Bacon, set the seal upon the superiority of empirical knowledge. He believed that a vast reformation in the understanding of nature could be effected only by a resolute and rigorous empiricism in matters of experiment or methodology. The pre-eminent method was to be that of induction, by which specific particulars were scrutinised in order to discover their form. Axioms were to be understood, therefore, only in terms of experience and of experiment; the investigator should then 'be able to meet the test of practice and bring about purposeful effects in the actions of nature'.[15]

Bacon's reliance upon practical detail and purposeful experiment seems to breathe an English spirit. He has been described as the originator of experimental science, and his critical empiricism heralded the native aptitude for scientific craftsmanship. He was the direct progenitor of the Royal Society, and his influence can also be traced in the Benthamism of the nineteenth century. A whole cluster of English attitudes and activities seems to form around his name. In his essays, too, he presents himself as an eminently practical scholar, collecting together many aphorisms or apophthegms and compressing them within a small space; he called it 'broken knowledge', just as English music divided into many parts for different instruments was known as 'broken music'. Two metaphors come to mind in any illustration of his prose. One is that of the Elizabethan miniaturist, who packs so much exquisite detail within so small a space. 'Ambition is like choler. . . . Virtue is like a rich stone, best plain set. . . . Reading maketh a full man; conference a ready man; and writing an exact man. . . . Fortune is like the market; where many times, if you can stay a little, the price will fall.' His essay 'Of Adversity' is less than 500 words in length. The other metaphor may be taken from English architecture, since Bacon's is an aggregate learning; he collects his sources and places them side by side, just as retro-chapels and cloisters were erected next to existing buildings without any formal or general design. In similar spirit Jacobean grand gardens were in fact 'small gardens linked to one another'.[16] This arrangement reflects a linear imagination, accustomed to consider matters in sequence rather than in system.

His literal and materialistic vision entered all the ramifications of his complicated life, as writer and courtier as well as experimental scientist. Bacon said of his essays that they 'come home to men's business and bosoms' where the 'business' is the most important consideration; his advice is politic, sage and cautious. It is aimed at 'the pragmatic intelligence'.[17] His own ascendancy at court, during the reigns of both Elizabeth I and James I, was achieved only by wiliness, hypocrisy and all the self-seeking counsels of pragmatic political wisdom. He became Lord Chancellor in 1618, but was summarily removed from his post after pleading guilty to taking bribes. Nevertheless his essays have been described as 'concerned with prudential expedients and instruction in appearances in the pursuit of self-interest'.[18] It should come as no extraordinary surprise, therefore, that 'his approach to moral philosophy was predominantly practical, looking invariably to use'. For this and for his other purposes he attempted to refashion the English language itself and, in his writing, to curb 'all ornaments of speech, similitudes, treasury of eloquence, and such like emptinesses'. He composed the *Advancement of Learning* in English (only at a later date did he translate it into Latin) precisely because he wished to sway his reader with his simple words. In one sense this must be an atavistic pursuit; to prune 'eloquence' is to remove Latinate or aureate diction in favour of Anglo-Saxon materiality and energy. It is as if in pursuing the doctrine of practicality and prag-matism Bacon was at the same time invoking the ancient spirit of the race. He also wished to discredit 'delicate learning', otherwise known as 'contentious learning' and 'fantastical learning', all of which could arguably be considered as importations from continental Europe; the native idiom of Bacon has territorial as well as philosophical contexts.

One exponent of the English tradition has formulated a number of key oppositions out of the Baconian model; from 'concrete/abstract' and 'practice/theory' come 'common sense/dogma' and 'amateur/ professional' as well as 'truth/pleasure', 'Protestant/Catholic' and 'English/French'. Another derivation is to be found in 'centre/ extreme'[19] from which may be adduced the English partiality for compromise and accommodation. In this context it is interesting that, in Bacon's discourse, knowledge comes not from feudalism 'in which inherited rank decides truth',[20] but from bourgeois individualism of a distinctively Protestant and democratic stance. The faith in com-promise has also been described as essentially English, simply because it manifests 'a belief in a self-evidencing reality which you can retrieve if you rid yourself of fantasy';[21] it is a question of things rather than of words.

Bacon can be considered the father of empirical philosophy and of experimental science in England, then, but his linguistic injunctions proved to be no less powerful. His denunciation of falsely affected prose, for example, was taken up by the early founders of the Royal Society and has been repeated ever since in the English distaste for rhetorical prolixity. The Royal Society was formally instituted in 1662 but had already existed for some years as a loose association of scientific experimenters, experimental philosophers and virtuosi intent upon practical resolutions concerning such diverse matters as barometric pressure and the migration of birds. In its diversity, and somewhat amateur status, it was a very English institution. In his *History* of the society Thomas Sprat declares that its members preferred 'a close, naked, natural way of speaking, positive expressions, clear senses, a native easiness, bringing all things as near the Mathematical plainness as they can, and preferring the language of Artizans, Countrymen and Merchants before that of Wits and Scholars'. The reference to 'Artizans' and 'Merchants' represents a powerful current of materialism and purely commercial speculation; at a later date, of course, Napoleon would denounce the English as 'a nation of shopkeepers'. In the *History* Sprat also advocated a 'return back to the primitive purity, and shortness, when men delivered so many *things* almost in an equal number of *words*', in which knowledge and judgement consist of a return to origins. Only in a 'primitive' linguistic community is truth to be found.

There may, therefore, only be a step between the scientific treatises of the Anglo-Saxons and the prevailing ethos of the Royal Society which, like other London institutions, was devoted to pragmatic and technical advancement. The experiments of the society were of a highly practical kind, since its fundamental project lay in the improvement of 'Manufactures, Mechanic practices, Engynes and Inventions'. No other scientific institution in the world so readily discarded questions of scientific theory or experimental philosophy. The concern, as outlined in the first issue of the *Philosophical Transactions* composed by the Secretary in 1666, was 'solid and useful knowledge'. Since the emphasis was upon 'legitimate Experiments' the members of the society felt able to criticise Descartes's 'geometric method' and deductive system, for example, on the thoroughly English grounds that 'he was for doing too great a part of his work in his Closet, concluding too soon, before he had made Experiments enough'. They doubted his concept of methodical doubt, principally because it smacked of speculation and theory. The assault upon Descartes was of course an assault upon France. As Sprat remarked of useful or applied knowledge, 'For the improvement of this kind of light, the English disposition is of all others the fittest.' The learned members of the Royal Society were not concerned with '*setling of Principles*' or '*Doctrines*' but with 'the way to attain a *solid speculation*'. It is the tone of the merchant or the broker, even of the stereotypical John Bull himself. 'Solid speculation' may be seen as equivalent, or complementary, to 'common sense' based upon a notion of shared responses and an implicit community of judgement; other native virtues, such as the tendency towards moderation, were also supposed to spring from the eschewal of general doctrines or abstruse theories.

In the roll-call of English philosophers we must include here Thomas Hobbes and John Locke. Of Hobbes it may be said that he felt the pressure of power upon his pulse and that, of all English philosophers, he harnessed the claims and exigencies of simple if brutal human experience. He disclaimed rhetoric, and repeatedly declined to quote from the wisdom of the ancients; his 'Discourse of Civil and Ecclesiastical Government', entitled *Leviathan*, was 'occasioned by the disorder of the present time' to which he would apply the balm of 'solid reasoning'. He has been described as 'the founding father of modern metaphysical materialism',[22] which consorts well with all the pragmatic tendencies of his age. It has been said that, for Hobbes, 'everything is a material process'.[23] He himself wrote that 'there is no conception in a man's mind which hath not at first . . . been begotten upon the organs of Sense'; imagination was 'nothing but *decaying sense*' and spirits themselves 'really Bodies'. His life was one of retirement and contemplation. Of humble origin, he lived in the houses of the nobility in the role of tutor and companion. He suffered from what Aubrey called 'a contemplative Melancholinesse', and translated his fearfulness into the doctrine of absolute power.

In the pragmatic tradition he was a social moralist as well as a philosopher, and his principles were indeed of a thoroughly practical kind. 'No man', he wrote, 'gives except for a personal advantage.' We pity others 'because we imagine that a similar misfortune may befall ourselves'. He made a metaphysics out of worldliness. 'Not he who is wise is rich, as the Stoics say; but, on the contrary, he who is rich is wise.' It can be assumed that *Leviathan* itself is a practical document, too, since it is concerned with the purpose and nature of political life. It has been suggested that Thomas Hobbes cannot be considered as representative of English philosophy because of his urgent desire to create a 'system' of knowledge based upon first principles. But this is not an Hegelian or Platonic 'system', which seems propelled by unearthly powers and by a desire to forge abstractions into truth, but a wholly earth-bound project designed to illustrate the social conditions of mankind. The work itself was prompted by the specific political circumstances of the period and, although Hobbes professed to despise the procedures of the Royal Society, he was equally concerned to demonstrate the practical efficacy of 'solid speculation'. He detested scholasticism, and distrusted rhetoric; he evinced also a 'profound suspicion of anything like authority in philosophy'.[24]

In *Leviathan* itself he argued that between men there is 'a perpetual contention for Honour, Riches and Authority', which in an ill-ordered world would create a condition of perpetual warfare; thus, to create civil order and stability, the will of each individual must be subsumed by a greater will. The fear of death and the promise of felicity also prompt men willingly to surrender their power to a supreme authority, which emerges in 'the generation of the great Leviathan, the King of the Proud'.[25] The Leviathan himself must be armed and potentially dangerous since 'Covenants, without the Sword, are but words'. This abbreviated résumé is not designed to introduce the reader to Hobbes's philosophy but, rather, to emphasise his often brutally pragmatic nature. The wisdom springing from such perceptions may then be considered 'the end and crown of experience'. It is a fitting conclusion for a philosopher who led the English imagination into unknown paths.

The native spirit of John Locke has never been in doubt. In his 'Epistle to the Reader', introducing *An Essay Concerning Human Understanding*, he places the origin of his treatise in 'five or six friends meeting at my chamber' who agreed after more than usually strenuous debate that 'it was necessary to examine our own abilities, and see what objects our understandings were or were not fitted to deal with'. There is no dogmatism or regimentation to be found, therefore, only the fruits of a modest enquiry. The *Essay* itself was 'begun by chance' and 'continued by entreaty'; it was 'written by incoherent parcels; and, after long intervals of neglect, resumed again, as my humour or occasions permitted'. It was 'spun out of my own coarse thoughts', and 'I am now too lazy or too busy to make it shorter'. Here are all the signs of that embarrassed modesty which has ever been the accompaniment of the English writer, together with a characteristic diffidence or detachment. Despite his lack of accomplishment, John Locke has emerged in print 'being on purpose to be as useful as I may'; he is content to be 'employed as an under-labourer in clearing the ground a little', particularly by identifying 'the learned but frivolous use of uncouth, affected or unintelligible terms introduced into the sciences'. This is an enterprise entirely in line with the English imagination, therefore, and the *Essay* itself, humbly presented, became 'the philosophical Bible of the eighteenth century'[26] in England, modifying the work of Sterne and Johnson, Reynolds and Addison.

In his *History of Western Philosophy*, first published in 1945, Bertrand Russell distinguishes Locke from European philosophers such as Leibniz or Descartes or Hegel by concluding that, in continental writing, 'a vast edifice of deduction is pyramided upon a pin-point of logical principle' whereas in Locke 'the base of the pyramid is on the solid ground of observed fact, and the pyramid tapers upward, not downward'.[27] His philosophy is established upon observation rather than speculation, and can justifiably claim a Baconian lineage. In this context it has also been asserted by Russell that 'British philosophy is more detailed and piecemeal than that of the continent',[28] eschewing system or authoritarian organisation; the significance of detail and organic accretion is once more underlined. It represents individual liberty of thought. In politics as well as in philosophy, therefore, Locke was 'tentative and experimental'; such diffidence encourages toleration and a trust in freedom of expression, so that the philosopher was 'not at all authoritarian'.[29] Here are the lineaments of native thought.

One of its conclusions would then run as follows. The desired goal is not that which is ideally or speculatively the best, but that which is most practical. This is, in a nutshell (to use the English phrase), also the history of the English constitution and of English common law. In the knowledge of nature, according to Locke, we possess only 'the twilight of probability'; but that is enough. In this condition our faculties must be 'accommodated to the use of life'. It is a philosophy of earnest practicality, one well suited to the accomplishments of Gresham College and the Royal Society. Engines may be less exciting than theorems, and utensils more homely than speculations, but they are somehow more appropriate. *An Essay Concerning Human Under-standing* is animated by a kind of inspired common sense, then, or by what Locke more elegantly terms 'the common light of reason'. He remarks in passing that 'it is the affectation of knowing beyond what we perceive that makes so much useless dispute and noise in the world'; this dislike of noise and dispute, the philosophical equivalent of not making a scene in a restaurant, also seems innately English. That is why Locke uses the most homely metaphors to make his point. He illustrates his theory of the association of ideas, for example, by citing the instance of a man who could dance only when there was a trunk in the room. The image might have come out of *Tristram Shandy*, and is an instance of that whimsicality which seems endemic to the native genius.

Out of Locke's self-deprecation, evinced in his 'Preface', irony may also spring. It has in turn been suggested that within 'the English discursive tradition, attending as it does upon empiricist attitudes, irony is pervasive'.[30] Irony suggests that there is some kind of collective experience which shadows any individual statement, and that there are certain shared sentiments which need only to be intimated rather than expressed. It also suggests the primacy of experience over theory. It might be put another way by declaring, with Locke, that 'all ideas have their origin in experience'.[31] No more radical exposition of English empiricism has been made. As Locke's editor suggests, 'the very word "principle" has evil associations for him';[32] it is as if all the theoretical arguments were purposeless. So 'Locke has written himself down as the founder of the English philosophy of experience', to which may be added the suggestion that 'English philosophy is instinctively the philosophy of experience, and the advance of English philosophy is the more precise definition of what experience means'.[33] It appears also in Francis Hutcheson's *An Enquiry into the Original of our Ideas of Beauty and Virtue* where he coined the phrase 'the greatest happiness for the greatest numbers', which was in turn co-opted by the English utilitarians. The sentiment was reasserted by Joseph Priestley who concluded that happiness is 'the great standard by which everything relating to that state must finally be demanded'.

We approach the nineteenth century with Jeremy Bentham, who appropriated and reformulated Hutcheson's proposition by suggesting that 'it is the greatest happiness of the greatest number that is the measure of right and wrong'. Bentham, like Locke and, indeed, like the humanists of the twelfth and sixteenth centuries, was preoccupied by civic conduct. In texts such as *Fragment on Government*, *Anarchical Fallacies* and the *Constitutional Code* he eschewed what he called the politics of 'abstract advantage' and speculation in order to concentrate upon practical, if radical, reform. His pre-eminence meant that 'philosophical radicalism in England, unlike the corresponding revolutionary doctrines in other countries, was based upon an empirical utilitarianism and not upon *a priori* ideas about natural rights'.[34] The same conclusion might be drawn of Bacon and of Hobbes, so traditional has it become.

But there is more than philosophy in the sphere of pragmatism. The French Revolution was considered by many English observers to be the direct consequence of 'French theory' and Arthur Young, in his *The Example of France a Warning to Britain*, urged a political ethic established 'merely upon experience'. Burke's animadversions against that revolution are well documented, but his sense of historical violation rendered his *Reflections on the Revolution in France* sympathetic to an English audience. The unspoken pact between past and present, in which the example of the dead earns the suffrage of the living, is the single most poignant note of Burke's exposition; it is the 'great melody' in which the voices of past orators mingle with Burke's own to furnish a savage denunciation of the French revolutionaries who thought to create a society *ab novo* and to extirpate the historical roots of their culture or nation. But English observers posited the power of practical as well as historical experience. The strength of the English Constitution, for example, according to one modern cultural historian, lay 'in its having no theory, in its being the gradual and patient accumulation of practice and precedent, in its being, above all, unwritten'.[35] A general aversion to 'rules', and a disdain for theoretical enquiry, mark English political discourse which accommodates the claims of individual liberty and individual circumstance more readily than abstract speculations about the 'rights' of those individuals.

That empirical temper can be found to be no less prominent in the art and music of England. Of eighteenth-century landscape painting it has often been suggested that 'in Italy the tradition of painting was one of idealisation and generalisation' where in England more attention was granted to 'revealing particularities of sky and water'.[36] The art of Stubbs and Joseph Wright is preoccupied with 'the nature of things'[37] and even the work of Turner has been described as 'not scientific but empirical'.[38] In eighteenth-century English music, too, the emphasis shifted 'from scientific and metaphysical speculation to empirical discussion of music itself'.[39] The triumphs of nineteenth-century architecture were those in which practical engineering played a formative role, as in the construction of the great railway stations of Newcastle Central, Paddington and King's Cross. The engineers themselves were celebrated for their 'inventive genius' and became the new heroes of Victorian England. 'These men', Samuel Smiles wrote, 'were strong-minded, resolute and ingenious.' In Germany the philosopher-scientist was king, but in England it was the technician. The Department of Practical Art was established in London as a direct consequence of the Great Exhibition of 1851, but it had already been anticipated by the Society for the Diffusion of Useful Knowledge and the British Association for the Advancement of Science. The 'science' was, as usual, 'applied'. As a character in Charles Kingsley's novel, *Two Years*

Ago (1857), explains, 'We doctors, you see, get into the way of looking at things as men of science; and the ground of science is experience.'

The same attitude is present in Matthew Arnold's belief that the English only exert themselves within 'the field of plain sense, of direct practical utility'. A Russian, Oloff Napea, wrote in *Letters from London* that 'in France every particle glistens, all is blandishment; in England all is utility, but no glitter'. This may account for the ugliness and lack of symmetry in London, contrasted with the elegance and formality of Paris; London grew instinctively and organically, while the centre of Paris was fashioned by administrative *fiat* and aesthetic principle.

The English possess moralists and psychologists rather than metaphysicians, and in England the tree of knowledge is prized only for its fruit in practice and activity. Thus A. J. Ayer, in *Logical Positivism in Perspective*, suggests that in England there has been 'an almost complete disregard of the current extravagancies of German speculative thought'.[40] He also describes the tendency of 'contemporary British philosophers . . . to deal with philosophical questions in an unsystematic illustrative way.'[41] The continuity of methods and preoccupations, from Bacon to the last century, would be astonishing if it were not for the fact that such remarkable continuities are found in every area of the English imagination. The discipline of logical positivism, associated with 'the Vienna Circle', for example, was welcomed and adopted in the English philosophical habitat; but it was subtly adapted for native circumstances. Its 'uncompromising positivism' and its 'blanket rejection of metaphysics' were modified. All extremes, in other words, were toned down. As a result of this process of assimilation, 'generalisations are distrusted, particular examples are multiplied . . . common sense reigns as a constitutional, if not an absolute, monarch, philosophical theories are put to the touchstone of the way in which words are actually used'.[42] A. J. Ayer calls the approach 'empirical in the political sense, the sense in which Burke was a champion of empiricism';[43] indeed his reference to 'constitutional' monarchy does suggest the larger context in which English empiricism prevails.

There is room in this cave of knowing for one other echo. Ayer himself adhered to the principle 'that general statements of science and those about the past can be meaningful if experience can show them probable',[44] which might be described as a doctrine of enlightened pragmatism. Such a statement would have been welcome to the members of the Royal Society. A further conclusion, that 'all scientific

393

propositions, however complex, are reducible to empirically verifiable propositions',[45] might have come out of the mouth of John Locke, rather than from his counterparts almost three centuries later.

Yet there is another way of regarding these tendencies within the English imagination. It is the nature of the language itself to be fluid and comprehensive, to cross the boundaries of Latin and Saxon, to compromise and moderate its various sources and origins. There are very few rules in English syntax and grammar which cannot be broken; the principles of its deep structure hold, but its local manifestations are often flexible and peculiar. It is an absorbent medium established upon the imperatives of usage and practice; words are introduced, or coined, and idiomatic changes are common. It carries a pragmatic force, therefore, and may bear a certain responsibility for English empiricism itself. One study of nineteenth-century literature has come to the conclusion that 'the most authentically "English" literature (and this was the preferred term, rather than "British") came to be more and more defined as that which was most resistant to theoretical epitome or to the language of theory in general'.[46] The language is deemed to be resistant to theory on every level; as the language, so the imagination which it carries and maintains. The paths of English empiricism have been long and wayward, but they have arrived at their destination.

Dedicated to the practicalities of scientific study: the Royal Observatory at Greenwich, 1675

CHAPTER 48

Prolix and prolific

Chaucer often used a pastiche of ornate or aureate style to mock the quiddities of theological controversy. On the doctrine of predestination he remarks in 'The Nun's Priest's Tale':

> That in scole is greet altercacioun,
> In this mateere, and greet disputisoun

only to add some thirteen lines later:

> I wol not han to do of swich mateere;
> My tale is of a cok, as ye may heere

The monosyllables, ultimately derived from Anglo-Saxon sources, are employed to emphasise practicality and individuality rather than the vapid learning traced within the polysyllables; there is a clear indication here that practical experience, and the specific circumstances of the story, are of more significance. The 'Nun's Priest's Tale' has in fact been described as a 'parody of the excesses of rhetoric'.[1] The word 'tale' itself comes from Old English, which may in turn suggest that Chaucer is drawing upon a stock of popular or common lore to match the Latinate quibblings of the 'clercs'. In 'The Canon's Yeoman's Tale' Chaucer also berates false learning in the guise of alchemy – 'Oure termes been so clergial and so queynte' – where the vocabulary of the pursuit is the principal object of scorn. This will be seen to be a characteristic English device, in a language which is so flexible and accommodating that it can parody its own excesses. In the miracle plays the comic pomposity of various 'Vertues' is delivered in aureate speech – 'My inwarde afflixyon yeldeth me tedyouse to your presens' – only to be deflated by the rough and homely demotic of the 'Vices'. It is such a common trait in English comedy that it almost passes unnoticed, but the incompatibility of styles is an important feature of the English imagination; it suggests that experience, and individual sensation, represent the true sources of the language.

There is a celebrated line from Sir Philip Sidney's sonnet sequence, *Astrophel and Stella*, which embodies the English disdain both for book-learning and for the ornamentation of mere words: 'Foole, said my Muse to me, looke in thy heart and write.' But we may also look to Sidney's contemporary, William Shakespeare, for a willing adumbration of this theme. One of his first plays, *Love's Labour's Lost*, is a satire upon pedantry and bookishness. When Ferdinand, King of Navarre, and his three lords pledge themselves to spend three years 'lyuing in Philosophie', their studies making up a 'lyttle Achademe', and to abjure the company of women, they are being impractical; they are sinning against common sense. In a similar false spirit the schoolmaster in the same play, Holofernes, addresses his companions in an obfuscatory style. 'Yet a kind of insinuation, as it were, *in via*, in way, of explication, *facere*, as it were, replication, or rather *ostentare*, to show, as it were, his inclination, after his undressed, unpolished, uneducated, unpruned, untrained, or rather unlettered, or ratherest unconfirmed fashion . . .' This is the comedy of aureate bookishness, which was already present in the mystery plays. It can be argued that the figure of the pedant was borrowed from the *commedia dell'arte* or the *commedia erudita*, but an instinctive disregard for the bookish scholar is also of native growth.

There was a form of English parody, in part deriving from More's *Utopia*, whereby a learned treatise was constructed as a standing joke against the learned themselves. Donne's 'Biathanatos', an essay upon suicide in which it is argued that 'Self-homicide is not so Naturally Sinne, that it may never be otherwise', is just such a work. It purports to be a learned disquisition upon the justification for suicide; since such an act would result in eternal damnation, however, it is clear that Donne is satirising the excesses of scholarly discourse. He even cites Sir Thomas More '(a man of the most tender and delicate conscience that the world saw since Saint Augustine) not likely to write anything in jest mischievously interpretable', a description in which irony is heaped on irony. Donne knew well that *Utopia* was written 'in jest', and his 'Biathanatos' is a production of the same type. He employs false logic and introduces false learning; his arguments are inconsistent and his conclusions bathetic; he employs a hundred allusions and quotations from obscure sources, with an apology that 'I did it the rather because scholastique and artificiall men use this way of instructing'. It is the method of Swift and Sterne. It allows him to pose as the diffident scholar advancing an absurd proposition, and also permits him to horrify his readers with such pronouncements as that upon the early Christians whose children were 'taught to vexe and provoke Executioners, that they might be thrown into the fire'. One of his editors has also suggested that 'the mere physical appearance of the book might suggest a satire on casuistry as each page in the original edition is so festooned with brackets and indices and marginalia', and that its style of 'bloated parentheses and meandering subordinate clauses' may be of similar comic intent.[2] It might be argued that John Donne's somewhat parlous circumstances at the time of composition – he had been dismissed from court service and forced into premature retirement – provoked him into the contemplation of self-murder. But that is precisely why he parodied the venture. It might as well be argued that Swift's *Modest Proposal* for the eating of children was authentic because there was a genuine Irish famine. If there is one characteristic aspect of the English imagination, it lies in mocking that which comes too close for ordinary self-expression. It is a question of satirising emotion, or even passion, itself.

Walter Raleigh's *History of the World* is replete with learned quotations and allusions – 'Peter Lombard, the schoolmen Beda, Lyranus, Comestor, Tostatus and others affirm . . .' Yet these words are a 'lift' from a Latin original. The invocation of many names is perhaps deliberately designed to impress, or confuse, the casual reader; in the English theatrical spirit, it represents a parade of learning. Yet it also suggests a certain detachment, a lack of complete seriousness, a whimsicality. Nikolaus Pevsner noticed a curious aspect of national sensibility in the sense that 'England was the first country to break the unity of interior and exterior'.[3] In Raleigh's panoply of 'exterior' learning, of adapted and assimilated knowledge, is not Pevsner's maxim comprehended?

It has been demonstrated by scholarly exegesis that throughout his *History* Raleigh depends upon the borrowing of other writers' material, upon unascribed translation and collation, to such an extent that one commentator has described the work as a 'patchwork of citations and quotations . . . with long lists of authorities presented in bewildering confusion'.[4] But this is by no means a specific or isolated instance. The history of literary learning in England is the history of inconsequence and random accretion. We may remark once more upon Robert Burton's *Anatomy of Melancholy*, the favoured book of Johnson and of Keats, which is replete with prolix and half-assimilated information. It is an encyclopaedic and synthetic work, marshalling sources and authorities with dexterity, but it is also curiously hesitant and ambivalent about any conclusions which might be plucked from this wealth of material; it leaves the reader, in the words of one critic, 'poised uneasily between two equally unauthorised authorities'.[5] Samuel Johnson declared that the *Anatomy* was filled with the 'scourings of the Bodleian'; the history of dreams might be followed by a disquisition upon genealogy, the transcription of a fever-fit succeeded by an encomium on marriage. Aphorisms and anecdotes are mingled with appeals to the ancients; quotations follow and surround para-phrases, while the course of a sentence proceeds uneasily through a maze or labyrinth of subordinate clauses. 'Yet re vera he was an illiterate idiot, as *Aristophanes* calls him, *irrisor & ambitiosus* as his Master *Aristotle* terms him, as *Zeno*, an enemy to all arts & sciences, as *Athenaeus*, to Philosophers & Travellers, an opiniative ass, a caviller, a kind of Pedant.' 'What madness ghosts this old man, but what madness ghosts us all? For we are, *ad unum omnes*, all mad, *semel insanivimus omnes*, not once, but always *& semel & simul & semper*; ever and altogether as bad as he'. The sentences spiral, take the form of a double helix, or, to use a less anachronistic metaphor, follow the serpentine line of English beauty. The *Anatomy* is a work of com-pilation and exegesis, not of analysis or speculation, so it becomes a thoroughly native product. Burton's unsystematic corpus grows by accumulation or aggregation in the manner of an early English cathedral. He poses as the bookish scatter-brain, an old English persona created by Geoffrey Chaucer; only out of embarrassment or humility does he offer his scholarship to the reader. In the English style, too, he deplores the pedantry of scholastic or speculative learning. 'What is most of our Philosophy, but a Labyrinth of opinions, idle questions, propositions, metaphysical terms . . . Philology, but vain criticisms? Logick, but needless sophisms? Metaphysicks themselves but intricate subtilties, & fruitless abstractions?' Instead he pursues the way of the antiquarian, citing the examples of history and the experience of the ages in order to demonstrate his theme. The English seem to relish unsystematic learning of this kind, in the same manner that they embarked upon 'Grand Tours' of Europe in pursuit of a peripatetic scholarship.

Burton's historical disposition also fostered in him a kind of fatalism which has already been noted in the Anglo-Saxons. As if by instinct, too, the same imaginative precepts are advanced. He invokes that trinity of preoccupations – the world as prison, the world as theatre, the world as dream – which seems to characterise one aspect of the English imagination. He mixes humour with his philosophy, however, and colloquialisms with his aureate periods. Hippolyte Taine described the

Anatomy as 'an enormous medley, a prodigious mass of jumbled quotations', but we have already discovered that 'medley' is precisely the English genre. Burton is entranced by details and minute particulars; he is prone to anecdote, and allured by digression. 'In this labyrinth of accidental causes, the farther I wander, the more intricate I find the passage, *multae ambages* & new causes as so many by-paths offer themselves to be discursed.' It seems a particular English trait, to wish to encompass everything, to fill a book or a stage with crowds, to list everything, and yet at the same time to lament that all is vanity and emptiness.

The *Anatomy* is also a parodic work which mocks its own learning. Burton invented several 'classical' quotations for the sake of euphony or sense. The meaning which he attempts to convey is also often lost in the labyrinth of metaphor and reference, so that eventually Burton seems to mean nothing at all. 'But where am I? Into what subject have I rushed?' The very structure of Burton's book, laid out as a 'synopsis' divided and subdivided into sections and categories, is an elaborate parody of continental discourse – such as that by Ramus – which similarly divides its content into theses and propositions. Thus in the 'synopsis of the first partition' one 'subsection' lists 'Dotage. Phrensy. Madness. Extasy. Lycanthropia. Chorus Sancti Viti. Hydrophobia. Possession or obsession of devils. Melancholy.' The principle is one of false methodology or, as one commentator has put it, 'the unsuitability of the intellectual approach to melancholy'[6] and thus 'the futility of scholarly learning'.[7] That is why the book is inconsistent and contradictory, with *non sequiturs* and egregiously false trails leading nowhere. Burton claimed that his book is '*nemenis nihil*', nothing from nobody. He coined neologisms or introduced deliberately archaic words; he chose the most obscure terms, and created a confusing syntax as if the whole exercise were no more than an elaborate joke. He was empirical, anecdotal, sensational.

He is also the best companion for Sir Thomas Browne, whose own prolix and prolific learning was not untouched by parody, and whose wit was tempered by fatalism and melancholy. Browne was trained in medicine, as we have seen, but in English fashion he was also an amateur scientist devoted to experiment; he weighed mice and chickens, before and after he had strangled them, to see if the release of their vital spirits lowered their weight. He put toads and spiders together in a glass vessel, to test their 'natural antipathy'.[8] He was firmly of the belief that witches were possessed by the devil and, even while studying the transactions of the Royal Society, was moved to ask his son 'what kind of stone is that wch stoned St Stephen, pebble, flint or freestone?' He had an infinite capacity for practical research and empirical learning. In other words he was unlike the continental philosophers, who worked from first principles or according to system. Like Burton and Sterne, he abjured the subtle mysteries of scholastics and metaphysicians. He wished 'to condemne to the fire those swarms and millions of *Rhapsodies*, begotten onely to distract and abuse the weaker judgements of Scholars, and *to maintaine the Trade and Mystery of Typographers*'.

In *Religio Medici* he discusses the principles of his faith in relation to his profession as a physician, but this is the merest excuse for a work that is digressive and theatrical, curiously knit and finely polished. Of other theological works he writes elsewhere that 'There are a bundle of curiosities, not onely in Philosophy but in Divinity, proposed and discussed by men of the most supposed abilities, which indeed are not worthy our vacant hours, much less our more serious studies; Pieces only fit to be placed in *Pantagruels* Library, or bound up with *Tartaretus De Modo Cacandi*', a sentence which itself may serve as a type or epitome of Browne's prose where an arresting cadence is filled with witty sententiousness and arcane allusion. His writing so abounds in intricate and convoluted argument that we might use the image of Anglo-Saxon interlace as the form of his thought; he revels in inconsistency and paradox in order to illustrate the limitations of scholastic argument and the infirmity of speculation. One passage, for example, affirms the union of opposites in the workings of creation and generation. 'God, being all things, is contrary unto nothing, out of which were made all things, as so nothing becomes something, and *Omneity* informed *Nullity* into an essence.' Coleridge wondered whether this sentence itself were an 'excellent *Burlesque* on some parts of the Schoolmen'. The element of burlesque is surely present, if only in an oblique fashion. Like Raleigh before him Browne borrows or steals without fully acknowledging the debt; in the process he builds up a patchwork of quotations and sources in a somewhat theatrical display of learning. It is Coleridge, too, who elucidates the native cast of Thomas Browne's thought when he describes him as 'Fond of the Curious, and a Hunter of Oddities & Strangenesses . . . a useful enquirer into physical Truth & fundamental Science'. His empirical tendencies are thereby aligned with his individualism and even his eccentricity.

Like Donne in 'Biathanatos', Browne parodies and mocks the language of pedantic learning. Humour emerges, too, in his discussion upon the lamprey, a fish resembling an eel. 'Whether Lampries have nine eyes, as is received, we durst refer it unto Polyphemus, who had but one, to judg it.' His scepticism, his delight in oddity, his humorous exaggeration, his plangent rhetoric, are all of a piece. Indeed his own work, like that of Burton, resembles some panopticon of the English imagination; in whichever direction we choose to look, we glimpse some fugitive historical trait.

CHAPTER 49

Some more dunces

The disdain for learned disquisition, or what has been termed 'useless' knowledge, is therefore an intrinsic aspect of the English imagination. One of the most popular comedies of the seventeenth century was Thomas Shadwell's *The Virtuoso* in which the virtuoso of the title is a scientific theorist, Sir Nicholas Gimcrack, who is found imitating the movements of a frog in order to learn how to swim. 'I content myself with the speculative part of swimming,' he declares, 'I care not for the Practick. I seldom bring anything to use; 'tis not my way. Knowledge is my ultimate end.' An intrinsic aspect of Gimcrack's dramatic character lies not so much in his pedantry as in his desire to carry all things to extremes. This is a sin against the common wisdom of the English imagination which maintains the importance of moderation and compromise. That is why Shadwell's satire on the 'new science' had political ramifications. Sir Nicholas Gimcrack decides to bottle the air from various parts of England so that it might be weighed. Pepys records meeting Charles II in the Duke's Chamber where the monarch passed 'an hour or two laughing . . . Gresham College he mightily laughed at, for spending time only in weighing of ayre, and doing nothing else since they sat'. Gimcrack, in thus becoming a dramatic caricature of 'fanaticks' and 'enthusiasts' of every kind, represents a distaste for the extremities of the civil war but also manifests an English aversion to feeling.

The character of Gimcrack, so obvious a dupe for English pragmatists, was elaborated by Pope and Gay in the deluded collector and scholar, Fossil, in their *Three Hours After Marriage*. Pope was an inspired opponent of false learning in a period which less deserves the epithet of 'the Age of Reason' than 'the Age of Sense'. The most fruitful forms were those of the parody, the burlesque, the satire and the mock-heroic. Works such as *A Tale of a Tub* (1704), *Gulliver's Travels* (1726), *The Dunciad* (1728), *Shamela* (1741), *Jonathan Wild* (1743) and *Tristram Shandy* (1759), parodied sentiment and innovation, scholarship and heroic posturing, enthusiasm and pedantry, metaphysics and theological speculation. In *The Dunciad* Pope berates false scientific learning as an instrument of 'Dullness':

> Impale a Glow-worm, or Vertu profess,
> Shine in the dignity of F.R.S.

The real wit of *The Dunciad*, however, emerges in the plethora of interpretations and commentaries with which Pope surrounds the poem. Its prefaces, letters, testimonies, prolegomena and marginalia far exceed in quantity the verses themselves. Even the title of the poem is immediately the subject of scholastic controversy. 'The DUNCIAD, sic MS. It may well be disputed whether this be a right reading: Ought it not rather to be spelled *Dunceiad*, as the Etymology evidently demands? *Dunce* with an *e*, therefore *Dunceiad* with an *e*' – which enquiry is followed by a disquisition upon Theobald's 'restoration' of Shakespeare.

Pope was part of the 'Scriblerus Club', among whose other members were Swift, Arbuthnot and Gay; it was a social club, a closed literary coffee-house on the English pattern, but its larger purpose was the promulgation of satires on 'party writers, critics, editors, and commentators . . . men of learning, whether philosophers or artists, antiquarians or travellers, teachers or poets, lawyers or dancers'.[1] All come under the title of 'Martin Scriblerus', a fictional dullard, who is deemed to have published or composed various works; real, as well as feigned, material could then be ascribed to him. The achievement of the Scriblerians, therefore, lay in 'the double process of putting out apparently serious works by their hero under his own and other names, and at the same time claiming for him things [and books] actually done by real people'.[2] This conflation of the artificial and the genuine, the blurring of distinction between fact and fiction, is a truly English joke; it combines 'ostensible solemnity' and 'frequent use of real material'.[3]

Amongst the publications composed by 'Martin Scriblerus' was Pope's *Peri Bathous: or the Art of Sinking in Poetry*, a disquisition upon the 'profound' in English poetry which has always been the object of English mockery – whether out of fear, or incapacity, is an open question. Pope defines paraphrase, for example, as 'another great aid to Prolixity; being a confused circumlocutory manner of expressing a known idea, which should be so mysteriously couched, as to give the reader the pleasure of guessing what it is that the author can possibly mean, and a strange surprise when he finds it'. Pope then adduces real examples, from John Cleveland to Ambrose Philips, to illustrate this tendency. In conventional English fashion, therefore, he mocks periphrasis and aureate diction as somehow repugnant to Anglo-Saxon common sense.

> '*Shut the door*' becomes in poetic diction:
> 'The wooden Guardian of our Privacy
> Quick on its Axle turn'.

It is funny, but it is also traditional and appropriate to the English imagination.

Thus, in *A Tale of a Tub*, Jonathan Swift mocks the wordiness of scholars which breeds '*an infinite Number of* Abstracts, Summaries, Compendiums, Extracts, Collections, Medulla's, Excerpta quaedam's, Florilegia's'. It is perhaps not surprising that, in the contemporaneous battle between the 'Ancients' and the 'Moderns', Swift should align himself with the 'Ancients'. The delusion of the 'Modern' is that 'every Branch of Knowledge has received such wonderful Acquirements since his Age, especially within these last three Years, or thereabouts'. Swift is assaulting the false learning of those who seem to believe that the world was created on the day they were born, and that whatever slight glimmerings of knowledge they since have acquired are of immense relevance and strength. They were the writers who 'cryed up' the latest text or the latest invention as the most important of its kind, and who argued seriously upon the merits of the vain ramblings of their contemporaries. All this was profoundly inimical to Swift, and also to those aspects of the English imagination which eschew innovation and avoid the self-congratulatory stance of those who deny the claims of history. Swift satirises one exponent of 'modern' learning for his strictures upon Homer – 'I mean, his [Homer's] gross Ignorance in the Common Laws of this Realm and in the Doctrine as well as Discipline of the Church of England. A Defect indeed, for which both he and all the Ancients stand most justly censored.' Here the vanity and foolishness of censoring the 'ancients' for not manifesting modern preoccupations are evident. So Swift berates certain of his contemporaries who 'have discovered a shorter, and more prudent Method, to become *Scholars* and *Wits* without the Fatigue of *Reading* or of *Thinking*'; their way is to adopt the fashionable vocabulary or terminology of the day, which they will learn from '*Systems* and *Abstracts*', and then to parrot it unthinkingly. In this world of chaos and of dullness the learned 'deal entirely with *Invention*, and strike all Things out of themselves, or at least, by Collision, from each other'. 'Invention' here covers the aptitude of modern thought to beget more fake learning, misperceptions and misunderstandings, all the time accompanied by a babble of errant voices; modern learning resembles 'A Man ever in Haste, a great Hatcher and Breeder of Business, and excellent at the Famous Art of *whispering Nothing*'.

And yet *A Tale of a Tub* is written by nobody. Throughout its several editions it remained an anonymous work, which somehow managed to parody all the mannerisms of the books which it attacked. It is, as one critic has put it, 'an anonymous book-compiling machine itself'.[4] This of course lends substance to Swift's further perception that the 'moderns' have no definable or decided personality. They are so much the creatures of their age, and repeat so faithfully its assumptions and conditions, that they have no self or soul to speak of. That is why he parodies those who claim 'inspiration' or the 'inner light', a species of modern idolatry which as a believer in the community of history he utterly despised. In another place he conjures up a windy picture in which 'the sacred *Aeolist* delivers his oracular *Belches* to his panting Disciples; of whom, some are greedily gaping after the sanctified Breath; others are all the while hymning out the Praises of the Winds'. It may be that the enormous concentration upon farts and farting in eighteenth-century literature is a somewhat noisome allusion to the fatuity of self-expression in the 'modern' fashion. It might also be suggested that Swift, as prescient as he was witty, was prophesying that change of consciousness which would one day be heralded as the 'romantic revolution' and that he already saw the first dim stirrings of that movement in the work of his contemporaries. For him it was a kind of madness incurring 'manifest danger of phlebotomy, and whips, and chains, and dark chambers, and straw. For what man, in the natural state or course of thinking, did ever conceive it in his power to reduce the notions of all mankind exactly to the same length, and breadth, and height of his own? Yet this is the first humble and civil design of all innovators in the empire of reason.' Once more the hostility to innovation is evinced.

But Swift was not entirely alone. In *A Tale of a Tub* he introduces blanks and asterisks into his narrative, and upon one digression he notes that 'if the judicious Reader can assign a fitter [place], I do here empower him to remove it into any other Corner he pleases'. The inescapable analogy here is with the narratives of Laurence Sterne. In *The Life and Opinions of Tristram Shandy* it is asked, 'What has this book done more than the Legation of Moses, or the Tale of a Tub, that it may not swim down the gutter of Time along with them?' Sterne's novel does indeed swim down with *A Tale of a Tub* because it is part of the same stream of wit, which may be paraphrased as learned wit.

Sterne borrows from the *Memoirs of Martin Scriblerus*, too, and lifts whole passages from Burton's *Anatomy of Melancholy*. In his gift for wholesale adaptation and assimilation he is a truly English writer.

Tristram Shandy is part burlesque, part parody, part satire; it includes sermon and farce, treatise and biography; it is in turn learned and obscene, pathetic and pantomimic. Its principles are misalliance and extravagance, shot through with a whimsical indifference to the conventional modes of reading and of writing, or, as Sterne put it in a 'Rabelaisian Fragment', 'in which the reader will begin to form a Judgement, of what an Historical, Dramatical, Anecdotical, Allegorical, and Comical Kind of a Work, He has got hold of'. Sterne himself was consistently drawn to encyclopaedic works, among them Ephraim Chambers's *Cyclopaedia* and the early volumes both of *Biographia Britannica* and of *An Universal History, from the Earliest Account of Time*; they emphasise his aversion to theoretical speculation and his delight in accumulative and unsystematic learning. His was a knowledge of fragments, as in some decorative mosaic; like Browne or Burton he was a delighted hunter of trifles. When, in *Tristram Shandy*, he quoted at length a French treatise on inter-uterine baptism, in the original language, it was widely believed that he had invented the matter entire. To dispel any confusion, however, in the second edition of the novel he appended a footnote on his original source. He delighted in theft and plagiarism, incorporating everything within the interlaced texture of his narrative. As Nietzsche said, 'he was familiar with everything from the sublime to the rascally'; it was this breadth of vision which truly constituted his genius. One contemporary noted that it was 'one of the odd qualities of this very odd person, to join contradictions'.

He was born in Ireland, in 1713, of an English military family; at the age of ten he returned to England, where he was eventually accepted at Cambridge. He was a whimsical, melancholic, sentimental man plagued by ill health. It was quite natural, therefore, that he should enter holy orders and he retained various livings in Yorkshire for the rest of his life. At the age of forty-six he began *The Life and Opinions of Tristram Shandy*, which caused an immediate sensation. He awoke and found himself famous, and remained in that happy condition until his death from pleurisy in his fifty-fifth year.

A critic in the *Monthly Review* understood his native genius very well, and had no hesitation in naming Harlequin as the father of Tristram Shandy and the novel itself as the 'PANTOMIME OF

LITERATURE'. As Sterne's most recent biographer has noted, the book 'is constructed on just such a principle of moving rapidly from one idea to another, in shifting from the serious to the light-hearted, of exploiting the possibilities for bawdy in the most innocent of ideas',[5] the latter characteristic being perhaps the most suggestive of national traits. Sexual matters can only be addressed in innuendo and smut, as if the idea of sexual passion itself were humiliating and embarrassing in the extreme.

The contradictoriness, or the rapid changes of tone and perspective, is also a matter of authorial detachment; that detachment or diffidence is compounded in Sterne's case by what his biographer calls 'the difficulty of knowing exactly what one's feelings are'.[6] The lack of 'inwardness' in English writing has often been discussed; it may be ascribed to embarrassment or absence of passion, but it can also be associated with the love of surface and surface decoration which is so integral to English art. It is sometimes suggested that this absence of interior feeling leads to loss of profundity or seriousness, but we have already seen that the 'profound' can be manifested in disparate ways. It is certain, however, that it leads to self-effacement. *Tristram Shandy* itself has been said to have 'created a generic self-mockery' which 'ostentatiously outfaced the parody of self-cherishing modernism in Swift's *A Tale of a Tub*'.[7] Sterne captured an English trait, and gave it immortal shape; that is why Byron wrote of his own *Don Juan* that 'I mean it for a poetical T Shandy'.

Yet at the time *Tristram Shandy* was received 'evidently as a prose *Dunciad*',[8] as exemplified in Sterne's own comment that he was satirising 'the Weak part of the Sciences, in which the true point of Ridicule lies'. In that sense, of course, he was continuing an old tradition in the witty dismissal of pedantry and speculative thought. In the novel there are parodies of legal language, of theological argument, and of abstruse learning in general. 'He had never in his whole life the least light or spark of subtlety struck in his mind, by one single lecture upon *Crackenthorpe* or *Burgersdicius*, or any *Dutch* logician or commentator.' Sterne acquired his own learning through volumes of 'popularised' thought and through entries in the encyclopaedia; he was not a 'serious' thinker and could thus brilliantly redeploy the arguments advanced by others. Like Browne and Burton before him, his was a triumph of the synthetic rather than the analytic imagination. He was a magpie, rather than an eagle soaring into the empyrean.

It is entirely appropriate that out of this parodic, unsystematic medley of a book should emerge one of the greatest of all English characters in Uncle Toby. This old soldier, who received a wound in his groin at the siege of Namur, has what Sterne describes as 'a HOBBY-HORSE' in the science and practice of fortifications. With the help of his servant and ex-corporal, Trim, Uncle Toby builds a model of French battlefields with their batteries, ditches, siege engines and pallisades. He is, in himself, a model of the eccentric in English fiction, close to Commander Trunnion in *Peregrine Pickle* and Mr Wemmick with his Walworth fortifications in *Great Expectations*. Here are the martial virtues of the English, fortitude and practical engineering, in miniature; once more there is something both deeply comic and deeply reassuring about their transposition to a smaller scale. Uncle Toby is abashed in the presence of women, and only really himself in the company of his corporal, but somehow he becomes ensnared in the matrimonial plans of Widow Wadman. 'These attacks of Mrs Wadman, you will readily conceive to be of different kinds; varying from each other, like the attacks which history is full of, and from the same reasons.' Mrs Wadman desires to wound Uncle Toby's groin in another sense, and Sterne joins the line of English humorists who cannot resist the caricature of the voracious female. It is a part of the tradition. But Uncle Toby himself is a genuine and singular creation who combines common sense and eccentricity, embarrassed delicacy and assumed gruffness, conviviality and melancholy. As one historian of the English, Peter Vansittart, has remarked in this context, 'contradiction, muddle, inconsistency and humour proved as necessary to the social psyche as fortitude, forbearance, decency'.[9] Indeed they help to define it. But then on a larger scale, as Hazlitt put it, Uncle Toby remains 'one of the finest compliments ever paid to human nature' and of course to the English imagination itself.

Green England

Sketch of Miss Gertrude Jekyll with sunflower. Doodle by Sir Edwin Lutyens

CHAPTER 50

The secret garden

Most houses in England possess a small garden; it is part of their natural state or, even, of their national inheritance from the prehistoric inhabitants of England whose small plots of cultivated land 'may be considered the first gardens of Britain'[1] where henbane and the opium poppy flourished.

The reconstruction of medieval settlements reveals peasant cottages with small back-gardens as well as streets of thatched houses with strips of garden 'all with private space fenced from their neighbours'.[2] The small Elizabethan garden is of the same lineage, and the study of local court records reveals many cases of trespass upon a neighbouring garden; it becomes the very image of defensive privacy which is so congenial to the English mind. The earliest maps of London reveal a city of gardens, each one carefully delineated. It has been remarked of the 'small seventeenth-century garden', also, that it exhibited 'a sturdily independent glory'.[3] 'Capability' Brown, that epitome of native ingenuity and practicality, was employed to create landscapes 'of privacy and seclusion'.[4] The same pattern of enclosure is repeated on the large, as well as the small, scale. That is why the walled garden became the model of secrecy and enchantment; the English imagination can grow only in a confined space. In the words of one historian of gardening, Jane Brown, 'the little garden becomes the key to a world of wonders and delights, of fabulous riches and wealth'[5] glimpsed in the pages of children's literature no less than in the myths and legends of the English. Gardens are places of safety as well as of delight, of security and privacy as well as of pleasure. As one early gardener put it, 'A garden is a sort of sanctuary, a chamber roofed by heaven . . . a little pleasaunce of the soil, by whose wicket the world can be shut.' This defines a native mood. The reclusive and unremarked spot of soil guards the *genius loci*. It is an image of self-sufficiency, and it is perhaps significant that 'garden' – otherwise 'garth', 'yerd' or 'yard' – itself springs from a root-word suggesting enclosure and protection.

Another historian of the garden has remarked in this context that the medieval garden, with its alleys and hedges, 'reflected in no small measure the sense of security of a walled town'.[6] It has always been considered an aspect of national sensibility that 'an Englishman's home is his castle' but the truism can be applied to the adjacent property. Jane Brown has suggested that 'the British taste for gardening has a great deal to do with a warlike past'[7] and that 'so many garden terms come from the art of warfare'; thus we have trenches and pallisades, cordons and covered ways. These are the insular gardens of an island race, complete with defensive fortifications, walls and outer ditches. We do not need the example of Uncle Toby in *Tristram Shandy*, with the fortified towns of France laid out on his bowling green, or of Mr Wemmick in *Great Expectations* with the battlements of his Walworth garden. Kensington Gardens itself was designed to resemble 'the lines, angles, bastions, scarps and counter-scarps of regular fortifications'.[8] Many plants have been granted military names, such as 'Blue Ensign' and 'Old Bloody Warrior'; the ubiquitous allotments of England, where vegetables are grown, are preserved in 'miniature parade-ground proportions, everything in impeccable rows'.[9] Several forces are at work here. The love of the small scale, of the miniature, is aligned with the need for seclusion and for privacy; but this may become a fierce protectiveness, with the English love of warfare somehow domesticated or displaced. But is there not also a trace of irony, a suggestion of self-mockery, in this mimicry of battle conditions among the lawns and flowers?

In the late eighteenth century Gilbert White remarked that 'every decent labourer also has his garden', and the brick cottages of the early nineteenth century were built with plots 45 feet wide and 225 feet long. In the same period there emerged the 'villa garden' as well as the 'cottage garden', the harbingers of the ubiquitous suburban garden. In *News from Nowhere* William Morris celebrates a future state enjoying a 'delicate superabundance of small well-tended gardens' just as Thomas More, in *Utopia*, reports that the inhabitants of his idealised community 'attached the greatest importance to their gardens' with 'keen competition between streets as to which has the best kept garden'. It is also worth observing that More's dialogue is set within a well-kept garden. It is a charmed space of the English imagination.

In indirect homage to *Utopia* the 'garden city' movement was essentially English in inspiration and, under the tutelage of Ebenezer Howard, developed an ethos in which 'the small garden, now so exceedingly worthy and desirable as almost to be sacred, reaches its apotheosis'.[10] One commentator of 1913 remarked that 'however various our occupations and tastes, however conflicting our opinions, in the garden we are united'. The popularity of gardening itself was markedly increased by the development of the 'semi-detached' house, within whose relatively secluded bounds emerged the English 'happy medium'[11] of a small front-garden and a large back-garden. The suburban phenomenon has been described as evincing 'the native urge to return to the land',[12] further imbued with an atavistic remembrance of the Tudor cottage garden. The resurgence of interest in allotments may owe something to the 'green' movement, but it is also part of a larger awakening. Bede possessed a copy of Pliny's *Historiae Naturalis*.

There are other specific examples from this long tradition. The contemporary revival of herb gardening has its 'roots' in the *Laecboc* or 'Leechbook' of Bald, composed in the tenth century, and in the Old English translation of the *Herbarium Apuleii* where 132 different plants are described. One of the earliest gardening legends concerns St Maurilius who in the fourth century worked the garden of an English prince. The knights who came to murder Thomas Becket in the cathedral of Canterbury 'threw off their cloaks and gowns under a large sycamore tree in the garden'. And then there are the flowers. In the first century Pliny was unsure whether England had acquired the name of Albion 'from the white roses with which it abounds'. A fifteenth-century poem celebrates 'the white rose of England that is freshe and wol not fade'. A prose text of the early seventeenth century, entitled *Paradisus*, extols roses white and red as 'the most ancient and knowne Roses to our Countrey'. Ancient, too, are the tools of the trade. They have changed very little from the rakes and spades employed by Celtic settlers to the shovels and lattices of the seventeenth-century gardener. In medieval illuminations Cain and Abel are shown with spades, picks and hoes, digging and delving after the Fall; a misericord in Lincoln Cathedral has the carving of a gardener carrying an unmistakeable spade.

Gardening, then, is a national pursuit with truly native characteristics. Thus Jane Brown celebrates 'our national preference for homelike rather than princely gardens'[13] and notes the fact that wherever the English go 'they establish gardens and always gardens of the type they left in the old country'.[14] The world itself is sometimes understood in this context. John Winthrop recorded in his diary, before he set foot upon the soil of Massachussets, that 'there came a smell off the shore like the smell of a garden'. The Indians of that region named plantain 'Englishman's foot' as if the race had an inalienable link with horticulture. In that sense 'the English garden was a nationalist icon',[15] with its disinclination for magnificence and its almost homely presence. The English have eschewed 'the frigid grandeur of Versailles'[16] and have avoided 'any hint of Mediterranean drama or French extravagance'.[17] The country has produced enthusiastic amateurs rather than botanical theorists. Practical men and women, such as 'Capability' Brown, Joseph Paxton and Gertrude Jekyll, are the epitome of the English gardener. 'Capability' Brown was self-made, and rose from gardening boy to companion of princes and statesmen. Joseph Paxton modelled his celebrated design for the glass hall of the Great Exhibition from the glass-houses that he had constructed for the Duke of Devonshire's tender plants. Gertrude Jekyll trained to be an artist but fading eyesight sent her into the nurture of gardens, where she delighted in broad sweeps and banks of colour – particularly in the wild gardens which she rendered fashionable.

The garden displays all the fruits of the English imagination, including the passion for intricacy and the love of the miniature. So it will not be wonderful to learn that the gardens of England have been described as 'jewelled miniatures'.[18] One history of gardening has concluded that the cottage garden of many centuries 'has much in common with hand needlework, for there is always the individual touch and lack of regularity';[19] here is an interesting confluence of taste. Anglo-Saxon embroidery, renowned for its intricate variety, was also recognised for its pattern of interlace, a native tendency which may help to explain the 'knot gardens' of the sixteenth century so curiously varied and with so many 'enknotted' flowers 'that the place will seem like a piece of tapestry of many various colours to encrease every one's delight'. Various plants 'were interlaced so that they were seen to weave in and out of each other', and these gardens were copied in sweetmeats to produce the ' marzipan knot'.[20] It is also worth noting here that the 'knot garden' displayed 'abstract and geometric designs'[21] and may in that respect also claim Anglo-Saxon ancestry. The English affection for 'medley' and heterogeneity is also evident in the range of gardens which proffer intricacy and variety in an enclosed or intimate space. John Aubrey described an English garden as 'full of variety and unevenness'. *The Theory and Practice of Gardening*, published in 1712, declared that 'the greatest beauty of gardens consists in variety'. In *Humphry Clinker* a garden is described as 'exhibiting a wonderful assemblage of the most picturesque and striking objects, pavilions, lodges, groves, grottoes, lawns, temples and cascades'; to use a phrase of Pope's, all is 'harmoniously confus'd'. In Stourhead, Wiltshire, we may admire 'the eclecticism of the English landscape school: the classic style side by side with English cottage "Gothick" '.[22] It may also be remarked that many fine English gardens 'grew piecemeal'[23] by that process of organic accretion which has been noticed elsewhere in this study.

The curved or serpentine line has also been a feature of this enquiry, and in Coleridge's 'Kubla Khan' there is a vision of 'gardens bright with sinuous rills'. In *The Pursuit of Paradise* Jane Brown suggests that English landscape gardening was 'obsessed with the serpentine line', in a manner of which Hogarth would have approved; Horace Walpole remarked of William Kent's landscapes that 'the gentle stream was taught to serpentine at its leisure'. Capability Brown's 'curves and serpentines were smooth and suave'.[24] The Georgian landscape garden has been described as 'enshrining the spirit of England' with 'the avoidance of straight lines and their invariable replacement by the amorphous serpentine' in lawns and paths and lakes.[25] It suggests a distaste for regimentation and a love of 'English liberty – that liberty of which the new [eighteenth-century] gardens themselves were a sort of symbol'.[26] Horace Walpole considered the art of the garden to be 'totally new, original and undisputably English', a development which he associated with 'English political liberties'.[27] Across the Channel 'the compressing geometry and regularity of the French avenues and bosquets had held down the pressure till France exploded'.[28] In 1753 Francis Coventry, writing in *The World*, asks whether 'a modern gardener would consent to enter heaven if any path there is not serpentine';[29] thirteen years later, in Garrick and Colman's *The Clandestine Marriage* a character revels in the fact that 'here's none of your straight lines here – but all taste – zigzag – crinkum crankum – in and out – right and left – to and again – twisting and turning like a worm, my lord'.

The pursuit of gardening fosters a native individualism; it is pre-eminently a solitary pleasure. It has been well said that 'in England we have always preferred high hedges, which make for privacy'.[30] A French aristocrat of the early nineteenth century observed that 'the English detest being seen and will gladly forgo any prospect beyond their own limited boundaries'. That is why, in coffee-houses of the same period, there were wooden partitions between each 'box'. It has been remarked, too, that 'secret gardens gain much fascination as remnants of old Catholic England and Scotland, lingering in intangible ways',[31] as if the enclosed and scented air were imbued with time past.

The lawn and the gravel path are also ancient features, and gardening does in a real sense touch the *genius loci*; the gardener makes contact with the soil, which is the ground of our being and becoming.

The garden is also an exercise in utility and practicality; the earliest gardening books were 'essentially practical'[32] and gardening itself was 'purposeful'[33] in the cultivation of herbs and vegetables. We may also introduce the English philosophical tradition here, in the words of William Lawson's *A New Orchard and Garden* published in 1618. 'We must count that art the surest, that stands upon experimental rules gathered by the rule of reason', under the guidance of 'mere and sole experience'. The elements of English diffidence or embarrassment may also be deemed to be present, since gardening may encourage the displacement of passion and even of sexuality itself. In her study of gardening Jane Brown has commented upon the fact that gardens are 'constantly demanding sweated exertions and a tender touch' while at the same time 'constantly offering sensual arousal'.[34] The innocence of children is therefore often conceived in the setting of an English garden, most notably in the animals and birds of Beatrix Potter. With their tales for children A. A. Milne, James Barrie, Kenneth Grahame and Lewis Carroll also linger in English gardens as if they had escaped into a refuge or a sanctuary.

Travel has also been seen, in this study, as a form of escape. The English gardener may also be a traveller, and has ranged from Japan to Central America, from China to Australia, from Borneo to South Africa, in pursuit of new or rare species. The Michaelmas daisy comes from Virginia, the convolvulus from Barbary, the tulip from Turkey. The fact that they have now been thoroughly acclimatised, and treated as native plants, is further testimony to the assimilative power of the English genius. It may be that the language of flowers takes as its model the English language itself. At Fulham Palace, for example, there are 'more than a thousand tender exotics'[35] which like the importations into the language flourish in a mild and accommodating climate. Jane Brown's insight into botanical practice uncannily echoes most other commentaries upon the English imagination itself. 'All plants and ideas which came home,' she writes, 'became instantly English, transmogrified as if they had no native roots at all: conversely *le jardin anglais* was exported and mysteriously became the rage.'[36] No better or more significant example could be found for the essential unity of English cultural practice. In the gardens of the late seventeenth and early eighteenth centuries 'we modified the new French style . . . in accordance with our traditional custom we adapted them to our insular taste'.[37] The emphasis rests upon a pattern of immigration and adoption, succeeded by ever renewed diversity. The Elizabethan chronicler, William Harrison, remarked that 'strange herbs, plants and annual fruits are daily brought unto us from all parts of the world'. A more recent commentator, Miles Hadfield, has remarked in his *Gardening in Britain* that 'our island was rapidly and readily absorbing theory and practice, as well as material, in the form of plants, from overseas. Thus it came about that our gardens, which we like to think of as singularly British, are in fact the most cosmopolitan in the Old World.'[38] The appetite for variety, and diversity, is thus very strong. One history of English gardens has in fact claimed that 'there is no part of the earth's surface as small in area as these islands where such a diversity of plants can be grown'[39] – smallness, heterogeneity and temperate accommodation have also been the grace notes of the present study.

It is therefore natural that the literature of gardens, and the gardens of literature, should be harmoniously united. Some of the best English prose has been preserved in gardening books, where communion with the spirit of place releases a note of native lyricism. William Kent in turn declared that 'he caught his taste in gardening from reading the picturesque descriptions of Spenser'; yet Spenser derived his plant names from *The New Herbal or History of Plants* translated by Henry Lyte in 1578. The pre-eminence of translation, as an aspect of the English imagination, has already been outlined; it need only be noted that the first gardening book in English, *A Most Briefe and pleasant treatyse teachynge how to dress, sowe and set a Garden . . . by Thomas Hyll, Londyner* (1563) was a translation and compilation of classical or continental European sources.

The legend of the twelfth-century 'Rosamond's Bower', described by Addison as a sacred spot where 'Amaranths and Eglantines with intermingling sweets have wove the particolour'd gay Alcove', evokes the enchantment which the English garden has cast upon poetry and prose. 'Of Gardens' is one of Francis Bacon's longest essays, with its delighted litany of plants and perfumes in 'gardens for all the months in the year'. He extols the delights of the English lawn, too, since 'nothing is more pleasant to the eye than green grass kept finely shorn'. In this setting Pepys remarked that 'the green of our bowling alleys is better than any they have'. This native pride, asserted here against the French and the Italians, is complemented by an instruction in *The*

Solitary Gardener that 'A Bowling Green should be incompassed with Great Trees' to ensure privacy and seclusion. The sports and pastimes of the English – among them bowling itself as well as cricket and snooker – take place upon 'greens' where an intricate game is played in a confined space.

It is the *hortus inclusus* of Chaucer's poetry – 'A gardyn saw I ful of blosmy bowes' – and in *The Legend of Good Women* he extols the virtues of the simple daisy 'of alle floures flour'. Violets scent the poetry of Shakespeare, and it has been calculated that the dramatist dilates upon the fairness of roses in some sixty separate passages. It has been asked, of the Elizabethan poets, 'in what foreign literature can one gather such handfuls of flowers?'[40] – through the cowslips of *A Midsummer Night's Dream* to the 'daffadowndillies' of Spenser. There were so many garden publications in the seventeenth century that one might conclude that England itself was one large garden. Abraham Cowley's 'The Garden' celebrates the 'blessed shades' and 'gentle cool retreat' of a secluded place, and much of Marvell's poetry is of course set among the prospect of flowers and gardens:

> Annihilating all that's made
> To a green Thought in a green Shade

Thus the English imagination is forever green.

Looking backwards

Title page of William Byrd's 'Psalms, Sonnets and
Songs of Sadness and Piety', 1588

CHAPTER 51

Forging a language

The art of forgery did not fully flower and prosper until the eighteenth century. It has been associated, in particular, with the emergence of the relatively new phenomenon of professional authorship as well as with the contextual arrangements of trade publishing and commercial marketing. But the single most important alignment has gone largely unremarked. The most significant connection is to be found between forgery and the burgeoning movement known as 'romanticism'. The forged document and the 'romantic' personality are manifestations of the same change in taste. We might advert here to Boswell's *Life of Samuel Johnson*, in which the first 'romantic' hero emerges out of faked conversations and dramatically staged encounters.

But there are more suggestive parallels. It is not inappropriate that the two greatest literary forgers of the eighteenth century, James Macpherson or 'Ossian' and Thomas Chatterton or 'Rowley', have been said to herald or inspire the new romantic movement in letters; with their transcription of a respectively Celtic and medieval past, they created that enchanted landscape which became a dominant influence upon the romantic poets.

James Macpherson was a Scottish poet and teacher who in 1758, at the age of twenty-two, published a long poem entitled *The Highlander* in part as a response to the intense interest in Celtic literature and mythology. That burgeoning movement of taste has been denominated 'the Celtic Revival' and can be taken to include Thomas Gray's ode upon the 'Bard', Mason's *Caractacus* and Evans's *Specimens of the Poetry of the Ancient Welsh Bards*. It has been estimated that in the forty years from 1760 one volume was published each year upon Celtic myth. It is also the context in which James Macpherson perpetrated his forgeries. He was a Jacobite with a profound instinct, and love, for his native culture. It took only the enthusiasm of another literary nationalist, John Home, to unleash his powers of historical imagination and creative reinvention. His first faked production was 'The Death of Oscar', which he claimed to be a translation from the manuscript of a Gaelic original in his possession; it was immediately recognised as a work of primitive genius. A year later Macpherson was able to publish *Fragments of Ancient Poetry*, the preponderance of which were also his own inventions. The appetite for Celtic folklore and verse already existed; it was only natural that it should be fulfilled. Two years later, therefore, Macpherson brought to light six books of *Fingal, An Ancient Epic Poem* composed by a bard named 'Ossian' in the more remote stretches of Scottish history. A specimen of Ossian reads, 'Our youth is like the dream of the hunter on the hill of the heath. . . . Her steps were the music of songs. He was the stolen sigh of her soul. . . . The horn of Fingal was heard; the sons of woody Albion returned.' Such plangent writing exerted an immediate and powerful effect, and Ossian was extensively quoted by Goethe in *The Sorrows of Young Werther*. A cult sprang up closer to home, too, and various eminent literary tourists explored Ossian's territory. Thomas Pennant discovered various Ossianic landmarks in the Scottish landscape, and the guide for Sir Joseph Banks on the island of Staffa pointed out 'the cave of *Fiuhn*' or '*Fiuhn Mac Coul*, whom the translator of Ossian's works has called *Fingal*'. Oyster shells were dated with reference to the Ossianic fragments. So the forged poetry of Macpherson engendered caves and rocks and crustacea. Pennant wrote also of the local songs, which 'vocal traditions state are the foundation of the works of *Ossian*'. A skilful faker had created a living communal tradition. It is testimony to the credulity of scholars and general readers alike, but it is also tribute to the creative power of Macpherson's imagination. His forged words forged – in another sense – a new reality.

In his 'Essay, Supplementary to the Preface' of *Lyrical Ballads* Wordsworth records that 'Having had the good fortune to be born and reared in a mountainous country, from my very childhood I have felt the falsehood that pervades the volumes imposed upon the world under the name of Ossian. From what I saw with my own eyes, I knew that the imagery was spurious' and from the lips of a 'Phantom . . . begotten by the snug embrace of an impudent Highlander upon a cloud of tradition'. At some point after his childhood, however, Wordsworth seems to have changed his opinion. The first lines of his poem entitled 'Glen-Almain; Or, The Narrow Glen' reflect that:

> In this still place, remote from men,
> Sleeps Ossian, in the NARROW GLEN;

The poem ends thus:

And, therefore, was it rightly said
That Ossian, last of all his race!
Lies buried in the lonely place

There is some ambiguity within the poem itself whether 'Fancy' creates the presence of death, but Wordsworth's overall ambivalence or confusion about Ossian reflects the general romantic sensibility. James Macpherson created a wild and sublime landscape of vision, from which emerged an ancient bard instilled with all the primitive simplicity of passion; here were romantic archetypes indeed. But if they were all faked or forged, what then? Could the products of the romantic sensibility themselves be fraudulent? Or, to put it in another manner, that which seems most genuine may be the most artificial.

In the same decade as James Macpherson was forging 'fragments of ancient poetry . . . translated from the Gaelic or Erse Language', Thomas Gray was in fact compiling his own authentic translations from Norse and Welsh poetry to add to his *Poems* of 1768; under these circumstances it is hardly surprising that Gray enthusiastically accepted the work of Ossian as that of a true original. Thus he joined William Blake and Johann Wolfgang Goethe in celebration of a notorious hoax which at the time satisfied the taste for the visionary sublime. The other most influential lyric poet of the period, William Collins, composed an 'Ode on the Popular Superstitions of the Highlands' ten years before Ossian himself furnished precisely those superstitions to an admiring public. As Samuel Johnson wrote of Collins, 'the grandeur of wildness, and the novelty of extravagance, were always desired by him'; but of course they were also desired by the two generations of romantic poets who professed their own debt to Gray and to Collins, to 'Ossian' and to Chatterton's Rowley. If forgery or fakery seem endemic to the whole enterprise, we will find it also in Collins whose 'Persian Eclogue' is composed in the 'pretence that he was translating from the Persian'.[1] His 'Song from Cymbelyne' has also been described by his editor as a 'skilful pastiche'.[2] In the same context Horace Walpole, the quondam friend and admirer of Thomas Gray, published his novel *The Castle of Otranto* as a relic of the sixteenth century some four years before the youthful Chatterton tentatively began his own forgeries.

It ought to be recalled that in the early years of the eighteenth century forgery could be celebrated as a form of masquerade or carnival, part of the endless shifting game of identities. It was nothing against the work of Defoe or Swift that they faked the character of the 'authors' of

Robinson Crusoe or *Gulliver's Travels*; in that ostensibly more stable and assured world, the notion of identity was neither precarious nor ambiguous. Daniel Defoe can plausibly and happily become 'Robinson Crusoe' in 1714 and 'Moll Flanders' in 1722; in the last decades of the century the subterfuge involved in such impersonations would become a matter for camouflage or indignant denial.

The latter half of the eighteenth century, however, the seed-bed from which the romantic movement emerged into the full light of the English imagination, has been well described as 'An Age of Forgery'.[3] The crime of forgery itself reached its apogee in the period 1750–80 but of more significance, in a literary context, was the passing of a Copyright Act in 1709 which confirmed the individual ownership of words as 'intellectual property'. Since the notion of individual ownership led in turn to the development of the literary personality and to the affirmation of the romantic selfhood, this act of legislation had aesthetic as well as economic consequences. It is often supposed that part of the 'irritability' of the romantic genius sprang from its immersion in the literary market-place, and its prostitution in commercial trading, but this disquiet can be traced back to the recognition of individual 'property' itself. It has been suggested by Paul Baines, an astute historian of forgery, that the new monetarism of the eighteenth century 'threatened basic ideas of value, and the security of human exchanges and interactions'.[4] Did not this new legislative sense of the individual, owning certain words and sets of words as private property, in turn threaten the old and more established ideas of selfhood as residing in a commonality of expression and perception? If the romantic self was first deemed to be a legal and financial unit, its origin might provoke deep unease and ambiguity in those who professed it. We will notice this in subsequent pages. If one anonymous discourse of the period can refer to 'that chimerical ill-founded Medium, Paper Money', then perhaps the individuality written upon paper might also possess a 'fluctuating, abstract and possibly evanescent value'.[5] As one historian has put it, 'Once property was seen to have a symbolic value, expressed in coin or credit, the foundations of personality themselves appeared imaginary or at best consensual: the individual could exist, even in his own sight, only at the fluctuating value imposed upon him by his fellows.'[6] It is interesting to observe in this light the assertion of personality in Wordsworth's poetry, which emerges only to be assailed by doubt and anxiety as to its true nature. If there did indeed run 'the need for a perfect, unassailable touchstone of human identity against which all falsifications could be measured',[7] the romantic 'I' offered only a tentative solution. If words as well as property have only 'a symbolic value' expressed in the 'coin or credit' which they obtain for their owner, then they too possess only a 'fluctuating value' dependent upon the manner in which they are recognised or received as the true coin of feeling or imagination.

Yet of course the rise of the 'individual author' long predates the work of Wordsworth and his contemporaries. Both Langland and Chaucer deliberately introduce themselves into their own narratives. The notion of individual authorship at this later time, however, extended beyond textual matters. It was also implicated in the relatively original notion of originality exemplified by Edward Young's *Conjectures on Original Composition* (1759), published two years after Edmund Burke's *A Philosophical Enquiry into the Sublime and the Beautiful* to which it remains a natural and faithful companion. As one study of poetics has put it, the concern for sublimity of expression, that artistry beyond the familiar reach of art, 'played no small part in the drift towards subjectivism . . . and ultimately in the rise of romanticism in poetry'.[8] The obscure and the dark, the aweful and the mysterious, became legitimised by Burke's enquiry in ways which he would have neither anticipated nor approved. They had a particular bearing, for example, upon Young's affirmation of 'original' composition. 'Our spirits rouze at an *Original*; that is a perfect stranger, and all throng to learn what news from a foreign land. . . . All eminence, and distinction, lies out of the beaten road.' In a similar spirit he enjoins the writer, 'Thyself so reverence as to prefer the native growth of thy own mind to the richest import from abroad.' Young's own interest is clearly aligned with the material and financial imperatives of his culture, with the encomium upon the original writer whose words 'will stand distinguished; his the sole Property of them; which Property alone can confer the noble title of an Author'. But his sentiments are no less clearly related to the burgeoning romantic movement in which spontaneity and originality are to be preferred over laboured imitation. The nature and nurture of Thomas Chatterton may be invoked here.

Some three years before Wordsworth composed his encomium upon Ossian he completed a poem, 'Resolution and Independence', which paid tribute to that paradigm of the romantic movement:

> I thought of Chatterton, the marvellous Boy,
> The sleepless Soul that perish'd in his pride

Thomas Chatterton was the most celebrated faker of the eighteenth century, and he shares with James Macpherson the palm also of being the most successful. Chatterton was born, in Bristol, in the winter of 1752; his father, an antiquarian and a collector of old trifles, died before his son was born. That death had a crucial effect upon Chatterton, since all his life he was searching for his patrimony. It would be easy to say that he had inherited his father's antiquarian passion, or that he identified antiquarianism with the invisible presence of his father. More significantly, however, he considered the past itself to be his true father. He learnt to read from sundry old folios scattered in his little house in Pyle Street, opposite the church of St Mary Redcliffe; his passion for antiquity was such that, even before he left his charity school, he had started to compose 'medieval' poetry. He may have been partly inspired by Percy's *Reliques of Ancient English Poetry*, published when Chatterton had reached the age of thirteen; it is ironic, too, that upon closer examination certain of Percy's own ballads were shown to be less than the genuine article. But the essential truth is that Chatterton was inspired and animated by the past; he devoured texts like a library cormorant and, when not reading or writing, devised genealogies and created heraldic emblems. He invented a fifteenth-century monk, Thomas Rowley, who had resided in St Mary Redcliffe and had written much poetry duly transcribed by the young Chatterton. On being challenged about the provenance of 'Rowley's' poems, Chatterton confessed that he had found them in an old chest within the muniment room of the church; he even managed to produce some stained antique documents to prove his assertions. His case was so plausible that, well into the nineteenth century, there were many who believed that no boy could have fashioned such masterpieces of an early date. But create them he did; the language of the past spoke through him, as it were, and his was a genius of assimilation and adaptation.

At the age of seventeen Chatterton travelled to London in order to find his fortune; he was noticeably successful, composing essays and satirical poetry on contemporary themes. Five months later, however, he was found dead in a Holborn attic with traces of arsenic poisoning in his teeth. It was necessary and inevitable that his death was deemed to be suicide, a last gesture to society from a doomed poet; more recent commentators have suggested that it was a botched effort to cure a bout of syphilis.

His apparent suicide added immeasurably to his stature, however, while his celebrity was maintained by the revelation that the 'Rowley' poetry was an imposture. There were pamphlets, essays and tracts issued by various interested parties. Almost immediately after his death he had been considered to be akin only to Shakespeare in his prolificity; Horace Walpole had commended him as a 'masterly genius' and Joseph Warton had described him as 'a prodigy of genius'. In 1780, ten years after his death, an epistolary novel on his life was published under the title of *Love and Madness*; in the following year Jacob Bryant's *Observations Upon the Poems of Thomas Rowley: in which the Authenticity of those Poems is Ascertained* were published in two volumes. Six hundred pages of scholarship and testimony led ineluctably to the conclusion that the poems were 'written too much from the heart to be a forgery'. That conclusion may still stand, if we deem the heart to be a capacious organ which includes inspiration, invention and historical memory. Chatterton composed as many fine lines of medieval poetry as came out of the medieval period itself; the language instinctively propelled him to this restoration, whereby ancient words and images float naturally if unexpectedly to the surface of consciousness.

His career as a forger, whose work was eventually compared with a 'forged note' presented to a banker, would certainly not be evident from the tributes lavished upon him by his romantic successors. Coleridge revised his poem, 'Monody on the Death of Chatterton', until his own surcease; he first began writing it at the age of thirteen, and the final text was not published until the year of his death. It began in Pindarics and ended in pentameters, all the while chanting in borrowed metres the fate of 'that heaven-born Genius'. Coleridge compared himself explicitly to the young poet, dead in a garret at the age of eighteen; apparently unwanted and unhonoured, Coleridge laments his 'kindred woes'. In his agonies he is possessed by 'the Ghosts of Otway and Chatterton' (Otway another penurious and unsuccessful writer) as if to confirm his own sense of doomed genius. Yet can 'Genius' subsist in forgery?

In his poem upon the death of Keats, *Adonais*, Shelley paid stately tribute to the 'solemn agony' of Chatterton; he is one of the 'inheritors of unfulfilled renown' who, in the unstated argument of the poem, will reach fruition by means of Shelley's productive genius. At a later date a memorial of Shelley was sculpted by Onslow Ford in the manner of Henry Wallis's *The Death of Chatterton*. Whatever the circumstances of Chatterton's compositions, that picturesque or theatrical pose survives as a token of romantic poetry itself. That is why Keats evinced the most effusive reaction to Chatterton's unhappy fate. He composed a sonnet in 1815, 'To Chatterton', and lamented the 'Dear child of sorrow – son of misery!' whose 'Genius mildly flash'd'. Three years later he inscribed *Endymion* 'to the memory of Thomas Chatterton' but, more significantly, in a letter of the following year he remarked that 'the purest english I think – or what ought to be the purest – is Chatterton's . . . Chatterton's language is entirely northern' and free from 'Chaucer's gallicisms'. He went on to declare that 'I prefer the native music of it to Milton's cut by feet.' Keats was acquainted with the controversy surrounding Chatterton's 'medieval' poetry, but he considered it to be of little consequence beside the dead poet's adoption and assimilation of a 'native' or 'northern' dialect – by which he means, in the context of Chaucer and Milton, an Anglo-Saxon cadence and vocabulary. In a letter of the same period he remarks that he has given up *Hyperion* because 'there were too many Miltonic inversions in it', but in the same paragraph he avers that Chatterton 'is the purest writer in the English Language . . . 'tis genuine English Idiom in English words'. His abandonment of *Hyperion* suggests that he understood the dangers of imitation or plagiarism, but then how are we to estimate his praise of Chatterton's forged verses as 'genuine English Idiom'? Here lie mysteries which may or may not be resolved. It may be worth noting in this context that the poem in which Wordsworth celebrated the memory of Chatterton, 'Resolution and Independence', is written in the same metre as Chatterton's fake medieval poem 'An Excelente Balade of Charitie'. Wordsworth also owned a portrait of the dead poet, which was itself a forgery.

The posthumous comparison of Chatterton with Shakespeare does suggest what all the evidence implies – the 687 pages of his extant poetry and prose, in the 'Oxford' edition of his works, is astonishing evidence of his precocity but it also bears testimony to the fact that he was a thoroughly English poet. If it were otherwise, his fame and fate would not be so congenial to the English imagination. There is, for example, the salient matter of Chatterton's reverence for the past. The influence of Percy's *Reliques* upon the young poet's burgeoning poetic imagination has already been suggested, but the antiquated diction and metre of Percy's specimens may have been less important than Percy's belief that there existed 'a peculiarly English characteristic of cultural history and national identity that derived from the Ancient Goths . . . the English minstrels were the inheritors of a national poetry'.[9] In this same spirit Chatterton declared in a letter to Horace Walpole, alas unsent, that 'However Barbarous the Saxons may be calld by our Modern Virtuosos; it is certain we are indebted to Alfred and other Saxon Kings for the wisest of our Laws and in part for the British Constitution'. He evinces all the antiquarianism of the English imagination, therefore, but out of it he fashioned works of genius; he wanted to re-create, rather than rescue, past time. Like Edmund Spenser he invented a language with which to restore the proximity as well as the mystery of the past. Or can we say that the language invented him?

He dwelled in another life. There were many antiquarians willing to forge material objects and produce medieval coins, rings or chamber-pots; but Chatterton spent the money, wore the ring, and shat into the pot. He restored the past, too, because he believed in its authority and efficacy. By the age of sixteen he had composed a long poem entitled 'Bristowe Tragedie or the Dethe of Syr Charles Bawdin', to which he appended a note claiming 'the following little Poem wrote by Thomas Rowlie Priest, I shall insert the whole as a Specimen of the Poetry of those Days, being greatly superior to what we have been taught to believe'. It is indeed a vigorous ballad:

> How oft ynne battaile have I stoode
>   When thousands dy'd arounde;
> Whan smokynge streemes of crimson bloode
>   Imbrew'd the fatten'd grounde;
>
> How dydd I knowe thatt ev'ry darte
>   Thatt cutte the airie waie
> Myghte notte fynde passage toe my harte
>   And close myne eyes for aie

Such diction materially affected the work of both Coleridge and Keats, to name only the two most celebrated examples. Only the foolish would dismiss it as pastiche. It is a genuinely new creation and, if genius may be defined as one who changes the nature of expression, then Chatterton has some claim to that honorific.

The question of plagiarism, however, presents itself. Chatterton was, in the native idiom, essentially a bookish writer who borrowed from a score of other English writers, most notably from Spenser, Pope, Dryden, Gay, Churchill and Collins. On occasions he seems to parody his own literary learning by indulging in exaggerated diction and over-elaborated tropes but, as one critic has maintained, 'there was a consistent dynamic of plagiarism working beneath the veneer of forgery'.[10] In one sense Chatterton was only doing that which all good English poets had previously done; he was stealing or lifting from great originals the material for his own verse. He cultivated a polyphonic personality. But as he was a great originator of the romantic myth, if not of the romantic sensibility, the accusation of plagiarism became a peculiarly sensitive one. We may discover, for example, how Coleridge and Keats themselves became preoccupied with just that charge.

There are other aspects of Chatterton's antiquarianism which are inevitably associated with the course of the English imagination. It has been noted that in 'poetry, prose and letters Chatterton makes use of the legends of Arthur, or the "Matter of Britain"'[11] so that in the process English history might then become 'both mythical and real'.[12] It is interesting in this context, therefore, that there are 'startling similarities between the respective canonisations of Chatterton and King Arthur'.[13] Both exist on the interstices of the invented and the authentic, and both embody the essential ebullition or presentness of the past. The assumption may be that, like Arthur who is not dead and will return, Chatterton lives on in the work of successive poets and novelists.

Of course the 'Rowley' poems are themselves set in the medieval rather than the Arthurian period, and provide a curious parallel with the 'Gothic' revival of the nineteenth century. There was a 'Gothick' style of the eighteenth century, but that was the work of connoisseurs and virtuosi. The medieval work of Chatterton was much more vigorous and invigorating, anticipating the strong and powerful Gothic of the Victorians. He believed in the presence of the past in part because it was the means of defining his own genius. This, again, is an abiding English preoccupation. The analogy with the master of early nineteenth-century Gothic, A. W. N. Pugin, is inescapable; it has been said that Pugin's 'knowledge of real medieval work was so profound that he could instinctively produce new designs . . . in a vivid Gothic detail, full of richness and variety'.[14]

Pugin is the true child of Chatterton in more than one sense. The young poet had written that 'the Motive that actuates me to do this, is, to convince the world that the Monks (of whom some have so despicable an Opinion) were not such Blockheads, as generally thought and that good Poetry might be wrote, in the days of Superstition as well as in these more inlightened Ages'. The letter, of 15 February 1769, was written in the same month as he composed a medieval eulogy on the churches of Bristol. It is as if the old religion were still very much in his head, as it was in that of Pugin. Chatterton's own recourse to 'Superstition' and to the supernatural in his poetry suggests that he had little respect for the 'inlightened' learning of his own time. His principal character is a Catholic monk and bard, and one critic has noted 'the religious atmosphere of Rowley's world'.[15] It allowed Chatterton to re-create in native fashion a world of visions and dreams, drawing material from the past in order to sustain his sense of the sacred; the antiquarians were the visionaries of the eighteenth century. It is appropriate that he should have appeared in vision to the nineteenth-century poet Francis Thompson, and dissuaded him from self-murder. 'I recognised him from the pictures of him,' Thompson said later. 'Besides I knew that it was he before I saw him.' Chatterton attained a kind of psychic or psychological reality, as a token of all that the eighteenth century had lost or abandoned; he was the wraith of faith.

It is not surprising, therefore, that Chatterton had a very powerful sense of place and of the *genius loci*. Certain spots were still holy. A posthumous account reveals how he stared at the church of St Mary Redcliffe, memorial of an earlier age, and said, 'This steeple was once burnt by lightning; this was the place where they formerly acted plays'; theatricality and supernatural visitation are in his imagination twinned. This intuitive sense of territory has been one of the objects of study in this volume, and the sole matter of the 'Rowley' poems is the city of Bristol itself – the medieval city, at least, which rises like a vision all around him. It is part of his patrimony. His father had once been singing-master in St Mary Redcliffe; Chatterton had never seen him, but in entering the old church he was also entering the house of his father. The establishment which Chatterton had attended as a boy, Colston's School, was erected on the site of an old Carmelite convent. So all the forces of his own past, and those of his territory, are aligned. This is the source of his historical mission. To restore a lost past and, at the same time, to restore a lost selfhood – here, once more, we may see how he impinged upon the romantic movement to which he bequeathed so much.

If we now draw the outlines of Chatterton and Macpherson together and see them as a compound figure, we glimpse the sublime and the fantastical mixed; the ancient and medieval landscapes of their imagination haunt their successors. Macpherson created 'Ossian', the inspired bard who sang of his own especial soil in tones of plangency and woe; Chatterton embodied the 'marvellous Boy' whose apparent suicide provoked contemplations of a solitary genius despised and neglected by contemporaneous society. These two poets, more than any others, created the romantic image. But it was of crucial significance to their literary successors that it should be deeply imbued with forgery and fakery, pastiche and plagiarism.

It might even be said that the recognition or detection of plagiarism and pastiche, in particular, began with the romantic movement itself. In previous centuries, as Walter Ong noted in his *The Art of Logic*, 'no one hesitated to use lines of thought or even quite specific wordings from another person without crediting the other person, for these were all taken to be – and most often were – part of a common tradition'. But when that tradition was broken or discontinued in the rise of the private and personal voice, then apparent originality of expression became of paramount importance. As a result, as if they were intense shadows created by a sudden light, the dangers of plagiarism and pastiche became evident in the first generation of the romantic movement. In one prefatory epistle Milton wrote: 'I have striven to cram my pages even to overflowing, with quotations drawn from all parts of the Bible and to leave as little space as possible for my own words.'[16] Wordsworth or Coleridge could never admit so much even if, in Coleridge's case, a similar confession might have been appropriate. The introduction to an important volume of essays upon English romanticism, *Romanticism and Language*, poses an interesting question: 'Is it pure coincidence, for example, that several of the essays [here] fix on the metaphor of theft?'[17] Romanticism and plagiarism occupy the same area of the English imagination.

CHAPTER 52

The romantic fallacy

English romanticism has no readily identifiable provenance. It has, of course, been traced back to the ancient sources of the native imagination. In particular the melancholy of the anonymous Anglo-Saxon poets may have been transmitted by indirect means to the poets of the late eighteenth and early nineteenth centuries. Certainly the interest in an ancient national poetry, in England no less than in Germany or Russia, was deemed to be at the expense of the classical tradition derived from Greece and Rome. Hence the division between the classic and the romantic. The romantics, unlike such predecessors as Pope and Dryden, were believed to be returning to some native source of eloquence. There are cultural historians who will then wish to establish their connection with the national Church which emerged after the Reformation. It is argued that the doctrinal emphasis upon individual conscience and private moral duty materially influenced the development of the romantic 'I'; Wordsworth is then the direct heir of those religious enthusiasts who were moved by the 'inner spirit'. The romantic movement in Catholic Europe took on a very different aspect. It became elaborate and symbolic, clothed in allegory and invaded by intimations of strange sins; it became, in other words, intensely Catholic. The image of Wordsworth striding across the rocks and vales of the Lake District is quite another thing. He epitomises that strain of moral earnestness, of right thinking and right feeling, avoid which characterises the Dissenting Protestant tradition.

If we look for earlier and perhaps less orthodox intimations of the romantic sensibility, however, we are sure to find them. The plight of the solitary poet, whose genius is akin to madness, can be witnessed in the unhappy experience of John Clare, Christopher Smart and William Cowper whose respective lunacies offer a disquieting footnote to the literary history of the eighteenth century. The cult of sentiment, the passion for antiquity, the attention to 'Gothick' and supernatural effects, the vogue for the ballad – all have their origins in that century, even if they found their apotheosis in the works of Wordsworth and his successors. The fixed production of generic verse upon classical models was replaced by an organic process of human transference and sympathy; poetic diction itself became 'less precise, more generally suggestive'.[1]

The retreat from statement and sententiousness, and the eighteenth-century movement towards a romantic sensibility, were marked by the fashion for sentimental feeling as exemplified by such novels as Henry Mackenzie's *The Man of Feeling*; sensitive sentimentality became known as 'the English malady'. The man of feeling dies because he is too good for this cruel world, and Mackenzie's novel was published just a year after the death of Chatterton. The harsh laughter of Congreve and Wycherley is replaced by the gentler amusement of Sheridan and Goldsmith.

Yet the lineaments of the romantic image were most decisively executed in the nineteenth century. The artist is then one surrounded by invisible powers, which by an act of rapt attention may be transformed into a permanent image or symbol. The poet is one set apart, the conscience and unacknowledged law-maker of human society who as a consequence of his solitariness is doomed to be misinterpreted and mistreated; he does not endure the world but re-creates it in the act of imagination, and must place his own sensibility at the heart of this enterprise because there is no other sure foundation of knowledge. The romantic poet is a lamp rather than a mirror, to use a celebrated antithesis, the source of illumination within his or her own breast. If this entails the re-creation of the self as well as of the world, then the divine afflatus of the bard may also be a mode of private transformation. A human being may be transfigured by god-like powers of the imagination. 'A Man's life of any worth is a continual allegory', Keats wrote. 'Shakespeare led a life of Allegory; his works are the comments on it.'

We may lower the temperature a little by recalling Coleridge's comment upon the acting of Edmund Kean; watching him upon the stage, he remarked, was 'like reading Shakespeare by flashes of lightning'. It is of some interest in this context that the romantic image, or at least the image of the romantic hero, was largely embodied in actors and in paintings of actors. They, rather than the poets themselves, seemed to fulfil the prerequisites of the part. Kemble as Coriolanus and as Hamlet, painted by Thomas Lawrence respectively in 1798 and 1801, set the mood and tone with 'these heroic figures, dark cloaked against murky skies' exhibiting 'Hamlet's introversion' and 'Coriolanus's humiliated pride'.[2] The connection of the romantic poets with the theatre is not confined to portraiture alone. All of them wrote verse dramas, and most of them speculated upon the nature of theatrical passion and dramatic performance. They associated their art with the techniques of impersonation. Coleridge may be said to set the scene of the dramatic action with his remark upon Shakespeare that 'he had only to imitate certain parts of his character, or exaggerate such as existed in possibility, and they were at once true to nature, and fragments of the divine mind that drew them'. In this passage the notion of imitation, and of exaggeration, is indistinguishable from that of creation.

The renown of actors such as Kean and Kemble, Macready and Mrs Siddons, was such that the nature of dramatic poetry itself was seen in the context of their art. Charles Lamb wrote even of a relatively minor actor, Robert Bensley, that he 'had most of the swell of soul, was greatest in the delivery of heroic conceptions, the emotions consequent upon the presentment of a great idea to the fancy. He had the true poetical enthusiasm.' Yet the terms of approbation are precisely those which were awarded to the poets themselves, so that there seems to be no difference at all between the poetic and theatrical 'delivery' of feeling. That may perhaps be sufficient cause for the ready identification of Shelley and Coleridge with the character of Hamlet, as if somehow their finest or most fugitive feelings were most nobly expressed by a dramatic persona. Coleridge described Hamlet as 'for ever occupied with the world within him, and abstracted from external things; his words give a substance to shadows: and he is dissatisfied with commonplace realities'. This might be a definition of Coleridge himself. Poetry itself is then fully explicated in the processes of the theatrical imagination. What is real, and what is feigned? As Coleridge puts it in *Table Talk*: 'I have a smack of Hamlet myself, if I may say so.'

If we turn from the part to the actor, then there is evidence of further confusion or conflation. Hazlitt comprehended the performance of Kemble as '*intensity*'; he was able to seize upon one feeling or one idea, 'working it up, with a certain graceful consistency, and conscious grandeur of conception, to a very high degree of pathos or sublimity'. Kemble 'had all the regularity of art' and lent 'the deepest and most permanent interest to the uninterrupted progress of individual feeling'. A casual reader might be forgiven for believing that Hazlitt was describing the imaginative procedures of the poet rather than the stage life of the actor. It is so common an identification in the period that it often passes without comment, but it is suggestive none the less. When Keats celebrates the 'sensual grandeur' which Kean brings to the 'spiritual passion' of Shakespeare's verse, he might have been describing his own practice; the poet then confirms and elaborates upon his point with the suggestion that 'Kean delivers himself up to the instant feeling, without a shadow of thought about anything else. He feels his being as deeply as Wordsworth. . . . We will say no more.' Enough has been said, however, to provoke the student of Wordsworth or of Keats himself into speculations about the theatrical management of passion.

The language of dramatic criticism was similarly of a piece with the language of literary criticism. Kean, as Iago, was praised for 'the ease, familiarity and tone of nature' of his delivery; as Timon of Athens he was criticised for want of 'sufficient variety and flexibility of passion'. The same vocabulary, and the same sentiments, were applied to the latest poetical productions of the period. Romantic acting, and romantic poetry, were considered to be equivalent. It throws curious light, too, upon Keats's conception of 'the poetical character' which 'is not itself – it has no self – it is everything and nothing . . . the camileon poet'; to which definition he adds: 'A poet is the most unpoetical of anything in existence, because he has no identity; he is continually . . . filling, some other body.' This might stand as a definition of the actor, too, as if the poet and performer shared the same identity – or, rather, shared the same absence of identity.

The equivalence may help to account for the modern critical assumption that in the romantic poetry of the early nineteenth century, particularly in that of Wordsworth, there exists 'artifice behind the postulate of nature'.[3] Just as an entire dramatic system lies behind the apparently unpremeditated art of Kean or Mrs Siddons, so dwell 'tradition, convention and genre behind the appearance of romantic spontaneity'.[4]

The claims of the romantic poets, however, were grand indeed. In his *Defence of Poetry* Shelley celebrated poets as themselves 'the happiest, the best, the wisest, and the most illustrious of men . . . men of the most spotless virtue, of the most consummate prudence'. It is not clear, however, if these remarks were made in the spirit of deepest irony. Wordsworth considered the poet to be a man 'endowed with a more lively sensibility, more enthusiasm and tenderness . . . a more comprehensive soul', so that 'the Poet binds together by passion and knowledge the vast empire of human society'. The natural virtues of the poet are here asserted in the spirit of what Keats called 'the Wordsworthian, or egotistical sublime', but the full ramifications of that phrase have not been properly understood. What, precisely, is egotism in the sphere of the imagination?

The term itself implies some weakness or insufficiency beneath apparent strength. It implies a trust in a deep and powerful subjectivity, but one which is also obsessive and defensive. Johnson defines an egotist as 'a talker of himself', and in his *Lectures* on Shakespeare Coleridge called egotism 'intense selfishness'. As one critic has remarked of the romantic poet in general, 'he is thrown back on himself, his status and nature'. In the case of Wordsworth, 'his chief preoccupation is with the question of the poet's function, his role, his power, his obligations'.[5] In turn the pose, or poses, which Byron adopted were 'a logical continuation of the Wordsworthian preoccupation with role'.[6] We revert inevitably to the vocabulary and manner of the stage.

In the largest sense romantic literature is the literature of personality, in which the writer imposes upon an unchanging landscape or a passing scene the contours of his or her own preoccupations; the world becomes an echo-chamber of the solitary voice. But this also may lead to a form of imposture, as if the romantic poet were indeed an actor trying to project to the 'gods' as well as the 'pit'. We have noticed how fragile the romantic image may become, touched with intimations of forgery and plagiarism as well as theatricality, but there is a subtler frailty. The cult of the 'egotistical sublime' – or, in a philosophical context, individualism – effectively destroyed, in the words of one eighteenth-century cultural historian, 'the organic metaphysics of earlier centuries and the archaic belief in the unity and wholeness of experience'.[7] It promulgated instead the instincts or doctrines 'of a solitary, increasingly alienated individual'.[8] Just as the Reformation severed the national Church from the consensus of a thousand years, so its natural child of romanticism abrogated the alliance between the artist and the larger settled community. That is why it has been argued that the 'central truth of romanticism is not joy and fulness of being but what Hegel . . . called "the unhappy consciousness . . . the consciousness of self as a divided nature, a doubled and merely contradictory being"'[9] relying upon the artificiality of language and its constructs to exemplify its dubious status. It is not irrelevant that Robert Browning parodied romantic sentiment through the voice of 'Mr Sludge', a fake spiritualist medium. One critic has discovered, in the narratives of British romanticism, a 'problematical self-consciousness' and a 'division in the self':[10] the main thematic and imaginative drift is not towards the affirmation of a certain and simple selfhood, but the nostalgia incumbent upon its loss of connection with the larger world. The solitary wanderers of Coleridge or Wordsworth or Byron are forms of self-projection and self-alienation.

To read through Wordsworth's collected works is to encounter strange stories of grief and loss, of death and forgetfulness, of isolation and failure, of dissolution and despair. In one edition of his poetry the 'Fragment of a Gothic Tale' is followed by *The Borderers – A Tragedy* succeeded a few pages later by 'The Three Graves', 'Address to Silence' and 'Incipient Madness'.[11] In *The Prelude* Wordsworth invokes the burden and the mystery of the 'Imagination'; the vision occurs at a moment when he and his companion are told they had crossed the Alps without realising that they had done so. In this moment of bewilderment and loss, the 'Imagination' wreathed itself around the poet

> Like an unfather'd vapour; here that Power,
> In all the might of its endowments, came
> Athwart me; I was lost as in a cloud,
> Halted, without a struggle to break through

The 'Imagination' here isolates and imprisons him; he is trapped in its vaporous obscurities. It is a power which seals off the world, leaving the traveller susceptible only to 'the might of its endowments'. The imaginative power is 'unfather'd'; it is not a natural force, and can be seen to work against the experience of the natural world as somehow irrelevant to its concerns. What Wordsworth is experiencing are the rising currents of his highest self, which lead in turn to anxiety and vertigo. There are times when he tries to flee from the reaches of his most profound mental consciousness but then he is confronted with images of death, loss and silence. The romantic image – the image of the romantic selfhood – was more fragile than its exponents seemed willing to comprehend.

It is perhaps appropriate that the great avatar of the romantic poets was Cain himself. He is invoked by Shelley in *Adonais*, by Byron in *The Giaour* and *Cain: A Mystery*, and by Coleridge in *The Wanderings of Cain*. The biblical murderer was one in whom the 'egotistical sublime' had dared to rear itself against God. When Cain became 'a fugitive and a vagabond in the earth' he set out upon a path of wandering and in his steps followed such great exilic romantic heroes as Manfred and Melmoth the Wanderer. But it was also decreed that 'thou art cursed from the earth'. The romantic personality can indeed seem curiously at a loss, sensitive of 'cultural discontinuity, of being nowhere in the movement of history, of being useless, ignored, misunderstood'.[12] As Schopenhauer wrote, 'we are lost in a bottomless void; we find ourselves like the hollow glass globe, from out of which a voice speaks whose cause is not to be found in it'. Or, as one historian of the romantic movement has put it, there emerges 'an infinite series of displacements of meaning' attendant upon 'incompleteness, fragmentation and ruin'.[13] Yet flowing beneath them, supporting them and moving them forward, is the steady current of English music itself.

CHAPTER 53

English music

There can be little doubt that the English music of the twentieth century was inspired and animated by the music of the sixteenth and seventeenth centuries; the old music awakened the new, and the new reawakened the old. Arthur Bliss composed his *Meditations on a Theme of John Blow*, which may be compared with Vaughan Williams's *Fantasia on a Theme by Thomas Tallis*; Gustav Holst's daughter has written of her father's 'wild excitement over the rediscovery of the English madrigal composers' which he considered to be 'the real musical embodiment of the English composers',[1] while Tippett's polyphony was directly modelled upon the madrigal compositions of John Wilbye. Delius's secretary and amanuensis, Eric Fenby, noted a connection between William Byrd's 'The Woodes So Wilde' and Delius's own *Brigg Fair*.

A critic, reviewing Ralph Vaughan Williams's *Fantasia on a Theme by Thomas Tallis*, observed that 'it seems to lift one into some unknown region' where 'one is never quite sure whether one is listening to something very old or very new';[2] the embrace of present and past time, in which English antiquarianism becomes a form of alchemy, engenders a strange timelessness. It is a quality which Eliot sensed in the landscape of England itself and to which he gave memorable expression in *Four Quartets*, 'Now and in England'. It is as if the little bird which flew through the Anglo-Saxon banqueting hall, in Bede's *Historia Ecclesiastica Gentis Anglorum*, gained the outer air and became the lark ascending in Vaughan Williams's orchestral setting. It is the skylark of Shelley's poem whose 'notes flow in such a crystal stream'. The same bird, in the words of George Meredith which Vaughan Williams used,

> rises and begins to round,
> He drops the silver chain of sound,
> Of many links without a break

The unbroken chain is that of English music itself.

The passion of Vaughan Williams for folk-music itself has now become a commonplace of English musical history. It began in Brentwood in Essex, in the winter of 1903; Brentwood was then a growing market town, where after giving a lecture he was invited to tea by the daughter of the local vicar. One of the villagers invited to this ancient ceremony, a seventy-year-old labourer named Charles Pottipher, began to sing the songs of the region. The first of them, 'Bushes and Briars', affected the young Vaughan Williams suddenly and profoundly with the force of revelation. On first hearing this song, in fact, Vaughan Williams confessed that he was invaded by a 'sense of familiarity . . . something peculiarly belonging to me as an Englishman'. The editor of his folk-songs has suggested that he 'experienced a deep sense of recognition, as though he had known it all his life'.[3] This is perhaps a strange conception. It is as if the land and the landscape had prepared him for this music; it is as if he had already heard it. The song is of ancestral voices. As a fellow enthusiast wrote, 'every country village in England was a nest of singing birds'. But theirs were not necessarily antique airs. 'In one aspect', Vaughan Williams wrote, 'the folk song is as old as time itself; in another aspect it is no older than the singer who sang it.' This is another aspect of the English imagination itself, which is endlessly renewed and is indeed 'new' again in each passing generation. The folk-song abides in Vaughan Williams's own music, where it has found fresh life and inspiration even if it has now fallen silent in fields and meadows. Of the English folk-song itself, Vaughan Williams has also written: 'We felt that this was what we expected our national melody to be.'

We may note the emphasis here upon melody. All authentic folk-music, as Vaughan Williams put it, 'is purely melodic'. It is also a striking intuition on the nature of English music itself. Of thirteenth-century chant, for example, 'the earliest phase of fully legible notation coincides in England with a flowering of melodic beauty so intense as to create the impression of a new and indigenous art'.[4] We read of the 'well balanced melodic lines' and 'rhythmic straightforwardness'[5] of fifteenth-century English music, which can profitably be compared with the native emphasis upon the flowing outlines and delicate linear compositions of the manuscript illuminations. Dunstable's music of that period is notable for its 'consonance and for melodic grace',[6] fully comparable with the description of Vaughan Williams's own music. Of the Eton Choirbook of English church music there has been noted 'the fluid yet vigorous melodic line that is so typical of this music',[7] and Taverner's sixteenth century compositions are celebrated for 'the flexibility of . . . melodic lines'. The songs of John Dowland, 'realised' at a much later date by Benjamin Britten, are characterised by 'such delicacy and refinement that their melodic material is invariably enhanced and transmuted into something precious'.[8] The pure line of melody is best expressed in the solo song, and so it is perhaps not surprising that 'simple songs or ballads' – in theatre productions no less than in street airs – take an 'indigenous' form.[9] In the context of eighteenth-century music, 'a wholly English turn of melody' has been remarked.[10] Victorian part-songs, resembling the polyphony of an earlier time, were also a native growth.

Vaughan Williams's own compositions in general are resplendent with 'prodigality of melody',[11] as if the singing birds had returned, and it has been said of A London Symphony that 'melodies in this work proliferate in a manner that makes disciplining them symphonically a constant problem to the composer'.[12] It is clear that the composer himself 'responded in an extremely sensitive and extraordinarily definite way to the expressive quality of melody'.[13] This is one definition of his Englishness, of course, and his preternatural attention to melody is part of his overwhelming responsiveness to folk-song. Thus his Pastoral Symphony is marked by melody or 'a free evolution of one tune from another . . . like streams flowing into each other';[14] the hidden stream itself is that of native song.

The 'melancholy lyricism' implicit in some of Vaughan Williams's finest work has already been described. A commentator in Musical Times compared Vaughan Williams's Pastoral Symphony to 'a dream of sad happiness', and of the Oboe Concerto a musicologist remarked that Vaughan Williams 'seems to be yearning for some lost and precious thing'.[15] What has been lost that excites so much lament? Could it be the idea of England itself? That would be the easy answer but not, perhaps, an altogether convincing one. The folk-songs collected and arranged by Vaughan Williams are also possessed by profoundly melancholy cadences which have been related to the line of the ancient landscape. It is a national mood, comparable to 'the eternal note of sadness' which Matthew Arnold heard on Dover Beach. It is that note of quietly and insistently 'throbbing melancholy'[16] which emerges in almost all of Vaughan Williams's orchestral compositions; it echoes the delicate melancholy of Dowland and the plangent sadness of Purcell. It lies within Elgar, too, in his 'beautifully poetic expression tinged with wistfulness'.[17]

Vaughan Williams gave a set of lectures in 1932, entitled 'National Music', in which he constructed a series of variations upon the theme of English music. In the first of them he asked whether 'it is not reasonable to suppose that those who share our life, our history, our customs, even our food, should have some secret to give us which the foreign composer, though he be perhaps more imaginative, more powerful, more technically equipped, is not able to give us? This is the secret of the national composer, the secret to which he only has the key . . . and which he alone is able to tell to his fellow countrymen.' Vaughan Williams was no narrow nationalist; he studied under Ravel in Paris, and his own thoroughly indigenous music is indebted to Debussy and Sibelius. Like that of Purcell and Elgar, his very 'English' music is in part inspired by continental models. Elgar was championed by Kreisler and Strauss before he found a thoroughly welcoming audience at home. In turn Vaughan Williams adduces the lives and careers of Bach and Beethoven, Palestrina and Verdi, to suggest that only a 'local' or even 'parochial' artist can become a 'universal musician'. He believed that 'if the roots of your art are firmly planted in your own soil and that soil has anything to give you, you may still gain the whole world and not lose your own souls'. It is a specific and significant perception, wholly shaped by his feeling for landscape and traditional English song.

In a lecture entitled 'The Importance of Folk-Song', for example, he stated that 'folk-songs contained the nucleus of all future development in music' and that 'national music was a sure index to national temperament'. It is what Elgar meant when he said, 'I write the folk-songs of this country.' He was testifying to the power and presence of these often ancient songs within the nation's musical life. It was a subject which preoccupied Vaughan Williams, too. 'It is extra-ordinarily interesting', he wrote, 'to see the national temperament running through every form of a nation's art – the national life and the national art growing together.' In his lectures upon national music he refined this sense of the native imagination with his description of a 'community of people who are spiritually bound together by language, environment, history and common ideals and, above all, a continuity with the past'. This insistence upon 'continuity with the past' is once more thoroughly English in its inspiration, since for Vaughan Williams it is a living past; it is exemplified by the freshness and spontaneity of the ancient folk-song and by the tradition of Byrd and Purcell, Tallis and Wilbye, revived in his own music. Yet it must be emphasised, too, that this belief and trust in a national 'community' did not preclude for him a faith in the larger possibilities of human civilisation; he professed a commitment, for example, to 'a united Europe and a world federation', but this global polity had to be established upon an attachment to a local ground since 'everything of value in our spiritual and cultural life springs from our own soil'. The medieval composers of England were part of a larger Catholic and European civilisation, but theirs was still a readily identifiable national art. It is the great perplexity, and mystery, of native consciousness.

Vaughan Williams's most recent biographer has suggested that the composer 'instinctively knew there were idioms of atavistic English music, whether of Tudor polyphony or of folk song, that bore a cultural fingerprint peculiar to his homeland'.[18] A musicologist has also remarked, of this 'national spirit in music', that 'the composer expresses some deeply-felt national characteristic with roots far back in social and cultural evolution'.[19] These may not be fashionable notions, but they are suggestive ones. How far does the *Norfolk Rhapsody* go back; to what atavistic longing does *A Sea Symphony* speak, and do the strangeness and serenity of *Sinfonia Antarctica* invoke an Anglo-Saxon fortitude in face of natural bleakness? The sense of place, so central to this study, is also evident. Peter Warlock's 'An Old Song' represented 'very much the Cornish moor where I have been living'.[20] A musical historian has in turn recovered this sense of place in the Norfolk landscape of Ernest Moeran's 'The Song of the High Hills' and in Frank Bridge's 'There is a Willow Grows Aslant a Brook'. The *genius loci* still sings. In the preliminary sketches for the *Ninth Symphony* Vaughan Williams drew upon memories of Stonehenge and Salisbury Plain; when he first saw the ancient stones he was suffused with 'a feeling of recognition' and 'the intuition that I had been there already'. His music is instinct with that sense of belonging, so that the act of listening to it becomes a form of home-coming.

It has been remarked of Delius and his contemporaries that, through their works, 'a wave of nature-mysticism swept like a rushing mighty wind'.[21] This great wave has been related to pagan nature worship and to elements of Celtic mythology, also; the possibilities of English music spring from the distant past, and can be expressive of it. But if the material is innate and instinctive, it must constantly be refashioned or refined. Thus in his Third Symphony, known as *The Pastoral Symphony*, Vaughan Williams wished to touch upon that 'nerve of English mysticism' by which he hoped 'the psyche of the nation might be made whole'.[22] His last symphony, completed shortly after he had set ten poems by William Blake for voice and oboe, is filled 'with an inner light' and a sound both 'unearthly and enigmatic'.[23] It is the inner light of the English tradition and the English imagination.

His understanding of that tradition was informed by his twin passion for folk-song and for Tudor music. He loved madrigals just as much as he loved 'Bushes and Briars' because he found in both of them an authentic, if unanalysable, English note. His deepest instinct was to draw both of them together in a music rich with harmony. He believed that the formal or ecclesiastical music of the Tudors drew its energy and strength 'from the unwritten and unrecorded art of its own country-side', and his purpose was to restore that grand symbiosis. 'There was a time', he once wrote, 'when England was always reckoned a most musical nation' and he wished to replenish his native culture with fresh melodies.

It has often been remarked how, in the music of Delius, the plangent harmonies convey an intense and intricate sense of loss or transience; it is an intrinsic part of the English imagination, first evinced in *Beowulf* and the Arthurian cycle. Warlock's 'Corpus Christi Carol', based upon an old English carol, contains 'a plaintive liquescent chromatic harmony of unutterable desolation'.[24] It is associated with lost childhood and the fugitive memory of the child's landscape `is related to the concept of innocence, precarious and fragile. The melancholy of Vaughan Williams's music 'set it apart from that of the continental masters',[25] and it may be that the island itself manifests the sadness of long-endured human occupation with all the cares and woes that it brings. Thus the music of Delius has a characteristically English tone which sets him apart from, for example, Mahler or Strauss – with its often searing nostalgia . . . 'its ever-frustrated yearning . . . its understated dreamy melancholy'.[26] It is aligned with the 'sense of weary desolation' attendant upon certain English songs of the thirteenth century,[27] and 'the undertone of intense sadness' glimpsed in Vaughan Williams's setting of the songs of A. E. Housman.[28] Pleasure and melancholy, lyrical beauty and desolation, are thus uniquely aligned in true English synthesis.

Another line of national music was continued by Vaughan Williams when he agreed to be the musical editor of *The English Hymnal* as an alternative to *Hymns Ancient and Modern*. He knew well enough that sacred music was one of the great glories of English composition, and that Tallis and Byrd and Dunstable were acknowledged to be the finest masters of their time. So, engaged upon his twin pursuit of reclaiming Tudor polyphony and folk-music as the true native arts, he fashioned a hymnal directly out of these elements. His concern was once more with the tradition. Church music provided the only consistent and continuous musical inheritance, however bowdlerised and inhibited it had become, and Vaughan Williams wished to revive it by incorporating 'tunes' by Lawes and Tallis as well as carols and traditional folk-melodies. When he took a psalm tune from that hymnal and composed his *Fantasia on a Theme by Thomas Tallis*, he created 'the ultimate expression of the English soul in music'.[29]

The sacred music of the past can be restored to life in more than one sense. Vaughan Williams received his first inspiration for the masque of *Job*, for example, from Blake's series of illustrations to that sacred book. Throughout his life he evinced a profound regard for Blake and the tradition of visionary writing in English, encompassing Bunyan as well as Herbert, Shelley as well as the King James Bible. His own visionary powers, intimated in the great symphonies, were enlarged by his reading of the English visionaries; he had pondered over Bunyan's pilgrim for fifteen years before completing *The Shepherds of the Delectable Mountains*, and thus associated himself with a tradition of ancient religious dissent and radicalism even while remaining for all intents and purposes an atheist. He could not escape his national inheritance, however, and his religious music is some of the finest ever created.

There are other elements of Vaughan Williams's native artistry which may be adduced here by way of explanation and interpretation. There is the question, for example, of his detachment and reticence. 'I don't know whether I like it,' he remarked of his Fourth Symphony, 'but it's what I meant.' Of another orchestral piece he said, 'Do what you like with it. Play it backwards if you want to.' All this was said in the context of his overwhelming artistry and professionalism. Pevsner has already noted this detachment as an intrinsic element of the English imagination. It is not a question of false modesty but, rather, a genuine aversion towards claiming too much. When a contemporary composer acknowledged that he had written a piece of music 'on his knees', Vaughan Williams replied that 'I wrote *Sancta Civitas* sitting on my bum.' It seems, like much in Vaughan Williams, to be a 'typically' English remark, eschewing any expression of deep emotion and siting the real strength of purpose in his posterior. It has all those elements of practicality and common sense which are considered to be characteristic, as well as a faint sense of earthy or ribald humour which comes (almost literally) with the territory.

Another example of his temperament has been explored by his friend and interpreter Michael Kennedy, who has remarked that 'at rehearsal and in performance his concern was always with technical matters . . . and never with the emotional content of the music'.[30] This emphasis upon the practical and pragmatic is wholly comprehensible in the English context, as is Vaughan Williams's taciturnity or diffidence concerning 'the emotional content'. He was not given 'to probing into himself and his thoughts or his own music'.[31] We may say the same of other English artists who have prided themselves on their technical skills and are decidedly reluctant to discuss the 'meaning' of their productions. Thus Mr Kennedy believes that the Sixth Symphony must have represented 'a deeply-felt, personal and impassioned utterance' precisely because Vaughan Williams's own programme-note 'studiously avoids any hint of emotional commitment'.[32] It is, once more, a question of English embarrassment.

There is in Vaughan Williams's work what has been described as 'a preoccupation with sonorities',[33] which may in turn be related to what one musical historian has called 'the English love of fullness of sound'[34] first noticed in the twelfth century. That fullness of sound, touched by melodic beauty, is a distinctive passion in Vaughan Williams just as it is in Purcell or in Tallis. We read of certain extant manuscripts where 'the English added their characteristically acute sense of vocal sonority' which could become 'a special concern for euphony (for which they were later to become especially noted)'.[35] It became apparent, too, in the employment of several lines of harmony meeting and parting in a musical structure like that of interlace.

That particular reverence for harmony might be variously interpreted at an aesthetic or social level; the English predilection for compromise and moderation, after all, is an aspect of the 'golden mean'. The rich harmonic texture of Vaughan Williams's music may thus be associated with the 'harmonic forces' of Purcell's compositions and the 'slow-moving harmonies' and 'fullness of instrumentation' in Elgar[36], or it may be related to a more primitive need for harmonious order arising from various competing elements. In either sphere, it is the true music of England. In 1994 the most acclaimed of contemporary English composers, Thomas Adès, completed a string quartet entitled *Arcadiana*; its most poignant and lyrical movement, the sixth, was entitled 'O Albion'.

The territorial imperative

And so the English imagination takes the form of an endless enchanted circle, or shining ring, moving backwards as well as forwards. I return again to Ford Madox Ford – returning being one of the central images of this book – who wrote that 'my private and particular image of English history in these matters is one of waving lines. I see tendencies rise to the surface of the people. I see them fall again and rise again.' These 'lines' of force or influence connect the present with the past. We draw half our strength and inspiration from the writers of the past. From their example we learn that the history of the English imagination is the history of adaptation and assimilation. Englishness is the principle of diversity itself. In English literature, music and painting, heterogeneity becomes the form and type of art. This condition reflects both a mixed language comprised of many different elements and a mixed culture comprised of many different races. That is why there is also, in the products of the English imagination, a characteristic mixing or blurring of forms; in these pages I have traced the conflation of biography, or history, and the novel.

The English have in that sense always been a practical and pragmatic race; the history of English philosophy, for example, has been the history of empiricism and of scientific experiment. There are no works of speculative theology, but there are many manuals of religious instruction. This native aptitude has in turn led to disaffection from, or dissatisfaction with, all abstract speculation. The true emphasis rests upon the qualities of individual experience, which are manifest in the English art of portraiture and in the English novel of character. The English imagination is also syncretic and additive – one episode leading to another episode – rather than formal or theoretical.

So there are many striking continuities in English culture, ranging from the presence of alliteration in English native poetry for the last two thousand years to the shape and size of the ordinary English house. But the most powerful impulse can be found in what I have called the territorial imperative, by means of which a local area can influence or guide all those who inhabit it. The example of London has often been adduced. But the territorial imperative can also be transposed to include the nation itself. English writers and artists, English composers and folk-singers, have been haunted by this sense of place, in which the echoic simplicities of past use and past tradition sanctify a certain spot of ground. These forces are no doubt to be found in other regions and countries of the earth; but in England the reverence for the past and the affinity with the natural landscape join together in a mutual embrace. So we owe much to the ground on which we dwell. It is the landscape and the dreamscape. It encourages a sense of longing and belonging. It is Albion.

Notes

Introduction: Albion

1 S. B. Greenfield and D. G. Calder, *A New Critical History of Old English Literature*, p. 58.
2 ibid., p. 61.
3 Michael Wood, *In Search of England*, p. 100.
4 ibid.
5 ibid., p. 16.

1 The tree

1 Joan Evans, *English Art 1307–1461*, p. 54.
2 Francis Spufford, *The Child that Books Built*, p. 24.

2 The radiates

1 K. R. Dark, *Civitas to Kingdom*, p. 184.
2 ibid., p. 191.

3 Listen!

1 E. M. W. Tillyard, *The English Epic and Its Background*, p. 171.
2 Kenneth Sisam, *Studies in the History of Old English Literature*, p. 28.

4 Why is a raven like a writing desk?

1 *The Exeter Book Riddles*, ed. and trans. Kevin Crossley-Holland, p. 68.
2 ibid., p. 24.
3 ibid., p. 28.
4 John Stephens, *Music and Poetry in the Early Tudor Court*, p. 17.
5 John Leyerle, 'The Interlace Structure of *Beowulf*', *University of Toronto Quarterly*, October 1967, p. 81.
6 *The Owl and the Nightingale*, trans. Brian Stone, p. 162.
7 John Caldwell, *The Oxford History of English Music*, Volume 2, p. 226.
8 ibid., Volume 1, p. 162.

9 A. R. Braunmuller, 'The Arts of the Dramatist', in *The Cambridge Companion to English Renaissance Drama*, ed. A. R. Braunmuller and Michael Hattaway, p. 73.
10 Graham Hough, *A Preface to the Fairie Queen*, p. 93.
11 Margaret Rickert, *Painting in Britain: The Middle Ages*, p. 47.
12 Joan Evans, *English Art, 1307–1461*, p. 5.

5 A rare and singular Bede

1 A. H. Thompson (ed.), *Bede, His Life, Times and Writings*, p. 62.
2 Kevin Crossley-Holland (ed. and trans.), *The Anglo-Saxon World*, p. 241.
3 J. F. Webb (ed. and trans.), *The Age of Bede*, p. 203.
4 S. B. Greenfield and D. G. Calder, *A New Critical History of Old English Literature*, p. 8.
5 Bede, *A History of the English Church and People*, trans. Leo Sherley-Price, rev. R. E. Latham, p. 205.
6 Edwin Jones, *The English Nation: The Great Myth*, p. 2.
7 Webb, p. 23.
8 ibid., p. 178.
9 D. Talbot Rice, *English Art, 871–1100*, p. 36.
10 Greenfield and Calder, p. 31.
11 D. Parsons (ed.), *Tenth-Century Studies*, p. 44.
12 ibid., p. 8.
13 Talbot Rice, p. 47.

6 The song of the past

1 Wilhelm Levison, 'Bede as Historian', in *Bede*, ed. A. H. Thompson, p. 142.
2 R. W. Southern, *Medieval Humanism*, p. 7.
3 All quotations are from Nennius, *History of the Britons*, ed. A. W. Wade-Evans.
4 Kevin Crossley-Holland (ed. and trans.), *The Anglo-Saxon World*, p. 35.

7 The lives of others

1 J. Boffey, 'Middle English Lives'. In *The Cambridge History of Medieval Literature*, ed. D. Wallace, p. 617.
2 *The Voyage of St Brendan*, ed. J. J. O'Meara, p. xiv.
3 J. F. Webb (ed. and trans.), *The Age of Bede*, p. 216.
4 ibid., p. 221.

5 John Wasson, 'The Morality Plays: Ancestor of Elizabethan Drama', in *The Drama of the Middle Ages*, ed. C. Davidson *et al.*, p. 322.
6. ibid., p. 325.

8 A land of dreams

1 Humphrey Carpenter, *J. R. R. Tolkien: A Biography*, p. 64.
2 R. W. Southern, *Medieval Humanism*, p. 146.
3 Bede, *A History of the English Church and People*, trans. Leo Sherley-Price, rev. R. E. Latham, p. 127.
4 ibid., p. 175.
5 ibid., p. 285.
6 ibid., p. 289.
7 J. F. Webb (ed. and trans.), *The Age of Bede*, p. 52.
8 M. Rickert, *Painting in Britain: The Middle Ages*, p. 172.

9 A note on English melancholy

1 S. A. J. Bradley (ed.), *Anglo-Saxon Poetry*, p. 359.
2 John Caldwell (ed.), *The Oxford History of English Music*, Volume 1, p. 31.
3 ibid., pp. 73–4.
4 E. K. Chambers, *Malory and Fifteenth-Century Drama, Lyrics and Ballads*, p. 198.
5 Caldwell (ed), Volume 1, p. 427.
6 Wilfred Mellers, 'Music: Paradise and Paradox', in *Seventeenth-Century Britain*, ed. Boris Ford, p. 196.
7 Ellis Waterhouse, *Painting in Britain 1530–1790*, p. 139.
8 John Murdoch, 'Painting: from Astraea to Augustus', in *Seventeenth-Century Britain*, ed. Boris Ford, p. 254.
9 Andrew Varney, *Eighteenth-Century Writers in Their World*, pp. 176–7.
10 Waterhouse, p. 235.

10 The rolling hills

1 W. G. Hoskins, *The Making of the English Landscape*, p. 285.
2 J. F. Webb (ed. and trans.), *The Age of Bede*, p. 56.
3 ibid., p. 69.
4 Christopher Woodward, *In Ruins*, p. 119.
5 ibid., p. 120.
6 William Gaunt, *A Concise History of English Painting*, p. 111.

11 It rained all night

1   Kevin Crossley-Holland (ed. and trans.), *The Anglo-Saxon World*, p. 242.
2   S. A. J. Bradley (ed. and trans.), *Anglo-Saxon Poetry*, p. 142.
3   ibid., p. 21.
4   ibid., p. 34.
5   Kenneth Sisam, *Studies in the History of Old English Literature*, p. 23.
6   Bede, *A History of the English Church and People*, trans. Leo Sherley-Price, rev. R. E. Latham, pp. 129–30.
7   Peter Conrad, *The Everyman History of English Literature*, p. 451.
8   Kenneth Clark, *On The Painting of English Landscape*, p. 14.
9   Margaret Drabble, *A Writer's Britain*, p. 189.
10 Peter Woodcock, *The Enchanted Isle*, p. 25.
11 ibid., p. 16.
12 ibid., p. 31.

12 The prose of the world

1   A. P. Smyth, *King Alfred the Great*, p. 549.
2   ibid., p. 560.
3   Patrick Wormald, 'Anglo-Saxon Society and Its Literature', in *The Cambridge Companion to Old English Literature*, ed. Malcolm Godden and Michael Lapidge, p. 19.
4   Smyth, p. 525.
5   ibid., p. 531.
6   ibid., p. 530.
7   S. B. Greenfield and D. G. Calder, *A New Critical History of Old English Literature*, p. 61.
8   W. P. Ker, *Medieval English Literature*, p. 55.
9   K. H. Jackson, *Language and History in Early Britain*, p. 107.
10 ibid., p. 108.

13 The first initials

1   Margaret Rickert, *Painting in Britain: The Middle Ages*, p. 19.
2   Christopher Kendrick, 'Preaching Common Grounds', in *Writing and the English Renaissance*, ed. William Zunder and Suzanne Trill, p. 179.
3   D. Talbot Rice, *English Art, 871–1100*, pp. 174–5.
4   ibid., p. 6.

5 Nikolaus Pevsner, *The Englishness of English Art*, p. 137.
6 ibid., p. 138.
7 Eric Mercer, *English Art, 1553–1625*, p. 156.
8 John Stephens, *Music and Poetry in the Early Tudor Court*, p. 100.
9 Margaret Whinney and Oliver Millar, *English Art, 1625–1714*, p. 22.
10 David Watkin, *English Architecture*, p. 67.
11 William Gaunt, *A Concise History of English Painting*, p. 200.
12 Rickert, p. 65.
13 ibid., p. 95.
14 Walter Oakeshott, *The Sequence of English Medieval Art*, p. 44.
15 *St Erkenwald*, trans. Brian Stone, p. 31.

14 Anglo-Saxon attitudes
1 J. W. Lever, '*Paradise Lost* and the Anglo-Saxon Tradition', *Review of English Studies*, Vol. 23, No. 90, p. 100.
2 ibid., p. 98.
3 D. Talbot Rice, *English Art, 871–1100*, pp. 95–6.

15 The alteration
1 Derek Brewer, 'Medieval European Literature', in *Pelican Guide to Medieval Literature*, Volume 2, p. 74.
2 R. W. Southern, *Medieval Humanism*, p. 161.
3 G. Zarnecki, '1066 and Architectural Sculpture', *PBA*, Vol. 52, 1966, p. 102.
4 Elizabeth Salter, *English and International Studies in the Literature, Art and Patronage of Medieval England*, p. 6.
5 D. Pearsall, *Old English and Middle English Poetry*, p. 76.
6 Lesley Johnson, 'Dynastic Chronicles', in *The Arthur of the English*, ed. W. R. J. Barron, p. 40.
7 W. F. Bolton, *A Short History of Literary English*, p. 35.
8 Norman Davies, *The Isles*, p. 425.
9 May McKisack, *The Fourteenth Century*, p. 525.
10 John Caldwell (ed.), *The Oxford History of English Music*, Volume 1, p. 108.
11 Sheila Lindbaum, 'London Texts and Literary Practice', in *The Cambridge History of Medieval English Literature*, ed. D. Wallace, p. 29.
12 ibid., pp. 284–5.

16 He is not dead

1 Ceridwen Lloyd-Morgan, 'The Celtic Tradition', in *The Arthur of the English*, ed. W. R. J. Barron, p. 3.
2 Richard Barber, *King Arthur*, p. 6.
3 ibid., p. 12.
4 Denis Hollier (ed.), *A New History of French Literature*, p. 41.
5 ibid., p. 51.
6 Barron (ed.), p. 24.
7 Rosamund Allen (trans. and intr.), *Brut*, p. 28.
8 ibid.
9 Barron (ed.), p. 71.
10 Hollier (ed.), p. 67.
11 Barron (ed.), p. 89.
12 Barber, p. 104.
13 Quoted in Barron (ed.), p. 195.
14 Thomas Malory, *Works*, ed. Eugene Vinaver, p. 7.
15 Barber, p. 122.
16 Barron (ed.), p. 245.
17 ibid.
18 W. P. Ker, quoted in E. K. Chambers, *Malory and Fifteenth-Century Drama, Lyrics and Ballads*, p. 198.
19 Chris Brooks and Inga Bryden, 'The Arthurian Legacy' in Barron, p. 250.
20 Beverly Taylor and Elizabeth Brewer, *The Return of King Arthur*, p. 69.
21 ibid., pp. 15–16.
22 ibid., p. 26.
23 ibid., p. 135.
24 Alfred, Lord Tennyson, *Letters*, ed. C. Y. Lang and E. F. Shannon, Jr, Volume 2, p. 267.
25 Barron (ed.), p. 263.

17 Faith of our fathers

1 G. G. Coulton, *Chaucer and His England*, p. 282.
2 *Sir Gawain and the Green Knight*, ed. Brian Stone, p. 147.
3 F. L. Utley, *The Crooked Rib*, p. 29.
4 R. P. Miller, 'Allegory in *The Canterbury Tales*' in *Companion to Chaucer Studies*, ed. Beryl Rowland, p. 348.
5 Jody Enders, *Rhetoric and the Origins of Medieval Drama*, p. 245.
6 Quoted in Martin Thornton, *English Spirituality*, p. 107.

7 J. A. W. Bennett and Douglas Gray (ed.), *Middle English Literature*, p. 268.
8 Thornton, p. 169.
9 ibid., p. 89.
10 W. K. Sorley, *A History of British Philosophy to 1900*, pp. 6–7.
11 T. S. R. Boase, *English Art 1800–1870*, p. 297.
12 R. W. Southern, *Medieval Humanism*, p. 177.

18 Old stone

1 Peter Brieger, *English Art 1216–1307*, p. 10.
2 Margaret Rickert, *Painting in Britain: The Middle Ages*, p. 181.
3 John Caldwell (ed.), *The Oxford History of English Music*, Volume 1, p. 174.
4 C. S. Lewis, *The Discarded Image*, p. 210.
5 Alex Clifton-Taylor, *The Cathedrals of England*, p. 88.
6 Brieger, p. 26.
7 Nikolaus Pevsner, *The Englishness of English Art*, p. 41.
8 Joan Evans, *English Art 1307–1461*, p. 9.
9 Quoted in Claude Rawson's 'Henry Fielding', in *The Cambridge Companion to the Eighteenth-Century Novel*, ed. John Richetti, p. 130.
10 Derek Pearsall, 'The Visual World of the Middle Ages', in *Medieval Literature*, ed. Boris Ford, p. 312.
11 Morton W. Bloomfield, 'Chaucerian Realism', in *The Cambridge Chaucer Companion*, ed. Pierre Boitani and Jill Mann, p. 187.
12 Peter Happé, *English Drama Before Shakespeare*, p. 29.
13 Kenneth Pople, *Stanley Spencer*, p. 67.

19 Part of the territory

1 Walter Oakeshott, *The Sequence of English Medieval Art*, p. 22.
2 J. C. Coldewey, 'The Non-Cycle Plays and the East Anglian Tradition', in *The Cambridge Companion to Medieval English Theatre*, ed. Richard Beadle, p. 189.
3 Alan MacFarlane, *The Origins of English Individualism*, p. 67.
4 ibid., p. 68.
5 Coldewey, p. 190.
6 ibid., p. 207.
7 Martin Thornton, *English Spirituality*, p. 203.
8 ibid., p. 214.
9 Coldewey, p. 193.

10 T. S. R. Boase, *English Art 1800–1870*, p. 35.

20 A song and a dance

1 R. T. Davies (ed.), *Medieval English Lyrics*, p. 32.
2 J. A. W. Bennett and Douglas Gray (eds.), *Middle English Literature 1100–1400*, p. 202.
3 John Stephens, 'Medieval Lyrics and Music', in *Medieval Literature*, ed. Boris Ford, Volume 1, p. 270.
4 Bennett and Gray (eds.), p. 138.
5 *Six Middle English Romances*, ed. Maldwyn Mills, p. xxii.
6 W. R. J. Barron (ed.), *The Arthur of the English*, p. 132.
7 Bennett and Gray (eds.), p. 18.
8 Rosemary Woolf, 'Later Poetry: The Popular Tradition,' in *The Middle Ages*, ed. W. F. Bolton, p. 277.
9 ibid.
10 ibid.

21 Fathers and sons

1 William Empson, *Seven Types of Ambiguity*, p. 74.
2 Piero Boitani, 'Old Books Brought to Life in Dreams', in *The Cambridge Chaucer Companion*, ed. Piero Boitani and Jill Mann, p. 41.
3 ibid., p. 53.
4 Barry Windeatt, 'Literary Structures in Chaucer', in Boitani and Mann (eds.), p. 198.
5 L. D. Benson (ed.), *The Riverside Chaucer*, p. 840.
6 ibid., p. 885.
7 Derek Pearsall, *The Life of Geoffrey Chaucer*, p. 245.
8 Nikolaus Pevsner, *The Englishness of English Art*, p. 31.
9 Paul Strohm, quoted in Pearsall, p. 132.
10 Pearsall, p. 112.
11 Pevsner, p. 79.
12 Paul G. Ruggiers, *The Art of The Canterbury Tales*, p. 17.
13 J. A. W. Bennett and Douglas Gray (eds.), *Middle English Literature 1100–1400*, p. 142.
14 John Caldwell (ed.), *The Oxford History of English Music*, Volume 2, p. 173.
15 Donald Cheney, 'Narrative, Romance and Epic', in *The Cambridge Companion to English Literature 1500–1600*, ed. A. P. Kinney, p. 207.

16 A. Easthope, *Englishness and National Culture*, p. 96.

23 The mysterious voice
1 E. K. Chambers, *Malory and Fifteenth-Century Drama, Lyrics and Ballads*, p. ci.
2 Richard Rolle, *The Fire of Love*, ed. and trans. Clifton Wolters, p. 32.
3 Frances Beer, *Women and Mystical Experience in the Middle Ages*, p. 110.
4 ibid., p. 112.
5 Marion Glasscoe, *English Medieval Mystics*, p. 165.

24 The inheritance
1 J. A. W. Bennett and Douglas Gray (eds.), *Middle English Literature 1100–1400*, p. 62.
2 ibid., p. 281.
3 John Carey, *John Donne: His Mind and Art*, p. 43.
4 ibid., p. 51.
5 Martin Thornton, *English Spirituality*, p. 226.
6 ibid., p. 236.
7 C. Palmer, *Delius: Portrait of a Cosmopolitan*, p. 160.
8 John Caldwell (ed.), *The Oxford History of English Music*, Volume 2, p. 477.
9 John Marshall, 'Modern Productions of Medieval English Plays' in *The Cambridge Companion to Medieval English Theatre*, ed. Richard Beadle, p. 290.

25 The female religion
1 M. W. Ferguson, 'A Room Not Their Own', in *Renaissance Poetry*, ed. Christina Malcolmson, p. 158.
2 ibid.
3 *Three Old English Elegies*, ed. R. F. Leslie, p. 10.
4 ibid., p. 12.
5 Christine Fell, *Women in Anglo-Saxon England*, p. 70.
6 Marilyn Desmond, quoted in L. A. Fincke, *Women's Writing in English: Medieval England*, p. 88.
7 Doris Stenton, quoted in Fell, p. 13.
8 ibid., p. 57.
9 ibid., p. 111.
10 ibid., p. 114.

11 ibid.
12 B. Lewalski, *Writing Women in Jacobean England*, pp. 6–7.
13 L. Eckenstein, *Women under Monasticism*, p. 9.
14 J. M. Ferrante, 'Marie de France', in *Medieval Women Writers*, ed. K. M. Wilson, p. 65.
15 ibid., p. 67.
16 ibid., p. 65.
17 Denis Hollier (ed.), *A New History of French Literature*, p. 51.
18 ibid., p. 52.
19 Jocelyn Wogan-Browne, 'Clerc u lai, muine u dame', in *Women and Literature in Britain: 1150–1500*, ed. C. McMeale, p. 74.
20 *The Oxford Companion to Christian Thought*, ed. Adrian Hastings *et al.*, p. 358.
21 Virginia Woolf, *A Room of One's Own*, p. 90.
22 Stevie Davis, *Emily Brontë: Heretic*, p. 65.
23 Norman Davies, quoted in Felicity Riddy, 'Women Talking about the Things of God', in C. M. Meale (ed.), p. 114.
24 Claire Harman, *Fanny Burney*, p. 57.
25 Catherine F. Smith, 'Jane Lead', in *Shakespeare's Sisters*, ed. S. M. Gilbert and S. Gubar, p. 4.
26 Elaine Hobby, quoted in B. S. Travitsky, 'The Possibilities of Prose', in *Redeeming Eve: Women Writers of the English Renaissance*, ed. E. V. Beilin, p. 249.
27 Beilin (ed.), p. 49.
28 ibid.
29 Germaine Greer, *Slip-Shod Sibyls*, p. 44.
30 Gary Waller, quoted in E. H. Hageman, 'Women's Poetry in Early Modern Britain', in *Women and Literature in Britain, 1500–1700*, ed. H. Wilcox, p. 194.
31 Beilin (ed.), p. 152.
32 ibid., p. 61.

26 But newly translated
1 Joan Evans, *English Art 1307–1461*, p. 133.
2 Ezra Pound, *Literary Essays*, pp. 34–5.
3 Robin Sowerby, *The Classical Legacy in Renaissance Poetry*, p. 220.

27 The Italian connection
1 Nicholas Von Maltzahn, *Milton's History of Britain*, p. 95.

2 Richard Helgerson, *Forms of Nationhood*, p. 1.
3 Graham Hough, *A Preface to The Faerie Queene*, p. 97.
4 Maurice Evans, (ed.) *The Countess of Pembroke's 'Arcadia'*, p. 21.

28 A short history of Shakespeare
1 Kenneth Muir, *The Sources of Shakespeare's Plays*, p. 12.

29 And now for streaky bacon
1 D. G. Scragg, 'The Nature of Old English Verse', in *The Cambridge Companion to Old English Literature*, ed. Malcolm Godden and Michael Lapidge, p. 68.
2 John Caldwell (ed.), *The Oxford History of English Music*, Volume 1, p. 74.
3 David Watkin, *English Architecture*, p. 40.
4 Margot Heinemann, 'Political Drama', in *The Cambridge Companion to English Renaissance Drama*, ed. A. R. Braunmuller and Michael Hattaway, p. 173.
5 Lee Bliss, 'Pastiche, Burlesque, Tragicomedy', in Braunmuller and Hattaway (eds.), p. 244.
6 J. A. Winn, 'Theatrical Culture: Theatre and Music', in *The Cambridge Companion to English Literature 1650–1740*, ed. S. N. Zwicker, p. 112.
7 Margaret Whinney and Oliver Millar, *English Art, 1625–1714*, p. 204.
8 William K. Wimsatt, in J. R. Damrosch (ed.), *Modern Essays on Eighteenth-Century Literature*, p. 142.
9 Watkin, p. 123.
10 ibid., p. 139.
11 ibid., p. 146.
12 Sally Jeffery, 'Architecture', in *Eighteenth-Century Britain*, ed. Boris Ford, pp. 253–4.
13 Nikolaus Pevsner, *The Englishness of English Art*, p. 75.
14 ibid., p. 48.

30 Among the ruins
1 L. A. Cormican, 'Milton's Religious Verse', in *From Donne to Marvell*, ed. Boris Ford, p. 233.
2 Nicholas Von Maltzahn, 'Milton's Readers', in *The Cambridge Companion to Milton*, ed. Dennis Danielson, p. 247.
3 William Levison, 'Bede as Historian', in *Bede*, ed. A. H.

Thompson, p. 142.

4 G. T. Shepherd, 'Early Middle English Literature', in *The Middle Ages*, ed. W. F. Bolton, p. 94.

5 Michael Wood, *In Search of England*, p. 118.

6 Melanie Hansen, 'Identity and Ownership', in *Writing and the English Renaissance*, ed. W. Zunder and S. Trill, p. 90.

7 James Sutherland, *English Literature of the Late Seventeenth Century*, p. 286.

8 Wood himself.

9 William Weber, *The Rise of Musical Classics in Eighteenth-Century England*, p. 56.

10 ibid., p. 5.

11 ibid., p. 3.

12 ibid., p. 73.

31 The conservative tendency

1 H. M. Taylor, 'Tenth-Century Church Buildings in England and on the Continent, in *Tenth-Century Studies*, ed. David Parsons, p. 167.

2 ibid., p. 195.

3 John Caldwell (ed.), *The Oxford History of English Music*, Volume 1, p. 27.

4 ibid., p. 379.

5 Andrew Saint, 'The New Town', in *Modern Britain*, ed. Boris Ford, p. 152.

6 Andor Gomme, 'Architecture', in *Seventeenth-Century Britain*, ed. Boris Ford, p. 28.

7 ibid., p. 79.

8 John Nelson Tarn, 'New Homes for Barons and Artisans', in *Victorian Britain*, ed. Boris Ford, p. 154.

9 Steen Eiler Rasmussen, *London: the Unique City*, p. 293.

10 ibid., p. 296.

32 A short history lesson

1 Bede, *A History of the English Church and People*, introduction by D. H. Farmer, p. 25.

2 Dorothy Whitelock, *The Audience of Beowulf*, p. 63.

3 Andrew Galloway, 'Writing History in England', in *The Cambridge History of Medieval English Literature*, ed. D. Wallace, p. 255.

4 Lesley Johnson, 'Dynastic Chronicles', in *The Arthur of the English*, ed. W. R. J. Barron, p. 34.
5 C. S. Lewis, *The Discarded Image*, p. 181.
6 Edwin Jones, *The English Nation: The Great Myth*, p. 151.
7 William Gaunt, *A Concise History of English Painting*, p. 163.
8 S. A. J. Bradley (ed. and trans.), *Anglo-Saxon Poetry*, p. 49.

33 The song of the sea

1 A. P. Smyth, *King Alfred the Great*, p. 570.
2 M. Godden and M. Lapidge, *The Cambridge Companion to Old English Literature*, p. 85.
3 D. Whitelock (ed.), *English Historical Documents*, p. 209.
4 S. B. Greenfield and D. G. Calder, *A New Critical History of Old English Literature*, p. 162.
5 Kevin Crossley-Holland (ed. and trans.), *The Anglo-Saxon World*, p. 53.
6 ibid., p. 288.
7 *The Exeter Book Riddles*, ed. and trans. Kevin Crossley-Holland, pp. 4 and 85.
8 J. A. W. Bennett (ed.), *Selections from John Gower*, p. xiv.
9 Harry Blamires, *Twentieth-Century English Literature*, p. 7.
10 C. Palmer, *Delius: Portrait of a Cosmopolitan*, p. 151.
11 ibid.
12 ibid., p. 158.
13 John Caldwell (ed.), *The Oxford History of English Music*, Volume 2, p. 409.

34 A brief excursion

1 J. F. Webb, *The Age of Bede*, p. 223.
2 Norman Davies, *The Isles*, p. 474.
3 Richard Helgerson, *Forms of Nationhood*, p. 153.
4 ibid., p. 165.
5 ibid.
6 ibid., p. 175.
7 ibid., p. 179.
8 C. Rawson and J. Mezciems, *English Satire and the Satiric Tradition*, p. 2.
9 John Mullan, 'Swift, Defoe and Narrative Forms', in *The Cambridge Companion to English Literature, 1650–1740*, ed. S. N. Zwicker, p. 254.

10 Roy Strong, *The Spirit of Britain*, p. 278.

35 A miniature

1 'The Phoenix', in *Anglo-Saxon Poetry*, ed. and trans. S. A. J. Bradley, p. 292.
2 Margaret Rickert, *Painting in Britain: The Middle Ages*, p. 44.
3 ibid., p. 47.
4 T. S. R. Boase, *English Art, 1800–1870*, p. 177.
5 Peter Brieger, *English Art, 1216–1307*, p. 79.
6 Boase, p. 299.
7 ibid.
8 Nicola Coldstream, 'Architecture', in *Medieval Britain*, ed. Boris Ford, p. 51.
9 J. A. W. Bennett and Douglas Gray (eds.), *Middle English Literature 1100–1400*, pp. 69 and 247.
10 Rickert, p. 178.
11 Joan Evans, *English Art 1307–1461*, pp. 7–8.
12 William Gaunt, *A Concise History of English Painting*, pp. 11–12.
13 Walter Oakeshott, *The Sequence of English Medieval Art*, p. 29.
14 Ellis Waterhouse, *Painting in Britain, 1530–1790*, p. 38.
15 Eric Mercer, *English Art, 1553–1625*, p. 5.
16 E. Auerbach, *Tudor Artists*, pp. 131–2.
17 Margaret Whinney and Oliver Millar, *English Art, 1625–1714*, p. 90.
18 William Vaughan, *British Painting: the Golden Age*, p. 44.
19 Boase, p. 163.
20 N. P. Messenger and J. R. Watson (eds.), *Victorian Poetry*, p. xiii.
21 Colin Manlove, *The Fantasy Literature of England*, p. 116.
22 ibid.
23 ibid.

36 I saw you Missis

1 Gerald Frow, *Oh Yes It Is: A History of Pantomime*, p. 149.
2 Enid Welsford, *The Fool*, p. 51.
3 Roly Bain, 'Clowns and Augustes', in *Victorian Britain*, ed. Boris Ford, p. 300.
4 Frow, p. 109.
5 David Robinson, *Chaplin*, p. 71.
6 O. M. Busby, *Studies in the development of the fool in Elizabethan drama*, p. 6.

7 Richard Axton, 'Church Drama and Popular Drama', in *Medieval Literature, Part Two: The European Inheritance*, p. 152.
8 ibid., p. 153.
9 Christopher Kendrick, 'Preaching Common Grounds', in *Writing and the English Renaissance*, ed. William Zunder and Suzanne Trill, p. 218.
10 ibid., p. 102.

37 In the beginning

1 Alister McGrath, *In the Beginning*, p. 31.
2 L. H. Wild, *The Romance of the English Bible*, p. 43.
3 Roger Scruton, *England: An Elegy*, p. 84.
4 Wild, p. 139.
5 Scruton, p. 99.
6 Wild, p. 154.
7 McGrath, p. 125.
8 ibid., p. 11.
9 ibid., p. 342.
10 C. R. Herworth, *The Literary Lineage of the King James Bible*, pp. 229 and 235.
11 Benson Bobrick, *The Making of the English Bible*, p. 253.
12 James Sutherland, *English Literature of the Late Seventeenth Century*, p. 315.
13 ibid., p. 335.
14 John Bunyan, *The Pilgrim's Progress* ed. and intro. N. H. Keeble, p. xxi.
15 William Weber, *The Rise of Musical Classics in Eighteenth-Century England*, p. 121.
16 Winton Dean quoted in *Eighteenth-Century Britain*, ed. Boris Ford, p. 291.
17 Weber, p. 121.
18 Helen Gardner, *Religion and Literature*, pp. 155–6.
19 ibid., p. 157.

38 London calling

1 D. S. Brewer, 'Chaucer's Poetic Style' in *The Cambridge Chaucer Companion*, ed. Piero Boitani and Jill Mann, p. 234.
2 ibid.
3 Andrew Gurr, *Playgoing in Shakespeare's London*, p. 147.
4 Colin Burrow, 'The Sixteenth Century', in *The Cambridge*

Companion to English Literature 1550–1600, ed. A. F. Kinney, p. 24.
5 Terry Castle, *Masquerade and Civilisation*, p. 204.
6 Wilfred Mellers, *Harmonious Meeting*, p. 227.
7 E. D. Mackerness, *A Social History of English Music*, p. 101.
8 James Sutherland, *English Literature of the Later Seventeenth Century*, p. 218.
9 Castle, p. 193.
10 Ronald Paulson, 'Life as Pilgrimage and as Theatre', in *Modern Essays on Eighteenth-Century Literature*, ed. L. Damrosch, p. 182.

39 An essay on the essay
1 Jane H. Jack, 'The Practical Essayists', in *From Dryden to Johnson*, ed. Boris Ford, p. 183.

40 The Hogarthian moment
1 James Sutherland, *English Literature of the Later Seventeenth Century*, p. 87.
2 William Vaughan, *British Painting: the Golden Age*, p. 25.
3 Ernest Barker, *National Character*, p. 101.

41 Some eminent novelists
1 see Terry Castle, *Masquerade and Civilisation*.
2 John Richetti, in *The Eighteenth-Century Novel*, ed. John Richetti, p. 7.
3 Richard West, *The Life and Strange, Surprising Adventures of Daniel Defoe*, p. 70.
4 Ian Watt, 'Defoe as Novelist', in *From Dryden to Johnson*, ed. Boris Ford, p. 155.
5 William Vaughan, *British Painting: the Golden Age*, p. 144.
6 John Preston, 'Fielding and Smollett', in *From Dryden to Johnson*, ed. Boris Ford, p. 320.
7 ibid., p. 321.
8 Paul Langford, *Englishness Identified*, pp. 10–11.
9 ibid., p. 10.
10 ibid., p. 294.

42 A character study
1 John Wain, *Samuel Johnson*, p. 276.
2 ibid., p. 295.

3   Ernest Barker, *National Character*, p. 217.
4   ibid., p. 216.
5   ibid., p. 220.
6   William Vaughan, *British Painting: The Golden Age*, p. 38.
7   William Gaunt, *A Concise History of English Painting*, p. 19.
8   Roy Strong, *The Spirit of Britain*, p. 164.
9   Margaret Rickert, *Painting in Britain: The Middle Ages*, p. 221.
10 Pieter Brieger, *English Art, 1216–1307*, p. 129.
11 Rickert, p. 185.
12 Eric Mercer, *English Art, 1553–1625*, p. 149.
13 ibid., p. 156.
14 ibid., p. 164.
15 Margaret Whinney and Oliver Millar, *English Art, 1625–1714*, p. 9.
16 ibid., p. 85.
17 Ellis Waterhouse, *Painting in Britain 1530–1790*, p. 60.
18 ibid.
19 Jean-Jacques Mayoux, *English Painting*, p. 14.
20 ibid., p. 23.

43 The fine art of biography

1   Adam Sisman, *Boswell's Presumptuous Task*, p. 165.
2   Richard Holmes, *Dr Johnson and Mr Savage*, p. 230.
3   ibid., p. 51.
4   ibid., p. 230.
5   Sisman, p. 174.
6   ibid.
7   ibid., p. 176.
8   William C. Dowling, in *Modern Essays on Eighteenth-Century Literature*, ed. L. Damrosch Jr, p. 370.
9   Sisman, p. 214.
10 Mrs Gaskell, *The Life of Charlotte Brontë*, ed. Alan Shelston, p. 29.
11 Jenny Uglow, *Elizabeth Gaskell*, p. 399.

44 Femality and fiction

1   S. M. Gilbert and S. Gubar (eds.), *Shakespeare's Sisters*, p. xvi.
2   ibid., p. xxi.
3   J. Todd, *The Sign of 'Angellica'*, p. 139.
4   Stuart Curran, 'Women Readers, Women Writers', in *The*

Cambridge Companion to British Romanticism, ed. Stuart
Curran, pp. 181–2.
5 Todd, p. 5.
6 S. M. Gilbert and S. Gubar, *The Madwoman in the Attic*, p. xi.
7 ibid., p. 476.
8 Betty S. Traviski, 'The Possibilities of Prose', in *Women and Literature 1500–1700*, ed. H. Wilcox, p. 259.
9 Curran, 'Women Readers, Women Writers', in Curran, p. 185.
10 Claire Harman, *Fanny Burney*, p. 58.
11 ibid., p. 385.
12 N. J. Waddell, quoted ibid., p. 58.
13 Todd, p. 127.
14 Elaine Showalter, *A Literature of their Own*, p. 36.
15 M. Cixous, quoted in *Authorship: From Plato to Post Modern*, ed. S. Burke, pp. 175–6.
16 Felicity Riddy, 'Women Talking about the Things of God', in *Women and Literature in Britain, 1150–1500*, ed. C. M. Meale, p. 114.
17 J. Spencer, *The Rise of the Woman Novelist from Aphra Behn to Jane Austen*, p. 135.
18 Quoted in *Persuasion*, ed. D. W. Harding, p. 7.
19 Claire Tomalin, *Jane Austen: A Life*, p. 117.
20 ibid., p. 173.
21 ibid., p. 139.
22 Gilbert and Gubar, *Madwoman*, p. 338.
23 A. Trodd, *Women's Writing in English: Britain 1900–1945*, p. 59.

45 Blood and gore
1 Tony Howard, quoted in Thomas Kyd, *The Spanish Tragedy*, ed. J. R. Mulryne, p. xxxiii.
2 F. P. Wilson, *The English Drama, 1485–1585*, p. 142.
3 John Donne: *Selected Prose*, ed. Neil Rhodes, p. 25.
4 *The Penguin Book of Horror Stories*, ed. J. A. Cudden, p. 37.
5 *The Oxford Book of Gothic Tales*, ed. Chris Baldick, p. xiii.
6 ibid., p. xxi.
7 ibid., p. xiv.
8 David Punter, 'Romantics to Early Victorians', in *The Romantic Age in Britain*, ed. Boris Ford, p. 23.
9 J. P. Carson, 'Enlightenment, Popular Culture and Gothic Fiction', in John Richetti (ed.), *The Eighteenth-Century Novel*, p. 262.

46 Ghosts

1 M. R. James, 'Casting the Runes' and Other Ghost Stories, ed. Michael Cox, p. xviii.
2 The Penguin Book of Horror Stories, ed. J. A. Cudden, p. 49.
3 Carole Weinberg, 'Dynastic Romance', in W. R. J. Barron, The Arthur of the English, p. 111.
4 Glen Cavaliero, The Supernatural and English Fiction, p. 122.
5 James, ed. Cox, p. xiii.
6 Jack Sullivan, Elegant Nightmares, p. 71.
7 James, ed. Cox, p. xxiii.
8 The Oxford Book of English Detective Stories, ed. P. Craig, p. xviii.

47 Practice makes perfect

1 S. B. Greenfield and D. G. Calder, A New Critical History of Old English Literature, pp. 50–3.
2 ibid., p. 107.
3 ibid., p. 116.
4 C. L. Wren, A Study of Old English Literature, p. 14.
5 N. Watson, 'Middle English Mysteries', p. 549.
6 Edwin Jones, The English Nation: The Great Myth, p. 9.
7 J. A. W. Bennett and Douglas Gray, Middle English Literature 1100–1400, p. 335.
8 L. G. Salingar, 'The Social Setting', in The Age of Shakespeare, ed. Boris Ford, p. 25.
9 John Caldwell (ed.), The Oxford History of English Music, Volume 1, p. 4.
10 ibid., p. 6.
11 ibid., p. 7.
12 ibid., p. 12.
13 ibid., p. 15.
14 Antony Flew (ed.), A Dictionary of Philosophy, p. 34.
15 Perez Zagorin, Francis Bacon, p. 38.
16 Miles Hadfield, Gardening in Britain, p. 69.
17 Zagorin, p. 141.
18 ibid., p. 143.
19 A. Easthope, Englishness and National Culture, p. 90.
20 ibid., p. 64.
21 ibid., p. 202.
22 Flew (ed.), p. 141.

23 Easthope, p. 66.
24 Thomas Hobbes, *Leviathan*, ed. Michael Oakeshott, p. xvii.
25 ibid., p. xxxix.
26 John Locke, *An Essay Concerning Human Understanding*, abridged and ed. A. S. Pringle-Pattison, p. x.
27 ibid.
28 Bertrand Russell, *The History of Western Philosophy*, p. 619.
29 ibid., p. 621.
30 Easthope, p. 96.
31 W. K. Sorley, *A History of British Philosophy to 1900*, p. 112.
32 Locke, ed. Pringle-Pattison, p. ix.
33 ibid., p. xix.
34 ibid., p. 230.
35 David Simpson, 'Romanticism, Criticism and Theory', in *The Cambridge Companion to British Romanticism*, ed. Stuart Curran, p. 4.
36 Jean-Jacques Mayoux, *English Painting*, p. 97.
37 ibid., p. 115.
38 ibid., p. 258.
39 William Weber, *The Rise of Musical Classics in Eighteenth-Century England*, p. 15.
40 A. J. Ayer, *Logical Positivism in Perspective*, p. 9.
41 ibid., p. 5.
42 ibid., p. 8.
43 ibid.
44 Flew (ed.), p. 33.
45 W. T. Jones and R. J. Fogelin, *A History of Western Philosophy: The Twentieth Century*, p. 246.
46 Simpson, p. 4.

48 Prolix and prolific

1 L. D. Benson, *The Riverside Chaucer*, p. 936.
2 John Donne, *Selected Prose*, ed. Neil Rhodes, p. 10.
3 Nikolaus Pevsner, *The Englishness of English Art*, p. 48.
4 Stanley Fish, *Self-Consuming Artefacts*, p. 204.
5 ibid., p. 357.
6 M. Heusser, *The Gilded Pill*, p. 3.
7 ibid., p. 6.
8 Joan Bennett, *Sir Thomas Browne*, p. 10.

49 Some more dunces

1 C. Kerby-Miller, *The Memoirs of the Extraordinary Life, Works and Discoveries of Martin Scriblerus*, p. 29.
2 ibid.
3 ibid.
4 Hugh Kenner, *Jonathan Swift: A Critical Anthology*, ed. Denis Donoghue, p. 265.
5 Ian Campbell Ross, *Laurence Sterne: A Life*, p. 407.
6 ibid., p. 410.
7 Claude Rawson, 'Unparodying and Forgery: the Augustan Chatterton', in *Thomas Chatterton and Romantic Culture*, ed. Nick Groom, p. 20.
8 Campbell Ross, p. 202.
9 Peter Vansittart, *In Memory of England*, p. 150.

50 The secret garden

1 Christopher Taylor, *The Archaeology of Gardens*, p. 25.
2 Jane Brown, *The Pursuit of Paradise*, p. 139.
3 ibid., p. 148.
4 ibid.
5 ibid., p. 3.
6 E. S. Rohde, *The Story of the Garden*, p. 235.
7 Brown, p. 82.
8 ibid., p. 90.
9 ibid.
10 ibid., p. 154.
11 ibid., p. 160.
12 ibid.
13 ibid., p. 67.
14 ibid., p. 138.
15 ibid., p. 303.
16 Rohde, p. 140.
17 Miles Hadfield, *Gardening in Britain*, p. 39.
18 Brown, p. 136.
19 Rohde, p. 12.
20 Charles Quest-Ritson, *The English Garden*, pp. 22–3.
21 Hadfield, p. 54.
22 ibid., p. 209.
23 ibid., p. 43.
24 ibid., p. 212.

25 ibid., pp. 170–80.
26 L. Whistler, quoted in ibid., p. 210.
27 Quest-Ritson, p. 124.
28 ibid.
29 ibid., p. 221.
30 Rohde, p. 161.
31 Brown, p. 57.
32 Hadfield, p. 31.
33 ibid., p. 30.
34 Brown, p. 133.
35 ibid., p. 174.
36 ibid., p. 303.
37 Rohde, p. 172.
38 Hadfield, p. 46.
39 Rohde, p. 234.
40 Brown, p. 87.

51 Forging a language

1 Roger Lonsdale (ed.), *The Poems of Thomas Gray and William Collins*, p. xvii.
2 ibid., p. xviii.
3 Paul Baines, *The House of Forgery in Eighteenth-Century Britain*, p. 7.
4 ibid., p. 11.
5 ibid., p. 13.
6 J. G. Pocock, quoted ibid., p. 14.
7 ibid., p. 15.
8 A. Preminger (ed.), *Princeton Encyclopaedia of Poetry and Poetics*, p. 819.
9 Nick Groom, 'Fragments, Reliques, & MSS: Chatterton and Percy', in *Thomas Chatterton and Romantic Culture*, ed. Nick Groom, p. 190.
10 Nick Groom, quoted in Groom, pp. 55–6.
11 Inga Bryden, 'The Mythical Image: Chatterton, King Arthur and Heraldry', in Groom, p. 64.
12 ibid., p. 65.
13 Nick Groom, 'Introduction', in Groom, p. 7.
14 Alexandra Wedgewood, 'Architecture', in *The Romantic Age in Britain*, ed. Boris Ford, p. 208.

15 Georges Lamoine, 'The Originality of Chatterton's Art', in Groom, p. 38.
16 Quoted Stephen B. Dobranski, 'Milton's Social Life', in *The Cambridge Companion to Milton*, ed. Dennis Danielson, p. 21.
17 Arden Reed, *Romanticism and Language*, p. 19.

52 The romantic fallacy

1 Eric Rothstein, *Restoration and Eighteenth-Century Poetry*, p. 145.
2 T. S. R. Boase, *English Art 1800–1870*, p. 12.
3 David Simpson, 'Romanticism, Criticism and Theory', in *The Cambridge Companion to British Romanticism*, ed. Stuart Curran, p. 17.
4 ibid.
5 Geoffrey Thurley, *The Romantic Predicament*, p. 113.
6 ibid., p. 139.
7 Terry Castle, *Masquerade and Civilisation*, p. 184.
8 ibid., p. 333.
9 Judith N. Shklar, *After Utopia: The Decline of Political Faith*, pp. 15–16.
10 Geoffrey Hartman, *Beyond Formalism*, pp. 300 and 303.
11 J. O. Hayden (ed.), *William Wordsworth: Poems, Volume One*.
12 Thurley, p. 138.
13 Thomas McFarland, *Romantic Cruxes: The English Essayists and the Spirit of the Age*, pp. 11 and 13.

53 English music

1 A. L. Bacharach (ed.), *British Music of Our time*, p. 52.
2 Fuller Maitland in *The Times*, quoted in Michael Kennedy, *The Works of Ralph Vaughan Williams*, p. 93.
3 R. Palmer (ed.), *Folk Songs Collected by Ralph Vaughan Williams*, p. ix.
4 John Caldwell (ed.), *The Oxford History of English Music*, Volume 1, p. 63.
5 ibid., p. 131.
6 ibid., p. 135.
7 ibid., p. 191.
8 ibid., p. 484.
9 ibid., p. 178.
10 ibid., Volume 2, p. 15.

11 Kennedy, p. 131.
12 ibid., p. 137.
13 ibid., p. 169.
14 ibid., p. 170.
15 ibid., p. 347.
16 J. Day, *Englishness in Music*, p. 18.
17 ibid., p. 25.
18 Simon Heffer, *Vaughan Williams*, p. 9.
19 Kennedy, p. 5.
20 C. Palmer, *Delius: Portrait of a Cosmopolitan*, p. 160.
21 ibid., p. 150.
22 Paul Holmes, *Vaughan Williams*, p. 57.
23 Kennedy, p. 370.
24 Palmer, p. 160.
25 ibid., p. 199.
26 ibid., p. 202.
27 Caldwell (ed.), Volume 1, p. 31.
28 ibid., Volume 2, p. 284.
29 Heffer, p. 37.
30 Kennedy, p. 157.
31 ibid.
32 ibid., p. 302.
33 Kennedy, p. 211.
34 Caldwell (ed.), Volume 1, p. 22.
35 ibid., p. 120.
36 Day, pp. 51 and 158.

Acknowledgements

The jacket and endpapers show details from the following images and are reproduced by courtesy of the Bridgeman Art Library, London:

Front jacket: Lucy Harrington, Countess of Bedford, in a masque costume designed by Inigo Jones by John Decritz the Elder, from Woburn Abbey, Bedfordshire; child up a tree picking fruit from the Luttrell Psalter, Add 42130 f.196v., from the British Library, London; detail from the Strickland Fibula from the British Museum, London.

Front flap: *Stonehenge* by John Constable from the Victoria and Albert Museum, London

Spine: needlework picture embroidered in silk from the Victoria and Albert Museum, London; Monk from *The Canterbury Tales* by Geoffrey Chaucer from the Huntingdon Library, San Marino, CA

Back jacket: music-hall artist (reproduced by courtesy Hulton/ Archive); Mr. Monks from *Oliver Twist* by Charles Dickens published by B. Pollock, from Dickens House Museum, London; picture panel, silk and wool petitpoint on canvas, from Lady Lever Art Gallery, Port Sunlight, Merseyside

Back jacket flap: St Matthew, Anglo-Saxon miniature from the Osterreichische Nationalbibliothek, Vienna

Endpapers: (front) Battle between King Arthur and Mordred from St Alban's Chronicle, Ms 6 f.66v, from Lambeth Palace Library; needlework details as on spine; (back) St Matthew as on back jacket flap; *A Tribute to Sir Christopher Wren* by Charles Cockerell from a private collection.

Bibliography

Auerbach, Erna, *Tudor Artists* (London: Athlone Press, 1954)

Austen, Jane, *Persuasion*, ed. D. W. Harding (London: Penguin, 1965)

Axton, Richard, 'Church Drama and Popular Drama', in *Medieval Literature*, ed. Boris Ford, The New Pelican Guide to English Literature I (London: Penguin, 1983)

Ayer, A. J., *Logical Positivism in Perspective: Essays on Language, Truth and Logic*, ed. Barry Gower (London: Croom Helm, 1987)

Bacharach, A. L. (ed.), *British Music of Our Time* (London: Penguin, 1946)

Bain, Roly, 'Clowns and Augustes', in *Victorian Britain*, ed. Boris Ford, The Cambridge Cultural History of Britain VII (Cambridge: Cambridge University Press, 1988)

Baines, Paul, *The House of Forgery in Eighteenth-Century Britain* (Aldershot: Ashgate, 1988)

Baldick, Chris (ed.), *The Oxford Book of Gothic Tales* (Oxford: Oxford University Press, 1992)

Barber, Richard, *King Arthur: Hero and Legend* (Woodbridge, Suffolk: Boydell Press, 1986)

Barker, Ernest, *National Character and the Factors in its Formation* (London: Methuen, 1927)

Barron, W. R. J. (ed.), *The Arthur of the English: The Arthurian Legend in English Life* (Cardiff: University of Wales, 1999)

Bede, *A History of the English Church and People*, trans. Leo Sherley-Price, R. E. Latham (London: Penguin, 1968)

Beer, Frances, *Women and Mystical Experience in the Middle Ages* (Woodbridge, Suffolk: Boydell Press, 1992)

Beilin, E. V. (ed.), *Redeeming Eve: Women Writers of the English Renaissance* (Princeton NJ: Princeton University Press, 1987)

Bennett, Joan, *Sir Thomas Browne: 'A Man of Achievement in Literature'* (Cambridge: Cambridge University Press, 1962)

Bennett, J. A. W. (ed.), *Selections from John Gower* (Oxford: Clarendon Press, 1968)

—— and Douglas Gray (eds.), *Middle English Literature 1100–1400*, The Oxford History of English Literature I (Oxford: Clarendon

Press, 1986)

Benson, L. D. (ed.), *The Riverside Chaucer* (Oxford: Oxford University Press, 1988)

Blamires, Harry, *Twentieth-Century English Literature* (London: Macmillan, 1982)

Bliss, Lee, 'Pastiche, Burlesque, Tragicomedy', in *The Cambridge Companion to English Renaissance Drama*, ed. A. R. Braunmuller and Michael Hattaway (Cambridge: Cambridge University Press, 1990)

Bloomfield, Morton W., 'Chaucerian Realism', in *The Cambridge Chaucer Companion*, ed. P. Boitani and Jill Mann (Cambridge: Cambridge University Press, 1986)

Boase, T. S. R., *English Art 1800–1870*, Oxford History of English Art X (Oxford: Clarendon Press, 1959)

Bobrick, Benson, *The Making of the English Bible* (London: Weidenfeld & Nicolson, 2001)

Boffey, J., 'Middle English Lives', in *The Cambridge History of Medieval English Literature*, ed. D. Wallace (Cambridge: Cambridge University Press, 1999)

Boitani, P., 'Old Books Brought to Life in Dreams', in *The Cambridge Chaucer Companion*, ed. P. Boitani and Jill Mann (Cambridge: Cambridge University Press, 1986)

Bolton, W. F., *A Short History of Literary English* (London: Edward Arnold, 1972)

Bradley, S. A. J. (ed. and trans.), *Anglo-Saxon Poetry: An Anthology of Old English Prose* (London: Dent, 1982)

Braunmuller, A. R., 'The Arts of the Dramatist', in *The Cambridge Companion to English Renaissance Drama*, ed. A. R. Braunmuller and Michael Hattaway (Cambridge: Cambridge University Press, 1990)

Brewer, Derek, 'Medieval European Literature', in *Pelican Guide to Medieval Literature*, ed. Boris Ford (London: Pelican Books, 1984)

Brieger, Peter, *English Art, 1216–1307*, Oxford History of English Art IV (Oxford: Clarendon Press, 1957)

Brooks, Chris, and Inga Bryden, 'The Arthurian Legacy', in *The Arthur of the English*, ed. W. R. J. Barron

Brown, Jane, *The Pursuit of Paradise: A Social History of Gardens and Gardening* (London: HarperCollins, 1999)

Brut, trans. Rosamund Allen (London: Dent, 1992)

Bryden, Inga, 'The Mythical Image: Chatterton, King Arthur and

Heraldry', in *Thomas Chatterton and Romantic Culture*, ed. Nick Groom (Basingstoke: Macmillan, 1999)

Bunyan, John, *The Pilgrim's Progress*, ed. and intr. N. H. Keeble (Oxford: Oxford University Press, 1984)

Burke, S. (ed.), *Authorship: From Plato to Postmodern, A Reader* (Edinburgh: Edinburgh University Press, 1995)

Burrow, Colin, 'The Sixteenth Century', in *The Cambridge Companion to English Literature 1500–1600*, ed., A. F. Kinney (Cambridge: Cambridge University Press, 2000)

Caldwell, John (ed.), *The Oxford History of English Music*, 2 vols (Oxford: Oxford University Press, 1998–9)

Carey, John, *John Donne: His Mind and Art* (London: Faber & Faber, 1981)

Carpenter, Humphrey, *J. R. R. Tolkien: A Biography* (London: Allen & Unwin, 1977)

Carson, J. P., 'Enlightenment, Popular Culture and Gothic Fiction', in *The Cambridge Companion to the Eighteenth-Century Novel*, ed. J. Richetti (Cambridge: Cambridge University Press, 1996)

Castle, Terry, *Masquerade and Civilisation: The Carnivalesque in Eighteenth-Century English Culture and Fiction* (London: Methuen, 1986)

Chambers, E. K., *Malory and Fifteenth-Century Drama, Lyrics and Ballads*, The Oxford History of English Literature III (Oxford: Clarendon Press, 1990)

Clark, Kenneth, *On the Painting of English Landscape* (London: British Academy, 1935)

Clifton-Taylor, Alex, *The Cathedrals of England* (London: Thames & Hudson, 1977)

Coldewey, J. C., 'The Non-Cycle Plays and the East Anglian Tradition', in *The Cambridge Companion to Medieval English Theatre*, ed. Richard Beadle (Cambridge: Cambridge University Press, 1994)

Coldstream, Nicola, 'Architecture', in *Medieval Britain*, ed. Boris Ford, The Cambridge Cultural History of Britain II (Cambridge: Cambridge University Press, 1988)

Conrad, Peter, *The Everyman History of English Literature* (London: Dent, 1985)

Cormican, L. A., 'Milton's Religious Verse', in *From Donne to Marvell*, ed. Boris Ford, The New Pelican Guide to English Literature III (London: Penguin, 1982)

Coulton, G. G., *Chaucer and His England* (London: Methuen, 1927)

Craig, P. (ed.), *The Oxford Book of English Detective Stories* (Oxford: Oxford University Press, 1990)

Crossley-Holland, Kevin (ed. and trans.), *The Anglo-Saxon World: An Anthology* (Oxford: Oxford University Press, 1984)

Cudden, J. A. (ed.), *The Penguin Book of Horror Stories* (London: Penguin, 1984)

Curran, Stuart, 'Women Readers, Women Writers', in *The Cambridge Companion to British Romanticism*, ed. Stuart Curran (Cambridge: Cambridge University Press, 1993)

Dark, K. R., *Civitas to Kingdom: British Political Continuity 300–800* (London: Leicester University Press, 1999)

Davies, Norman, *The Isles: A History* (London: Macmillan, 1999)

Davies, R. T., (ed.), *Medieval English Lyrics: A Critical Anthology* (London: Faber & Faber, 1963)

Davis, Stevie, *Emily Brontë: Heretic* (London: Women's Press, 1994)

Day, J., *Englishness in Music: From Elizabethan Times to Elgar, Tippett and Britten* (London: Thames, 1999)

Dobranski, Stephen B., 'Milton's Social Life', in *The Cambridge Companion to Milton*, ed. Dennis Danielson (Cambridge: Cambridge University Press, 1999)

Donne, John, *Selected Prose*, ed. Neil Rhodes (London: Penguin, 1987)

Dowling, William C., 'Structure and Absence in Boswell's "Life of Johnson"' in *Modern Essays on Eighteenth-century Literature*, ed. L. Damrosch Jr (Oxford: Oxford University Press, 1988)

Drabble, Margaret, *A Writer's Britain: Landscape in Literature* (London: Thames and Hudson, 1979)

Easthope, Anthony, *Englishness and National Culture* (London: Routledge, 1999)

Eckenstein, Lina, *Women under Monasticism* (New York: Russell & Russell, 1963)

Empson, William, *Seven Types of Ambiguity* (London: Penguin in association with Chatto & Windus, 1995)

Enders, Jody, *Rhetoric and the Origins of Medieval Drama* (Ithaca: Cornell University Press, 1992)

Evans, Joan, *English Art 1307–1461*, Oxford History of English Art V (Oxford: Clarendon Press, 1949)

Evans, Maurice (ed.), *The Countess of Pembroke's 'Arcadia' by Sir Philip Sidney* (London: Penguin, 1977)

The Exeter Book Riddles, ed. and trans. Kevin Crossley-Holland (London: Penguin, 1979)

Farmer, D. H., 'Introduction' to Bede, *The Ecclesiastical History of the English People*, ed. Leo Sherley-Price, R. E. Latham and D. H. Farmer (London: Penguin, 1990)

Fell, Christine, *Women in Anglo-Saxon England* (London: British Museum Publications, 1984)

Ferguson, M. W., 'A Room Not Their Own', in *Renaissance Poetry*, ed. Christina Malcolmson (London: Longman, 1998)

Ferrante, J. M., 'Marie de France', in *Medieval Women Writers*, ed. K. M. Wilson (Manchester: Manchester University Press, 1984)

Fincke, L. A. (ed.), *Women's Writing in English: Medieval England* (London: Longman, 1999)

Fish, Stanley, *Self-Consuming Artefacts* (London: University of California Press, 1972)

Flew, Antony (ed.), *A Dictionary of Philosophy* (London: Pan Books, 1979)

Ford, Boris (ed.), *Eighteenth-Century Britain*, The Cambridge Cultural History of Britain V (Cambridge: Cambridge University Press, 1988)

Frow, Gerald, *Oh Yes It Is – A History of Pantomime* (London: BBC, 1985)

Gardner, Helen, *Religion and Literature*, (Oxford: Oxford University Press, 1983)

Gaskell, Elizabeth, *The Life of Charlotte Brontë*, ed. Alan Shelston (London: Penguin, 1975)

Gaunt, William, *A Concise History of English Painting* (London: Thames & Hudson, 1964)

Gilbert, S. M., and S. Gubar (eds.), *Shakespeare's Sisters: Feminist Essays on Women Poets* (London: Indiana University Press, 1979)

——, *The Madwoman in the Attic: The Woman Writer and the Nineteenth-Century Literary Imagination* (London: Yale University Press, 1980)

Glasscoe, Marion, *English Medieval Mystics: Games of Faith* (London: Longman, 1993)

Godden, Malcolm, and Michael Lapidge (eds.), *The Cambridge Companion to Old English Literature* (Cambridge: Cambridge University Press, 1991)

Gomme, Andor, 'Architecture', in *Seventeenth-Century Britain*, ed. Boris Ford, The Cambridge Cultural History of Britain IV (Cambridge: Cambridge University Press, 1988)

Greenfield, S. B., and D. G. Calder, *A New Critical History of Old*

English Literature (New York: New York University Press, 1986)

Greer, Germaine, *Slip-Shod Sibyls: Recognition, Rejection and the Woman Poet* (London: Viking, 1995)

Griffiths, Paul, 'Music', in *Modern Britain*, ed. Boris Ford, The Cambridge Cultural History of Britain IX (Cambridge: Cambridge University Press, 1988)

Groom, Nick (ed.), *Thomas Chatterton and Romantic Culture* (Basingstoke: Macmillan, 1999)

Gurr, Andrew, *Playgoing in Shakespeare's London* (Cambridge: Cambridge University Press, 1987)

Hadfield, Miles, *Gardening in Britain: An Historical Outline to 1939* (London: Hutchinson, 1960)

Hageman, E. H., 'Women's Poetry in Early Modern Britain', in *Women and Literature in Britain, 1500–1700*, ed. Helen Wilcox (Cambridge: Cambridge University Press, 1996)

Hansen, Melanie, 'Identity and Ownership', in *Writing and the English Renaissance*, ed. William Zunder and Suzanne Trill (London: Longman, 1996)

Happe, Peter, *English Drama Before Shakespeare* (London: Longman, 1999)

Harman, Claire, *Fanny Burney* (London: HarperCollins, 2000)

Hartman, Geoffrey, *Beyond Formalism: Literary Essays 1958–1970* (London: Yale University Press, 1970)

Hastings, Adrian, Alistair Mason and Hugh Pyper (eds.), *The Oxford Companion to Christian Thought* (Oxford: Oxford University Press, 2000)

Hayden, J. O. (ed.), *William Wordsworth: Poems, Volume One* (London: Penguin, 1977)

Heffer, Simon, *Vaughan Williams* (London: Weidenfeld & Nicolson, 2000)

Heinemann, Margot, 'Political Drama', in *The Cambridge Companion to English Renaissance Drama*, ed. A. R. Braunmuller and Michael Hattaway (Cambridge: Cambridge University Press, 1990)

Helgerson, Richard, *Forms of Nationhood: The Elizabethan Writing of England* (London: University of Chicago Press, 1994)

Herworth, C. R., *The Literary Lineage of the King James Bible 1340–1611* (Philadelphia: University of Pennsylvania Press, 1941)

Heusser, M., *The Gilded Pill – A Study of the Reader–Writer Relationship in Robert Burton's Anatomy of Melancholy* (Tubingen: Stauffenburg, 1987)

Hobbes, Thomas, *Leviathan*, ed. Michael Oakeshott (Oxford: Blackwell, 1946)

Hollier, Denis (ed.), *A New History of French Literature* (London: Harvard University Press, 1989)

Holmes, Paul, *Vaughan Williams* (New York: Omnibus Press, 1997)

Holmes, Richard, *Dr Johnson and Mr Savage* (London: Hodder & Stoughton, 1993)

Hoskins, W. G., *The Making of the English Landscape* (London: Penguin, 1985)

Hough, Graham, *A Preface to The Faerie Queene* (London: Duckworth, 1962)

Jack, Jane H., 'The Practical Essayists', in *From Dryden to Johnson*, ed. Boris Ford, The New Pelican Guide to English Literature IV (London: Penguin, 1982)

Jackson, K. H., *Language and History in Early Britain* (Dublin: Four Courts, 1994)

James, M. R., *'Casting the Runes' and Other Ghost Stories*, ed. Michael Cox (Oxford: Oxford University Press, 1987)

Johnson, Lesley, 'Dynastic Chronicles', in *The Arthur of the English*, ed. W. R. J. Barron (Cardiff: University of Wales Press, 1999)

Jones, Edwin, *The English Nation: The Great Myth* (Stroud: Sutton, 1998)

Jones, W. T., and R. J. Fogelin (eds.), *The Twentieth Century to Quine and Derrida*, A History of Western Philosophy V (London: Harcourt Brace Publishers, 1997)

Kendrick, Christopher, 'Preaching Common Grounds', in *Writing and the English Renaissance*, ed. William Zunder and Suzanne Trill (London: Longman, 1996)

Kennedy, Michael, *The Works of Ralph Vaughan Williams* (Oxford: Oxford University Press, 1980)

Kenner, H., 'The Gulliver Game' in *Jonathan Swift: A Critical Anthology*, ed. D. Donoghue (London: Penguin, 1971)

Ker, W. P., *Medieval English Literature* (Oxford: Oxford University Press, 1912)

Kerby-Miller, C., *The Memoirs of the Extraordinary Life, Works and Discovery of Martinus Scriblerus* (Oxford: Oxford University Press, 1989)

Kyd, Thomas, *The Spanish Tragedy*, ed. J. R. Mulryne (London: A & C Black, 1989)

Lamoine, Georges, 'The Originality of Chatterton's Art', in *Thomas*

Chatterton and Romantic Culture, ed. Nick Groom

Lever, J. W., '*Paradise Lost* and the Anglo-Saxon Tradition', *Review of English Studies* 23 (1990)

Levison, Wilhelm, 'Bede as Historian', in *Bede, His Life, Times and Writings*, ed. A. H. Thompson (New York: Russell & Russell, 1966)

Lewalski, B., *Writing Women in Jacobean England* (London: Harvard University Press, 1993)

Lewis, C. S., *The Discarded Image: An Introduction to Medieval and Renaissance Literature* (Cambridge: Cambridge University Press, 1964)

Leyerle, John, 'The Interlace Structure of *Beowulf*', *University of Toronto Quarterly* (October 1967)

Lloyd-Morgan, Ceridwen, 'The Celtic Tradition', in *The Arthur of the English*, ed. W. R. J. Barron

Locke, John, *An Essay Concerning Human Understanding*, abridged and ed. A. S. Pringle-Pattison (Oxford: Clarendon Press, 1924)

McFarland, Thomas, *Romantic Cruxes: The English Essayists and the Spirit of the Age* (Oxford: Clarendon Press, 1987)

MacFarlane, Alan, *The Origins of English Individualism* (Oxford: Blackwell, 1978)

McGrath, Alister, *In the Beginning: The Story of the King James Bible and how it Changed a Nation* (London: Hodder & Stoughton, 2001)

Mackerness, E. D., *A Social History of English Music* (London: Routledge & Kegan Paul, 1964)

McKisack, May, *The Fourteenth Century* (Oxford: Oxford University Press, 1959)

Malory, Sir Thomas, *Works*, ed. Eugene Vinaver, rev. P. J. C. Field (Oxford: Clarendon Press, 1990)

Manlove, Colin, *The Fantasy Literature of England* (Basingstoke: Macmillan, 1999)

Mayoux, Jean-Jacques, *English Painting: From Hogarth to the Pre-Raphaelites* (London: Macmillan, 1975)

Mellers, Wilfrid, *Harmonious Meeting: A Study of the Relationship between English Music, Poetry and Theatre* (London: Dennis Dobson, 1965)

Mercer, Eric, *English Art, 1553–1625*, Oxford History of English Art VII (Oxford: Clarendon Press, 1962)

Messenger, N. P., and J. R. Watson (eds.), *Victorian Poetry* (London: Dent, 1974)

Miller, R. P., 'Allegory in *The Canterbury Tales*', in *Companion to Chaucer Studies*, ed. Beryl Rowland (Oxford: Oxford University Press, 1979)

Muir, Kenneth, *The Sources of Shakespeare's Plays* (London: Methuen, 1977)

Mullan, John, 'Swift, Defoe and Narrative Forms', in *The Cambridge Companion to English Literature, 1650–1740*, ed. S. N. Zwicker (Cambridge: Cambridge University Press, 1998)

Nennius, *History of the Britons*, ed. A. W. Wade-Evans (London: Church Historical Society, 1938)

A New History of French Literature, ed. Denis Hollier (Cambridge MA: Harvard University Press, 1989)

Nicholas of Guildford, *The Owl and the Nightingale*, trans. Brian Stone (London: Penguin, 1977)

Oakeshott, Walter, *The Sequence of English Medieval Art* (London: Faber & Faber, 1950)

The Owl and the Nightingale, Cleaness, St Erkenwald, ed. and trans. Brian Stone (London: Penguin, 1977)

Palmer, C., *Delius: Portrait of a Cosmopolitan* (London: Duckworth, 1976)

Palmer, R. (ed.), *Folk Songs Collected by Ralph Vaughan Williams* (London: Dent, 1983)

Parsons, D. (ed.), *Tenth-Century Studies* (London: Phillimore, 1975)

Paxman, Jeremy, *The English. A portrait of a people* (London: Penguin 1998).

Pearsall, Derek, *Old English and Middle English Poetry*, The Routledge History of English Poetry I (London: Routledge and Kegan Paul, 1977)

——, *The Life of Geoffrey Chaucer* (Oxford: Blackwell, 1992)

Pevsner, Nikolaus, *The Englishness of English Art* (London: Penguin, 1976)

Pople, Kenneth, *Stanley Spencer* (London: Collins, 1991)

Pound, Ezra, *Literary Essays*, ed. T. S. Eliot (London: Faber & Faber, 1985)

Preminger, Alex (ed.), *Princeton Encyclopaedia of Poetry and Poetics* (Princeton NJ: Princeton University Press, 1973)

Punter, David, 'Romantics to Early Victorians', in *The Romantic Age in Britain*, ed. Boris Ford, The Cambridge Cultural History of Britain VI (Cambridge: Cambridge University Press, 1988)

Quest-Ritson, Charles, *The English Garden: A Social History* (London:

Viking, 2001)

Rasmussen, Steen Eiler, *London: the Unique City* (London: Jonathan Cape, 1937)

Rawson, Claude, 'Unparodying and Forgery: the Augustan Chatterton', in *Thomas Chatterton and Romantic Culture*, ed. Nick Groom

——, and J. Mezciems, *English Satire and the Satiric Tradition* (Oxford: Blackwell, 1984)

Reed, Arden (ed.), *Romanticism and Language* (London: Methuen, 1984)

Rhodes, Neil (ed.), *John Donne: Selected Prose* (London: Penguin, 1984)

Rice, David Talbot, *English Art, 871–1100*, Oxford History of English Art II (Oxford: Clarendon Press, 1952)

Richetti, John (ed.), *The Cambridge Companion to the Eighteenth-Century Novel* (Cambridge: Cambridge University Press, 1996)

Rickert, Margaret, *Painting in Britain: The Middle Ages* (London: Penguin, 1954)

Riddy, Felicity, 'Women Talking about the Things of God', in *Women and Literature in Britain, 1150–1500*, ed. C. M. Meale (Cambridge: Cambridge University Press, 1993)

Robinson, David, *Chaplin: His Life and Art* (London: Penguin, 2001)

Rohde, E. S., *The Story of the Garden* (London: Medici, 1989)

Rolle, Richard, *The Fire of Love*, ed. and trans. Clifton Wolters (London: Penguin, 1972)

Ross, Ian Campbell, *Laurence Sterne: A Life* (Oxford: Oxford University Press, 2001)

Rothstein, Eric, *Restoration and Eighteenth-Century Poetry 1660–1780* (London: Routledge & Kegan Paul, 1981)

Ruggiers, Paul G., *The Art of The Canterbury Tales* (Madison: University of Wisconsin Press, 1967)

Russell Bertrand, *The History of Western Philosophy* (London: Routledge, 2000)

Salingar, L. G., 'The Social Setting', in *The Age of Shakespeare*, ed. Boris Ford, The New Pelican Guide to English Literature II (London: Penguin, 1982)

Salter, Elizabeth, *English and International Studies in the Literature, Art and Patronage of Medieval England*, ed. D. Pearsall and N. Zeeman (Cambridge: Cambridge University Press, 1988)

Scragg, D. G., 'The Nature of Old English Verse', in *The Cambridge*

Companion to Old English Literature, ed. Malcolm Godden and Michael Lapidge (Cambridge: Cambridge University Press, 1991)

Scruton, Roger, *England: An Elegy* (London: Chatto & Windus, 2000)

Shepherd, G. T., 'Early Middle English Literature', in *The Middle Ages*, ed. W. F. Bolton (London: Sphere, 1986)

Sir Gawain and the Green Knight, ed. Brian Stone (London: Penguin, 1959)

Sisam, Kenneth, *Studies in the History of Old English Literature* (Oxford: Clarendon Press, 1953)

Sisman, Adam, *Boswell's Presumptuous Task* (London: Hamish Hamilton, 2000)

Six Middle English Romances, ed. Maldwyn Mills (London: Dent, 1982)

Smith, Catherine F., 'Jane Lead', in *Shakespeare's Sisters*, ed. S. M. Gilbert and S. Gubar

Smyth, A. P., *King Alfred the Great* (Oxford: Oxford University Press, 1995)

Sorley, W. R., *A History of British Philosophy to 1900*, ed. D. M. Mackinnon (Cambridge: Cambridge University Press, 1965)

Southern, R. W., *Medieval Humanism* (Oxford: Blackwell, 1970)

Sowerby, Robin, *The Classical Legacy in Renaissance Poetry* (London: Longman, 1994)

Spencer, Jane, *The Rise of the Woman Novelist from Aphra Behn to Jane Austen* (Oxford: Blackwell, 1986)

Spufford, Francis, *The Child that Books Built* (London: Faber & Faber, 2002)

St Erkenwald, in *The Owl and the Nightingale, Cleaness, St Erkenwald*, ed. and trans. Brian Stone

Stephens, John, *Music and Poetry in the Early Tudor Court* (Cambridge: Cambridge University Press, 1979)

Strong, Roy, *The Spirit of Britain: A Narrative History of the Arts* (London: Pimlico, 2000)

Sullivan, Jack, *Elegant Nightmares: The English Ghost Story from Le Fanu to Blackwood* (Athens, OH: Ohio University Press, 1980)

Sutherland, James, *English Literature of the Late Seventeenth Century*, The Oxford History of English Literature VI (Oxford: Clarendon Press, 1969)

Taylor, Beverly, and Elizabeth Brewer, *The Return of King Arthur: British and American Arthurian Literature since 1900* (Cambridge: D. S. Brewer, 1983)

Taylor, Christopher, *The Archaeology of Gardens* (Aylesbury: Shire Archaeology, 1983)

Tennyson, Alfred, Lord, *Letters*, ed. C. Y. Lang and E. F. Shannon Jr, 3 vols (Oxford: Clarendon Press, 1982–1990)

Thompson, A. H. (ed.), *Bede, His Life, Times and Writings* (New York: Russell & Russell, 1966)

Thornton, Martin, *English Spirituality* (London: SPCK, 1963)

Three Old English Elegies, ed. R. F. Leslie (Exeter: University of Exeter Press, 1988)

Thurley, Geoffrey, *The Romantic Predicament* (London: Macmillan, 1938)

Tillyard, E. M. W., *The English Epic and Its Background* (London: Chatto & Windus, 1954)

Todd, Janet, *The Sign of Angellica* (London: Virago, 1989)

Tomalin, Claire, *Jane Austen: A Life* (London: Penguin, 2000)

Trodd, Anthea, *Women's Writing in English: Britain 1900–1945* (London: Longman, 1998)

Uglow, Jenny, *Elizabeth Gaskell: A Habit of Stories* (London: Faber & Faber, 1993)

Utley, F. L., *The Crooked Rib* (Columbus, OH: Ohio State University Press, 1944)

Vansittart, Peter, *In Memory of England: A Novelist's View of History* (London: John Murray, 1998)

Varney, Andrew, *Eighteenth-Century Writers in Their World: A Mighty Maze* (Basingstoke: Macmillan, 1999)

Vaughan, William, *British Painting: the Golden Age from Hogarth to Turner* (London: Thames & Hudson, 1999)

Von Maltzahn, Nicholas, *Milton's History of Britain: Republican Historiography in the English Revolution* (Oxford: Clarendon Press, 1991)

——, 'Milton's Readers', in *The Cambridge Companion to Milton*, ed. Dennis Danielson (Cambridge: Cambridge University Press, 1999)

The Voyage of St Brendan, trans. J. J. O'Meara (Buckinghamshire: Colin Smythe, 1991)

Wain, John, *Samuel Johnson* (London: Macmillan, 1980)

Wasson, John, 'The Morality Play: Ancestor of Elizabethan Drama', in *The Drama of the Middle Ages*, ed. C. Davidson *et al.* (New York: AMS Press, 1982)

Waterhouse, Ellis, *Painting in Britain 1530–1790* (London: Yale University Press, 1994)

Watkin, David, *English Architecture: A Concise History* (London: Thames & Hudson, 2001)

Webb, J. F., and D. H. Farmer (eds.), *The Age of Bede* (London: Penguin, 1983)

Weber, William, *The Rise of Musical Classics in Eighteenth-Century England* (Oxford: Clarendon Press, 1992)

Weinberg, Carole, 'Dynastic Romance', in *The Arthur of the English*, ed. W. R. J. Barron

Welsford, Enid, *The Fool: His Social and Literary History* (London: Faber & Faber, 1935)

West, Richard, *The Life and Strange, Surprising Adventures of Daniel Defoe* (London: HarperCollins, 1997)

Whinney, Margaret, and Oliver Millar, *English Art, 1625–1714*, Oxford History of English Art VIII (Oxford: Clarendon Press, 1957)

Whitelock, Dorothy, *The Audience of Beowulf* (Oxford: Clarendon Press, 1951)

—— (ed.), *English Historical Documents c.500–1042* (London: Eyre & Spottiswoode, 1955)

Wild, L. H., *The Romance of the English Bible: A History of the Translation of the Bible into English* (Garden City NY: Doubleday, Doran & Co., 1929)

Wilson, F. P., *The English Drama, 1485–1585*, ed. G. K. Hunter, The Oxford History of English Literature IV (Oxford: Clarendon Press, 1969)

Wimsatt, W. K., 'Rhetoric and Poems: The example of Swift' in *Modern Essays on Eighteenth-Century Literature* ed. L. Damrosch Jr (Oxford: Oxford University Press, 1988)

Windeatt, Barry, 'Literary Structures in Chaucer', in *The Cambridge Chaucer Companion*, ed. P. Boitani and Jill Mann (Cambridge: Cambridge University Press, 1986)

Wood, Michael, *In Search of England: Journeys into the English Past* (London: Viking, 1999)

Woodcock, Peter, *This Enchanted Isle* (Glastonbury: Gothic Image, 2000)

Woodward, Christopher, *In Ruins* (London: Chatto & Windus, 2001)

Woolf, Rosemary, 'Later Poetry: the Popular Tradition', in *The Middle Ages*, ed. W. F. Bolton (London: Sphere, 1986).

Woolf, Virginia, *A Room of One's Own* (London: Flamingo, 1994)

Wordsworth, William, *William Wordsworth: Poems, Volume One*, ed.

J. O. Hayden (London: Penguin, 1977)

Wormald, Patrick, 'Anglo-Saxon Society and Its Literature', in *The Cambridge Companion to Old English Literature*, ed. Malcolm Godden and Michael Lapidge

Wrenn, C. L., *A Study of Old English Literature* (London: Harrap, 1983)

Zagorin, Perez, *Francis Bacon* (Princeton NJ: Princeton University Press, 1998)

Zarnecki, G., *1066 and Architectural Sculpture* (London: British Academy, 1968)

Index

abbeys, 130; *see also* monasteries
'Academy of Ancient Music', 250
acting and actors, 434–5
Acton, John Emerich Edward
  Dalberg, 1st Baron, 38
Adams, William, 62
Addison, Joseph: and sensitivity to
  weather, 74; on Dryden's
  translation of Virgil, 203; prose
  style, 204; on Shakespeare's
  fantasy characters, 223; hymn-
  writing, 303; on world as theatre,
  314; as essayist, 318; Fielding
  imitates, 332; on women and
  thinking, 362; influenced by
  Locke, 389; on 'Rosamond's
  Bower', 417
Adès, Thomas: *Arcadiana*, 447
Aelfric ('Grammaticus'), 80–1, 291
Aethelbert, 77, 183
Aethelflaed, 184
Aethelwold, 36
Ailred of Rievaulx, 108
Alamanni, Luigi, 209
Alan of Lynn, 139
Alban, St, 38
Albion: origins of, xvii–xviii;
  Milton on, 47; Blake on, 49; myth
  of, 107
Alcuin, 127
Aldhelm, 20, 24, 32
Alfred the Great, King: Englishness,
  xviii; genealogy, 15; on
  monasteries, 30; on learning, 32;
  and architecture, 36; dreams, 49;
  and winter cold, 72; translations,
  77–9, 126; use of prose
  vernacular, 77–80, 383;

inheritance, 96; historical
  research, 243; represented in
  paintings, 257; nautical imagery,
  263
All the Year Round (journal), 333
allegory, 124, 165, 434
Allestree, Richard: *The Ladies
  Calling*, 181
alliteration: in Anglo-Saxon
  literature, 20–1, 36, 95; in
  Spenser, 57; in Hopkins, 75; in
  Middle English, 99–100; in
  Layamon's *Brut*, 111–12; in
  popular verse, 145–8;
  characteristics, 146–7; in *Piers the
  Plowman*, 163; in Richard Rolle,
  171; Virginia Woolf uses, 187;
  encourages paradox, 230; Auden
  uses, 253; revived, 253; in Bible
  translations, 291
allotments (garden), 412
'Amara' (imaginary hill), 269
Ambrose, St, 33
America: Tudors and, 213
Anales Cambriae, 108
Ancrene Wisse (*Ancrene Riwle*), 86,
  170
Andreas (Anglo-Saxon poem), 30
Anglo-Saxon Chronicles, xviii, 40,
  78–80, 263
Anglo-Saxons: art, xix, 10, 85–6,
  274; temperament and character,
  11; literature, 15–17, 20–5, 54–5,
  67, 72, 88–91, 206, 327; musical
  instruments, 17; riddles, 23, 25,
  277; scholarship and learning,
  32–5, 82, 95; and landscape, 65;
  and prevalence of winter, 72;

Birtwistle, Sir Harrison: *Gawain*, 177
Biscop, Benedict *see* Benedict Biscop
'Bishops' Bible', 298–9
Black Book of Carmarthen, 107
Black Death, 101
Blake, William: on Albion, xviii;
 visions, 4, 47–9, 53, 164, 307–9;
 and locality, 68; art, 85–6; on
 leaping, 87; and Langland, 164–5;
 on small moment, 173; admires
 Milton, 241; sea imagery, 264; on
 Chaucer, 309; images, 309;
 invective and polemic, 310–11;
 background, 329; accepts Ossian
 as genuine, 423; Vaughan
 Williams sets poems by, 444, 446;
 'Auguries of Innocence', 276; *The
 Four Zoas*, 53; *Jerusalem*, 38, 49;
 Milton, 68; *Songs of Innocence*,
 46; 'A Vision of the Last
 Judgement', 7
Bligh, William, 273
Bliss, Sir Arthur: *Knot of Riddles*,
 24; *Meditations on a Theme of
 John Blow*, 440
'blue' humour, 24
Blue-Stockings, 363
Blunden, Edmund, 68
Boccaccio, Giovanni, 155–6, 158,
 197
Boerhaave, Hermann, 348
Boethius: *Consolation of Philosophy*,
 78–9, 96, 126, 154, 198
Boniface, St, 34
Book of Durrow, 30, 84
Borges, Jorge Luis, 23
Bors, 113
Boswell, James, 134, 341, 346; *Life
 of Johnson*, 347, 350–3, 421
bowling greens, 417–18
Boydell, John: *Shakespeare Gallery*,
 257
Brendan, St, 42, 268
Brian, Havergal, 68; *The Gothic
 Symphony*, 373

Bridge, Frank, 444
Bridget, St, 139
Brighton Pavilion, 236
British Association for the
 Advancement of Science, 392
Britten, Benjamin: and use of older
 musical elements, 253; realises
 Dowland's songs, 441; *Billy Budd*,
 267; *Noye's Fludde*, 177; *Peter
 Grimes*, 267
Brontë sisters: juvenile stories, 277;
 adopt male names, 360; writings,
 361, 374
Brontë, Branwell, 355
Brontë, Charlotte: on Emily as
 'nursling of the moors', 70;
 feminine status, 186; Mrs
 Gaskell's life of, 352–5; fiction
 writing, 360; anger and
 frustration in, 366; *Jane Eyre*, 3,
 7, 74, 190, 366–7; *Villette*, 366
Brontë, Emily: melancholy, 63;
 Charlotte on, 70; mystical
 expression, 190; fiction writing,
 360, 363; ghosts in, 376;
 Wuthering Heights, 65, 187, 367
Brontë, Patrick, 355
Brooke, Rupert, 372
Brown, Jane, 411–13, 416; *The
 Pursuit of Paradise*, 415
Brown, John: *Athelstan*, 257
Brown, Lancelot ('Capability'), 411,
 414
Browne, Sir Thomas: meditations as
 poetry, 21; literary style, 27, 32,
 62, 233, 399–401, 406–7;
 background and career, 61,
 399–400; Johnson on, 62, 233; on
 eating, 372; faith and beliefs,
 399–400; *Hydriotaphia, or Urne-
 Buriall*, 61–2; 'A Letter to a
 Friend', 8; *Religio Medici*, 51, 400
Browning, Robert, 21, 437; 'Childe
 Roland to the Dark Tower Came',
 52

Odoric, Friar, 269
Of Arthour and of Merlin (poem), 102, 113
Ohthere, 80, 268
Old England (journal), 334
Old English (West Saxon) language, 15, 17–18, 97, 206
Old Mother Hubbard and her Dog, 279
Old Walsingham, Norfolk, 62
Oliver, Isaac, 276
Ong, Walter: *The Art of Logic*, 432
optimism, 128, 147
opus anglicanum (embroidery), 26, 275
Orange prize for women's fiction, 359
original sin (doctrine), 127
Orosius: *Seven Books of Histories against the Pagans*, 78
Orwell, George: *Animal Farm*, 52, 177
'Ossian' *see* Macpherson, James
Otranto Cathedral, 107–8
Otway, Thomas, 427; *Venice Preserv'd*, 234
Ovid, 205, 222
Owen, Wilfred, 119
Owl and the Nightingale, The (poem) *see* Nicholas of Guildford
Oxford, 1st Earl of *see* Harley, Robert
Oxford University: use of Latin, 102

painting: and landscape, 69, 75–6, 392; history, 257; marine, 264–6; medieval, 275; and empiricism, 392; *see also* art; portrait painting
Palmer, Samuel, 4, 70
Pankhurst, Emmeline and Sylvia, 185
pantomime, 279–80, 284, 286, 372–3
Paradisus, 413

Paris, Matthew, 59; *Chronica Majora*, 129
parody, 396–9, 402–7
Parr, Katherine, 191
Paston letters, 189
pastoral poetry, 206
pathways, 66–7
pattern and decoration, 26–7, 84–5, 130–1, 274
Paxton, Sir Joseph, 414
Pearl (poem), 49, 124, 145
Peasants' Revolt (1381), 150
Pelagius, 34, 127
Pembroke, Mary Sidney, Countess of, 192; *Psalmes*, 194
Pennant, Thomas, 422
Pepys, Samuel, 286, 402, 417
Percy, Thomas, Bishop of Dromore: *Reliques of Ancient English Poetry*, 55, 243, 249, 426, 428
Perpendicular architecture, 130, 253
Persius, 33
Peter Martyr, 270
Petrarch, Francesco, 209
Petrondinus, Petrus, 204
Pevsner, Sir Nikolaus: on Hogarth's reticence, 159; on English breaking of unity of exterior and interior, 397; on detachment, 446; *The Englishness of English Art*, 85, 132, 235
Philips, Ambrose, 403
philosophy, 384, 388–91, 393, 398
picturesque, the, 69, 243
Pierce, Edward, 343
pilgrimages, 172, 191–2, 268; *see also* travel
Pine, Robert Edge, 257
Piper, John, 76
place: power of, 303, 448–9; identification with authors, 354; and gardens, 416; Chatterton and, 431
plagiarism, 429–30, 432, 437; *see*